Korean War Leadership

and

Leftist Revolution –

America Betrayed

Richard Masella

2

Contents

3

4

Abbreviations

AEC – US Atomic Energy Commission

CIA – US Central Intelligence Agency

CCF – Communist Chinese Forces

CHEKA, original comprehensive Soviet intelligence agency, predecessor of OGPU, NKVD, and KGB

CPUSA – Communist Party of the United States of America

DMZ – Demilitarized Zone separating North and South Korea

FBI – US Federal Bureau of Investigation

FDR – Franklin Delano Roosevelt

FEAF – US Far East Air Force

GI – 'Government Issue,' a US soldier

GRU – Soviet military intelligence, smaller and less powerful than main OGPU, NKVD

HUAC – US House Un-American Affairs Committee

IMF – International Monetary Fund

IPR – US-based Institute of Pacific Relations, a pro-Soviet Communist-front group

JCS – US Joint Chiefs of Staff

KATUSA – Koreans Attached to the US Army

KGB – successor name of main Soviet intelligence agency NKVD

MI5, British domestic intelligence agency

MI6, British foreign intelligence agency

MLR – Main Line of Resistance

MSR – Main Supply Route

NATO – North Atlantic Treaty Organization

NKPA – North Korean People's Army

NKVD – replacement name for OGPU, main Soviet intelligence agency

NSA – US National Security Agency

NSC – US National Security Council

OGPU – successor name for the 'CHEKA,' main branch of Soviet intelligence

OSS – World War II-era Office of Strategic Services, first formal US Government
intelligence agency, replaced by Central Intelligence Agency

PLA – Communist China's People's Liberation Army

POW – Prisoner of War

PPSh – Soviet submachine gun, 'burp' gun, used by CCF and NKPA

PRC – People's Republic of China

RCT – Regimental Combat Team

ROC – Republic of China, Taiwan

ROK – Republic of Korea, South Korea

SCAP – post-World War II Supreme Command Allied Powers office in Tokyo, Japan

UN – United Nations

UNC – United Nations Command

USAF – United States Air Force

8

USSR – Union of Soviet Socialist Republics

VOA – Voice of America radio programming

MAPS, following text page numbers

Preface

America's tradition of military victory died in Korea, along with 54,262 mostly young men. Both perished at the hands of politically-powerful American leftist revolution.

This book rose from desire for war history truth and justice. It tells a story unknown to the American people. The story involves foreign control over the United States Government.

Disappointing reality brought Korean War research passion: true War causation, American War conduct, and lasting, serious outcomes, are publicly unknown. Blood of dead Americans, South Koreans, and allies demands better.

History texts, popular media, and government routinely fail to report war realities. Censorship is a well-worn tool of political and military leaders.

War misunderstanding and confusion undercut public ability to restrain leader behaviors and promote accountability. Similar challenge arises in discovering hidden political agendas underlying leader war policies destructive to national and popular interests.

Presidents may need to serve a higher cause, a greater political power. Then, war leader inattention to common good and common sense brings needless spending of life and limb, departure from "consent of the governed," and endless national calamity. War in Korea is a perfect, if tragic, example.

President Harry Truman openly and frequently admitted a continual fear of igniting World War III with Communist-bloc nations. His memoirs reveal World War III phobia just a few years after World War II's end. This is pure fact and settled history. It cannot be argued away.

Something is drastically wrong with this picture. *War fought victoriously with full national strength and huge losses of life should bring a long peace*. Why was aftermath of World War II a time of world instability, leading less than five years later to renewed American and Asian bloodshed?

The truthful answer is very politically incorrect and not commonly understood. Of central importance, Korean War is witness to, and proof of, powerful leftist revolution in America. Such power assured disastrous World War II political results for America and the West, guaranteeing

Korean explosion. Examination of US war leadership in both reveals strange disregard of national interests, senseless decisions, deep incompetence, and treason in United States Government. American boys died in droves, so that half the world would know Communist domination.

Red revolutionary success in Washington meant masking America's tragic World War II political outcomes and pitching Korean fighting as not real war. Bloody, extended Korean War might cause people to ask, 'Why so soon?', and blame Roosevelt and Truman for Asian, and European, messes. Hence the major leftist deception of 'Korean Police Action' and 'Conflict' as official Government descriptions. Insult to American soldiers, especially killed and wounded, and their families, lasts forever.

The text treats great leftist revolution not as allegation, but pure fact for all to see, appreciate, and fear, a driving reality of American political life and Korean War conduct. Revolutionary mandate comes straight from core Communist literature of Marx, Lenin, Trotsky, and Stalin. The plan calls for internal Red sharing of US Government power ('Dual Power'), as prelude to complete control. Secret, non-stop Government infiltration, and Red political muscle, keyed mission success.

During Franklin Roosevelt and Truman administrations, a three-headed monster of Communism, Socialism, and Internationalism waged a campaign of destruction against traditional society. Feasting on institutions and people, radical leftists achieved dominance in academia, communication media, labor, law, and politics. State and Treasury departments, and the White House, knew strong Red policy influence. Today, under pleasant-sounding labels of "progressive," "liberal," and "democratic socialism," leftist rebels are more numerous and dangerous than ever.

Dual Power meant rotten deals for Americans in World War II and Korea. As a matter of deadly principle, every revolutionary US Government official held sole allegiance to Soviet and Chinese Communist interests – to Stalin and Mao Zedong, not reviled America or US presidents.

Truth of Dual Power's "extent, depth of penetration, and fierce vindictiveness of its revolutionary temper," would tarnish revered, foundational political reputations, so deception ruled the day. Franklin Roosevelt must be hailed as "savior of humanity," Harry Truman the "gutsy, gritty national champion." Public unawareness of polar-opposite truth, actual reality, simply reflects pro-Red media and academic conditioning. Hero Stalin's inflexible maxim guides the faithful: "We alone determine what is true and what is not."

Reds have no equals at mind-bending propaganda, nor in abhorrence of Judeo-Christian moral and ethical standards. Radical left media cannon barrages are important tools of destruction, aimed at suppressing knowledge of enormous hidden revolutionary power, while creating widespread inability to distinguish true from false, right from wrong, reality from unreality. After all, leftist revolution is at covert and perpetual war with the United States. Impermissible common knowledge of civilian and military leadership incompetence and anti-American Executive, Legislative, and Judicial Branch actions might expose the revolution and Democrat Party to political ruin.

Regarding Democrats, 1940 and 1944 presidential elections clearly reveal huge Roosevelt and Truman debts to leftist political power, a fertile source of electoral votes. In both elections, Communist-run American Labor and American Liberal parties provided Roosevelt margins of victory in New York State and many northeastern and midwestern industrial states. A 100% Socialist labor boss, Sidney Hillman, assured Truman's 1944 vice-presidential nomination, and therefore, of course, his presidency.

Resulting World War II and post-War political leadership meant global Communist ascendance, Truman-imposed US military impotence, dangerous power imbalance in Far East Asia, and war in Korea. Both presidents served as Korean War matchmakers.

Undeniably, for minds and eyes open to seeing, Roosevelt fathered Korean War through pro-Soviet World War II actions, detailed shortly. Americans, expecting long peace given full commitment to world war victory, never learned of Commander in Chief Roosevelt's dedication to building Soviet world power. US Soviet specialist George Kennan related the "long series of concessions we had made, during the course of World War II and just after it, to Russian expansionist tendencies."

Instead, 70 years of media praise and historical adulation assured Roosevelt's permanent status as world and nation savior. The fact that truth stands at 180-degree variance testifies to leftist political and media brainwashing power.

All sides agree on Truman's post-World War II conventional and nuclear US military gutting. In Korea, the recently mighty, atomic-capable US Army knew embarrassing rout at North Korean, then Chinese Communist hands. When shifting War tides brought American battlefield domination and wholesale Red slaughter and retreat, Washington abruptly called off the rousing offensive and dropped pursuit of Korean military victory.

Instead of winning, Truman chose the course of "holding on" in Korea, described by historian John Toland as "alien to our national experience."

The incredible truth is that a Communist Chinese Army using horse cavalry and pack animal transport, lacking air cover, imposed a military draw on so-called modern, mechanized, *nuclear-capable*, air-covered US forces. Horse power stopped atomic power in its tracks. Talk about civilian and military leadership embarrassment!

Many such Korean-related presidential leadership acts are popularly unknown, radical departures from prior national military practice. A New Order ruled in Washington.

Presidential world war and Korean War leadership led America down a path toward internationalism. The United States would be closely and permanently tied to Western Europe and the United Nations. Civilian leaders now exercised unprecedented control over the military. George Kennan told of "conscious effort within the Truman Administration to concentrate power in civilian hands, including control and possession of atomic weapons." The new reality assured dominance of political interests over all aspects of war-fighting, even if this meant gross and needless slaughter of young Americans.

The American people should know that a devoted leftist ideologue Secretary of State, Dean Acheson, a lawyer, not a general, ran US/UN Korean military operations during Truman's presidency. His War micromanagement extended to field operations and traveled the full US fighting force chain of command. Generals through lieutenants could not breathe without State Department permission. Joint Chiefs of Staff generals and admirals served compliantly, under tight thumb. Junior Pentagon officers secretly referred to them as 'The Five Silent Men.'

As proven in Korea and Vietnam, consequences to US war fighting would be extremely negative and long-lasting.

Before becoming Truman's right-hand Korean War director, Acheson strongly and openly encouraged US sharing of nuclear secrets and bomb materials with Soviet Russia. This also is settled history.

For all who would see, end of World War II and Korean fighting (South Korea excepted), proved major disappointments – world peace and security still a distant dream, Communism in place of Nazism, ever-present threat from the Soviet Union (or Russian Federation) and Chinese and

North Korean peoples' republics. Americans live today at the mercy of these terrible war outcomes.

SOMETHING FOUL IN WASHINGTON

The American people are clueless about Russian spying and Government policy influence during Roosevelt and Truman presidencies. The following Washington leadership acts are unique, surprising, and in fact, history-making. They represent only a small sample of Red US Government infestation and associated treason. They demand truthful explanation:

- President Truman's 1946 appointments of influential US Government Soviet agents Harry Dexter White and Frank Coe to important International Monetary Fund posts, ignoring written reports from FBI Director Hoover about their rich Red spy histories;

- Truman's August 1948 press conference statement, "The Alger Hiss Case is just a red herring" – a false issue. The Case centered on high-level espionage within US Government. The comment reflected official disinterest and "active hostility among the most powerful sections of the Truman Administration" in publicizing and rooting out Reds in Government;

- identical "near-total absence of Executive-level interest in exposing and eliminating Communists in Government" disappoints FBI agents working to uncover the truth;

- despite hard evidence of US Government treason, the Justice Department announces on December 1, 1948 that without additional proof, no legal action would be taken against Communist spy Hiss;

- when new, irrefutable proof of treason meant the Justice Department could no longer stonewall filing of formal charges against Hiss, two US Supreme Court justices, Frankfurter and Reed, testify as character witnesses at his 1949 perjury trial. Their appearances are unprecedented in Court history;

- Truman Secretary of State Acheson's 1949 public statement personally backing then-convicted perjurer Hiss, whose legal troubles centered on espionage against America. Acheson is the only prominent US Government leader openly expressing support for a convicted Communist Washington spy. Fierce political criticism over the remarks hurt the Truman Administration forever after;

- Franklin Roosevelt brushes off entreaties of Assistant Secretary of State Berle, Ambassador William Bullitt, and prominent reporter Walter Winchell about widespread Communist penetration in US Government;

- great and unspoken Roosevelt and Truman administration (1942 – 1949) material support in enabling Soviet nuclear bomb creation and mass production. Much help came straight from the White House under the "Lend-Lease" umbrella and included multiple uranium shipments to Soviet Russia. Important Government figures in both administrations, Harry Hopkins, Robert Oppenheimer, David Lilienthal, and Acheson, favored sharing all atomic information and materials with Moscow. The American people financially paid for the senseless largess, then paid for decades in Soviet nuclear threat to America, always blind to Washington's great help in building Red atomic bombs.

In the words of Communist underground agent turned American patriot Whittaker Chambers, Americans "might understand the evidence, they might reject it, but the hard fact was that the evidence was in. What they did with it, would be a shrewd measure of popular ability or inability to save themselves," and their nation.

A particular revolutionary success is control of American courts of law. As Chambers reminded, "Reds use the means of justice to defeat the ends of justice." To radical leftists, the American court system, especially the US Supreme Court, represents the 'enforcement arm,' the hammer crushing American freedom. Totalitarianism smothers the vote and representative democracy. The few rule the many.

Any person, group, or institution standing for right and truth is the enemy of leftist revolution. Perhaps our saving grace is very low Red regard for popular American intelligence. Yet, if this revolution "grinds existing social institutions into dust, it will prove that common people lost the instinct of self-preservation."

With rapid passing of Korean War veterans, their families and all concerned Americans, armed with truth, must step forward in loud, constant protest of disgraceful US Government treatment of loved ones. Reds must be stopped from completing the job of American destruction. May a great, resounding 'Yes' fill the air for patriotism, freedom, Constitution, truth, and America first, not last.

Readers will examine unknown information on presidents Franklin Roosevelt, Truman, and

Eisenhower; Secretary of State Acheson, US Joint Chiefs of Staff, and generals MacArthur, Ridgway, Van Fleet, Collins, and Bradley; wisdom of Winston Churchill, US diplomat Kennan, war strategist Bernard Brodie, and nuclear arms specialist Fred Iklé. Focus is also on the American Red spy host faithfully laboring for savior Stalin.

To ease subject and person searches, a comprehensive, reader-friendly Index is provided. The author takes full responsibility for text content and style errors.

Deepest thanks and appreciation are expressed for 41 years of love and patience from wife, Dr. Joanne Masella, and for an education-centered upbringing by late parents Aldo and Jessie Masella.

Personal thanks are also due for timely and important help given by technology consultant Jake Gustavsson of Boynton Beach, Florida.

In the ancient Roman Republic, statesman Cato the Elder preached necessity of a third Punic War (146-143BC) against Carthage. He ended every Senate speech with the warning, "*Ceterum, censeo, delendam esse Cartaginem* – Besides, I also believe that Carthage must be destroyed." Once, to underscore the message before the Senate, Cato removed from his toga a rich cluster of Carthaginian figs, a symbol of growing alien power.

Today's 'enemy within' enjoys vast political harvest from well-cultivated fields of chaos and destruction. Saving the United States of America requires popular determination for total alien political defeat. Everything hinges on people knowing, and acting on, the truth.

Dedication

To family and friend war veterans:

Petty Officer Frank Ali IV, US Navy, Scottsdale, AZ – Vietnam, 1967*

Cpl. James P. Ali, US Army, Elizabeth, NJ – World War II, Europe, 1944-45*

PFC Dominic Branca, US Army, Aston, PA – Korea, 1951-53

Private Giuseppi Branca, US Army, Philadelphia, PA – World War I, 1917-18*

Lt. Col. E. Monroe Farber, US Army, Delray Beach, FL – Korea, 1951-53*

Gunnery Sgt. Richard Masella Jr., US Marine Corps, Los Angeles, CA – Operation Iraqi Freedom, 2003

Private Vincenzo Masella, US Army, Fifth Infantry Regiment, New York, NY – Civil War, 1864-65*

Cpl. Benjamin McGuire, US Army, Chester, PA – World War II, Europe, 1944-45*

Sgt. Armand Palestini Sr., US Army, Philadelphia, PA – World War II, Europe, 1943-45*

*deceased

18

Part I

American Political Backdrop, 1915 – 1950

<u>Chapter 1: Politically – Dominated War Leadership</u>

"Politics is everything."

- Anonymous.

"The years will pass. Not a stone will remain unturned of the cursed capitalistic structure, of its wars, its reaction, its vileness, its bestiality, and its progressive savagery. People will think back on the days of capitalism as on a bad dream."[1]

- Communist International (Comintern) boss Dmitri Manuilski, 1939.

Washington-imposed political constraints made Korea unique in American war history. For the first time, and contrary to highly favorable battlefield results, US forces would be intentionally denied the prospect, and achievement, of military victory.

Martial departures from normality had a common root: political primacy. Gaining, holding, and exercising power is the political "reason for being." Politics is a world of unreality, determining presidential and governmental commentary and decision-making. Supreme civilian power over America's military establishment means the reality of 100%-politicized American war-fighting. Possibly excepting Vietnam, nowhere is this more evident than in Korean War leadership.

Communist-Internationalist tenets featuring deep animosity toward traditional American life gained political traction before US entry into *World War I,* flowering into powerful leftist forces during Franklin Roosevelt and Harry Truman administrations. In fact, Roosevelt and Truman presidencies reflected and helped foster strong leftist political power, an efficient machine for turning out Democratic votes and financing campaigns.

Communists, Internationalists, and Socialists made up left-labor union leadership and radical political, academic, legal, and media activism. All shared belief in the *Communist Manifesto,* a no-holds-barred approach to "proletarian" revolution over despised capitalism. All were anti-American – vociferously hostile to traditional national institutions and people.

Leftist politics steered the contested 1944 vice-presidential nomination to Missouri Senator Truman. Just four months and one week later, he would be called "Mr. President." Far-reaching political debts must always be repaid.

A handful of perceptive insiders and former subversives knew the far-left threat. By time of Korean War, leftist Executive Branch politics ruled military affairs. Laws passed in 1947 and 1949 brought new military command structures assuring tight civilian control of armed forces. Generals and admirals served as political pawns under State and Defense Department secretaries. As a result, the military could not implement strategy and tactics necessary to win the War. Nor could armed services physically possess nuclear weapons, sole purview of the civilian, left-dominated Atomic Energy Commission.

Common-sense-defying civilian orders prohibited US attack on Red Chinese territory, despite mass counter-attack by People's Liberation Army "Volunteers" on American, South Korean, and allied troops within Korea. Communist Chinese Forces (CCF) enjoyed comfortable Manchurian marshalling zones for injecting divisions and supplies into North Korea. Manchurian-based anti-aircraft weapons fired over the Yalu River to down American aircraft and kill pilots in North Korea, while safe from US counter-fire. Reds knew a no-lose situation: freedom to attack at will, sanctuary from home attack. Politics created a deadly world of military unreality in Korea and environs.

War leadership analysis rightly recognizes the role of anti-Americanism in important Korean War strategies. Socialist-Internationalist-Red leadership – America's radical left intelligentsia – decreed limited strengths and missions of US/UN ground, air, and naval forces. Civilian-leader minds embraced leftist ideological sympathies identical to core Communism, assuring dampers on American military power in Korea, ruling out decisive and necessary war with the People's Republic of China (PRC). Communist China and North Korea were then cast in stone. Pro-Red lens also mandated paralyzing leadership fear of Soviet Russia as militarily un-opposable, despite huge American nuclear advantage. Truman would not dare offend political godfathers in countering European and Asian Soviet Army ground supremacy with nuclear threat.

Besides hatred of American people and institutions, Internationalism meant "collective security" and United Nations reverence. Great allied nation influence in Washington War decisions, disproportionate to relatively small troop commitments, helped keep US military power in Korea under wraps. Internationalism insisted on American Euro-centrism – preponderant economic and military support for Western Europe (Soviets controlled Eastern and Central Europe), at expense of second- or third-rank consideration for Pacific-Far East Asia interests. Regarding Korea, Truman stuck to leftist precepts such as minimal troop and supply commitment, ruling out of military victory and nuclear threat, Chinese territorial sanctuary, United Nations umbrella, and desperate grasping at peace negotiations. Continual unproductive shedding of American blood could not change the misguided approach. Politics rules all.

Recently, former Virginia Democratic US Senator James Webb told a reporter, "The duty of a writer is to live in the real world." For 75 years, American brains have drowned in war-related unreality. Our political masters created a fantasy world, a national/international fairy-tale, to "explain" and mask tragic World War II and Korean War outcomes. One has only to read war history books or watch current television programs to appreciate the deception. Speaking or writing about half the post-war world under Communism is most incorrect. So is emphasis on endless Washington propaganda about "making the world safe for democracy." We didn't even come close.

EXPONENTIAL INCORRECTNESS

Sixty-year-old Bolshevik scholarship by professor Philip Selznick, 1990s work by Herbert

Romerstein and Stanislav Levchenko, writings of Fred Charles Iklé, leavened by two-dozen excellent books on Soviet espionage in America, FBI and Venona Project files, and secret 1953 Congressional Executive Session transcripts only released in 2003, funnel into shocking truth. From the late-1930s through President Truman's January 1953 departure from office, a state of *Dual Power* existed in Washington. Directly put, a second, clandestine federal government, Moscow-planned and run by American Reds and pro-Reds, existed alongside "legitimate" US Government, purposely steering national policy toward Soviet ends.

The following Two Governments – Dual Power chapter, and additional treatments in chapters 35, 43, and 44, sufficiently detail Red-Socialist-Internationalist power in America, and its great influence on Korean War causation and conduct. Absent this background, politically-conducted American war may never be understood, and reality of barbaric, never-ending revolutionary assault on America will remain beyond public awareness, just as destroyers wish.

Late Soviet specialist George Kennan nailed down Red operating principles better than any 20th-century or contemporary author. His wisdom provides full knowledge of the motives and *modus operandi* driving the century-old campaign of American destruction. As Kennan explained,

> "The American people would find socialist words and actions easier to understand if they would bear in mind the character of socialist aims. Socialist assault is directed to only one goal: power. It is a matter of indifference whether a given area is "communistic" or not. The main thing is that it should be amenable to socialist influence and authority. If this can be achieved inconspicuously ... and through a concealed form, so much the better.[2]

> It is not our lack of knowledge which causes us to be puzzled by impending socialism. It is that we are incapable of understanding the truth about socialism when we see it.[3] We must understand that for socialists, [internationalists, and all radical leftists,] *there are no objective criteria of right and wrong. There are not even any objective criteria of reality and unreality* (italics added).[4]

> What do we mean by this? We mean that right and wrong, reality and unreality, are determined in the socialist mindset not by any God, not by any innate nature of

things, but simply by men themselves. Here men determine what is true and what is false.

Bolshevism has proved some strange and disturbing things about human nature. It has proved that what is important for people is not what is there but what they *conceive* to be there. It has shown that with unlimited control over people's minds – and that implies not only the ability to feed them your own propaganda but also to see that no other fellow feeds them any of his – it is possible to make them feel and believe practically anything. And it makes no difference whether that 'anything' is true, in our conception of the word" (italics added).[4]

Above facts provide the springboard for accurate evaluation of presidential Korean War decisions and related battle outcomes. One finding is clear: the people may never assume routine Washington leader action to promote American interests. Actual decision-making effects are often anti-American, a disturbing theme unchanged from Roosevelt's 1933 inauguration. Despite Truman's founding of the North Atlantic Treaty Organization (NATO), the 20-year presidential leadership span preceding and including Korean War routinely favored advancement of Soviet and world Communist power at American and Western expense.

OPPORTUNITY FOR NATIONAL LEADERSHIP ANALYSIS

The Korean War teaches many important lessons in civilian and military leadership. With the gift of ample hindsight, we may compare leader words to actions and results, and assess long-term impact of decisions. Presidents, secretaries of state and defense, top generals and admirals, national security advice groups, and intelligence agencies made decisions and left legacies worthy of analysis.

Two 20th-century world wars brought solemn presidential pronouncements about "just peace and self-determination of peoples," neither of which materialized. Instead, instability and global confrontation followed both. Every right-thinking person is justified in cynicism about presidential promises, especially those referencing war and peace. Leaders just can't be trusted to tell the truth, it would expose poor performances.

AVENUES OF EVALUATION: CIVILIAN AND MILITARY LEADERSHIP

The Korean War student may assess effectiveness of American civilian and military leadership on a number of levels: one, in determining the impact of pre-war American foreign policy on Far East stability; two, in defining and solving major combat-related problems; three, in judging truthfulness of government-citizen wartime communications; four, in evaluating consequences of decision-making to future generations; and finally, in predicting leadership performance and national implications in future crises. We may never trust culturally-accepted projections of international or domestic issues. Most electronic and print media are politically-driven and intentionally propagate untruths, superficiality, and sensationalism.

Political elitists frown on objective facts or truth. Our rulers consider truth as extremely dangerous. *Truth is held to threaten political power*, an uncomfortable prospect for the ruling class. Better for America to live a fantasy existence regarding momentous international happenings, such as World War II and its offshoot, the Korean War.

Starting with World War II, American society, if not the Western world, was forced to embrace the tenets not only of socialism, but Soviet Communism. This is unsurprising, given a relentless campaign of destruction waged at least since 1915 by fanatically dedicated and well-funded political activists who evidenced true hatred for traditional America. Of course, politically acceptable descriptors now replace bludgeoning words of old. Internationalists and Communists have evolved into "progressives," while "social and health equality," "social justice," "right to privacy," and "choice," mask contempt for pillars of Capitalist society.

IMPORTANCE OF GEOGRAPHY

A book learning objective is knowledge of Far East Asian geography. Americans do well in becoming familiar with the region's land and sea features and relations. Proper understanding of Korean War events requires frequent reference to regional and national maps. These are included within the text as necessary adjuncts to learning. Readers are encouraged to frequently reference these maps. World atlases and globes are other important aides to physical orientation and understanding.

Factors such as national boundaries, bodies of water, topographic features of rugged mountain ranges, rivers and valleys, and man-made barriers, played vital Korean War roles at all times. Vastness of East Asian land masses and Pacific Ocean, and proximity of Japan, Soviet Russia, and Communist China to War theater, hugely affected Korean War conduct (MAPS 1, 2).

Far from the secondary status of Korean War days, today's Far East is an economic, political, scientific, and military powerhouse. Much of global future will be written there. The past century's regional ignorance and disdain by Western countries must yield to enlightenment and sense of equality. Equal partnership is a necessary and realistic goal.

A COMMENT ON HISTORICAL NICETIES OF LANGUAGE

Most historical writing is couched in super-diplomatic, delicate terminology. Literally earth-shaking points and conclusions are typically sweetened with great, genteel sensitivity. For example, one widely respected American historian characterized global post-World War II tragedy as "dubious political gains" for America. Human implications of half the world under Communism demand more realistic and pointed language.

When historical outcomes involve wholesale human slaughter and misery, much from incompetent political leadership, the author believes strong condemnatory language is appropriate. The same holds in describing treasonous conduct. This book treats incompetent and dishonest civilian and military leaders, whose actions needlessly cost many lives and much blood, with stark and justifiable frankness, and condemns as inappropriate the muted criticism of literary historical protocol.

Decisions of American civilian and military Korean War leadership often placed foreign interests, particularly those of Communism and Internationalism, far ahead of spending native sons. Misplaced leadership brought needless suffering to GIs and families. The author

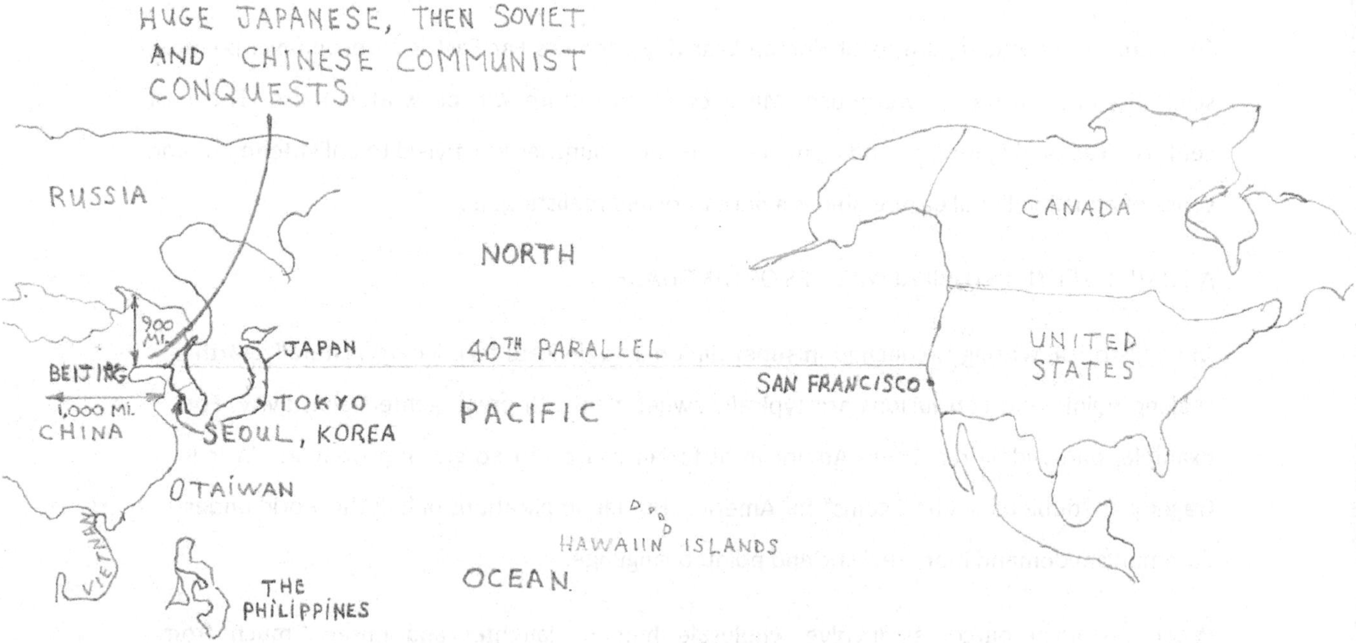

HUGE JAPANESE, THEN SOVIET
AND CHINESE COMMUNIST
CONQUESTS

RUSSIA

NORTH

CANADA

40TH PARALLEL

JAPAN

BEIJING

900 MI.

TOKYO

1,000 MI.

CHINA

SEOUL, KOREA

PACIFIC

SAN FRANCISCO

UNITED
STATES

O TAIWAN

VIETNAM

HAWAIIN ISLANDS

THE
PHILIPPINES

OCEAN.

VASTNESS   OF   PACIFIC   OCEAN
SAN FRANCISCO TO SEOUL 6,500 MILES

MAP 1

RM

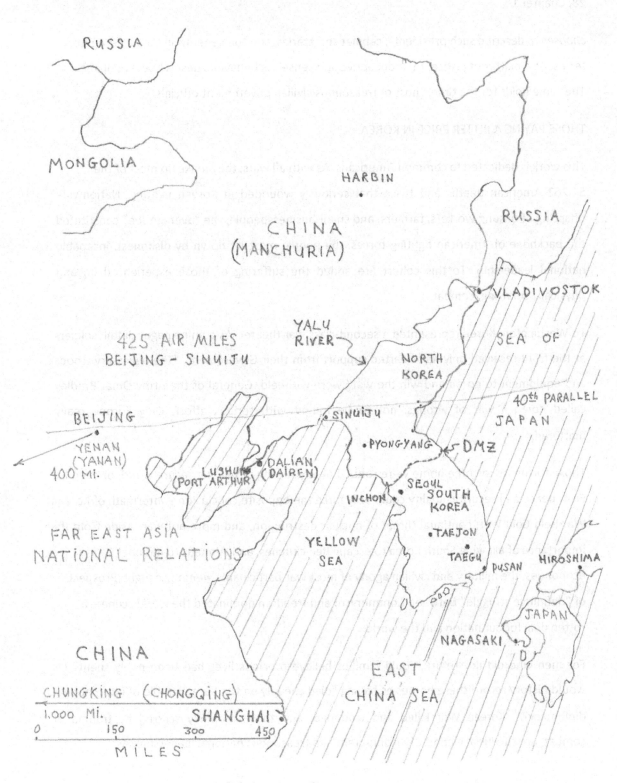

RUSSIA

MONGOLIA

CHINA
(MANCHURIA)

HARBIN

RUSSIA

VLADIVOSTOK

SEA OF

YALU
RIVER

425 AIR MILES
BEIJING - SINUIJU

NORTH
KOREA

40th PARALLEL

JAPAN

BEIJING

SINUIJU

YENAN
(YANAN)
400 MI.

PYONGYANG

DMZ

LUSHUN
(PORT ARTHUR)

DALIAN
(DAIREN)

SEOUL

INCHON

SOUTH
KOREA

FAR EAST ASIA
NATIONAL RELATIONS

YELLOW
SEA

TAEJON

TAEGU

HIROSHIMA

PUSAN

JAPAN

CHINA

NAGASAKI

EAST
CHINA SEA

CHUNGKING (CHONGQING)

1,000 MI.

SHANGHAI

0   150   300   450

MILES

MAP   2

RM

chooses to describe such presidents, cabinet secretaries, and top generals in harsh, derogatory terms. As a matter of justice, their deceptive and senseless behaviors deserve severe blame. The same holds for the time's host of treasonous civilian government officials.

THOSE PAYING A BITTER PRICE IN KOREA

This work is dedicated to common Americans. As with all wars, they make up most of the 54,262 American deaths and twice that seriously wounded in Korean fighting. Nationwide offspring of unsung workers, farmers, and small-businesspeople, the "average Joe" constituted the backbone of American fighting forces, the people most let down by dishonest, incapable national leadership. To this cohort are added the suffering of those experienced in, and physically surviving, combat.

To Washington, Korea represented a second-class war theater. As coming pages detail, soldiers at the front received only half-hearted support from their Government. "The necessary troops and equipment to go on and win the war" were withheld. General of the Army Omar Bradley called Korea a war of wrongs, not to be fought with serious effort. Only Europe really mattered.[5]

Those fortunate to come home were robbed of any feeling of helping secure world, or even Far East, peace and security. Reality could only force the opposite conclusion – aftermath of Korean War held Cold War, continual threat of nuclear destruction, and more hot war. Aside from the importance of allowing South Korea to escape Red clutches, and stimulus to national economies, the military and civilian agony of most war participants went for naught. Prospect of "definitive struggle" between Communism and freedom dominated the world scene – a rotten deal for our nation and the world.

For men who did not return, could families believe precious lives had been nobly spent? Or would history record these heroes as having "died cheaply on the bargain table of international diplomacy?"[6] Korean War killed and wounded, and those mentally scarred by trauma of combat, are sacrificial victims of incompetent and treasonous national leadership. As discussed in the text, there is sound basis for accusation of treason.

Finally, by way of explanation, this book is anything but a blow-by-blow, detailed account of Korean War combat. While preparatory events and every major stage of fighting are given their due, the emphasis is on decisions of top American civilian and military leaders relative to their effect on Korean events, and major 21st-century international problems.

A bit of Biblical advice is appropriate in entering the realm of Korean War leadership analysis. May all those caring about God, country, and family, "Forsake foolishness that you may live; advance in the way of understanding.[7] Take no part in the fruitless works of darkness; rather expose them ....[8] Live as children of light, for light produces every kind of goodness and righteousness and truth."[9]

Chapter 2: Two Governments – Dual Power

"History's a funny thing, isn't it? History can be changed. The past can be changed and distorted and used for propaganda purposes. Things we've been told happened might not have happened at all. And things that we were told didn't happen actually might have happened. Newspapers do it all the time; history books do it all the time. Everybody changes the past in their own way. It's habitual, you know?

We always see things the way they really weren't …."[1]

- Bob Dylan, The *Rolling Stone* Interview.

The following statement on American shadow government is true. It does not represent hyperbole. It is contrary to leftist correctness and so publicly unknown. As the saying goes, "Friends of Soviet Russia do not tell the truth about Soviet Russia." Perhaps 10% of those performing these monstrous acts are known, the remainder undiscovered. Most lived and worked in Washington and New York.

Two United States governments existed before, during, and after World War II. President Franklin Roosevelt visibly headed the first and overt Government, followed by President Truman. This Government is popularly and mistakenly understood as the real and only US Government.

A second federal government flourished at this time, secret and invisible, staffed by over 2,000 Soviet spies and sympathizers masquerading as loyal Americans. Right under noses of Roosevelt and Truman, these traitors controlled sections of the State and Treasury departments, exercised influence in *all* Executive agencies, Congress, and the Judiciary, and operated with impunity in the White House and supposedly super-secret Manhattan Project. Plundering of America knew no bounds. Collective disloyalty and resultant damage are unparalleled in US and possibly world history.

In fact, the secret regime served as a branch of Soviet Government grafted onto the structure and function of American Government, existing solely to satisfy mandates of Kremlin rulers to promote Soviet world power. Communist power in Washington to steer US policy toward ends desired by Moscow represented the culmination of 20 years of incessant pressure for penetration, influence, and control of Federal agencies.[2] These acts took place in an incredibly naïve and unprotected American society whose leaders, presidents Roosevelt and Truman, refused to acknowledge any Soviet espionage problem and profoundly misunderstood, or intentionally overlooked, Soviet motives and actions.

Whether digging in heels to delay and defeat existing US policies harmful to Russian interests, or formulating new policies to promote Red world objectives, Stalin always stood as the shadow's true hero, not FDR, Truman, or the reviled US Constitution.[3]

DENIAL AND PROOF

Thought of two Federal governments appears unrealistic and beyond possibility: "No one could carry off such an audacious operation." But Soviets viewed this as standard operating procedure. Writings of seminal Communist revolutionary Leon Trotsky attest to the *Dual Power* stratagem as necessary in overthrowing hostile, reactionary government. According to US diplomats working in 1930s Moscow, Russian Communists had mastered the dual governance technique. Open Soviet government accessible to US Embassy officials had only form, not substance, while real power lay in the hands of secret police and their controllers. The concept came naturally to fear- and suspicion-obsessed Soviet leaders.[4]

So Moscow marched on two paths in advancing its world position. One "depended on the official actions of the Soviet Government as represented by its leaders and diplomats. The other used personnel of secret police and espionage agencies within foreign countries who recruited pro-Soviet operatives within and without government, for all of whom the Russian Government denied any responsibility."[4]

Examining the true state of 1930s and 40s US-Russian relations validates the expectation and reality of massive clandestine Soviet attack on America. Writers Daniel Patrick Moynihan, Simon Montefiore, William Bullitt, and George Kennan likened Red espionage onslaught to the act of an enemy only briefly at peace with a perceived adversary, with whom they would shortly be at war.[5,6,7] Kennan related "the defiant and provocative attitude taken at all times by the Moscow regime toward non-Communist governments: regarding them by definition as enemies, viewing peaceful relations with them only as a sort of provisional abnormality – an armistice or 'breathing space' between conflicts."[8]

Author Katherine A.S. Sibley described "systematic Communist infiltration and penetration of countless critical positions in US government and industry." Some planted sources took years to develop valuable contacts, information, and influence.[9] A 1947 report prepared by Truman White House Chief of Staff Clark Clifford cited "thousands of invaluable Soviet sources of information in various industrial establishments as well as in the Government."[10] Reds held licenses to steal, bend, distort, manipulate, undermine, and control. As attested by confessed American spy Hede Massing, the Roosevelt administration's blind eye encouraged a golden Soviet espionage era. The same unwillingness to see, or inability to act because of political constraints, clearly afflicted the Truman presidency.

A 1947 book by Richard Hirsch, "The Soviet Spies: the Story of Russian Espionage in North America," helped blow the lid off secret war. By then the FBI had jumped in with both feet. Hirsch castigated Roosevelt and Truman for "no action taken on data readily available, and insensitivity to persistent violation of security rules." Eisenhower later described "a shocking deficiency … in the field of intelligence."[9] But not even intense publicity of 1948 Congressional spy hearings could prevent Truman stonewalling: politics and upcoming presidential election demanded the whole assault be passed off as "red herring," a false issue. Rightfully, Truman should have exercised proper leadership in making the Red spy issue one of prime national security, instead of partisan politics.

According to retired KGB officer Oleg Gordievsky, as soon as World War II ended the US began to be referred to in internal agency communications as the "MAIN ADVERSARY." The term remained in daily use for the next 40 years.[11]

Even before 1933 onset of diplomatic relations between Washington and Moscow, the powerful Red espionage apparatus set its highest goal as worming its way into the heart of American Government. The White House represented a special target.

OPEN SEASON FOR RED INFILTRATION

That a hostile foreign power, the Soviet Union, could control important levers of American policymaking represented a focused and highly disciplined undertaking. A ruthless, Kremlin-generated plan followed a pattern successfully employed in numerous countries. All went according to schedule. Russian revolutionary leader Trotsky's "Dual Power" scheme did the trick, the Communist blueprint for seizing national control. Central to the strategy is gradual, continuous implanting of revolutionary power within legitimate government. Eventually, the host government crumbles from within.

Layers of cells or groups of spies existed throughout America and Canada, most numerous in New York and Washington. Infestation began in 1919-20.[12] Cell supervisors consisted of Moscow-trained Russian professional intelligence agents of the world's largest and most effective spy operation. Some NKVD (the most powerful agency, first called the CHEKA, then OGPU, later the NKVD, then KGB) and GRU (military intelligence) spy bosses worked under the "legal" category, meaning covert intelligence roles played under cover of diplomatic, business, or cultural status. So-called "illegal" professionals having no diplomatic or business cover supervised other spy operations.

Americans made up cell membership, which included the New Deal's brightest and best minds, ideologically devoted to Soviet Communism. Many such agents, and/or their parents, were Russian-born. Government boarding took place during the Warren Harding, Calvin Coolidge, and Herbert Hoover presidencies, with droves arriving under Franklin Roosevelt. These included a host of aggressive and capable operators holding important New Deal government posts. Red power grew with each new Roosevelt term.

FBI historian John F. Fox, Jr. described, "A general leftist tilt in government, which meant that these ideologues blended well into the Washington bureaucracy while keeping their strong Soviet sympathies largely hidden."[13] Franklin Roosevelt's third-term vice-president, Henry Wallace (1941-45), exemplified the dedicated Socialist fitting comfortably in New Deal politics. Wallace served as Secretary of Agriculture in Roosevelt's first two terms.

Despite ample evidence of mass murder, American liberal enthusiasts felt powerfully attracted to the Soviet Union. The same held for British and Canadian establishment figures. George Kennan reported Moscow surprise over Western Red fascination. Kremlin police authorities adeptly used US Communists and sympathizers as vehicles for modifying American foreign policy to fit Soviet aims.[14] Considered "agents of Soviet power," American devotees of Red Russia always stood ready to promote Communist interests while helping tear down those of anti-Communism.[15] No opportunity could be missed to weaken capitalist powers.[16] To Reds, and their "retracted claws" cousins, the Socialists and Internationalists, America exemplified "The classic Marxist predicament: the blood-sucking, corrupted capitalist versus the downtrodden, exploited, but socially pure worker."[17]

Ironically, many traitors came from wealthy families and some were *Mayflower* descendants. The group "who profited most, materially and culturally, from the free American system" had no compunction about destroying that system.[18] Spy cadres held loyalty only to Russian Communism, totally uncaring about welfare of Americans or threats to American security. The US stood as a detested foreign power holding an alien way of life, to be exploited and beaten down. For clandestine agents, Communism represented the one true faith, mankind's shining star.

An FBI comment illustrated the effect of Franklin Roosevelt's welcome-mat approach: "In 1942, Communist Party branches were formed which contained groups of employees from particular government agencies." One spy, Max Elitcher, "joined the *Navy* branch of the Communist Party!" (italics added).[19]

Along similar lines, Roosevelt ordered Secretary of the Navy Frank Knox to lean on the Chief of Naval Operations to mandate hiring Communist radio operators on American warships. The order was to be unquestioningly obeyed. There is no indication of shortage of non-Communist shipboard radio operators. The US knew Moscow aggressively sought classified information on US Navy operational plans. But Roosevelt practiced "Help Reds, hurt Americans," a reckless absurdity.

When publicly identified in 1948 by turn-coat American spy and Vassar graduate Elizabeth Bentley, traitors squealed outrage and innocence. One, William Remington, filed suit against Bentley for libel. Later found guilty of perjury and sent to federal prison, he was killed there by an inmate. Pressed to testify before Congressional committees in the late 1940s, devotees of Stalin such as Harry Dexter White offered outrageously patriotic pitches on their stellar Americanism, the exact opposite of truth.

But shedding light into these dark and sinister recesses could not be tolerated, nor could truth. Anti-Communism represented a sin of epic proportions. In today's historical literature, academia, and media, it still does. It was, and is, quite improper to suggest Soviet influence in Washington. Those who dared expose Reds in government suffered withering fire from the left. The first US Secretary of Defense, James Forrestal, commented privately in 1947 on the pro-Russian nature of American news media.[20] Publicity about Soviet espionage in America could only represent "Fascism" and must be crushed under massive pressure campaigns and relentless character assassinations. The more inconspicuous and concealed the pro-Soviet work, the better.[21]

Grounded in *realpolitik,* only actual power relationships concerned Reds; they didn't care about postwar plans for a United Nations, establishment of collective security, or other naïve, misguided abstractions mesmerizing weak-minded American leaders.

Increasing Soviet power in practice meant satisfaction of Russian political interests throughout the world at expense of US and Western interests. The 20th-century knew no greater political disaster for free peoples than the outcome of World War II, which saw a huge shift in the global power balance toward Soviet Russia, along with generalized political instability.[22]

THE UNFOOLED

At the time, a number of Americans surmised hidden government based on endless pro-Soviet and anti-American actions taken by the United States under Roosevelt and Truman, inexplicable in common sense. Esteemed Soviet specialist Kennan proved most perceptive in diagnosing the problem, detailing the infective Soviet control apparatus. Kennan's unmatched knowledge of Communism and Soviet methods included the Red essence of promoting world revolution. He accurately portrayed "democratic-progressive" traitors doing Stalin's bidding as "disciplined and unscrupulous minorities pledged to the service of the political interests of the Soviet Union in the United States."[23] These accurately resembled a small and viciously hostile internal enemy army.

FBI Director J. Edgar Hoover preached likewise in December 1953 testimony before the Senate Subcommittee on Internal Security: "There is more involved here than the charges against one man. This situation has a background of some 35 years of infiltration of an alien way of life into what we have been proud to call our Constitutional Republic. These Red Fascists distort, conceal, misrepresent, and lie to gain their point. Deceit is their very essence. This can never be understood until we face the realization that to a Communist there are no morals except those which further the world revolution directed by Moscow."[24]

Hoover relayed Washington spy cell composition and actions in numerous FBI reports to President Truman. A November 8, 1945 letter revealed "14 persons employed by the Government of the United States who have been furnishing data and information … to espionage agents of the Soviet Government." A December 4, 1945 report to Truman went into more detail; copies went to Cabinet officials, including the Attorney General. A comprehensive FBI summary presented to the White House October 21, 1946, "Underground Soviet Espionage Organization (NKVD) in Agencies of the United States Government," told chapter and verse, backed by 32 reliable sources. None deterred Truman from appointing two highly documented Reds, Harry Dexter White and Virginius Frank Coe, to vital international posts that year, and in 1948 to relegating Soviet espionage to the political farce of "red herring."[25]

Naturally, Reds pulled all stops in attacking Hoover for audaciously speaking truth. The character assassination campaign against Hoover by Communism's many press foot-soldiers extended long past his 1972 death.

Before World War II, Congressman Martin Dies of Texas chaired a House committee that exposed deep Red penetration and political activity in the US labor movement. He soon became the object of press ridicule. In September 1939, former domestic Red spy Whittaker Chambers revealed much information and many names to Assistant Secretary of State Adolf Berle, to no effect. Postwar confessed spies Elizabeth Bentley and Hede Massing identified dozens of US traitors and details of spy apparatus organization and mission. In 1949, US Marine Lt. Gen. Pedro del Valle correctly diagnosed Red/Internationalist power in Washington as behind attempted sacking of Gen. MacArthur's Japanese occupation leadership.[26] Truman Secretary of State Dean Acheson worked in this effort.

During the 1940s and 50s, the House of Representatives Un-American Affairs Committee exposed many traitors to public examination. California Congressman and Committee member Richard Nixon played an important role, especially in the Alger Hiss investigation.

RED TRAITORS IN WASHINGTON

President Roosevelt's influential White House assistant Lauchlin Currie served as a chief participant in Red Government for six years (1939-45). The Harvard-educated economist enjoyed FDR's complete trust and took on roles far outside economic expertise, serving as chief liaison for US-China affairs and head of Lend-Lease to China. Currie also knew many military secrets, and frequently met with notorious Red agents Nathan Gregory Silvermaster, wife Helen Witte Silvermaster, and Abraham George Silverman. Currie also found time to visit top Russian NKVD officials posted to the Soviet Embassy to discuss "cultural" matters.

In the wartime White House, Currie hired British emigrant and Communist Michael Greenberg as *his* assistant. This neatly reflected Red philosophy: once an opening had been made, it should be worked assiduously. Given China-related assignments, Greenberg freely used Currie's power and White House stationary to impress contacts. He later fled back to England to avoid Congressional scrutiny.

Currie and Greenberg worked alongside White House presidential assistant David K. Niles, mentioned in a deciphered Soviet cable as a source of fake passports for Red friends in need. Fraudulent papers by the hundreds each year allowed free movement of spies, a thriving and important side industry. Niles recruited Philleo Nash from the Office of War Information as personal assistant (June 7, 1945). Upon Niles's White House departure, Nash ascended to presidential aide "in charge of minority problems," keeping the "Red Seat in the White House" tradition alive under Truman. Nash came from Toronto, where his home served as an early-1940s Communist-cell meeting and housing place. According to the FBI, he "maintained close contact with the Communist underground in Washington."[27]

Testifying at August 1948 Congressional committee meetings on Communist espionage, Currie naturally denied any impropriety, while smartly securing legal counsel from Secretary of State Acheson. Currie had entered the business world, heading an import-export company with offices on Manhattan's Park Avenue. Now a political hot potato, Currie "exported himself to Columbia," in the words of author Ted Morgan, where he bought a farm, relinquished American citizenship, and gained a new wife.[28] Revered guest at the 1974 People's Republic of China 25th-anniversary celebration in Beijing, Currie lived into his nineties, never touched by US law

Photo File – Spies and Traitors

Figure 1. Alger and Priscilla Hiss, CPUSA members. Alger worked for Soviet Military Intelligence, the GRU. *National Archives.*

Figure 2. Alger Hiss prison mug-shot after perjury conviction. *National Archives.*

Figure 3. Harold Ware, founder 1930s-40s Washington Red spy cell 'Ware Group.' *National Archives.*

Figure 4. Virulent British spy Donald Maclean, Cambridge family-man. Washington years (1944-48) provide Moscow rich atom bomb information. 'What evil lurks ….' *gettyimages.*

Figure 5. British arch-spy Kim Philby warrants Soviet postage stamp. Made KGB general, he made fools of British and American governments. *Britannica.*

Figure 6. George Koval, key Soviet spy within Manhattan Project, not discovered by US until 2007. Two Soviet spies within Manhattan Project headquarters remain undisclosed. *Wikipedia.*

Figure 7.British Intelligence Service MI5 chief Sir Roger Hollis, with wife, Lady Valentine. Peter Wright believed Hollis a decades-long Soviet agent. *RonMorgansblog5poL*

Figure 8. American academic prodigy Ted Hall, long-time Manhattan
Project traitor for Soviet Russia. Intelligence code-name *Youngster.*
In his thirties, moved with family to England. Proud that Soviet nuclear
bombs may have prevented US atomic attack on China. *National Archives.*

Figure 9. British MI5 Counter-Intelligence agent Peter Wright. Super-bright,
ruffled many feathers. Authored excellent book on his life. *Wikipedia.*

Figure 10. Four of 'Cambridge Five': top left, Kim Philby; top right, Sir Anthony Blunt; lower left, Guy Burgess; lower right, Donald Maclean. Burgess and Maclean fled to Soviet Union 1951. Philby waited until 1968. Their spying killed American and British soldiers in Korea. *Wikipedia.*

Figure 11. Key FDR White House advisor (1939-45) Lauchlin Currie, Stalin henchman. Fled to Columbia 1949 in heat of Congressional investigations. Never touched by law enforcement. *National Archives.*

Figure 12. David K. Niles, Harvard Law graduate, White House Administrative Assistant to presidents Roosevelt and Truman, 1942-51. Decrypted Venona Soviet message New York to Moscow stated, "Around Niles is group of his friends who will arrange anything for a bribe." Fake passports his specialty. *Conservapedia.com.*

Figure 13. Philleo Nash, White House Assistant to President Truman 1946-52, in Key West for Truman vacation. During World War II served as Office of War Information liaison to White House. Canadian Communist ties continued in Washington. *Truman Library Photographs.*

Figure 14. William Weisband, Sr. Soviet agent implanted in 'super-secret' National Security Agency, tipped off Moscow in 1948 about American Venona decryption project. Soviets then changed cipher systems, causing immediate US intelligence blindness before start of Korean War. Weisband spent year in jail for refusing to divulge Red contacts to grand jury, suffered no other legal consequence. His treason directly led to dead American soldiers in Korea. *Wikipedia.*

Figure 15. Duncan Chapin Lee, Yale Law School, Soviet spy in OSS top leadership. All OSS agent information throughout world passed over Lee's desk. Moscow then quickly knew everything. *Wikipedia.*

Figure 16. Lee testifying before US House Committee on Un-American Activities, 1948.
Die-hard Red agent showed typical characteristics: early commitment to
Communism, personal presence in Soviet Russia, graduation from elite
schools, spouse as Communist Party member, vehement denial of
wrongdoing, total loyalty to Stalin, profession of stellar Americanism.
Amazon.com.

Figure 17. Whittaker Chambers (center), devout Soviet spy in America, revealed secret life,
espionage activities and contacts to Congressional committee, grand jury,
and Alger Hiss perjury trial. Proof of long-term Hiss friendship and turning
over classified microfilms and paper documents sealed Hiss guilty verdict.
Chambers book *Witness* eloquent testimony to deep Red infestation throughout America and inherent danger to US survival. *National Archives.*

Figure 18. Arch-spy Nathan Gregory Silvermaster headed extremely productive Soviet spy ring in Washington. Moved into Government jobs at will, used Roosevelt White House aide Lauchlin Currie to forestall Civil Service Commission trouble, acted as owner of US Government. Numerous Venona revelations testify to his importance to Moscow.

American leftist revolutionary champion Silvermaster became a hero to the powerful and wealthy elite leftist establishment. Highly protected and super-politically correct, unknown monster Silvermaster was never prosecuted for any crime.

After meeting Silvermaster March 15, 1944, chief NKVD agent in America Iskhak Akhmerov described him to Moscow as "a man sincerely devoted to the Party and the Soviet Union … politically literate, knows Marxism, a deeply Russian man … known in Washington as a *progressive liberal"* (italics added).

According to Allen Weinstein's book *The Haunted Wood, Soviet Espionage in America,* "By 1951, Silvermaster had become a wealthy home builder on the New Jersey shore." *Historic Images.*

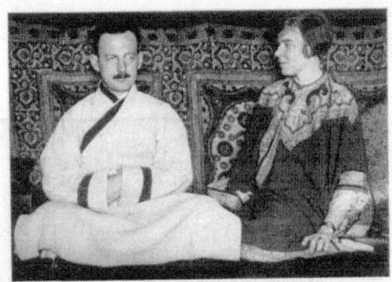

Figure 19. Owen Lattimore wedding, China, March 4, 1926. *Courtesy of David Lattimore.*

Figure 20. Vice-President Henry Wallace, Owen Lattimore, John Carter Vincent, John Hazard, in China June 1944. First 3, ardent backers Chinese Communism. Vincent key Red cog in Two Governments State Dept. machine. Lattimore long-time Red propagandist, held Johns Hopkins University position though never graduated high school. *publishing.cdlib.org.*

Figure 21. Nathaniel Weyl, Soviet agent in America until Sept. 1939 Hitler-Stalin Pact. Authored number of books about Communist reality, at great variance to public understanding. Shunned by academia and media. Truth must be tightly managed for Red advancement. *Wikipedia.*

enforcement.

The State Department's Alger Hiss stood as an influential, highly respected, and key underground operative. Graduate of Harvard Law School and Supreme Court clerk under protean Justice Oliver Wendell Holmes, Hiss started working for Soviet military intelligence, the GRU, in 1935. He rose in State to Director of the Division of Special Political Affairs, receiving the prestigious assignment of chairing United Nations formation.

Hiss also joined Roosevelt as personal advisor at the February 1945 Yalta Conference. There he had the honor of meeting his Moscow-based handler, General Mihlstein. On leaving Yalta, Hiss traveled to Moscow to receive personal congratulations and thanks from a grateful Kremlin intelligence official. A Washington-to-Moscow Soviet cable message sent March 1945 and deciphered by the US Venona Project confirmed Hiss's important role as "leader of a small group of spies who were mostly relatives, [who] worked in the State Department and gathered information on military issues."[29]

After 11 treasonous years in government, Hiss accepted the presidency of the Carnegie Endowment for International Peace. He waged war against former Red agent and chief accuser, Whittaker Chambers, lied under oath about his actions, and suffered the rare indignity of trial and conviction on perjury charges. Hiss served four years in federal prison and for decades counted on a reflexive sycophant cadre to trumpet protestations of innocence. Venona revelations, not made public until 1995, sealed his guilt. Hiss also lived into his nineties and survived demise of his beloved USSR.

HARRY HOPKINS – MORE RED THAN ARTERIAL BLOOD

After Roosevelt himself, close confidant Hopkins represented the most powerful Communist influence in the Executive Mansion and nation. Referred to by insiders as "Associate President," Hopkins enjoyed Roosevelt's full confidence and acted directly on presidential behalf. He lived at the White House for three years, appointed by Roosevelt to head Lend-Lease.

Unstinting in Moscow support, Hopkins routinely gave orders to top military brass, including Gen. George Marshall. Bypassing Manhattan Project director Gen. Leslie Groves, Hopkins provided Soviets with tons of uranium and other nuclear-specific metals necessary for making atomic bombs. Going over the head of Secretary of State Cordell Hull, Hopkins arranged for the sacking of pro-American US Ambassador to Soviet Russia Laurence Steinhardt in favor of pro-Red Joseph Davies. Former KGB agent Oleg Gordievsky called Hopkins *"nash,* one of ours," an agent of Soviet intelligence.[30]

MOST RED DEPARTMENT OF GOVERNMENT

Astute George Kennan knew that "Nowhere in Washington had the hopes entertained for postwar collaboration with Russia been more elaborate, more naïve, or more tenaciously (one might say ferociously) pursued than in the Treasury Department."[31] Assistant Secretary of the Treasury Harry Dexter White, right-hand to Secretary Henry Morgenthau, Jr., prolifically aided secret Government while belonging to Nathan Gregory Silvermaster's productive spy cell. By 1950, the FBI identified 29 Silvermaster ring members.[32] White received, and forwarded to Silvermaster's home, classified directives issued by US military chief Gen. Marshall and sensitive information on "policy of the US Government with respect to both domestic and foreign issues of almost every description."[33]

White's clout in Washington allowed him to block World War II US gold shipments to the Chinese Nationalist Government. Congress had approved gold delivery to shore up China's war-ravaged, inflation-ridden economy. White found every excuse to delay this support and thwart Congressional will, helping bleed Nationalist China to death.[34]

White set up the important Bretton Woods Conference that planned post-World War II international financial recovery, and played key roles in creating the International Monetary Fund (IMF) and World Bank as vehicles for delivering American money to needy or favored nations.

As mentioned, ample evidence of White's deep involvement in Soviet espionage, including two comprehensive FBI reports sent by Director J. Edgar Hoover to the White House, did not deter President Truman from appointing him on January 23, 1946 as US Executive Director to the IMF. The following June, Truman appointed another devout Red agent from Treasury, Frank Coe, as IMF Secretary. A second White favorite, twice-FBI-documented Treasury Red Harold Glasser, soon joined them.[35] Coe remained in that important post until 1952! The next year brought true colors to light, Coe emigrating to the People's Republic of China, along with Treasury Department traitor Solomon Adler. They joined "Peking Joan," defected US nuclear scientist Joan Chase Hinton, recently of the Los Alamos bomb development site, who "held the atomic bomb in her hands," and happily spewed hatred for America in Korean War radio broadcasts.

White, Silvermaster, Currie, and Hiss had power to hire anyone they wanted into scores of government posts having "strategic importance." White in particular served as a one-man Red employment agency, "carefully seeding sensitive American and international agencies with known Soviet agents and conscious instruments of the Kremlin."[36] Reds could dominate divisions, hire, promote, recommend themselves as they wished, and basically run their own shows. The World War II-era Office of War Information, parts of the US Army Signal Corps, especially at Fort Monmouth, NJ, and CIA-forerunner Office of Strategic Services, knew rich Soviet infestation.

Perceptive author David Dallin noted Red penetration of "Six Congressional committees, the Office of the [Military] General Staff, Bureau of Ordnance, National Labor Relations Board, Works Progress Administration, Office of Education, Federal Emergency Relief Administration, Federal Public Housing Authority, Government Printing Office, Library of Congress, Maritime Labor Board, SCAP [postwar Japan's allied military command headed by Gen. MacArthur], Securities and Exchange Commission, and the Veterans Administration."[37]

The US delegation at one postwar international meeting near San Francisco, devoted to world financial recovery, featured the Government's version of the Red All-Stars. Representing "America" were spies Harry Dexter White, Alger Hiss, Maurice Halperin, and Nathan Gregory Silvermaster. It is no mystery the meeting approved a US-backed $90 million "loan" to Communist Poland, over objection of US Ambassador Arthur B. Lane. The FBI revealed that Donald Hiss, Alger's brother, devout Communist and partner in then-Undersecretary of State Acheson's law firm, earned a $50,000 origination fee in the transaction, equivalent to some $600,000 today.[38] The US Treasury never saw a single repayment penny from Red Poland.

The John Earl Haynes and Harvey Klehr book, *Venona: Decoding Soviet Espionage in America*, disclosed the importance of Silvermaster's potent ring. In closeness to seats of power and sheer numbers of high-value documents stolen, it could not be matched. For at least six years, Silvermaster worked closely with Harry White and Lauchlin Currie. Moscow references to Silvermaster in *64* decrypted Venona cables, four times those of White, the second-most mentioned, attest to his high valuation.[39]

Reality is that traitors boldly and literally hijacked key parts of overt US Government and used them to achieve ends set by Stalin and Kremlin henchmen.

TAPPING DOMESTIC RESOURCES

The FBI documented extensive Moscow use of Communist Party USA (CPUSA) Chairman Earl Browder for spy recruitment and facilitation of American operations. Browder assisted in "infiltrating government agencies" and frequently met with and advised underground agents.[40] In the early 1940s, Browder's secretary made 38 trips to the Roosevelt White House, recorded in the visitor's log. Roosevelt pardoned Browder in May 1942 after conviction for using false passports on frequent trips to Moscow and a subsequent four-year prison sentence, one of innumerable and completely useless "goodwill" gestures toward Soviets thought important in modifying Red behavior.

OSS INVASION

A hotbed of Soviet spy activity, the Office of Strategic Services (OSS), CIA forerunner, held perhaps the highest Red percentage of any government agency. The FBI identified at least 16 OSS "penetrations" by Red intelligence. A key source, fore-mentioned Maurice Halperin, held a doctorate from the Sorbonne in Paris, served as direct OSS contact with the Secretary of State, and worked closely with chief officers of America's United Nations delegation.[41] Under Joint Chiefs of Staff direction, Halperin chaired a special combined Army [Department]-Navy [Department]-OSS intelligence project. For years he delivered secret OSS reports and State Department cables to Elizabeth Bentley.[42]

University of Virginia and Yale graduate Duncan Chapin Lee, related to Confederate General Robert E. Lee, served as New York law partner of OSS Director William "Wild Bill" Donovan. Donovan brought Lee into the OSS as his right hand, "privy to most of the material directed to General Donovan."[43] Dues-paying Communists Lee and wife provided Moscow highly-important information on identification, duties, and covers of all OSS agents in foreign countries. Lee befriended OSS traitor Donald Wheeler, member of the Victor Perlo Washington spy ring, employed in the Research and Analysis Division.[43] OSS traitress Helen Tenney also supplied much information to Moscow on worldwide agent activities.

Well-known Washington attorney and Congressional committee advisor John Abt also served the Victor Perlo spy apparatus. One of his clients was politically-powerful Sidney Hillman's Amalgamated Clothing Workers Union.

TRUMAN'S HIDDEN GOVERNMENT – HELPING MOSCOW WITH CHINA

Covert Red Government survived Roosevelt's death and lived for years within the Truman presidency. With exception of Roosevelt's time, America never knew a more favorable environment for treason.

Blatant appointment and retention of Communists in important Government posts spoke of heavy Truman political debts. There is no doubt the President would have better served America by making Soviet espionage a national security matter, instead of letting the issue wallow in political filth. After Truman left office, FBI Director Hoover accused him of "exercising extremely poor judgment" in handling the problem, and *"assumed that Reds who remained in government did so with Truman's blessing"* (italics added).[44] Press-slamming and stonewalling had to follow such shocking incorrect truth.

In December 1953, Attorney General Herbert Brownell told the Senate Committee on Internal Security, "The records available to me fail to show that anything was done which interfered with the continued functioning of the espionage ring of which Harry Dexter White was a part."[45] Truman's blindness to Soviet espionage reflected a political balancing act aimed at satisfying the Democrat Party's powerful left wing while preserving the image of bold patriotism. As mentioned, Truman owed his 1944 vice-presidential nomination, and therefore his presidency, to labor boss and avowed Socialist Hillman. *Hillman* selected Truman over a number of vice-presidential contenders. To paraphrase FBI Director Hoover, America suffered from extremely poor presidential leadership as traitors held sway in Washington.

Noted historian Barbara Tuchman reported the November 25, 1945 resignation of US Ambassador to China Maj. Gen. Patrick Hurley, who made the unprecedented public charge that "A considerable section of our State Department is endeavoring to support Communism generally as well as specifically in China."[46,47] He referred in part to US China specialists John Stuart Service, John Paton Davies, and John Carter Vincent, strong advocates of Mao Zedong's revolutionary movement and demise of Chiang's "feudal and corrupt" Nationalist government. Ambassador Hurley's surprising action expectedly earned rapid and everlasting condemnation from leftist media and historians.

As Douglas MacArthur observed, "While Chiang might be all the things he was accused of, he was also a good friend of the United States." In their zeal to see Communism triumph in China, "China Hand" diplomats ignored the threat to their home country and employer. Despite nonsensical statements by US pro-Communists about Mao's openness to American friendship, the devout Marxist Great Helmsman held only hatred and distrust for the "imperialist" foe.

Importantly at this time, Moscow's Far East policy centered on "acquiring sufficient control of all areas of North China dominated by the Japanese to prevent other foreign powers from repeating the Japanese incursion."[48] George Kennan boiled out the essence: "To the Russian mind, this meant maximum possible exclusion from that area of Americans and British."[48] Roosevelt's huge mistake of encouraging massive Soviet invasion of North China, Manchuria, and Korea, formalized at Yalta, sealed disaster. Undersecretary of State Sumner Welles rightly equated such Soviet control with Communist Chinese victory over Chiang Kai-shek's Nationalists. It also assured US-Soviet confrontation on the Korean peninsula leading to bloody Korean War.

Vehement Red John Carter Vincent, holding the important post of State Department Far Eastern Division Director, wrote a 1945 memo "strongly urging establishment of coalition governments in North Korea and South Korea."[49] Unsurprisingly, Vincent recommended State Department support for a Moscow-trained individual as *South Korean* president while arguing for US abandonment of American-educated and Christian Syngman Rhee. Chapter 43 contains recently declassified State Department Congressional testimony on Vincent's damaging treason.

Europe knew the same sorry state. Fascism's defeat immediately brought Communist hegemony in Central and Eastern Europe. American pro-Nationalist China leader Alfred Kohlberg noted Washington backing of "the magic motto of *coalition government* in Czechoslovakia, Romania, Bulgaria, and Hungary, coined for us by the avowed and secret dupes of Moscow. The Iron Curtain has enfolded and garroted our friends – the friends of democracy and freedom – in all those countries. That has not prevented us from pursuing the same old will-of-the-wisp in China" and Korea (emphasis in original).[50]

Proof is in outcomes. Barbara Tuchman spoke truth with brutal clarity: "Within 18 months of 'victory' in the Far East," the great American military triumph over Japan, "the goal it had been meant to achieve had receded beyond reach, *in mockery of the American effort* ... as if the Americans had never come" (italics added).[51] These words, profound in political incorrectness, are unspoken in popular written and televised Pacific War accounts, shunned in academia, and therefore publicly unknown.

Moscow's Far East wishes corresponded exactly to China policy promulgated by the State Department and endorsed by Truman. Currie, HD White, Acheson, State's China Hands, and press minions faithfully executed Russian mandate. A host of pro-Red "American" authors, including Theodore H. White, Owen Lattimore, and Edgar Snow, waxed eloquently over the brave and just people's world birthing in China. To grease public acceptance of Chinese Communism, the CPUSA dictated use of the descriptor "agrarian reformer" to camouflage Mao's classic Marxism-Leninism.[52]

State Department public pitch emphasized purely humanitarian motives and moral indignation in burying "corrupt" Nationalist China. Supporting human repression and feudalism was unthinkable. American words and directions came straight from Moscow's playbook.[53,,54] As proven by William Bullitt, one need only read excerpts from the time's *Daily Worker* CPUSA newspaper to follow the desired course. The Kremlin called the tune and puppets danced.

ASIAN BALANCE OF POWER DISASTER

While softening up public opinion, the US abandoned Nationalist China at time of dire need. The world's most populous nation quickly became a US-hostile "titanic Red monster." The People's Republic of China (PRC) wasted no time concluding a mutual assistance pact with Soviet Russia after its November 1949 founding, creating "America's worst nightmare," two continent-encircling Communist giants. Huge trouble brewed in Far East Asia. For Roosevelt, and Truman until Korean War, Red interests in Asia clearly took precedence over those of

America.

As with his predecessor, Truman withheld from the American people the deep national security danger inherent in a Communist China. His Secretary of State, Dean Acheson, slickly managed the sleight-of-hand. Another hostile behemoth now stood on the world stage, but why not mask its true role? It is obvious whose interests benefitted from the deception.

In fact, Acheson told State Department officials to downplay the issue in public statements of US non-interference in pending PRC conquest of Taiwan, a vital island-link in Western Pacific US defense plans. As James Forrestal knew, a friendly China and Manchuria represented the best guarantee of Far Eastern peace.[55] Moscow-allied Communist China guaranteed the opposite, as proven in Korea. Truthful linkage, where art thou?

There is no defense, no excuse for the dishonorable, deeply disappointing result of full national commitment to World War II. The outcome represented something terribly wrong and unworthy of popular and national sacrifice. The American people have been shielded from this reality for 70 years, while sending sons to fight, die, and be maimed in bloody, related Asian wars in Korea and Vietnam. Link to terrible leadership under Roosevelt and Truman is clear yet forbidden ground. Unreal, corrupt politics vanquished most-unpleasant reality.

MANHATTAN PROJECT PICKED CLEAN

History's finest example of espionage excellence is Moscow's total consumption of America's "super-secret" atomic bomb project. The Soviet coup further proves the truth of Two Governments.

From world balance of power and national security perspectives, nothing except Communist victory in China compared to lost US nuclear monopoly. Treating America with typical disdain, Reds marched into the Manhattan Project as conquerors and co-owners. Nothing and no one stopped them. The left could never allow long-term US military advantage over the USSR, which must have at least equal capability in atomic weapons.

First-and-foremost loyalty of some American citizens to Soviet Communism is finely illustrated in the 1997 words of Manhattan Project Los Alamos scientist and nuclear traitor Theodore Hall (Holtzenberg), whose family emigrated to America from Russia. His treasonous gifts encompassed at least four years and included key bomb information. Ending the conspiratorial life, Hall and family moved to Britain, from which he penned the following comments:

> "During 1944 I was worried about the dangers of an American monopoly of atomic weapons …. To help prevent that monopoly I contemplated a brief encounter with a Soviet agent, just to inform them [sic] of the existence of the A-bomb project. Now I am castigated in some quarters as a traitor, although the Soviet Union at the time was not the enemy but the ally of the United States …. It has even been alleged that I 'changed the course of history.' Well, if I helped to prevent the bomb [being] dropped on China in 1949 or the early fifties …, I accept the charge."[56]

Soviets exploded their first A-bomb August 1949. Door opened wide to Korean War June 1950. Russia pounced on America's nuclear bomb idea in 1941, before creation of the Manhattan Engineer District (MED), the project's official title. In appreciation of its significance, Soviets attached the code name "ENORMOZ" to the American effort. The attention is remarkable, given concurrent German Army onslaught threatening to overwhelm the Soviet nation. But the Red apparatus promptly bit into the project's heart and never let go. We can only describe the mission's success in terms of a finely-tuned, efficient, continually smooth-running machine attached to US Government to strip bare its nuclear cupboard.

The Kremlin quickly identified the most important *personal* sources of atomic bomb knowledge from American and European physicists and other scientists, then methodically evaluated their usefulness in providing information. All American, British, and Canadian physical facilities involved in bomb design, research, testing, and production were penetrated in depth. These included the University of California Berkeley Radiation Laboratory, Columbia University

Substitute Alloy Metals Laboratory, University of Chicago Substitute Metals Laboratory, and massive, novel plants developed at Oak Ridge, Tennessee; Hanford, Washington; Los Alamos, New Mexico; and Chalk River in Canada. Reds covered all bases.

The apparatus unrelentingly scoured people and institutions for written materials on nuclear fission and bomb development. An estimated 10,000 pages of stolen American information enriched the Soviet bomb program.[57] Reds soon knew the vital US breakthrough in mass production of fissile (atomic chain reaction) material Uranium-235 through the "gaseous diffusion process," arrived at through costly and intense research. This particular theft saved Moscow years of work. Cart-loads of diagrams, plans, drawings, research findings, uranium samples, and production secrets that turned theoretical concepts into workable atomic bombs, quickly found their way to Moscow through the Great Falls, Montana, Army airbase, eliminating other years of trial-and-error. Treasure included theoretical knowledge of the far more deadly, fusion-based *hydrogen* bomb.

The Soviet Army officer supervising loading of Russia-bound American aircraft at Great Falls brooked no delays. Prospect of US Army inspection of the regular mountains of document-containing luggage brought immediate phone calls of protest to Harry Hopkins at the White House. Hopkins promptly ordered Army officers not to interfere. The hard-to-swallow reality: a Red Army officer could issue orders to a US Army Air Corps officer, on an American air base within the United States, which must be obeyed. Now that is Red control!

Completing the nuclear espionage picture is awareness of another important and unknown American venue encouraging Soviet nuclear bomb development: the Lend-Lease program shipping uranium, scarce bomb metals, and more to the Soviet Union. The main actor here is Roosevelt's closest advisor and operative, Hopkins, called by government insiders the second-most-powerful man in America. Russians rightly called the incredible gifts "Super Lend-Lease." Hopkins told a pro-Russia World War II mass rally at New York's Madison Square Garden, "We are going to give you all that we have." He wasn't kidding.

While atomic espionage is anything but humorous, interplay of Russian and American leaders during World War II often featured lines of farcical theater. At the July 1945 Potsdam Conference, President Truman notified Stalin of the successful US atomic bomb test at Alamogordo, New Mexico. Courtesy of traitor and key bomb developer Klaus Fuchs, Stalin already knew. Reserved in comments and acting unsurprised, the Generalissimo merely wished Truman luck in using the bomb. He owned Fuchs lock, stock, and barrel. Voracious reader Stalin's personal library held at least 5,000 pages of secret information on nuclear weapons. Soviet secret police boss Lavrenti Beria initially informed his leader about the US nuclear bomb project in March 1942, over three years before Truman knew![58] Stalin could have lectured pathetically innocent Truman for hours on the bomb.

J. ROBERT OPPENHEIMER

US Army Maj. Gen. Leslie Groves served as MED administrative head. Project security fell to Army investigation, intelligence, and counter-intelligence officers. Physicist J. Robert Oppenheimer led the scientific end. Although a security check on Oppenheimer revealed significant Communist connections, Groves ignored the risk and approved him to head bomb development work. Given Harry Hopkins' White House political pressure, he had no choice in the matter.

During Eisenhower-era hearings on Oppenheimer's loyalty, former Army Los Alamos security officer Peer da Silva testified that Oppenheimer facilitated Soviet atomic espionage by allowing "a tight clique of known Communists or Communist sympathizers to grow up about him within the Manhattan project."[59] The following information validates da Silva's testimony.

In the late 1930s, Robert Oppenheimer regularly attended San Francisco-area Communist Party meetings and belonged to numerous Red "front groups." Local Party leader Isaac Folkoff considered him a Party member.[60,61] Oppenheimer contributed $150 per month to the Party, a considerable sum in those days, easily equal to $1,800 a month today.

Oppenheimer had Manhattan Project freedom to hire as he pleased. Talented physicist brother Frank Oppenheimer joined the Project from the Berkeley Radiation Laboratory and spent two years at the Los Alamos bomb manufacturing site. Frank Oppenheimer and wife belonged to the Communist Party, along with Robert Oppenheimer's wife Kitty and Robert's girlfriend. The Oppenheimers were not alone: prominent Manhattan Project scientist and Nobel Prize winner Harold Urey belonged to 12 Communist-front organizations.[62]

In 1946, Robert Oppenheimer told the FBI of frequent visits to his Berkeley home, before and during the war, by important West Coast Communist Party organizer Steve Nelson (original last name 'Mesarosh').[63] Police departments and Army and Naval intelligence units from Seattle to San Francisco had long known about Nelson.

FBI agents observed a 1943 Nelson meeting in San Francisco with NKVD American spy chief Vassili Zubilin, during which Nelson provided a folder believed to contain nuclear secrets.[64] The Justice Department prohibited any arrests to avoid unfavorable diplomatic publicity. All must be well between US and USSR. The FBI notified Harry Hopkins of the meeting, "with little effect." Hopkins informed Soviet Ambassador Oumansky about FBI probing.

San Francisco again served as backdrop for atomic espionage in July 1944 at Bernstein's Fish Grotto restaurant. Berkeley Radiation Laboratory scientist Martin David Kamen met there with two Soviet consular officials. Earning a PhD at age 23 from the University of Chicago, Kamen "worked on highly classified nuclear experiments, and freely discussed his Berkeley work and experience at Oak Ridge" with the Russians.[65] FBI agents sitting in an adjacent booth taped the conversation. Absence of Radiation Laboratory security encouraged open conversations about atomic research, often in the facility cafeteria.[66]

Four years later, Kamen told the House Un-American Affairs Committee his comments represented "mere discussion of cultural matters," standard traitor response. Reminded about taped comments on "such cultural highlights as the uranium pile, classified atomic experiments, and safety considerations in nuclear work," Kamen denied any wrongdoing and displayed the dedicated Soviet spy's typical *chutzpah*.[65] He knew the inadmissibility of clandestinely-taped remarks in American courts.

Author Katherine Sibley noted FBI awareness of Soviet wartime penetration at Berkeley, Chicago, and Columbia that took five more years to fully understand. Likely reflecting thoughts of Director J. Edgar Hoover, the Bureau passed on "an alarming but prophetic rumor: Slowly but surely an alien control is creeping through the [Berkeley Radiation] Laboratory unseen and unsuspected, *an espionage effort of major proportions which may develop into a national catastrophe*" (italics added).[67] As it turned out, however, Red presence at the MED's vital Los Alamos bomb development and assembly facility remained unknown years after the fact, a "stunning example of espionage excellence."[68]

PLEDGING NUCLEAR GOOD-FAITH

Oppenheimer frankly shared his "enlightened philosophy" about nuclear secrets: there shouldn't be any. His December 31, 1947 letter to President Truman clearly advocated international control of atomic energy, which in reality meant sharing all with the Soviets.[69]

Manhattan Project Theoretical Physics Division chief Hans Bethe spoke for many of the time's nuclear specialists: "We scientists are of the world, we work for the world," not the United States. Bomb scientists, including Robert Oppenheimer, joined politically sophisticated Washington Internationalists Supreme Court Justice Felix Frankfurter, then-Undersecretary of State Dean Acheson, and David Lilienthal, first chairman of the new Atomic Energy Commission, in insisting America "should place at Moscow's disposal, as a pledge of good faith, complete information on the new weapon and methods of its production."[70,71] Necessity of "good faith" *always* devolved on America, never Russia.

Correct politics caused reality to be stood on its head. George Kennan observed the "unshakeable faith of Berkeley atomic researchers that if only the Soviets could be enlightened about the nature of atomic weapons, all would be well."[72] He warned against American assumption of Soviet leader restraint through belief in nonexistent "scruples of gratitude or humanitarianism" that "fly in the face of overwhelming contrary evidence on a matter vital to the future of our country." Kennan called such unreality "a frivolous neglect of vital American interests." Meanwhile, the February 13, 1946 *New York Times* quoted the "correct" Party line version by State Department roving ambassador Philip Jessup: "The US should stop production of atomic bombs and atomic material, and destroy existing atomic material."[73] Reds and minions aimed to put brakes on US nuclear work while Russia caught up, precisely what happened.

Distinguished Soviet affairs author Simon Montefiore revealed rampant Kremlin paranoia over Hiroshima atomic bombing. Stalin observed, "There was no need to use it. Japan was already doomed! A-bomb blackmail is American policy. The balance has been destroyed. That cannot be."[74] The Soviet A-bomb "project was the most important in Stalin's world, code-named 'Task Number One.'" Red god had spoken – let worshippers act.

According to former Manhattan Project scientist Robert Bacher, from 1946 to 1948 America had not a single functional nuclear bomb in its "arsenal." No stockpile of uranium existed from which to make bombs, and US conventional forces barely constituted an administrative, let alone field-grade, army.[75,76] These facts embarrass Commander in Chief Truman, reflecting poorly on his leadership. They can't be publicly known. Moscow, however, had full awareness of American weakness.

Despite the bonanza of stolen and freely-provided materials, including tons of uranium, cobalt, aluminum tubing, and whole factories devoted to A-bomb development, Moscow pushed for full and immediate US release of nuclear bomb secrets. Task Number One mandated all stops be pulled. Truman Administration and Manhattan Project officials faithfully complied, issuing the 'how-to' Smyth Report, *Atomic Energy for Military Purposes,* August 9, 1945, the day of

Nagasaki nuclear bombing and Soviet Far East invasion. The booklet can be purchased today from Amazon.com for about $48. With its help, college students have designed workable atomic bombs.

At the same time, Reds dared not neglect non-nuclear matters. A month later, cell head Julius Rosenberg told underling Max Elitcher that even with war's end, Moscow still needed classified American information on jet aircraft, radar, associated electronics, and every other military advance. This treason would have deadly effects on US Air Force, Navy, and Marine pilots and crews flying in Korea.

The September 1945 defection of KGB decryption clerk Igor Gouzenko from the Ottawa, Canada Soviet Embassy should have alerted Truman to the depth of Red espionage. Gouzenko delivered classified papers to Canadian authorities and implicated 14 trusted public officials as active Red spies belonging to just one "ring" or apparatus.[72] He mentioned evidence of nine other undiscovered rings in Canada alone. It took four months to arrest the traitors, a year more to convict them. Canadian Prime Minister Mackenzie King proved as naïve as Roosevelt and Truman about Russian spying, or perhaps, *equally indebted to socialist political power*.

<u>Chapter 3: Tragic World War II Leadership Begets Korean War</u>

"It is every citizen's duty to attempt, on the basis of what he is permitted to know, to evaluate the foreign-policy problems that face us, to utter his honest views, and to be mindful of the many erroneous assessments … promulgated from Washington in the recent past."[1]

- Gen. Matthew B. Ridgway, The Korean War.

In 1953, American parents asked pertinent questions of their Government: "Why were our boys sent to fight and die in Korea? Why are they sent to Germany and other danger spots of Europe and Asia?"[2] Common people wondered why World War II was *not* followed by a long peace. The pax Americana had lasted less than five years. Something was wrong with this picture. The same questions are raised today about trouble spots in Asia and Africa, and the fact of perpetual US war, with identical lack of truthful Washington response.

Since the people's lives and those of loved ones are at stake, and rarely those of presidential, cabinet secretary, and congressional children, grandchildren, nieces, and nephews, Americans must ask for and demand answers to these important questions. Pat responses, such as "The rogue North Koreans decided out of nowhere to attack South Korea," will not suffice.

For at least a hundred years, the closer we look at presidential leadership in international crisis situations, the worse that leadership looks. When the subject is war leadership, incompetence grows 10 times. Truth about America's wars would unmask great deception and failure on the part of presidents and high government officials. Truth would bring political disaster. Utterly false but sacred, power-foundational political reputations would be threatened, most exemplified in the case of Franklin Roosevelt.

The truth is, we live under a system of pervasive and subtle censorship, "of turning black into white and white into black.[3] We are a nation where government and media control not only the present, but the past."[4]

UNWARRANTED DEFERENCE

People and press give US presidents and cabinet officials far too much estimation in decision-making ability and not enough attention in accountability. High-ranking officials are typically held in awe, as endowed with super-human qualities, when reality beyond image often reveals clay feet. Historian Barbara Tuchman wisely observed that statesmen have no innate quality permitting prediction of future events: "Their actions are taken in contemporary context with no view over the hill."[5] Dreadful Korean War civilian and top military leadership suggests that a careful and doubting eye be cast on all Washington public statements. Lies flow as water from our presidents and Government and indeed define our political system. Truth has devolved into a Stalinist perversion of reality aimed at gaining and advancing political power. Mere truth is nothing compared to political necessity.

A Chinese saying well describes the lasting state of affairs between American Government and the public: "Politics is just the same as it has been since Confucius, a matter of manipulating people."[6] For the last century, truth about world events has been withheld from Americans. Reasons for whole-cloth treatment boil down to politics, economics, even spirituality. A long-waged domestic campaign of destruction seeks to eliminate traditional American life in favor of a "New Order" controlled by a secular, wealthy liberal elite. Widespread knowledge of truth impedes this control.

Lest desire for popular ignorance be viewed as a recent phenomenon, powerful French statesman Cardinal Richelieu (1585-1642) advised that, "A nation whose every subject should be educated would be as monstrous as a body having eyes in every part; pride and presumption would be general, and obedience almost disappear."[7]

Late distinguished US diplomat George Kennan, and two military officers playing important roles in the Korean War, Army Gen. Matthew Ridgway and Admiral C. Turner Joy, are among those who learned first-hand how America's New Order manages information. The first law of political leadership requires, and maintenance of power demands, that "We ourselves determine what is true and what is not."[8]

For the sake of political power, millennia-old principles of truth are abolished in favor of standardized "distortion, deception, and falsehoods."[9] Truth is destroyed through continual barrages of "lies and bigger lies, which when repeated long enough and loud enough will be believed by the people."[9] Any person or group opposing the "change" agenda receives a rain of vile insults. The right to set moral standards is denied the public majority, held as discriminatory, unjust, oppressive to minorities. Those favoring retention of moral standards as necessary to humane society are castigated as bigots and tyrants. The majority may only hold moral values deemed acceptable by the minority. They can't choose their own.

As is clear from historical literature, purveyors of New Order rile against America's version of freedom and democracy as abomination against humanity. Antiquated, useless conceptions of patriotism, belief in God, practice of religion, especially Christianity and Judaism, use of the Bible, and reverence for home and family, are objects of endless ridicule. Amply proved in Europe and Asia, full national "progressive" control equates with destruction of Judeo-Christian principles, teachings of Christ, clergy, churches, temples, and followers. These must be banished from the face of the earth. Destroyers seek and attain a new system, featuring absence of objective truth and dominance of moral relativism – an "anything goes" mandate. People are brain-washed to accept the politically-correct agenda as key to social salvation, to wiping out centuries of "evil" tradition. In true Marxist practice, competing sources of authority are strictly prohibited.

Our rulers profess strong faith in "One World," a universal government under which major wars will supposedly be impossible. The process depends on leveling out differences between the United States and the rest of the world, which necessitates bringing the American people down many notches economically and socially to a level of non-uniqueness. Laying waste to America also includes the concept of people's gods, a necessary element of popular control, but these "gods" must be selected and correct men and women, not a heavenly Deity. Marx, Lenin, Franklin Roosevelt, and Barack Obama fit the mold.

Government and press lie merchants are heavily invested in the New Order's Communist ideology masquerading as "socialism" and "social justice." A favored public tranquilizer is the naturally welcome word of "peace," used during and after World War II to numb the masses, as preparations continued for slaughter to a higher cause. Despite six years of promised universal freedom, democracy, and self-determination, packaged in Franklin Roosevelt's "Four Freedoms," bloody combat returned to the world stage in Korea too soon after the greatest war ended.

In the sense of actual World War II and Korean War outcomes, this book attempts to "provide a glimpse into the nature of truth and reality," bearing in mind the words of Palm Beach Atlantic University educator Gene Fant, Jr.: "No one has ever created truth. Truth is discovered and described, but … independent from human affirmation … and unchanged by discovery."[10] In a corollary view, truth also cannot be destroyed, unless every mind be deprived of reason, reflection, reality, observation, perception, and conclusion. We embark on a journey to uncover what is intentionally hidden from public view. Much discovery awaits.

FOR POWER-MAD, KEEPING PEOPLE DUMB IS SMART POLITICS

Ancient Greek and Roman mythology featured hosts of gods with super-human powers. We wonder over backwardness and unsophistication of peoples apparently believing such tales. Yet today's citizens are immersed in a similar sea of myths that define understanding of national and world events. The particular mythology associated with World War II is 75 years in the making.

MONUMENTAL DECEPTION – ENSHRINING 'THE LIE'

In his March 25, 2014 radio program, Rush Limbaugh quipped, "It may require an act of courage to believe the truth." Leftists commonly portray truth as hate speech, uttered only by radical fringe, right-wing "extremists" and "nut jobs." Saturation lying helps create an atmosphere hostile to truth. Mainstream media are always there to pitch the favored line. Correct people and causes receive the most sympathetic attention.

Leftists specialize in legitimizing untruths. Prominent politicians, including presidents, are frequently brought before the public to attest to the loyalty, greatness, and pro-Americanism of favored sons and daughters. Prestigious awards are bestowed on leftist champions, impressive testaments to high achievements in country and world. For example, two weeks into his first term, President Obama astoundingly received the Nobel Peace Prize. Actual accomplishment, the truth, meant nothing to the award. Likewise, before leaving office, President Lyndon Johnson dutifully honored nuclear scientist J. Robert Oppenheimer before the cameras for lifelong loyal service to America. Johnson knew where his bread was buttered. That Oppenheimer created a years-long, fast-flowing conduit of secret atomic weapons information to Moscow during and after World War II, later confirmed in opened Soviet files, didn't matter one bit. Neither did his Manhattan Project recruitment of dozens of pro-Soviet scientists and workers, nor professed wish to pass all atomic secrets to Russia. The special treatment shows how documented histories of disloyalty are overcome in public minds.

Another favorite device crushing truth is building of grand monuments to leftist icons in Washington, New York, and other places of prominence. Words and statements embodying lofty principles are carved in massive blocks of granite, emphasizing honoree importance and everlasting impact on a grateful nation. Such monuments tell people that only truth could be portrayed in such impressive manner, only the most noble and honest could sit alongside Washington, Jefferson, and Lincoln. Surely, massive physical manifestations of greatness could not grow from deception or grand lies. National Government stands behind these testaments to lofty ideals, so they must reflect truth and justice.

Meanwhile, leftists labor hard to eliminate traditional American practices: complementary words about Founding Fathers, verbal and written references to cross, Bible, and Judeo-

Christian underpinnings, and popular feelings of profound national love and gratefulness. In their stead come pitches for class and gender conflict, increasing dependence on government, higher taxes, and supposed gross unfairness and discrimination in social, educational, and employment fields.

Monumental devices of leftist political control represent brilliant mechanisms of popular brainwashing. The process has a 100-year operational history in America, with no signs of receding. Why should it? From the Red view, results are outstanding.

WORLD WAR II BEGETS KOREAN WAR

A vital yet unknown core fact begs appreciation: the Korean War is a direct product of World War II. Korean War came about *only* because of World War II. Almost every popular Second World War and postwar history, including those of Korea, avoids this understanding. A major point of popular history is to keep people from thinking, especially about World War II – Korean War linkage. Modest public knowledge about reasons for fighting these wars, when joined to their outcomes, must soon lead to reader amazement at American senselessness, obvious disjunction between truth and public knowledge, and deep sense of let-down by government.

Among probing questions sure to arise are, "Why did we trade Nazism for Communism in Europe? If Pacific War sought to prevent Japanese domination of China, why was it OK for Communists to control China? Didn't the people expect and deserve a long period of peace after the Second World War? Why didn't that peace happen? Did American boys fight, die, and be maimed in World War II, and so many families suffer anguish, for nothing? What is going on here?"

Very few Americans know the reality of World War II military victory and political disaster.[11] Media emphasis on American military victory ignores the postwar political debacle infecting international life and bringing 45 years of Cold and sometimes hot War. Television history programs continually portray the many scenes of military action and US victory on European and Pacific fronts. Unfortunately, horrendous political outcomes are disconnected from success-oriented battle narratives. The same holds for almost all popular World War II history books. Public thinking about the outcomes would threaten the reputation of an iconic president who did his nation dirty on a global scale, hence irrelevance and shunning of truth.

Historian D. Clayton James faulted restricted American vision during the Second World War on achieving military victory, while the Soviet Union and Great Britain focused on maximizing political interests in the new postwar environment. Franklin Roosevelt tended to ignore difficult and unpleasant matters, "unwisely delaying settling of major political issues with the Soviets."[12] Resulting Red domination of Eastern and Central Europe, and shortly the huge expanse and population of China and Manchuria, set up Western-hostile power throughout the world. We strain to find any historical or cultural references to Roosevelt's defining role in this mess.

President Truman's memoirs attest to the tragic state of world affairs in Spring 1948, while never mentioning his predecessor. It was a bleak landscape: "We knew that Korea was one of the places the Soviet-controlled Communist world might choose to attack [an outright lie; no such awareness existed. North Korea's attack on the South came as a devastating surprise]. We could say the same for every point of contact between East and West, from Norway through Berlin and Trieste to Greece, Turkey, and Iran; from the Kuriles in the North Pacific to Indo-China and Malaya."[13] North Pacific and Indo-China references proved especially ominous.

In short, the world was split in two. For America, this reality cast sadness and tragedy on reasons for fighting World War II. Roosevelt's abominable handiwork stood for all to see. But as today's esteemed Dr. Ben Carson notes, "The left can't argue the actual facts," so unpleasant truth must be managed and buried. Frank-speaking British intelligence officer Peter Wright described a "Looking-glass world, where simple but unpalatable truths [are] wished away."[14] Better to show more pictures of wildly happy Times Square crowds celebrating Japanese surrender.

Also absent in American understanding, part of the same issue, is the uncomfortable fact of Korean War as a direct consequence of terrible presidential leadership during and after World War II. But prospect of this unpleasant truth soon brings charging white steeds and circling of wagons around the past century's most revered, truly sacred American political reputation, that of Franklin Roosevelt. The reflexive word comes down from secular heaven, inscribed on massive granite blocks in boldest letters, reminding all of Roosevelt's eternal sanctioning as "Savior of Mankind." When you mess with FDR, you mess with the bedrock foundation of socialist and Red power in America.

Roosevelt's promotion of world Communism at every opportunity is held unworthy of public attention. With "peristaltic vengeance," the power base must and will be protected at all costs. Thinking about half of mankind doomed to live under Communist tyranny because of Roosevelt is most incorrect, sure to bring merciless stomping or shunning. After all, great Stalin taught as a national and international necessity, "One must sometimes correct history."[15]

POLITICAL FIREWALL PROTECTS TRUE KOREAN WAR CAUSATION

Although we strain in historical literature to find evidence of direct linkage between the Second World War and war in Korea, the connection is clear, strong, incontrovertible. North and South Korean nations came into existence only as a consequence of the great war. Franklin Roosevelt's insistence on bringing a huge Soviet Russian army to Far East Asia to defeat already-defeated Japan brought Red and US armies face to face on the Korean peninsula. The peninsula must then be divided forthwith to head off military unpleasantness.

In a rare gesture of ready acceptance, Kremlin leaders agreed to Washington suggestion of the useless, insignificant 38th Parallel as the Korean and US-Soviet dividing line. The line had no economic, geographic, or political meaning to Korean peoples. US Army Lt. Col. Dean Rusk, soon to be President Truman's Assistant Secretary of State for Far Eastern Affairs, made the recommendation which led to one of the 20th-century's worst foreign policy decisions (Rusk later became President Kennedy's secretary of state). *Korea was set up as a real-life chessboard, East versus West, Communist versus Capitalist, a battleground* on which American and allied boys and Korean and Chinese peoples would shed blood.

Few Far East Asian scholars spoke about, or published information on, the dangerous power imbalance attending China's Communist domination. American Government maintained silence on the issue, the people ignorant of any consequences. One author who stepped forward, visionary David Dallin, penned a chillingly perceptive assessment of regional prospects: "For the Far East the fighting is not yet over. The Far East stands on the threshold of a new series of hostilities which will exact a heavy toll in human lives before stability and progress return there."[16]

The prophetic words came in 1948, two and a half years before war in Korea, 16 years prior to Vietnam. Dallin dealt in reality, so different than fantasies of US presidents and power brokers. In this book, the author attempts to emulate such realism in assessing Korean War causation, conduct, and consequences.

Part II

Korea Explodes, June 25, 1950

Chapter 4: North Korean Surprise Attack

"We're sitting on a keg of dynamite in Asia. I think we can hold them off

until we get strong ...."[1]

- President Truman, Journals of David E. Lilienthal.

The North Korean People's Army (NKPA) launched full-scale invasion of South Korea June 25, 1950. Despite numerous small incursions and skirmishes by both sides over the prior 18 months, the mass attack caught President Truman and his administration completely off guard. Some officials believed the claim of US Korean Military Assistance Group (KMAG) Maj. Gen. William Roberts that South Korean forces could easily handle any threat posed by the North.[2] Unreality aside, Truman, Secretary of State Dean Acheson, and US military chiefs of staff knew North Korea possessed far greater armed force than the South.

Since 1945 partition of the Korean peninsula, US troops had occupied the South and Soviet forces the North. Governments, politics, economic policies, and cultures of each side directly reflected strong Soviet and American influences. Russia created North Korean Communism by bringing in some 300,000 Korean Reds from Siberia and Manchuria, many trained in Moscow, while American diplomats worked to create a stable South Korean government.[3] August 1948 proclamation of the southern Republic of Korea (ROK) brought the feisty presidency of Syngman Rhee. State departments under presidents Truman and Eisenhower viewed Christian, US-educated Rhee as an unstable zealot bent on peninsular unification. Because of fears Rhee's government would take major aggressive action against the North, the US refused to arm the ROK with planes, tanks, effective anti-tank arms, and artillery. South Korea had more of a police force than an army.

Foundation of the northern Democratic People's Republic of Korea quickly followed. Courtesy of the Soviets, the NKPA had the above arms in abundance. Ample manpower came from military draft of all 17- to 25-year-old North Korean males. Soviet T-34 tanks, master of World

War II German armor, spearheaded invasion routes. Air attacks and artillery bombardments preceded armor and infantry. Unsurprisingly, North Korean forces crushed southern resistance. After a few days, the key objective of Seoul, the South Korean capital, fell to the North. It appeared all South Korea would shortly follow (MAP 3).

US INTELLIGENCE BLINDNESS

Korean War students agree that Northern surprise attack represented a huge American intelligence failure. Neither the Central Intelligence Agency (CIA), State Department sources, nor Far East military intelligence predicted the disaster. Starting February 1950, reports revealed intense Soviet targeting of South Korean communications from Vladivostok listening posts, plus North Korean and Manchurian receipt of large Russian shipments of bandages and medical supplies. No alarm sounded.[4]

As post-World War II Soviet-American relations deteriorated and world tensions grew, US intelligence capability in Russian affairs suffered a disabling blow with far-reaching consequences. As revealed by David Hatch and Robert Benson, "Soviet intelligence had placed an agent inside the US Armed Forces Security Agency," forerunner of today's National Security Agency, who in 1948 informed Moscow about extensive US penetration of Soviet cipher or coding systems. The Soviet KGB had recruited American traitor William Weisband in 1934. By 1945 Weisband worked as supervisor in the super-secret AFSA Russian section, that by 1947 had partially cracked Soviet codes. Based on their spy's warning, Moscow quickly shut down all existing message systems. Hatch and Benson described the result as US intelligence "Black Friday": There was no American decryption ability in the period leading up to the Korean War. It was perhaps the most significant intelligence loss in US history."[5] It took almost 50 years for the American public to learn about US breaking of Russian codes through the "Venona Project."

Roosevelt administrations ignored vast Soviet espionage attack on the United States, while Truman politically downplayed the barrage as "red herring." Finally arrested in 1950, Weisband, KGB-codenamed "Zveno," stonewalled a grand jury and wound up serving only a

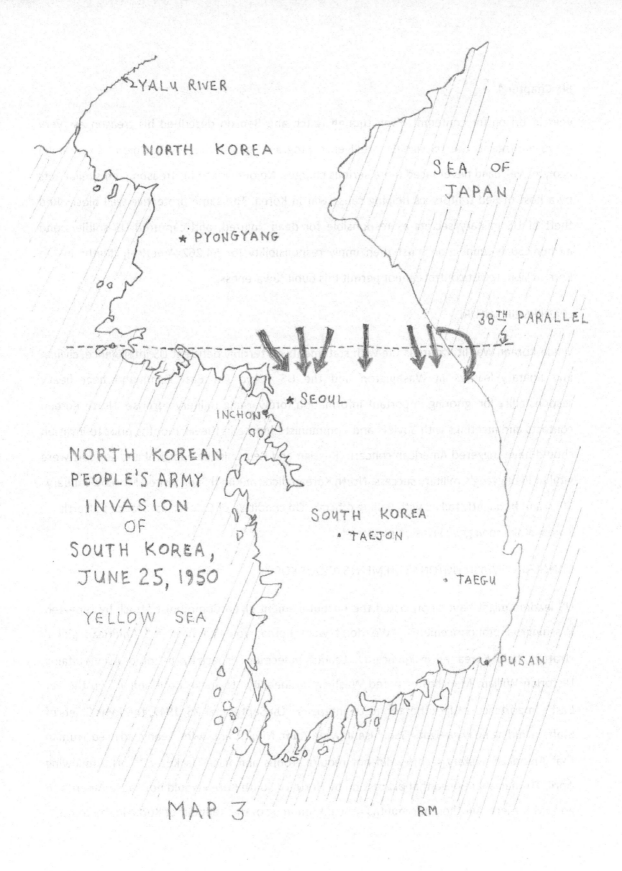

YALU RIVER

NORTH KOREA

SEA OF JAPAN

★ PYONGYANG

38TH PARALLEL

★ SEOUL

INCHON

NORTH KOREAN
PEOPLE'S ARMY
INVASION
OF
SOUTH KOREA,
JUNE 25, 1950

SOUTH KOREA
• TAEJON

• TAEGU

YELLOW SEA

• PUSAN

MAP 3   RM

year in prison for contempt. Even though Hatch and Benson described his treason as "very grave damage to the US signals intelligence program against the Soviet Union," loyal Stalin acolyte Weisband never faced more serious charges. No one linked his treason, and similar acts by a host of Red traitors, as helping cause war in Korea. The same protective wall blocks Red theft of US military secrets as responsible for dead, injured, and captured US soldiers and airmen. Such connection must then imply responsibility for 54,262 American deaths in the Korean War. Leftist control cannot permit this public awareness.

LEADERSHIP FAILURE

While Korean War literature is rife with statements on terribly deficient US intelligence, civilian and military leaders in Washington and the US Tokyo Far East Command bear heavy responsibility for ignoring important information forewarning military surprise. North Korean contacts and meetings with Soviets and Communist Chinese in the six months prior to invasion should have triggered American concern. Russian and Red Chinese approval and support were vital to Pyongyang's military success. North Korean dictator Kim Il Sung visited Moscow January 1950 and frequently talked with Beijing officials. On condition of Chinese assistance to North Korea, Stalin soon gave invasion go-ahead.[6,7]

DANGEROUS WASHINGTON STATEMENTS ABOUT KOREA

US leaders might have appreciated the encouragement given Communist attack by repeated Washington pronouncements, "We don't want Korea, you can have it." American global strategy held Korea as insignificant.[8] Leader indecision especially haunted Asian affairs. Historian William Manchester noted Washington inability "to make up its mind" on the Far East's importance, or lack thereof, to US interests.[9] On September 25, 1947, the Joint Chiefs of Staff, including heavyweights Gen. Eisenhower, Adm. Nimitz, and Adm. Leahy, advised Truman that American military security did not require troops and bases in Korea.[2,10] The following April, Truman announced that aggression by North or South Korea would not cause America to go to war there. Another four months brought founding of the Republic of Korea in the south, countered the next month (September) by establishment of the northern DPRK. On June 29, 1949, the last American combat troops departed Korea, with only a small KMAG remaining. Its commander, Gen. Roberts, gave a false and self-serving estimate of potent southern fighting capability. The US got not quite a year's respite before the roof caved in.

Secretary Acheson iced the cake with his January 12, 1950 National Press Club speech placing Korea outside the US Western Pacific defense perimeter.[11] The Communist side took American leaders at their word, not appreciating the depth of uncertainty plaguing US Far East policy. For Washington, Europe held center stage, not the Pacific.[11,12] Seeds so well planted by Franklin Roosevelt and nourished by Harry Truman grew into "the first limited war between the Cold War powers, both directly and by proxy."[13]

Five days into invasion, President Truman sent US Far East Commander Gen. Douglas MacArthur to assess the Korean battle situation. Visiting the Han River's south bank opposite Seoul, MacArthur observed wholesale retreat of ROK army remnants and fleeing civilian hordes (MAP 4). Organized resistance had disappeared. MacArthur advised the president that air and sea support would not suffice to save the South. Only US infantry would do. Truman quickly agreed, authorizing elements of three US divisions on occupation duty in Japan to confront and stop North Korean invaders south of Seoul.

Less than five years after World War II, American blood would again flow in battle. The American people expected a long peace following total national commitment to global war, but only gained a brief break. Roots of this unpleasant, illogical, and undeniable fact are largely left untouched by historians. Blame is typically, wholly, and falsely assigned to "irrational North Korea." We are not supposed to think otherwise. In truth, we are not supposed to think at all.

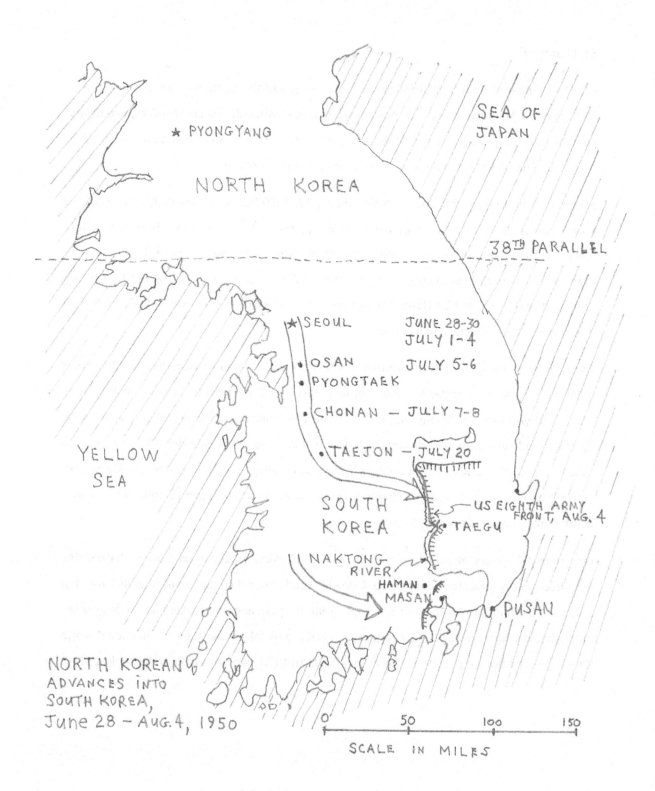

★ PYONGYANG

NORTH KOREA

SEA OF JAPAN

38ᵀᴴ PARALLEL

★ SEOUL   JUNE 28-30
                 JULY 1-4
• OSAN   JULY 5-6
• PYONGTAEK
CHONAN — JULY 7-8
• TAEJON — JULY 20

YELLOW SEA

SOUTH KOREA

US EIGHTH ARMY FRONT, AUG. 4

• TAEGU

NAKTONG RIVER

HAMAN •
MASAN

• PUSAN

NORTH KOREAN ADVANCES INTO SOUTH KOREA, June 28 – Aug. 4, 1950

0   50   100   150
SCALE IN MILES

MAP 4

RM

Chapter 5: Twin Albatrosses - United Nations "Legitimacy"

and Revised Chain of Command

At urging of Secretary of State Acheson, avowed internationalist and protégé of influential Supreme Court Justice Felix Frankfurter, President Truman sought a United Nations umbrella for Korean military action. Internationalists favored US intervention in Korea only under UN aegis. The US must support the UN at every opportunity as the only bulwark against world war. But the fact is, America did not need UN approval to defend South Korea.

As World War II ended the US stood as sole occupying power in the southern half of Korea. American troops stayed in South Korea until 1949, American government always closely associated with the South's legitimate government. America had every right and obligation to defend South Korea on its own. International mandate for this action was unnecessary. Going in under the UN banner simply reflected Truman-beholden Internationalist power in America.[1]

For the US, UN war affiliation proved anything but innocuous. Joint Chiefs of Staff Chairman Gen. Bradley referred to "the outlook of our allies, in particular, [as] a major consideration."[2] The UN tie significantly restricted American freedom of action in the Korean War, far in excess of allied manpower and logistic contributions. Continual "need to consult with allies" hampered prompt battlefield responses. On numerous occasions, allied nations withheld approval and necessary combat steps were not taken.[3] Wars can't be fought successfully by politically-dominated committees, but that was reality for America in Korea. Only one example is prohibition of UN aircraft from pursuing Communist jet fighters operating in North Korea back across the Yalu River to Manchurian bases.

High-performing Soviet MiG-15 jets could attack at will below the Yalu, then secure safe refuge at south Manchurian airfields simply by re-crossing the river. No "hot pursuit" by US or allied planes allowed, courtesy of the UN.[4] D. Clayton James also believed hot pursuit flew in the face of "several efforts by the US government, presidential statements, and UN overtures, to signal Beijing that UNC operations in North Korea posed no threat to Communist China," and so must be denied.[4] Red airbases were also off-limits, along with North Korean hydroelectric power plants and northern halves of Yalu River bridges. These are unique restrictions in the annals of aerial warfare. "Thirteen allies against a particular American military action" became a regular cry and excuse for avoiding common-sense air and ground responses.

Britain's influence on war strategy especially transcended any physical assistance.[3] Gen. Bradley related the Joint Chiefs view of British equal-partner status, her views "at all times given full consideration in Washington."[2] Britain very much sought to preserve economic interests in Hong Kong, and so resisted firm action against the People's Republic of China after it entered the war. Joint Chiefs shared the belief that "war should not spread to Red China."[2] In early December 1950, Prime Minister Clement Attlee tried to push Truman into granting Communist China a number of concessions to put the brakes on her successful counter-attack, in reality a surrender package. Attlee insisted Truman rule out threat or use of nuclear weapons in Korea or China. Moscow promptly received the full Truman-Attlee meeting transcript and learned the President would not resort to nuclear attack in Korea under any circumstances, a comforting assurance. Churchill's description of Attlee may be apt: "A sheep in sheep's clothing."

Britain did send an infantry regiment to Korea, plus an aircraft carrier and other warships, while Australia provided an air squadron for ground combat support. Turkey, France, Greece, Canada, and The Netherlands contributed combat battalions; Italy, Ethiopia, and other countries logistical and medical support. British, Turkish, and French infantry units performed bloody missions with great bravery. But non-US and ROK manpower comprised less than 2% of allied strength. This help would likely be forthcoming without UN sanction, in recognition of American effort in the Second World War.[1]

The model of Internationalist influence in American foreign affairs holds to this day. President Obama's 2014 Secretary of Defense Chuck Hagel and Joint Chiefs of Staff Chairman Gen. Martin Dempsey were adamant in "need for endorsement of NATO allies" before any economic measures could be taken against Russian imperialism in the Ukraine or military response to Islamic terrorists. As always, the political component of these important defense positions is overwhelming. Leader side-stepping seeks to mask unpleasant realities from public view.

NEW MILITARY CHAIN OF COMMAND

After World War II, powers-that-be decreed complete civilian control of military operations, even in the realms of strategy and tactics. Political control had to be tightened to make this possible, hence push for new laws to reorganize the military chain of command. The resulting hierarchy presented a far different picture of civilian control than existed in the great war.

Now chiefs of Army, Navy, and Air Force (later to include the Marine Corps), sitting as Joint Chiefs of Staff, reported to an overseeing civilian secretary of defense, appointed by the president and confirmed by Congress. The defense secretary in turn appointed civilian secretaries for each service branch, and military chiefs acceptable to the president. A 1949 law amendment created a Joint Chiefs chairmanship, which served as the formal communication link between chiefs and secretary of defense. The JCS chairman also served as the political lever keeping chiefs under thumb. If politics meant operational excellence instead of power fixation, we should be living close to martial paradise.

Starting with Truman's presidency, the secretary of state weighed in as an important authority on military affairs. By 1950-51, Dean Acheson's State Department enjoyed "unprecedented influence in military affairs."[5] It was unthinkable for Roosevelt's long-time Secretary of State Cordell Hull to exercise *any* military influence – he had trouble enough staying in the diplomatic loop. Truman served as an artillery officer in World War I but knew little of international affairs on assuming the presidency. D. Clayton James and David McCullough commented on his personal hostility to generals, excepting George Marshall, and military education.

While Defense Secretary Louis Johnson languished in Truman's political doghouse, Acheson enjoyed unparalleled sway with his president. That the Secretary of State had no expertise in military strategy, tactics, and operations, in fact no military experience whatsoever, didn't matter. *Control* was the important thing.

The military command chain now grew to Byzantine complexity. Assistant- and under-secretaries of state and defense had input, along with counterparts in offices of civilian service secretaries and military chiefs of service. Another civilian executive body reporting to the president topped off the stew, the National Security Council. Still later, the office of National Security Advisor placed yet another civilian at the president's ear.

Unsurprisingly, imposition of command hodge-podge helped assure US inability to win wars in Korea and Vietnam. Field command knew strict political oversight and terribly convoluted civilian-military leadership. Since political systems function as promoters and protectors of power, high-functioning combat officers, real warriors in ability, boldness, and honesty unwilling to sacrifice personal morals, pose a threat to civilian power and usually do not rise above the rank of colonel. To put it crudely but accurately, most promotions to general and admiral, eventually rising to service chiefs, are to politically-minded "rear-end kissers."

So, the system demanded that Korean-era Chiefs play lap-dogs and violate common sense and wise military strategy in agreeing to eliminate highly successful, wide-scale mobile offensive operations as peace negotiations beckoned. Ground threat to their rear now gone, major military pressure off, willing to trade blood at a 10-to-1 ratio, time stood on the Communist side. Mao and Zhou played Truman and Acheson like well-hooked fish. It was one of the darkest points in US civilian and military leadership history.

Recent examples prove continuation of the Truman-Acheson model. President George W. Bush's Defense Secretary Donald Rumsfeld, and Joint Chiefs, failed to appreciate and act on Iraqi armed hostility threatening gains of hard-won 2004 invasion and capitulation of the Saddam Hussein regime. Only on Rumsfeld's departure did the situation improve. Likewise, President Obama micromanaged the saving of an American ship captain from Somali pirates, repeatedly refusing Navy requests to eliminate the pirates. The on-scene commander stuck his neck out to order Navy Seals to shoot the pirates and free the captain. Afterward, politics had the last word as the president played the ill-fitting role of brave, decisive commander in chief. The brave combat commander is not likely to gain an admiral's star.

Consequence of the military's political domination is evident in Obama's second-term Secretary of Defense Hagel. The former Nebraska US Senator's public utterances project weakness and confusion. He struggles to effectively communicate. From the standpoint of leadership competence, Hagel appears a complete dud. How he managed to gain election to the Senate and appointment as the nation's top defense official is a matter of amazement. But he fills the desired role of dutiful water carrier. Foreign aggressors are sure, and right, to hold him in complete disregard. (President Obama fired Hagel November 2014).

Chapter 6: Military Reality – Outnumbered, Outgunned, Undertrained

Combat capability of the Japan-based US 2nd and 24th infantry and 1st Cavalry divisions well-reflected the state of American conventional military power. President Truman had gutted not only the recently mighty US Army, but the entire defense establishment. Dwight Eisenhower equated post-World War II "demobilization" with destruction, observing in December 1946, "We have no real military formations."[1] Chief of Staff Gen. Bradley described the army he inherited from predecessor Gen. Eisenhower as a 552,000-strong *administrative* force, in "shockingly deplorable" condition, "with almost no combat effectiveness." As Bradley related, "The Army of 1948 could not fight its way out of a paper bag."[2] Two years later nothing had changed. On February 12, 1948, Truman Secretary of State George Marshall told the National Security Council, "We are playing with fire while we have nothing with which to put it out."[3]

The first Secretary of Defense, James Forrestal, bemoaned the "anguished problem of how to deal with an ominous world power situation when one's own power had been laid aside."[4] He encouraged President Truman to frankly tell the nation the dire state of international relations. George Kennan agreed, believing Truman should level with the American people on realities of the Russian problem, "the sooner, the better."[5]

Protection of Franklin Roosevelt's sacred political reputation meant "the trumpet call never came."[5] The simple, deadly truth was that international Communism equaled intractable advocacy of world revolution. Truman's adoption of America's "containment policy" for Soviet Russia, Kennan's brainchild, required military muscle to work. As Gen. Bradley reported, "Exactly the opposite was taking place."[6]

That Truman blamed Congress and people for headlong destruction of American military might did not square with his clear national security responsibility as Commander in Chief. The second volume of Truman memoirs, "Years of Trial and Hope," contains the outrageous statement, "I was against hasty and excessive military demobilization. The press and Congress drowned us out."[7] Military neglect is more remarkable given concurrent growth of worldwide Soviet threat.

Truman writings admitted revolutionary Communist danger in 1948, "from the Baltic in northern Europe to Trieste, to Middle and Far East Asia," but failed to mention the April 1950 National Security Council policy paper number 68 (NSC 68), "the first significant post-1945 statement on American global strategy."[8,9] The NSC detailed serious increase in Soviet military power that along with American weakness might presage "conventional and nuclear warfare by 1954."[8] The USSR and Communist China had already signed a long-term mutual assistance pact. NSC 68 urged immediate and extensive American military buildup, with *four-fold* increase in military expenditures for fiscal 1950. Truman ignored the advice and threat, locking the paper in a safe. Then came Korean War and a US Government caught militarily with its pants down. Red interests appeared to benefit from US military weakness, leader indecision, and complacency.

THE KOREAN PENINSULA AND ILL-CHOSEN 38TH PARALLEL

Geographically, North and South Korea hold some 84,000 square miles, half the area of Greece. The north-south expanse, from the Yalu River to peninsular tip, is about 600 miles. Excluding the much wider continental portion of North Korea, extending "as the crow flies" 375 miles from southwest to northeast, maximum peninsular width is 150 miles.[9] The Yalu and Tumen rivers comprise the 880-mile, continually twisting North Korean-Chinese border[10] (MAP 2).

South Korea is a bit larger than the state of Indiana, its 1950 population of 20 million twice the North's. Traditionally, the North contained most of the region's heavy industry, the South dominant in agriculture. Korean rice is considered among the world's finest.

Importantly, the State Department's hastily chosen dividing line between north and south, the 38th Parallel, held no significant geographic features such as major rivers or other bodies of water, defined mountain ranges, or any other notable aspects of terrain. Militarily, politically, economically, and historically to Korean peoples, it was meaningless. Washington, in the person of State Department-assigned US Army Lt. Col. Rusk, made a very poor choice that soon caused severe disturbance to the normal lives of millions of Koreans. Traditionally undivided people were now split in two. Japanese control of Korea yielded to Soviet and American control. The 38th Parallel may have looked like a natural line of division on a map, but surely helped set the stage for Korean War.

Now chickens set loose by Roosevelt in Far East Asia came home to roost. There is no evidence of presidential appreciation of profound geo-political changes unleashed by insistence on massive Soviet entry into the Pacific War. Communist imperialism quickly replaced that of Japan in mainland Asia. From the standpoint of preventing one tyrannical nation from controlling China and East Asia, US sacrifice in the Pacific War came to nothing.

CHARACTERIZING THE JUNE 1950 US ARMY

A modest-sized theater of action by world war standards, America would be hard pressed to fight effectively in Korea, or anywhere else. The US had exactly one combat-fit reserve division, the 82nd at Fort Bragg, NC.[2] Washington civilian and military leaders, and Japan-based US Army officers and soldiers tasked with saving South Korea, overestimated the meager capabilities of occupation-softened troops. Garrison life in Japan meant parades and "a crisp set of khakis with polished brass and shoes that would reflect your face."[11] It meant cleanliness and peacefulness, a comfortable army cot with "clean ironed sheets," and fried chicken on Sunday. A brief walk to the "club" offered a few games of pool, a fine dinner, and later a couple of sets of tennis. As one Army lieutenant recalled, "It had been so pleasant ...."[12] Now, at war in Korea, that same soldier lived in a hole, covered in dirt, ate cold rations, and faced an enemy intent on blowing him to pieces.

THE TYPICAL GI ENTERING KOREA

American ground-fighting units could be accurately summarized as an "under-force:" undermanned, undertrained, under-weaponized, and unprepared for combat realities. Identical deficiencies characterized the Navy and Air Force. Since words are easier to muster than abilities, troops about to enter Korea substituted bravado: "Once North Koreans saw US uniforms they would drop their arms and run away."[13] Blind confidence would shortly vanish; tough war with Japan should have eliminated the bane of racial chauvinism toward Far East Asians. The misperception proved a persistent, inappropriate, embarrassing and counter-productive theme in America's 20th-century wars.

Importantly, 18- and 19-year-olds comprised the majority of American infantrymen in Korea, drawn from the "bottom rung of the social and economic ladder: poor and uneducated whites, blacks, and yellows."[14] These became prime candidates for slaughter. Many Second World War veterans filled non-commissioned and commissioned-officer ranks. Yet, freshly minted second lieutenants entered the line in droves, the West Point Class of 1950 losing 34 of 670 graduates in Korea. Author Rick Atkinson described most of them as "green as grass when they died."[15]

Given dire manpower straits early in Korea, the US military activated a large number of World War II veterans on reserve status. This group had given years-long loyal and courageous service in European and Pacific theaters and returned home to marry and start families. With overwhelming victory on both fronts, few worried they would ever have to leave the reserves for active duty. Americans expected a long, deserved peace. Then came a host of men, either heads of families, key workers in war production, or a bit on the old side, who had not served in the great war, had no reserve commitment, and did not get called for Korean service.

Activation of combat-veteran reserves engendered much family unhappiness and charges of unfairness. Regardless of reserve status, medical personnel such as physicians and dentists were routinely drafted out of private practice or professional school graduation to meet field demands.

STEPPING INTO THE RING

The morning of July 1, 1950, 24th Infantry Division Commander Maj. Gen. William F. Dean ordered his 21st and 34th regiments to move post haste from Japan to Korea. Both held only two depleted battalions instead of the normal three.[16] These were airlifted into Pusan at Korea's southeast tip, the first to arrive.[17] The enemy had now marched far into the southern part of the Korean peninsula (MAP 4).

Departing July 4 by train from Pusan, the 21st Infantry's 1st Battalion, led by Lt. Col. Charles B. Smith, moved northwest to engage the North Koreans. Among other geographical features, the Battalion crossed the Naktong River on its way up (MAP 4). The Army and historians called the initial combat group "Task Force Smith." A battery of three 105-millimeter artillery guns enhanced the force. Lack of hand grenades and recoilless rifle (rocket) rounds somewhat diminished firepower, but "wouldn't be needed." Neither would well dug-in defensive positions.

Officers and grunts shared a positive mood. Backward soldiers of North Korea would be routed, the unit "back at Sasebo [Japan] after a short police action." Rout indeed described the encounter. Combat, with its many uncontrolled variables, does not allow guaranteed outcomes.

Chapter 7: American Combat Begins

Joint Chiefs Chairman Bradley long considered "piecemeal commitment of our ground forces the worst possible way to enter a fight."[1] Yet the US did just that in Korea (and Vietnam). Sending the 82nd Airborne Division was unthinkable – national combat reserve would then be at zero. The 82nd must be saved for Europe, the far more important theater to Washington, in case of Soviet attack. Of course, a stand-alone 82nd would be eaten whole by the European Red Army. Military weakness and lack of presidential will invite many terrible scenarios.

Even six months into Korean fighting, Gen. Bradley bemoaned a "US still militarily unprepared for general war – we could still not save Western Europe."[2] To Truman and Joint Chiefs of Staff, Korea was a relatively minor irritation.

First US fighting took place the morning of July 5 north of Osan (MAP 4). Hardy North Korean T-34 tanks rolling south brushed aside the 400-strong "blocking" Task Force Smith, deployed along hillsides overlooking the main north-south highway. Puny 2.36-inch bazooka rounds bounced harmlessly off sturdy tank hulls.[3] Battle, as it was, lasted four hours, after which Lt. Col. Smith ordered withdrawal south. Smith's artillery would likely have wreaked havoc on enemy T-34s and following infantry, but after taking a few tank cannon rounds, artillerymen abandoned their guns and ran for their lives. Much of Task Force Smith did likewise. North Koreans executed unfortunate soldiers trying to hide in foxholes, a continual war barbarity.

Army historian Russell Gugeler disturbingly reported, "As many wounded as possible were carried out, but the unit abandoned its dead," a kind way of stating wounded and killed-in-action were left behind. Failure to retrieve dead and injured comrades represented great combat code violations.[3] Presaging US practice during Communist Chinese mass invasion, soldiers also threw down guns and equipment, including personal gear such as steel helmets, boots, ponchos, and ammunition belts.

The first round of combat had ended. US showing could not have been more disgraceful. Grim realization set in: "Of the two armies, the North Korean force was superior in size, equipment, training, and fighting ability."[4] How far the World War II American Army had fallen!

Debacle continued. On July 6 a 34th Infantry rifle platoon ineffectually took on the southbound Red tank and infantry column between the towns of Osan and Pyongtaek (MAP 4). Now Americans were digging in, but heavy night-time summer rains filled fighting holes and brought soldiers "up to their necks in cold, stagnant water." Advancing North Koreans were mistaken for fleeing Americans and not fired on.[5] Many GIs refused to raise their heads above holes in order to fire. Gugeler noted, "Even after 15 minutes of combat, less than half the men were firing their weapons. Squad and platoon leaders did most of the firing. Many riflemen appeared stunned and unwilling to believe enemy soldiers were shooting at them" and trying to kill them.[6]

Almost half a 31-doughfoot platoon had inoperable rifles. A sergeant examined the guns and found them "broken, dirty, or incorrectly assembled."[7] Embarrassingly, and dangerously, soldiers simply didn't know how to care for their guns. While some men neglected to carry canteens into battle, panic caused those that did to throw them aside, then in exhaustion drink from ditches and rice paddies fertilized by human excrement.[8] Gastrointestinal disease soon flourished. Those who attempted surrender received North Korean bullets to the head.[8]

LAX DUTY, DISGRACEFUL PERFORMANCE

Unrealistic training and soft occupation living took their toll on preparedness. One infantryman described an enemy formation as, "Like the entire city of New York moving against two little under-strength companies."[6] Again, potent weapons such as 4.2 inch mortars lay unused as panic held sway. Men didn't know the difference between sounds of their own mortar fire and that of enemy tank guns. Terrorized by North Korean machine gun fire, troops readily shed personal weapons. Few heeded officer calls for order in the rush from reality.

Befitting sorry performance, North Koreans captured 24th Infantry Division Commander Maj. Gen. Dean, held as a prisoner of war the next three years, the Korean War's highest ranking American POW.

ELEMENTS OF INDIVIDUAL AND UNIT FAILURE

Exceptional Korean combat leader and later Army Col. David Hackworth recognized, "There are no bad outfits, only bad officers.[9] An outfit is only as good as its commander."[10] Army leadership from training to field commands bears blame for the debacle. Leaders neglected the responsibility of "mentally training every soldier for the shock of battle" and instilling the reflex of instant personal and unit defense.[11] Army training not only lacked intense and realistic experiences mimicking battlefield conditions, it failed abysmally in marksmanship. Incredibly, many men in early Korean fighting "had never fired their weapons." M-24 tank crews could not practice-fire their 75-mm guns due to lack of barrel recoil lubricant, "on backorder for two years."[12]

Failure to carry sufficient ammunition proved another common and deadly infantry problem reflecting combat inexperience and terrible leadership. Soldiers went into battle with relatively few clips of rifle rounds, machine-gunners with only a couple of boxes of shells. Even before reaching the combat zone, green troops riding South Korean trains north would get "trigger happy" at sundown and begin indiscriminate firing. Nervousness at start of action also caused much needless shooting – with hours of combat remaining, troops then found themselves short of, or out of, ammunition.

It is interesting that under similar battle stress situations, US Marines in Korea did not "cut and run." One explanation is found in realistic training. Legendary Marine combat commander Col. Lewis "Chesty" Puller arranged for training companies to sit under artillery practice-fire barrages to get used to booming and intimidating sounds.[13] The practice held danger, but far less than sending green combat troops to early graves. Puller frankly told his units: "I know something about the strain of combat. Why does the louder nose of a fight with heavy artillery and bombs make such a difference? I think the difference is entirely in the mind, in the preparation of men for combat. If we make our men tough in mind, *before* they go to war, and give them an honest idea of what war is like, we won't have so much of this shell-shock trouble" (italics added).[13]

Army battalion, company, and platoon field officers routinely failed to establish forward combat outposts to warn of trouble; to place platoons in positions of mutual fire support; to personally communicate and coordinate with adjacent units; and in preparing secure defensive positions.[14] All reflected embarrassing unprofessionalism.

Too many Korean battalion, regiment, and division commanders had lost the fire in their bellies. Prime years left on World War II battlefields, now "too old for the job," the spark of keen, creative leadership could not be rekindled.[15] Their wrong tactics often led green units to "sheer bloodbaths."[15] The phenomenon manifested at the highest level in the timid and defeatist Joint Chiefs of Staff. The ghost of ancient Roman military commander Pompeius Magnus, Pompey the Great, lived on.

COMBAT LEADERS AS HEROES

A strong sacrificial element exists in excellent small-unit combat leadership. Given demand of roving personal presence in close proximity to enemy force, "Correct and successful command at platoon and company levels is not conducive to long life."[16] The combat leader, especially the platoon second lieutenant, "must constantly expose himself in order to lead and maintain control."[17] Enemy gunners all too often note the exposure. Hackworth, who earned *five* Purple Hearts in Korea, bluntly estimated platoon leader life expectancy as "no longer than a month."[16]

Months later, after personal experience with Eighth Army leaders and troops, Gen. Matthew Ridgway summarized the state of military reality and *esprit de corps*:

"If ever we were unprepared for war, we were on this occasion. Before the Eighth Army could return to the offensive it needed to have its fighting spirit restored, to have pride in itself, to feel confidence in its leadership, and have faith in its mission.[18]

Every command post I visited gave me the same sense of lost confidence and lack of spirit.[19] [Army] leadership I found in many instances sadly lacking, and I said so out loud. Reliance on creature comforts, timidity about getting off of scanty roads, reluctance to move without radio and telephone contact, and lack of imagination in dealing with a foe whom they soon outmatched in firepower and dominated in the air and on the surrounding seas – these were not the fault of the GI but of the policymakers at the top.[20]

In combat, every unit commander is absorbed in the accomplishment of his own mission. Be he in command of a squad, a platoon, a company, or any unit all the way up to Corps, his assigned task requires all the professional competence, all the physical energy, and as much strength of spirit as he possesses.[21] By proper foresight and correct preliminary action, he knows he can conserve the most precious element he controls, the lives of his men. So he thinks ahead as far as he can. He keeps his tactical plan simple. He tries to eliminate as many variable factors as he is able.[22]

The ability to make prompt decisions and to execute them vigorously is best bred in men who, through confidence in their troops and in their superiors, have persuaded themselves that they are unbeatable."[22]

Soldierly incompetence reached beyond ground action. An American plane mistakenly strafed the two-mile column of hapless retreaters with .50 caliber machine gun bursts. The only casualty was a South Korean soldier suffering a blown-away lower jaw.[23] According to Hackworth, incidents of friendly fire accounted for a staggering 15 to 20% of dead and wounded in both Korea and Vietnam.[24]

DATED EQUIPMENT AND WEAPONS

Hackworth made a depressing comment on combat communications: "10% [of troops] never get the message."[25] This failure rate is frighteningly high and must compromise infantry success. Regularity of radio failure added to communication woes. Bulky, obsolete 1943-vintage radios routinely failed to work, while an updated version had not yet been issued to GIs in Korea. With radios out, artillery forward observers could not relay enemy positions and strength to battalion commanders, along with important firing coordinates. Army 27th Regiment (25th Division) 2nd Lt. Addison Terry related sighting North Korean tanks but inability to call in artillery strikes, sadly observing, "in 62 days of combat the SCR-610 radio worked for only one mission."[26] Soldiers had to lay down wire between outposts and field headquarters to enable electronic communication. Within a day or so, the enemy would cut the wire and GIs again had to risk life and limb rejoining cut sections.[27] Whomever had responsibility for Army radio communications, especially for providing combat units with non-functional, dated equipment, should have been relieved of duty and held accountable for compromising combat effectiveness and costing needless casualties.

Poor quality extended to American artillery pieces. Bread-and-butter 105-mm howitzers, the main weapon at this time for keeping the NKPA at bay, were old and worn, commonly 50 to 200 yards off target despite best efforts of competent crews and fire directors. Self-propelled guns would be more rapidly moved and set up, but the US had only truck-towed artillery at this time in Korea. North Koreans, however, had a complement of self-propelled cannons, courtesy of Soviet Russia.[26]

Manpower proved a most troubling US deficiency. The four divisions on occupation duty in Japan (24th, 25th, and 7th infantry, and 1st Cavalry) all stood at two-thirds strength. Instead of holding the specified three battalions per regiment, they held only two. Combat losses quickly drove strength below 50% of "authorized" levels. While Gen. Bradley's 1948 words about the US Army reduced to an "administrative" force came back to haunt, the American people never knew the seriousness of manpower shortage, because the guardian press never pounded the point home. *American national security had been sacrificed for Western European economic and military support, and continuation of Fair Deal and New Deal domestic policies.* Tragically, this huge, costly mistake did not rise to the threshold of national news.

POLITICS VERSUS MILITARY REALITY

According to pre-Korean War boasts of Defense Secretary Louis Johnson, seconded by President Truman and Secretary of State Acheson, the United States Army "would strike back decisively within an hour after being attacked," wherever this might happen – the "powerful, well-equipped, well-trained, and well-manned Eighth Army," bereft of fat but resplendent with potent muscle.[26,27] Lt. Terry joined many GIs in mocking these ridiculous political falsehoods. Representing "the United Nations in its first adventure in international policing" was proving a rather unpleasant undertaking.[28]

Abandoning company radios, the retreating Army horde lacked any chance at communication with battalion, regimental, or division headquarters. The "plan" was simply to go south, then east.[29] Survivors found brief refuge in soon-overrun Pyongtaek. The 24th Infantry Division, along with the *24th Regiment* of the 25th Division, took awful beatings at NKPA hands, "entire battalions wiped out and artillery positions and regimental command posts overrun." Reflecting poor leadership, the 24th Regiment routinely cut and ran at first sign of enemy fire, leaving "bazookas, 81 mm mortars, Browning Automatic Rifles, heavy and light .30 caliber machine guns, and M1 rifles by the dozen," along with matching ammunition. No spent brass from fired rounds at "fighting" positions meant no resistance.[30]

Displaying savagery that must have reflected command policy, "Enemy tanks ran through aid stations, shooting GI wounded as they lay on litters."[31] Retreating troops suffered "murderous fire" from T-34 tank machine guns and cannons, causing en masse abandonment of division vehicles and "a mad rush to outdistance" the rampaging enemy.[32] Scores of soldiers, still with weapons, lay in ditches and other cover, yet failed to return fire "while lead thumped into the ground all around them."[33] Machine gun strafing, bombing, and rocketing by Air Force, Navy, and Marine planes could not stop the enemy host. The important road center of Taejon in southwestern South Korea fell one month into war (MAP 4).

Brutality extended beyond actions of North Koreans. The US rained artillery shells and tank cannon fire on many South Korean villages suspected of housing enemy. On at least one occasion during night fighting, hamlets were set afire and burned to the ground by white phosphorus rounds, the light helping expose North Koreans. The mentality appeared to be, "Let's get them before they get us." In this phase of fighting, the author has not learned of any efforts to evacuate civilians prior to shelling. Fortunately, as documented later in the text, the US showed exceptional consideration for *North* Korean civilians when battle safety permitted.

Three days after 24th Regiment battlefield abandonment at Haman, deep to the south, only one infantry company of its original six could be found (MAP 4). The rest melted into surrounding towns (Masan for one) and countryside.[34] Military police scoured roads and villages for the remnant.

For true warriors carrying the combat burden, among them the 27th Regiment, cynicism provided an outlet for frustration. The Army's *Stars and Stripes* newspaper ran a whole cloth story about the 1st Cavalry Division's bravery and defeat of North Koreans. A 27th Wolfhound trooper observed, "This morsel of information brought hope to our hearts, for we had been under the impression that the 1st Cav was on the Yankee [North Korean] side, especially since their artillery had continually shot at us all the time we were fighting the rear guard down Heartbreak Highway. In fact, we were practically sure, for hadn't the 5th Regiment of the 1st Cav left all their equipment on the road behind us so that our fighting withdrawal would be more difficult? No, it couldn't be true that they were on our side. But, the paper said they were winning the war for us. We were much encouraged by this revelation."[35]

NEVER TRUST GOVERNMENT AND PRESS WAR REPORTS

A vital lesson emerges from the above incident and so many others. Press coverage of combat and war, and official government war statements, simply cannot be accepted as truth. Realities of censorship and bias are permanent features of mass communication. War reportage is packed with 180-degree lies, exaggerations, and whole-cloth treatments, meant as political balm for troubled people. Father Government knows best. Political leaders must *appear* as competent, wise, displaying just the right leadership. Truth is not allowed to impede power.

Round two of fighting showcased US ineptitude and decisive North Korean ground superiority.[36] The enemy continued to roll, gobbling big chunks of South Korea. Boots on the ground no longer talked about "police action."[37] Col. Hackworth told the truth: *"Never had American arms performed so badly in time of war than in the first months of the Korean War* (italics added)."[38]

Chapter 8: Combat Second Phase - Naktong (Pusan) Perimeter

FIRST US COMBAT VICTORY

July 24, 1950 brought a momentous event: for the first time in the Korean War, the month-long US Army losing streak against the NKPA ended. As the battle for Taejon raged, multiple NKPA divisions took up positions to the east and blocked the Poun Road (MAP 5). The US 24th Division came dangerously close to being trapped.

Unknown to the enemy, the two-battalion 27th Regiment (25th Infantry Division), the "Wolfhounds," was ordered to deploy on either side of the Road. Eight T-34s spearheaded southern NKPA infantry advance, brazenly marching in close formation. Timely and accurate artillery fire tore into the Red advance, while World War II-vintage Australian Air Corps P-51 Mustangs knocked out the tanks and wreaked havoc on enemy artillery. The all-important element of surprise lay with the UN. The Wolfhounds saved the day, a new day at that — parts of the North Korean Army had finally been "defeated and stopped" in battle.[1]

By no means eliminated as a major threat to Eighth Army survival, NKPA forces continued to roam South Korea at will. Battle momentum still favored the Reds. US/UN opposition kept falling back toward the southeast. As artillery forward observer Addison Terry frankly put it, "There was always the road — 'Heartbreak Highway.' We fought on the hills around it, swam and waded the rivers that it crossed, burned the towns it went through, ate on it, ran on it, and died on it."[2]

Importantly for the US/UN, August 1 marked the end of the Korean War's first phase. President Truman generously referred to the first month as "trading space for time," meaning yielding most of South Korea in order to allow build-up of a fighting force capable of defeating the

NORTH KOREAN ATTACK

NAKTONG RIVER

SEA OF JAPAN

POUN

TAEJON

SANGJU

NAKTONG-NI

YONGDOK

SOUTH KOREA
(SOUTH-EAST CORNER)

ROK ARMY

P'OHANG

NORTH KOREAN ATTACK

⊙ TAEGU - (EIGHTH ARMY HQ)

EIGHTH ARMY

NAKTONG RIVER

1 CAV. DIV.

24 DIV.

NAKTONG RIVER

25 DIV.

NORTH KOREAN ATTACK

CHINGDONG-NI

MASAN

PUSAN

KOREA STRAIT

KOJE DO

0   10   20   30

SCALE IN MILES

MAP 5   NAKTONG (PUSAN) PERIMETER

AUG. 4 - SEPT. 15, 1950

RM

NKPA. The daunting task took every remnant of America's depleted martial fiber. Wars always started poorly for the United States – Korea was no exception.

By now, GIs well-appreciated North Korean battle preferences. The NKPA avoided daylight attacks, American firepower exacted too heavy a toll. It appeared the enemy slept during the day. Better for North Koreans to sneak up "between four and five in the morning and get in close before being discovered."[3] Then short-range, round-magazine, Russian-made 7.6 millimeter "burp" guns, efficient gangster-style submachine guns, plus hand grenades, could be used to deadly effect.[4] NKPA patrols came out the hour before sundown, looking for UN formations; attacks in force would come after dark, and usually break off by midnight.

American tactics quickly adapted to enemy habits, the key to taking advantage of US firepower supremacy. In night action, GIs stayed in deeply-dug holes on high ground, threw hand grenades liberally, and let friendly artillery wreak havoc on exposed NKPA. Friendly and enemy cannon fire often came frighteningly close to US positions. In cases where the enemy broke through the American perimeter and roamed in force about fighting holes, platoon leaders called in artillery strikes on their own positions, shell fuses set for detonation six to eight feet or so above ground. Hot shards of steel whizzed in all directions, exacting a heavy toll on the enemy, while GIs sat in great fear, glued to the bottoms of their holes.

US/UN retreat continued across the Naktong River, a natural barrier helping cordon off the southeast corner of South Korea. At its south coast stood Pusan, the only major peninsular port and supply base in American and South Korean hands (MAP 5). The Korean War's second phase now began. The Naktong Perimeter must be held at all costs. Its fall meant sure Communist victory and control of all Korea. Shorn of overconfidence, combat-experienced American troops and leaders "settled down to a grim defense."[5]

COMBAT REALITY WITHIN NAKTONG ZONE

Korean War battle accounts, excepting that of Addison Terry, paint a deceptive picture of the "Naktong Perimeter." Most sources portray a line of battle with North Koreans on one side and

US, South Koreans, and allies on the other. This is not the reality of Naktong fighting. The 140-mile, inverted 'L' perimeter was surely not a sealed, continuous main line[6] (MAP 5). Strong NKPA divisions infiltrated the territory within, and serious combat took place *within the zone* from the August 1 perimeter creation to September 15 UN breakout. See-saw battles raged near the centrally-located hub of Taegu, site of Eighth Army headquarters. The command itself lay within North Korean artillery range. If able, enemy tanks could reach the Eighth's headquarters in less than an hour.

In short, the concept of front and rear areas, the latter considered safe and secure, did not apply within the Naktong Perimeter. The enemy might appear in strength at any place, any time, including the so-called "rear." As one platoon leader put it, "No one was really safe, the front was everywhere."[7]

The Naktong line began at the east coast town of Yongdok, went almost due west about 50 miles, then generally followed the southern course of the Naktong River until that wide, lazy flow broke east. At this point the front continued south to Chingdong-ni on Korea's southern coast, facing the Western Channel of the Korea Strait (MAP 5). Defense of the far northern part, including a mountainous region some 60 miles above Pusan, fell to reconstituted ROK divisions. Eighth Army's 1st Cavalry Division occupied the zone immediately below. The US 24th Division held the next segment south, with the 25th Division and its 27th Regiment Wolfhounds anchoring the far southern region bordering the Korea Strait.

In early August, Eighth Army Commander Lt. Gen. Walton Walker welcomed the freshly-arrived Marine Provisional Brigade for three weeks of important Naktong duty. Wisely, Gen. MacArthur allowed Walker temporary use of the new force, just arrived from California's Camp Pendleton and shortly to be fighting on another, unexpected front. For now, Walker had a sorely needed fire brigade ready to respond to daily emergencies.

Given progressive US/UN retreat to this final redoubt, the American press carried stories of a pending "Korean Dunkirk," expecting massive sea-lift of Eighth Army and ROKs off the peninsula to Japan, akin to 1940 British Army evacuation from the northern French coast. Many GIs shared the gloomy thought, unaware Inchon invasion would soon be launched.[8]

American bases throughout the world strained to provide men and supplies to fill out grossly undermanned Army divisions. Supremely confident North Koreans lost their manpower advantage early August 1950, both sides now fielding some 75,000 troops. One month of fighting funneled into a do-or-die, six-week slug-fest.

To his credit, Eight Army Commander Gen. Walker, World War II armored corps (multi-division) leader under Gen. George Patton, ordered aggressive US movements in force, seeking out the enemy. Much Naktong combat resulted from such probes — fighting was not solely defensive. This Korean War phase clearly showcased North Korean dedication to defeating the US Army through repeated employment of multi-division attacks led by armor and backed by artillery and mortars. The NKPA often attacked simultaneously on two or even three fronts. Fortunately, US air attacks had neutralized most of the North's air support capability.

Once UN forces had coalesced within the perimeter, North Koreans attempted to sneak through the back door, hitting the far southwestern edge at Chingdong-ni as other NKPA divisions pressed from the north and northwest. Determined 27th Regiment resistance kept the back door closed. Heading toward Masan for much needed rest and relaxation, the 27th Wolfhounds made an about-face and sped north to defend Taegu. Unswayed by the bloody nose, North Koreans now sought to batter down the front. Two Red divisions backed by tanks and self-propelled artillery attacked down the Sangju-Taegu Road August 10, while two other North Korean divisions smashed through the ROK 3rd Division to reach P'ohang on the east coast (MAP 5). The retreating ROK 3rd left the South Korean 8th and Capital divisions vulnerable. To top off Eighth Army's nightmarish trouble, the US 1st Cavalry came under attack on the west and fell back all along its sector.

On August 18, 1950, Reds launched another night attack down the north-south Sangju-Taegu Road, their infantry covering east and west hill flanks, only 10 miles from Eighth Army headquarters. The objective was forced entry into Pusan and "running the US Army into the sea."[9] Red spearheads broke into the 27th regimental command perimeter and sought unsuccessfully to destroy its artillery battalion. As Lt. Terry related, "use of illuminating star flares and prearranged artillery fire on the road saved the day."[10]

Terry described the "hair-raising sound" of dueling artillery "going back and forth through the air, and awful explosions of the bursting shells accentuated by the manner in which sound waves were funneled up and down the valley. This sound of artillery shells rushing through the smoke-filled air and exploding with a terrible crash prompted one GI to refer to the valley as the 'Bowling Alley.'"[11]

Two days later, the enemy was nowhere to be found, but their dead littered the Sangju-Taegu Road. Infantry and artillery of the proud, fighting Wolfhounds had severely punished two NKPA divisions and a tank company. Gen. Walker thanked 27th Regiment Commander Col. Mike Michaelis for saving Taegu, Eighth Army Command, and maybe, Eighth Army.

Gen. Walker's superior, Tokyo-based Far East Commander in Chief Gen. MacArthur, regularly flew across the Sea of Japan to visit the front and consult on strategy. Even with US equality of numbers, North Korean Communists stood close to total victory by late August.[12] US Eighth Army defense of the 140-mile Naktong front meant unit concentration along expected avenues of attack. This often meant travelling on dirt roads running up and down mountains connecting South Korean cities and villages. These turned to treacherous mud alleys with summer rains. At least two trucks loaded with GIs tumbled off slippery mountain roads to deadly crash far below.[13]

Walker's line proved quite porous, the River wide, shallow, muddy, and easily forded, especially at night. Determined North Koreans regularly infiltrated regiments in the Taegu vicinity, smack in the middle of Naktong redoubt. New pitched battles late August to early September again came within a short march of Walker's command. But importantly, the US Army's Naktong action, with vital Marine and air help, stopped the pattern of continuous North Korean infantry and armor victory and advance. The example gave a desperately needed boost of confidence to US, ROK, and allied forces.

Still, backs to the Sea of Japan, Eighth Army occupied only the limited ground within the Naktong Perimeter, a tenuous, flesh-grinding pocket. Repeated NKPA probes and river crossings in strength were beaten back at great cost in blood. Gen. Walker exhorted officers and men to hold firm, no retreat allowed. Any more lost ground would leave nothing *but* the Sea of Japan. Walker proved adept at shuffling units "just-in-time" to plug weak spots in the front.

Meanwhile, US carrier- and Japan-based air support helped blunt Communist thrusts while pounding rear troop and supply concentrations. Without this help, North Korea stood a good chance of defeating Eighth Army and successfully capturing all South Korea.

AN ARMY SECOND LIEUTENANT'S BATTLEFIELD MUSINGS

As mortar rounds exploded in the distance and Naktong fighting beckoned, Georgia-born artillery forward observer Lt. Terry philosophized about the war from his outpost hole. The war

> "seemed to have all the characteristics of a great fiasco." He recalled excitement and shock "over the news of American intervention in the Korean War. Only a few months before we had been told … there probably would be a conflict in Korea, but that our State Department had decided we would not intervene. I was curious to know the circumstances leading to such obvious indecision in the State Department, [and] indignant over the seeming nonchalance with which we were committed to action. *It seemed as though our entire Far East Command was being steered from one course of action to another on the individual whims of a small number of politicos in Washington* (italics added).

> It seemed absurd that the army should have such a 'hands-off' attitude toward politics. We had men to advise our government, men who had spent 30 years in the military and who had gone to our best schools. Their viewpoints as to what might or might not be necessary and advisable from a military standpoint should be a little more closely scrutinized by our State Department planners – specifically Gen. MacArthur's viewpoint as to the defense of Formosa.

> For us in Japan during March and April 1950, it seemed Secretary of State Acheson's pronouncement that Formosa was not militarily nor politically important to our

national interest was *an open invitation for the Communists to parade into French Indochina and Korea*. If the United States chose not to defend Formosa, … we certainly would not … defend Korea and Indochina (italics added).

This Formosa policy … brought about a considerable loss of face to the Asian people …. The reversal of our State Department's thinking concerning Korea seemed extremely late, and certainly unnecessarily costly."[14]

<u>Chapter 9: Phase 3 - MacArthur and Inchon</u>

"It is difficult to tell the hero from the great man at war. Both have military virtues. However, the former is generally young, enterprising, gifted, self-controlled even in danger, and courageous; the latter has much judgment, foresees events and is endowed with much ability and experience. … one might say Alexander was only a hero and Caesar was a great man."

- Jean de la Bruyère (1645-1696), Characters – On Men and Books.[1]

General of the Army Douglas MacArthur can be summarized as a highly-experienced, brave, patriotic, and arrogant military genius. MacArthur appreciated the present dilemma of US and ROK forces trapped within the bloody Naktong foothold. His solution reflected confidence borne of repeated success at World War II Pacific amphibious assault operations that bypassed Japanese land strong-points.

In planning since early July, MacArthur proposed the audacious Operation Chromite to Pacific theater commanders and Joint Chiefs of Staff, an amphibious landing far to the enemy's rear that would cut supply lines and force the NKPA to abandon the Naktong and South Korea. Seoul would be liberated and North Koreans put into full retreat north. While the concept lay within general understanding of most high brass, the landing site brought surprise: Inchon on the Yellow Sea, the port nearest Seoul (MAP 6). Yet surprise was the whole point.

MacArthur's plan called for a new Tenth (X) Corps, commanded by his Tokyo Chief of Staff Lt. Gen. Edward "Ned" Almond. X Corps consisted of the Army 7th Division, four ROK divisions, and the reinforced Marine First Division, headed by Maj. Gen. Oliver P. Smith. The strong Marine Provisional Brigade would be removed from the Naktong to join First Division invasion. Navy gunfire support ships and landing vessels would converge on Inchon mid-September. A three-pronged Marine harbor assault would overwhelm port and city, the 7th Division would land, then both march to free Seoul and trap the North Korean army. Concurrently, Walker would

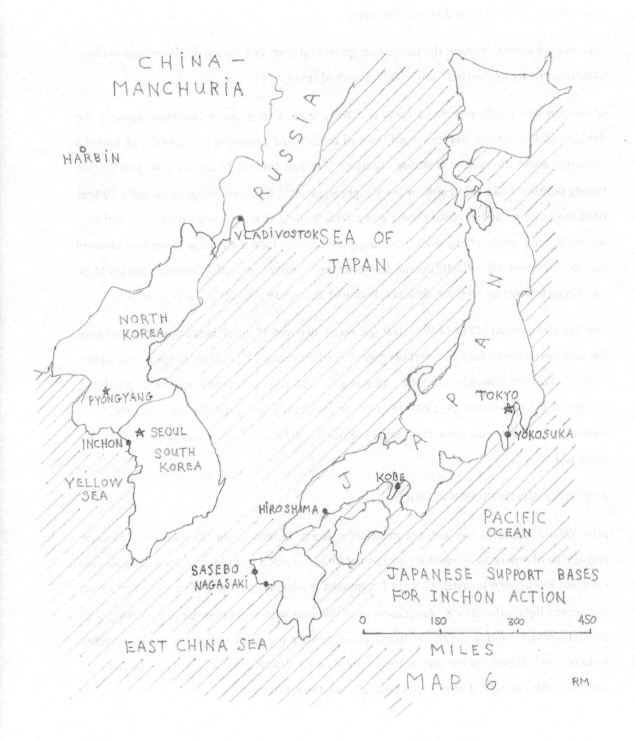

CHINA-
MANCHURIA

RUSSIA

HARBIN

VLADIVOSTOK SEA OF
JAPAN

NORTH
KOREA

PYONGYANG

SEOUL

INCHON
SOUTH
KOREA

YELLOW
SEA

J A P A N

TOKYO

YOKOSUKA

KOBE

HIROSHIMA

PACIFIC
OCEAN

SASEBO
NAGASAKI

JAPANESE SUPPORT BASES
FOR INCHON ACTION

0   150   300   450

EAST CHINA SEA

MILES

MAP 6   RM

lead Eighth Army break-out across the Naktong and northern thrust against a fleeing enemy. The NKPA would be surrounded and annihilated.

Time did not permit dry runs, the plan would go on first shot. In a typical display of hyperbole, MacArthur himself called it a "1 in 5,000" chance of success.

MacArthur masterfully convinced Army and Navy leaders to endorse Chromite, swaying the doubtful with extended, passionate off-the-cuff remarks. At a meeting of top brass, he issued a challenge about the current Naktong situation: "Are you content to let our boys stay in that bloody perimeter like beef cattle in the slaughterhouse?"[2] Doubters stressed Inchon's 29-foot tides that would hamper naval access and strand landing vessels in mud-flats for a half day, leaving them, literally, sitting ducks. Landing groups would take the narrow Flying Fish Channel into port, covered by a North Korean island fortress. Supposedly safer landing sites could be found south of Inchon on the Yellow Sea, in one of near-endless coves or inlets (MAP 6).

The General's record of Pacific War strategic excellence and 49 amphibious operations without failure contributed to high personal prestige. Key support came from Chief of Naval Operations Admiral Forrest Sherman. Despite misgivings, Operation Chromite received go-ahead, scheduled for September 15, 1950. Joint Chiefs reluctantly approved the plan only the week before! Most naval units came from Japanese ports and bases at Kobe, Sasebo, and Yokosuka (MAP 6A).

RED SPIES KNEW OF INCHON ASSAULT

John Toland is one of few authors mentioning North Korean leader Kim Il-Sung's advance knowledge of American amphibious invasion at Inchon, gained from Mao Zedong's supposedly excellent intelligence analysis. Chinese Communist leadership passed the news to Kim about two weeks before the attack.[3] American-based Red intelligence sources, closely working with US policymakers and generals, in many cases *serving as policymakers,* typically provided Moscow and Beijing timely and accurate warning of Washington and Tokyo plans. Many American officials did not want their country to win the Korean War.

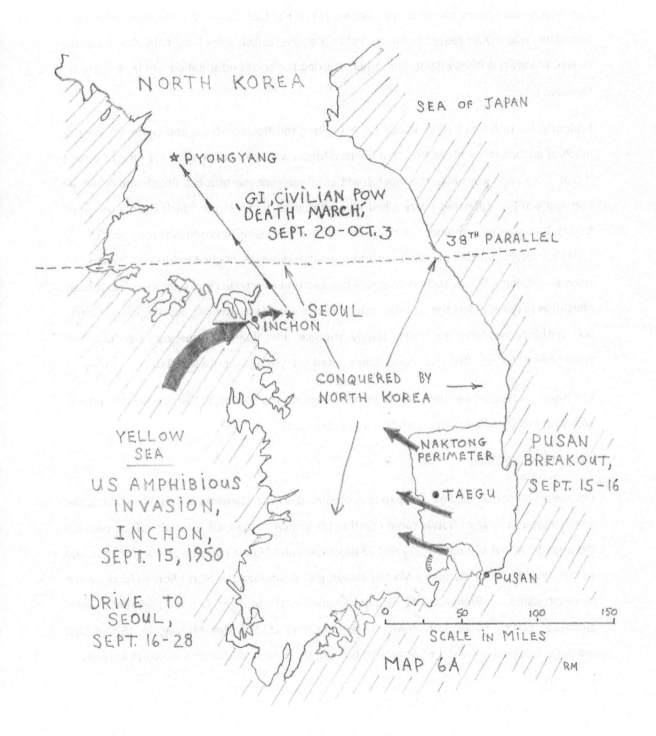

OPERATION CHROMITE

NORTH KOREA

SEA OF JAPAN

★ PYONGYANG

'GI, CIVILIAN POW
DEATH MARCH,'
SEPT. 20 - OCT. 3

38TH PARALLEL

★ SEOUL
INCHON

CONQUERED BY
NORTH KOREA

YELLOW
SEA

NAKTONG
PERIMETER

PUSAN
BREAKOUT,
SEPT. 15-16

● TAEGU

US AMPHIBIOUS
INVASION,
INCHON,
SEPT. 15, 1950

DRIVE TO
SEOUL,
SEPT. 16-28

● PUSAN

0   50   100   150
SCALE IN MILES

MAP 6A   RM

In the case of Inchon, Moscow's advanced knowledge permitted enlightenment of Mao and Kim. MacArthur shared his plans with British Tokyo Far East Command colleague Sir Alvary Gascoigne, who loyally passed them to London. Devoted British spies Kim Philby, Guy Burgess, Donald Maclean, Anthony Blunt, and others, carried the secret information ball from there to Moscow.[4,5,6]

Evidently, North Korea had its hands full assaulting the Naktong front and could not muster much of an Inchon counter-force. Red Chinese forces were too far away at the time to pose a threat. But Toland gives Mao too much credit as intelligence mastermind: British and American Red and pro-Red spies fed every allied communication to Moscow, which shortly informed Beijing. Red pipeline continued the documented pattern existing in World War II, when all 1,700 Roosevelt-Churchill classified wartime messages promptly made it to Moscow.[7] Stalin knew everything – agents such as London American embassy code clerk Tyler Kent felt solemn obligation to quickly alert the Kremlin about all American plans. The only loyalty that mattered was faithfully rendered to Stalin. Happy to take advantage of American freedom and governmental largess, Red spies nonetheless hated everything America stood for.

Kim Il-Sung messaged his NKPA before Inchon: "Protect and defend all liberated areas. Defend with your blood and life every mountain and every river!"[8]

OPERATION CHROMITE

Despite a typhoon in the Sea of Japan in preceding days that damaged a number of ships, the naval, marine, and army flotilla came together off Inchon as planned. Four aircraft carriers led the armada, joined by two cruisers and 25 destroyers providing a two-day preparatory gun and air barrage. On D-Day morning a Marine assault group subdued the North Korean force on the blocking island of Wolmi-do. At 5:00PM landing craft brought Marine regiments under command of Col. Puller, Col. Homer Litzenberg, and Lt. Col. Ray Murray, to 15-foot-high seawalls; ladders improvised while on ship brought them over. Within Inchon, North Koreans offered only light resistance. The first day's fighting took "20 Marines killed and 170 wounded," considered a light toll by commanders.[9] Amphibious assault achieved the all-important element of surprise. A jubilant MacArthur announced, "The Navy and Marine Corps have never shone brighter."[10]

The 1st Marine and Army 7th divisions consolidated outside Inchon and overran the key airfield of Kimpo, Korea's best. The first week of combat brought 165 1st Marine Division dead, 1,000 wounded, five missing.[11] Then began tough street fighting to liberate Seoul (Map 6). Now North Koreans fought back with vigor. ROK marines helped flush out the enemy in house-to-house combat devastating people and city. It took the best efforts of X Corps to return Seoul to President Rhee September 29, 1950. North Korea had invaded the South just over three months before.

The last five days of fighting accounted for 40% of casualties.[12] All told, 414 Marines gave lives and 2,016 suffered wounds over 15 days of "one of the most demanding operations in Corps history." Tenth Corps took 4,800 NKPA prisoners, inflicted an estimated 13,000 enemy casualties, and captured "vast stores" of US Army weapons and supplies abandoned by GIs and taken by North Koreans.[12]

Walker's Eighth Army broke from the Naktong perimeter as the NKPA learned of Inchon invasion. North Koreans quickly fled toward home. Planes dropped thousands of leaflets on enemy troops announcing the landing and emphasizing their hopeless situation and advisability of surrender. Many were captured and killed, and except for guerrilla units in mountain strongholds, organized North Korean forces were driven from South Korea. However, hoped-for crushing of enemy forces between Eighth Army and X Corps never materialized. The "hammer and anvil" leaked big-time. Perhaps 30,000 NKPA escaped to upper North Korea and Manchuria to fight again. Marine First Division Commander Maj. Gen. Smith blamed "failure on the part of Far East Command to plan adequately for the closure."[13]

Other disturbing news did not emerge until war's end. A group of 340 GI and civilian prisoners of war, some of them Christian missionary workers, had been held at a Communist camp in Seoul. Before Tenth Corps could reclaim them, North Koreans imposed a brutal, 130-mile forced march from Seoul to Pyongyang, the North Korean capital, starting September 20. Cold weather, difficult up-and-down terrain, and criminally abusive NKPA guards made for a nightmarish journey. No medical care or clothing was provided, and very little food and water. The sick were forced to march until they died or could no longer be carried. Those who refused orders to march, and the very sick, were shot. Those who lost the will to live readily died from harsh conditions. *Thirty* prisoners made it alive to Pyongyang October 3.[14] History refers to this tragedy as the 'Korean Death March.'

This information came from survivors testifying before Congress after the War about savage North Korean treatment. While transcripts of Congressional hearings on POW abuse are readily accessible, little or no attention is paid to North Korea's barbaric treatment of American and UN prisoners. History has mostly focused on mistreatment of Red Chinese and North Korean POWs by Americans and South Koreans.

For Douglas MacArthur, an ancient Roman commander's maxim now reared up: "All glory is fleeting."

Chapter 10: Genius Run Amok – Push to the Yalu

Inchon represented Gen. MacArthur's zenith of success. What followed proved militarily senseless, a deviation from prior unmatched vision and rapid descent from Olympus.

MacArthur ordered another amphibious invasion for Tenth Corps, this time at Wonsan, far up North Korea's east coast (MAP 7). First Division Marines marched back to Inchon for naval outloading down, around, and up the peninsula. Inchon's modest port became clogged, unable to logistically support Eighth Army "decisive hot pursuit" that might destroy the fleeing NKPA.

Unable to contend with Inchon bottleneck, the 7th Infantry Division rode trains and vehicles 200 miles south and outloaded by ship from Pusan to Wonsan. A frustrated Gen. Bradley later wrote, "The enemy himself could not have concocted a more diabolical scheme to delay our pursuit."[1] Post-Inchon combat operations came "to a standstill for almost three weeks."

It turned out that a mostly-unopposed ROK Army group marched rapidly up North Korea's east coast to take the Wonsan objective. The marvel of Inchon would not be repeated. As the saying went, "Even Bob Hope's USO show got to Wonsan before MacArthur." Hope joked, "This is the first time I've ever been on shore waiting for the Marines."[2] Importantly, three weeks of reasonable weather were wasted in musical chair maneuvers. Bitter Korean winter came early in 1950.

Exasperated Gen. Bradley observed, "Had a major at [Army] Command and General Staff School turned in this solution to the problem, he would have been laughed out of the classroom."[1] Long after the fact, Bradley lambasted MacArthur for depriving Eighth Army the chance to knock the NKPA out of the War.

US/UN ENTER THE NORTH

Success at Inchon allowed US and ROK forces to throw North Koreans out of South Korea. The

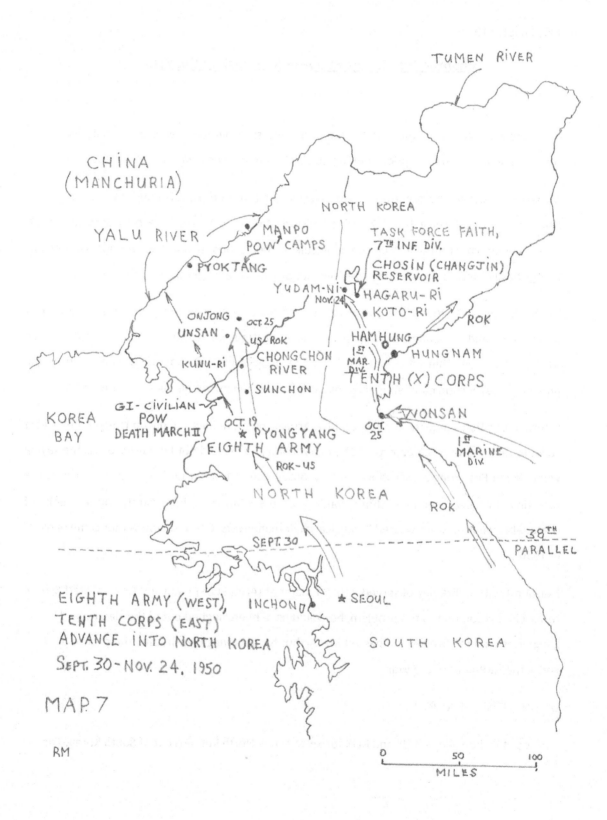

TUMEN RIVER

CHINA
(MANCHURIA)

NORTH KOREA

YALU RIVER

MANPO
POW CAMPS

TASK FORCE FAITH,
7TH INF. DIV.

• PYOKTANG

CHOSIN (CHANGJIN)
RESERVOIR

YUDAM-Ni•
NOV. 24

HAGARU-Ri

ONJONG
• OCT. 25

KOTO-Ri

UNSAN

US-ROK

ROK

KUNU-Ri

CHONGCHON
RIVER

HAMHUNG

1ST
MAR.
DIV.

HUNGNAM

TENTH (X) CORPS

• SUNCHON

KOREA
BAY

GI-CIVILIAN
POW
DEATH MARCH II

OCT. 19

★ PYONGYANG

EIGHTH ARMY

WONSAN

OCT.
25

1ST
MARINE
DIV.

ROK-US

NORTH   KOREA

ROK

38TH
PARALLEL

SEPT. 30

EIGHTH ARMY (WEST),
TENTH CORPS (EAST)
ADVANCE INTO NORTH KOREA
SEPT. 30 - NOV. 24, 1950

INCHON

★ SEOUL

SOUTH   KOREA

MAP 7

RM

0   50   100
MILES

Photo File – Combat

Figure 22. Marine Maj. Gen. Oliver P. Smith, 1ˢᵗ Division Commander, pays respects to fallen comrades at Marine cemetery in Korea. *National Archives.*

Figure 23. Eighth Army Commander Lt. Gen. Matthew Ridgway exemplifies leadership excellence. Note signature hand-grenade on left, medical kit on right. *gettyimages.*

Figure 24. Gen. Ridgway awards combat decoration, March 1, 1951, to French Commander Lt. Col. Ralph Monclar for heroism at Battle of Chipyong-ni. *gettyimages.*

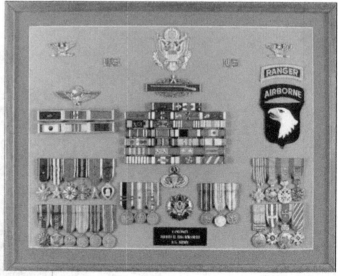

Figure 25. US Army Col. David Hackworth, Korean and Vietnam combat hero *par excellence.* **Eight Purple Hearts, 8 Bronze Stars, 10 Silver Stars, 2 Distinguished Service Crosses attest to unique warrior status.** *jeffgoerig.com*

Figure 26. General of the Army Douglas MacArthur, Far East Commander in Chief for Korean War, June 1950 – April 1951. Advocated politically-incorrect decisive war with People's Republic of China. Leftist power forbid the showdown. Twenty-first century consequences are profound. *National Archives.*

Figure 27. Gen. George Marshall and Mao Zedong in China, 1946. US policy is "bang heads together" for coalition government. Despite phony Acheson claims to contrary, US-imposed cease-fire and arms embargo on Nationalist China greatly encouraged Red victory in Chinese civil war. *National Archives.*

Figure 28. Navy F9F Pantherjet landing on USS Boxer. Wing tanks added operational range and increased time-on-target. *National Archives.*

Figure 29. Navy F4 Corsairs return from Korean mission, Sept. 4, 1951. World War II-vintage planes served well in close ground support at and near MLR. *National Archives.*

Figure 30. F-86 Sabrejets, best air-to-air fighter in US inventory. Very limited allocation to Korea. *National Archives.*

Figure 31. Russian-made MiG-15 flown into South Korea by defecting Red pilot. Soviets sent 60,000 air support personnel to Manchurian bases during Korean War, including pilots. Red spies provided Moscow latest information on American aircraft development. *National Archives.*

Figure 32. Bell helicopters and C-46 transports provided rapid medical care to wounded GIs. Speedy treatment reduced wound mortality 50% from World War II level. Helicopters well-suited to Korean mountain and valley flying. *National Archives.*

Figure 33. US Air Force B-26 bombers outfitted for night operations, sporting 14 forward-firing .50 cal. machineguns, being tested for accuracy. US needed much-enhanced night air attack capability. *National Archives.*

Figure 34. Marine H-19 Sikorsky helicopter featured greater operating radius and passenger capacity compared to predecessor. *National Archives.*

Figure 35. Inchon landing site, LSTs (Landing Ship, Tanks) at beachhead. Minimal enemy resistance changes to fierce fighting in march on Seoul. *gettyimages.*

Figure 36. PLA "Volunteers" in quilt winter garb. Red Star emblem on soft caps hard to see. Hardy, disciplined, brave souls. *National Archives.*

Figure 37. Rugged, pock-marked Heartbreak Ridge, North Korean killing ground for US and Chinese fighters. "The heartbreak was in the meaningless carnage." *National Archives.*

Figure 38. Ridgway instilled US Army "can-do" spirit, encouraging effective counter-attacks. Patrol watches bombing of enemy-held area, Feb. 1951. *National Archives.*

Figure 39. Bloody Ridge, northeast of Hwachon Reservoir, taken Sept. 4, 1951 by US/UN after 3 weeks bitter fighting. Over 2,700 friendly casualties. Welcome to limited objective, die-for-tie war. Soldiers noted at ridge-top. *Wikipedia.*

Figure 40. UN POW camp, rice by the barrel. *National Archives.*

Figure 41. American GIs with NKPA prisoner. *National Archives.*

Figure 42. US/UN peace talks delegation about to board helicopter for first Kaesong session, July 10, 1951. Generals Ridgway and Almond long coats; left to right, Vice Adm. C. Turner Joy, delegation chairman; Air Force Maj. Gen. Laurence Craigie; distinguished South Korean commander Maj. Gen. Whitey Paik; Rear Adm. Arleigh Burke; Army Maj. Gen. Henry Hodes. *National Archives.*

Figure 43. Plutonium-based 'Fat Boy' atomic bomb, identical to Nagasaki bomb dropped Nov. 9, 1945, and first 4 Soviet-developed nuclear bombs starting 1949. 10,000 pounds. Deadly nuclear/thermonuclear weapon evolution toward compact, light-weight, human-carried explosives. *National Archives.*

US/UN had convincingly defeated North Korea. Prospect of crossing the 38th Parallel and invading the North received due consideration from Truman, Acheson, and JCS. They decided to permit MacArthur's attack north and "unify the peninsula." Unification became official UN policy, MacArthur so notified. Now came push to the Yalu River, separating North Korea from Red China's massive province of Manchuria (Map 7). Conquering a good part of the North would not do – leadership mindset appeared fixed on all-or-none.

A number of Korean War historians incorrectly accuse MacArthur of masterminding invasion of North Korea. Many of these sinister-oriented treatments reflect pro-left bias. Two who knew better, D. Clayton James and Anne Wells, likened dispelling of false charges against MacArthur "to scraping barnacles off ship hulls: Many in number and hard to dislodge."[3] In today's parlance, MacArthur was considered politically incorrect in displaying patriotism, anti-Communism, concern about Red Chinese threat to America, desire to *win* the Korean War, and caring about expenditure of American lives.

Four days prior to Inchon landing, September 11, President Truman formally approved National Security Council Paper 81/1, authorizing MacArthur "to conduct various military operations north of the 38th Parallel on approval from Washington, and urg[ing] political unification of all Korea by free elections."[4] The reader notes that formal request for military action came from a civilian agency, the NSC, not from Joint Chiefs. As Bradley commented, "the President, Acheson, the JCS and MacArthur were in full agreement on these fundamental policies." Clearly, MacArthur was not a lone ranger in carrying the war into North Korea.

On September 26, Truman issued specific orders to MacArthur that in Bradley's estimation "amounted to the most extraordinarily detailed and limiting set of instructions ever given a military field commander."[5] This remarkable statement from an iconic US Army "good soldier" testified to a new level of political control in the Korean War.[6] These were new and unpleasant days for an American military accustomed to greater freedom of action than allowed in the new defense scheme (the Defense Reorganization Act passed into law in 1947). The "unique and complex set of restrictions" basically manifested greater civilian powers coupled with tremendous fear throughout top civilian and military leadership.

Bradley frankly saw the relatively new National Security Council as "tending to degrade and diminish the power and policymaking role of the Joint Chiefs of Staff."[7] Korean fighting could never be allowed to escalate into "general war" against Soviet Russia and Communist China. The US could not fight such war given its military weakness. People might also question why another general war could follow so closely the recent conclusion of the greatest war. *Extended peace should be a reasonable outcome of successful all-out war.*

The public might pose the same question about Korean fighting. Much of actual war-related happenings in Washington were not suitable for public consumption. America often played the role of war supplicant instead of battlefield equal, let alone superior. For example, as will be detailed, Truman, Acheson, and Joint Chiefs gave serious consideration to suing Communist China for peace in December 1950, despite grave implications. And America, not the Soviet Union, started the 1951 peace negotiation ball rolling in Korea. But these particular bits of truth, reflecting negatively on Franklin Roosevelt's successor, must be secreted away. Better a fairy-tale be concocted and people live in a fantasy world. Then bloody war in Korea could merely be labeled a "police action," or "conflict."

In consideration of MacArthur's fetters, Secretary of Defense George Marshall messaged him September 29: "We want you to feel unhampered tactically and strategically to proceed north of the [P]arallel."[5] MacArthur likely relied on this advice as a green-light to the Yalu River.

Truman's political choke-hold on Korean military action is also illustrated in the case of heavy Chinese troop passage across the Yalu through most of October into early November 1950. Heretofore assured but now highly alarmed MacArthur promptly ordered B-29 bombing of Yalu bridges on November 6, to cut means of enemy ingress. When Acheson got word of the plan, he immediately acted to stop the mission. At that very time the State Department had been trying to push through a "UN resolution calling for halt to Red Chinese aggression in Korea."[8] As the Western world repeatedly learned and promptly forgot, resolutions have no effect on a determined aggressor's plans.

Truman cancelled the B-29 attack and wanted MacArthur to tell Joint Chiefs "why he found this dangerous step necessary." The President then instructed Chiefs to order MacArthur to "postpone all bombing of targets within five miles of the Manchurian border." Yalu dams and electric power plants were also off limits; heaven forbid cutting North Korean and Manchurian electricity.[8] Omar Bradley feared Soviets and Chinese might consider Yalu bombing as frank attack on Manchuria and be moved to overt war entry. Yet, to Bradley, Acheson, and Truman, the recently concluded Chinese First Phase Offensive and soon-to-come full-bore Second Phase did not constitute war on America and the West. In politics truth does not exist.

Joint Chiefs took another bath in absurdity in allowing air bombing of *only the southern half* of Yalu bridges, an exceedingly difficult and dangerous task. Aircrews then faced deadly fire from gun emplacements just across the Yalu. Bradley seemed consumed by necessity for "diplomatic delicacy" and "maintaining optimum position with the United Nations."[9] Based on his writings, winning the Korean War did not matter to Gen. Bradley. The man appeared to have no teeth. Keeping the political boat in Washington on an even keel seemed of far greater importance.

On November 9, a JCS-NSC meeting brought agreement on desirability of UN-mediated political settlement of "the problem of Chinese Communist intervention in Korea," including "reassurances to China with respect to our intentions." US/UN diplomacy "demanded prompt withdrawal of Chinese forces from North Korea."[10] This must have brought guffaws from Soviet, Chinese, and North Korean leadership. Red China's war intentions were cast in stone and unfolding as scheduled. Identical dainty-fingered Washington leadership statements stained the Winter 2014 post-Olympic Russian invasion of Crimea and other parts of the Ukraine.

WE CAME, WE SAW, WE CONQUERED … NOT!

Gen. Bradley is credited with truthful summary of JCS activity and Caesarian comparison: "We read, we sat, we deliberated, and … we reached drastically wrong conclusions and decisions."[11]

Politically-imposed Joint Chiefs form of military leadership fostered "Pompeyization," a gathering of spent warriors akin to ancient Roman commander Pompey, whose stamping of feet toward the end of his army career brought dust, not military potency. Joint Chiefs Korean War behavior reeked of timidity and defeatism. Put mildly, the first war fought under the new US defense system did not inspire confidence in civilian and military leadership.

After Inchon, divided commands and armies beset US/UN military effort. The formidable Taebaek Mountains are a prominent north-south Korean terrain feature, a rugged spine thought impossible by US commanders. Mountainsides often presented the challenge of 50- to 70-degree inclines, ruling out motorized approach and necessitating use of hands and feet in climbing, and bringing exhaustion in reaching ridge-tops.

With extensive and steep mountain ranges on either side of the spine, Marine Gen. Smith found "practically all movement in Korea was along corridors," or valley roads. Smith noted the "accepted principle that in advancing along a terrain corridor, the shoulders [hillsides] must be occupied or otherwise denied the enemy before movement can be safely made."[12] "Denial" includes application of heavy, continuous firepower, elimination of enemy formations through direct infantry attack, mortar, artillery, and tank fire, and air bombing and strafing.

US Main Supply Routes (MSRs) typically snaked along valley floors, the Army often derelict in "taking to the hills" to neutralize threatening enemy forces, then paying a heavy price in blood. The most disturbing example is the post-Chinese-invasion slaughter attending 2nd Infantry Division retreat south through the seven-mile North Korean Kunuri – Sunchon terrain corridor or "gauntlet," ordered by division commander Gen. Keiser (Map 9). US Army historian Brig. Gen. SLA Marshall detailed the tragic shooting-gallery action in his superb book, "From River to Gauntlet." Beset by paltry communication and reliance on assumption instead of first-hand knowledge, an already Chinese-battered division moved "into a fire gauntlet more than six miles long via the valley road."[13] Road blocks and heavy broadside machinegun attacks destroyed 80% of the 2nd Infantry Division.

But the combat situation looked rosy in early October 1950. With Seoul secured and adequate logistics re-established, Eighth Army's 2nd and 24th infantry and multiple ROK divisions attacked west of the Taebaek divide, capturing the North Korean capital, Pyongyang, October 20 (Map 7). A rare parachute jump by the 187th Regiment added punch. Prior-mentioned Red-held US and allied POWs were again put on the march ('Death March II'), now to the Yalu River, an even more-formidable, nearly impossible task.

By now it was obvious many North Korean units and government officials had fled to the Yalu vicinity and eluded the UN trap.[14] MacArthur ordered continued Eighth Army advance beyond the Chongchon River toward the final destination, the Yalu, another 50 air-miles north (MAP 7).

Starting from the eastern side at coastal Wonsan, Hungnam, and Hamhung, Gen. Almond's Tenth Corps fought north to Hagaru-ri at the Chosin Reservoir's southern edge (MAPS 7, 8). There Army 7th Division Regimental Combat Team 31 turned up the Chosin's eastern shore while strong elements of the Marine 5th and 7th regiments marched west, their objectives also the Yalu. Morale was high, "Home by Christmas" the refrain. At least to Gen. MacArthur, the daunting task of subduing all North Korea seemed within close reach.

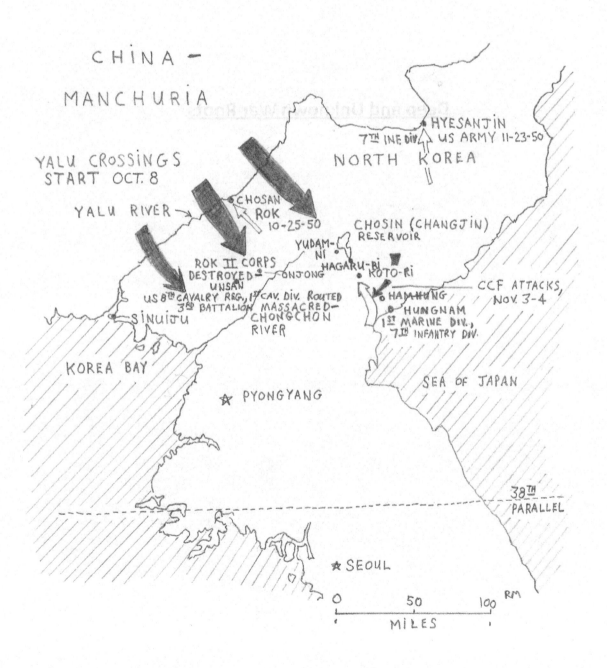

CCF FIRST PHASE OFFENSIVE
OCT. 28 - NOV. 6, 1950
MAP 8

CHINA -
MANCHURIA

YALU CROSSINGS
START OCT. 8

YALU RIVER →

CHOSAN
ROK
10-25-50

HYESANJIN
7TH INF DIV ← US ARMY 11-23-50
NORTH KOREA

CHOSIN (CHANGJIN)
RESERVOIR

YUDAM-
NI
HAGARU-RI
KOTO-RI

ROK II CORPS
DESTROYED
UNSAN
ONJONG

US 8TH CAVALRY REG, 1ST CAV. DIV. ROUTED
3RD BATTALION MASSACRED-
CHONGCHON
RIVER

SINUIJU

CCF ATTACKS,
NOV. 3-4

HAMHUNG
HUNGNAM
1ST MARINE DIV.,
7TH INFANTRY DIV.

KOREA BAY

SEA OF JAPAN

★ PYONGYANG

38TH
PARALLEL

★ SEOUL

0   50   100   RM

MILES

Part III:

Deep and Unknown War Roots

Chapter 11: Traditional Mistreatment of the Chinese People

Before discussing the People's Republic of China's role in the Korean War, it is appropriate to emphasize historical facts underlying the 19th- and 20th-century relationship of Western powers, China, and all Far East Asian nations. We may then understand the animus underlying and driving PRC entry into the War.

As superb writer Barbara Tuchman pointed out, the United States joined Great Britain, France, Italy, and other European states in regular violation of Chinese territory for purposes of economic advantage.[1] Each country posted military detachments in China to secure respective commercial interests. Chinese were treated more like slaves than equals. Douglas MacArthur cited a Far East "long exploited by the so-called colonial powers, with little opportunity to achieve any degree of social justice, individual dignity, or a higher standard of life ...."[2] The General knew "Asian peoples covet[ed] the right to shape their own free destiny" and attain "the dignity of equality, not the shame of subjugation."[3]

The harsh nature of early- to mid-20th-century Chinese life should be appreciated. Half the population "died before reaching the age of 30." The majority of premature deaths came from "preventable diseases, mostly filth-borne."[1] To compound misery, the Nationalist Government outdid the outrageous ancient Romans in taxation – "a peasant could be subjected to 44 different taxes, often collected years, even decades, in advance ...."[1] Chinese Communists obviously had fertile grounds for popular support. Rock-bottom peasants had nothing to lose.

PATTERN OF WESTERN, AND AMERICAN, LYING

Twice in pre-Communist years, America and the West promised self-determination to the Chinese people in return for help with world war. In the first instance, President Woodrow Wilson's assurance of postwar Chinese autonomy meant nothing, as World War I ended with the Treaty of Versailles that shamefully ignored her interests. Promise of self-determination "withered at the touch of hard realities."[4] The West cared only about the West. Racial chauvinism flourished.

Chinese students then reacted in strenuous public demonstrations against empty Occidental promises, Japan's brutal treatment, and continued warlord rule. Nationalistic fever spread through China as intellectuals spearheaded political activity. On May 4, 1919, a particularly spirited student protest took place in Beijing that encouraged even more political action. Known today as the May Fourth movement, the Chinese Communist Party marks the date as beginning the process leading to the Party's 1921 foundation.[5]

At the time, Marxism proved a powerful attraction for the young – "new and exciting, the latest and best panacea" for the world's ills.[5] Not only budding Chinese leaders Mao Zedong and Zhou En-lai came under Red spell; substantial numbers of Americans, British, Germans, French, and Italians joined them.

Franklin Roosevelt and Harry Truman unfortunately followed Wilson's China path, performing the same slight-of-hand during and after World War II. Prior assurance of "equal" status in the postwar world did not stop Roosevelt from abandoning China at the December 1943 Tehran Conference. Tuchman told of Roosevelt's "sacrifice of [Nationalist China leader] Chiang Kai-shek to Stalin," his "new partner at the dance."[6] At the Yalta Conference Roosevelt drove nails into China's coffin, again "casting his lot" in favor of the Soviet Union. There, without Chiang's knowledge, let alone consent, Roosevelt secretly gave away major Chinese territorial rights to Stalin. These included China's vast frontier territory of Manchuria, north of the Great Wall, developed by Japan to be rich in modern industry, and blessed with abundant natural resources, both later plundered by the Kremlin.

Russia's Far East mainland "curved around Manchuria like a horseshoe"[7] (MAP 2). For at least a century, Japan and Russia vied for dominance there. End of Pacific fighting in 1945 meant a power vacuum created by Japan's imperial dissolution, filled in two weeks by Roosevelt-requested massive Russian armies. No comparable counter-force confronted the Asian Soviet giant. By carelessness, intention, or both, Roosevelt created a Red tidal wave soon engulfing the Far East mainland. Wheels now spinned for Communist domination of China and Manchuria, severe Far East power imbalance, and wars in Korea and Vietnam.[8]

Chiang didn't learn about extensive Roosevelt-mandated territorial concessions to Russia until June 15, 1945, four months after Yalta, with the president two months dead. The Chinese people waited until February 1946 to get news of Moscow's bonanza. Authors Chang and Halliday reported "anti-Soviet demonstrations in many Chinese cities."[9]

Protests could just as well have been directed at America. Roosevelt practiced a searing mixture of paternalism and contempt for Chinese feelings, pride, and most importantly, national interests. Stab-in-the-back well kept alive the US record of "shabby treatment of an ally."[10] This proved especially cruel given widespread devastation wreaked on China by 13 years of war with Japan (1932-45). According to MacArthur, a poor Chinese pre-war living standard had now sunk "infinitely lower."[3]

Chapter 12: "Colossal Presidential Fraud" –

Red Russia Takes Far East, East and Central Europe

"They are in great error who imagine that a man's happiness consists in things as they are. No; it consists entirely in his opinion *of what they are. Man is so constituted that falsehood is far more agreeable to him than truth."*[1]

- Erasmus (1466 – 1536), The Praise of Folly.

Clearly, through vast concessions to Soviet Russia in Far East Asia, Franklin Roosevelt fathered the Korean War. With Japan on its knees, regional balance of power now heavily favored the Communists. Communism had no counter-balance on the East Asian mainland. Big trouble brewed. Historical and media accounts have erected a stone wall to block this unpleasant, highly significant fact from the American people.

Heavily publicized "historic" Allied war conferences provided Roosevelt rich opportunities for domestic deception. An obliging press amplified the impact of propaganda pitch. Roosevelt first met Stalin at the Tehran (Iranian capital, spelled "Teheran" in 1940s-50s literature) Meeting November 27 – December 1, 1943, also attended by Churchill. A year earlier, Roosevelt tried his best to get Stalin to attend a Big Three meeting in Casablanca, the Moroccan Atlantic coast city some 200 miles southeast of the Gibraltar Straits. Stalin refused – he "could not leave his direction of the war" in Moscow.[2] Casablanca hosted only the Big Two, January 14-24, 1943. For the supposedly momentous Yalta (February 1945) and Potsdam (June-July 1945) meetings, the latter a Truman responsibility, the same restrictions held. Both US presidents had to come to Stalin.

Perhaps another factor accounted for Stalin's stubbornness. Churchill messaged Stalin March 9, 1942, about willingness to side with Roosevelt in insisting on a Big Three treaty defining Russia's post-war European frontiers. This was still a time of great Soviet fear of continued Nazi plundering and invasion. The war was in a very precarious position, a favorable time if ever to seek Communist agreement on territorial limits. (The best time was Summer 1941, as Nazi surprise attack advanced deep into Russia along a massive front). But Stalin need have no fear the two allies would gang up on him.

Accentuating the hat-in-hand nature of Churchill's dealings with Roosevelt, the President shortly leveled a barrage on his British partner: "I think I can personally handle Stalin better than either your Foreign Office or my State Department. Stalin hates the guts of all your top people. He thinks he likes me better and I hope he will continue to do so."[3] Unfortunately for Roosevelt, all "top-secret" communications between Washington and London, including letters and notes exchanged with Churchill, would shortly end up on Stalin's Moscow desk, courtesy of British Soviet spies Kim Philby, Guy Burgess, and Donald Maclean, and US counterparts Lauchlin Currie, Harry Dexter White, Alger Hiss, Nathan Gregory Silvermaster, Tyler Gatewood Kent, and many others. Supreme Bolshevik ideologue Stalin could never forgive the bourgeois insult of this and other condescending messages. Roosevelt's paternalistic arrogance never stood a chance of swaying Stalin and Soviet oligarch behaviors. Stalin could only feel general contempt for capitalist imperialists. He wound up with Roosevelt eating out of his hand.

PASSING FANCIES: FOUR FREEDOMS AND FOUR POLICEMEN

With his January 1941 State of the Union message to Congress, FDR first proclaimed the "Four Freedoms" phase of necessary world direction, with Europe 17 months into World War II. Mankind should enjoy "Freedom of speech and expression, ability of all people to worship God as they pleased, freedom from want, and from fear."[4] Finalized understanding awaited a North Atlantic Ocean, Roosevelt – Churchill shipboard meeting. No formalized Four Freedoms document or "official signed copy" ever existed. The final draft consisted of "mimeographed sheets given ship radio operators." The British regarded the statement as merely "a publicity handout."[5] It received huge American press attention.

The President opened the first Tehran session with reference to "a family circle." Per standard Roosevelt practice, no agenda was used, assuring "rambling from topic to topic."[6] The same deficiency prevailed at White House cabinet meetings, along with prohibition on note-taking. Roosevelt mentioned to Stalin the "six- to seven-million Polish-American votes he did not want to lose," which prevented him from "taking part in any decision on Polish frontiers until after the November 1944 presidential election."[7]

Roosevelt came away from Tehran very impressed by Stalin, who gave assurance the Soviet Union "would join the war against Japan after defeat of Germany."[8] The American people learned from the President that "Cooperation of the three nations [Russia, US, and Britain] would outlast the war by *generations*," then the wondrous news, "We proved here at Tehran that the varying ideals of our nations can come together in a harmonious whole (italics added). We leave here friends in fact, in spirit and in purpose."[9,10]

Conference end brought Roosevelt's gushing topper: "enduring peace" would be won, "tyranny and slavery, oppression and intolerance" eliminated. A *Life* magazine editorial cut through the rhapsody – "If it can be believed, it solves everything; if it cannot, it is a *colossal fraud*" (italics added).[11] For three generations, effusive words of deceit remained sheltered under the cloak of "great presidential war leadership."

Roosevelt revealed a new grand world strategy at Tehran: the concept of "Four Policemen." The latest vision represented "quite a contrast to the United Nations Declaration of the previous January, the Four Freedoms, which promised equality of all nations."[12] While prior-pitched universal freedoms melted away, Roosevelt now adopted the merits of four great world powers, the US, USSR, Britain, and China, assuring global peace and tranquility in the post-war era. Apparently, all other nations would disarm and defer in security matters to the four world cops. A global "general assembly" would meet once per year to allow "smaller powers to blow off steam."[13] The Big Four would join "six to eight" lesser nations in an "advisory council," charged with settling "any international questions." The President did not appreciate that long-fighting and exhausted Great Britain and China emerged from the war with their skins, and little else. Only two policemen could exert strong global influence, the United States and Soviet Union. As D. Clayton James observed, their world views and philosophies of government were "so antipodal as to preclude any general agreement on the post-war fate of nations."[14] Stalin and henchmen knew only unwavering dedication to Communism's world revolution creed. A huge mess of conflict awaited World War's end.

ABYSMAL WAR LEADERSHIP

Despite mountains of literature and rhetoric praising FDR's war leadership record, the President continually made appalling national and world decisions fraught with disastrous consequences. William Neumann courageously pursued this incorrect truth in his 1967 book, "After Victory: Churchill, Roosevelt, Stalin, and the Making of the Peace." Telling criticism of Roosevelt's careless, self-centered, completely unrealistic leadership style assured the work would never win prestigious historical writing awards or gain public attention.

In the chapter, "The Personal Equation," Neumann provided a remarkable, frank, and comprehensive treatise on Roosevelt's diplomatic deficiencies. Domestic political abilities that proved so effective for so long, did not work anywhere near as well internationally. Personal charm that swayed legislators and public, and helped bring national compromises on difficult issues, proved ineffective in solving the "conflicting interests of the Big Three."[15] Neumann compared Roosevelt's "dynamism" in recruiting an "array of talent to manage domestic problems," to distrust of State Department sources and desire to run foreign affairs as a personal fiefdom, a one-man show.[15]

Roosevelt greatly erred in believing major international issues, especially related to Communist interests, "could be dissolved by an atmosphere of good fellowship alone."[16] Surely, Soviet conference attendees, including Stalin and his ruling circle, enjoyed toasting their objectives, national interests, and guests at dinner meetings. Vodka flowed freely at such events. But hard-nosed negotiations were ingrained in Bolshevik politics, in the words of Foreign Minister V.M. Molotov, "the best possible training ground for world diplomacy"[17] (In the Russian language, "Molotov" means "hammer-man," "Stalin" the "man of steel"). Roosevelt the "cordial and entertaining raconteur" may have dominated Washington, but performed with woeful inadequacy on the world scene. As Neumann observed, "Russians never responded in any marked degree to this side of the President. Realties of basic differences" between Washington and Moscow were left untouched.[15]

Pending defeat of Nazi Germany, evident by Summer 1944, dissolved any bonds linking Washington, London, and Moscow. Reds now disdained helping Warsaw rebels fight off Nazis, or permitting the US to help Polish freedom fighters. Roosevelt made "amorphous statements in support of a [free] Polish state from which Polish exiles were able to maintain a faith that the US would eventually stand between them and their Russian neighbor."[18] Of course such protection never materialized. The President would say anything to save the votes of millions of Polish-Americans and gain a fourth term.

The handwriting stood perfectly clear for all who *wanted* to see. "Efforts to raise Roosevelt's doubts over viability of the Russian-American relationship," such as former Ambassador to the USSR William Bullitt's personal, impassioned entreaties, "met with great presidential self-assurance."[19] But "No matter how frequent the professions of amity and unity, each side was fighting a war for different ends from a background of conflicting interests."[20]

LEADING BY INACTION

Neumann cited Roosevelt's propensity for "push[ing] off into the future as many issues as possible where Russian and American interests were likely to clash."[21] The characteristic closely followed the President's common response to politically dangerous domestic issues: do nothing. Neumann called the policy, "Propensity for Postponement."[22] Roosevelt believed today's festering political problem would in time change "in a way that would relieve him of his difficulty." Neumann condemned this form of leadership: "Not to make some decision in regard to foreign affairs *during a war*, however, did not always have the same beneficial result. Then the decision was either left in the hands of the other nation or nations involved, or the sequence of events determined the outcome" (italics added).[16] As the case of Soviet Russia clearly demonstrated, the US was then commonly "faced with a *fait accompli*."[22] As his health deteriorated in 1944-45, along with personal energy, Roosevelt practiced more and more un-benign neglect.

Unfortunately, this "unfinished business became the underlying grievances of the Cold War," and uncontested Russian control of major parts of the world.[23] So Poland joined the Baltic states of Estonia, Latvia, Lithuania, plus Romania, Bulgaria, Hungary, East Germany and other European countries, as Soviet vassals bereft of vaunted Four Freedoms. Wishful thinking took the place of realism in foreign relations. Roosevelt told Congress and people after returning from Yalta that "spheres of influence and balances of power" would no longer beset national relations. A new world would emerge from the ashes of world war, the history of millennia replaced by an all-encompassing United Nations. As Henry Kissinger remarked, the prediction proved especially ironic given Roosevelt's recent granting of a huge sphere of Far East Asian influence to Soviet Russia, guaranteeing Communist rule in China, ideological split in Korea, and Korean War.[24]

SUPREME PATERNALISM

Neumann described another "domestic talent that served Roosevelt ill on the international front," the penchant for keeping "ultimate decision-making power in his own hands." The President liked to assign "several people to the same task," and give aides "ambiguous instructions or uncertain authority. If blunders were made, Roosevelt was still able to avoid direct responsibility, while taking credit for successes."[22]

Real power of international diplomacy lay not at the State Department, but in the White House. Roosevelt's right arm, Harry Hopkins, served as de facto secretary of state, although lacking any diplomatic experience. Hence Secretary of State Hull would attend an October 1943 Moscow meeting, unaware of official US policy and bereft of authority to act. The scenario repeated endless times. At Roosevelt's instruction, ambassadors commonly bypassed Hull's office and the State Department in direct White House communication.

The last day at Casablanca, January 24, 1943, brought a surprise Roosevelt announcement. Without consulting Churchill, the President proclaimed necessity of *unconditional surrender* of Germany, Japan, and Italy. As Neumann related, "the phrase 'unconditional surrender' had just popped into Roosevelt's mind and he associated it, mistakenly, with Grant's dealings with Lee at Appomattox. Grant had not used the term with Lee."[25]

Secretary of State Hull thought it a grave mistake, expecting stiffened Axis determination and "prolonged war." As it turned out, Nazi Minister of Propaganda Joseph Goebbels "did use the phrase in efforts to strengthen German morale."[26] Other observers linked Roosevelt's mandate to "complete destruction of German power, thus creating *a political vacuum that later seemed so favorable to extension of Russian power*" in Europe. Roosevelt used this particular "folly ... as a technique for creating a stable Europe favorable to Anglo-American interests and ideals" (italics added).[27]

Unsurprisingly, and "unrealistically, the President hoped in March 1943 [that] postwar division of Germany would be the product of indigenous separatist movements and not have to be imposed by the victors." British Foreign Secretary Anthony Eden then asked Roosevelt at Casablanca, "what he favored doing if no separatism developed. The President said he favored a division of Germany *under any circumstances*" (italics added).[27] As Neumann emphasized, "Without much consideration of the political and historical factors involved, Roosevelt appeared ready to make quick decisions that disposed of the fate of many lands."[28]

The Four Policemen concept, the view of everlasting US-Soviet concord, wishful thinking on and incomprehension of world power balances and spheres of influence, and careless mandate for unconditional surrender, caused Neumann to characterize Roosevelt's ideas as "loose and shaky ..., so remote from realities as to be irrelevant."[15,22] Roosevelt also acted with condescension in failing to "educate the American public to the necessity" of political compromise with the Soviet Union.[22] As Neumann noted, "As the gap between Soviet and American outlook[s] became wider and more obvious in the last year of war, the President, his physical powers declining rapidly, faced a political task requiring great intellectual and political energies."[22] Sadly for America and the world, these personal qualities no longer existed.

FDR's close aides, including Hopkins and White House Chief of Staff Adm. Leahy, failed to "press him to undertake this difficult intellectual task. *Roosevelt never worked seriously and sustainedly on drafting a blueprint for the postwar world that would be acceptable to his two allies and also politically acceptable to the American public. His ideas, to the extent that they have been recorded, were too often nebulous and superficial*" (italics added).[29]

WHAT WAS THE MAN THINKING?

Roosevelt did find time in October 1944 to commence "a secret collaboration between the US and USSR" to develop Soviet naval strength in the Pacific. According to author Joseph Persico, through "Operation Hula," America "would covertly turn over to the Soviet Union a flotilla of 30 US frigates, 60 minesweepers, 56 submarine chasers, and 30 large landing vessels." Courtesy of Washington, US Navy personnel "housed, fed, and trained 15,000 Soviet naval officers and enlisted men at Cold Bay, at the tip of the Alaskan Aleutian peninsula."[30]

Two points deserve mention relative to this revelation. Two months before, Stalin denied America permission to directly support Polish resistance fighters in Warsaw, then engaged in a fight-to-the-death against the German Army. Stalin feared creation of anti-Red Polish political leaders who would impede Soviet control of all Poland. Obviously, no consequence accrued to the Red Tsar for this refusal to a "friend and ally." Then comes the fact of US Seventh Fleet minesweeper shortage early in the Korean War which significantly delayed MacArthur's post-Inchon amphibious landings at mine-seeded North Korean east coast ports of Wonsan and Hungnam. Most US Far East Pacific Fleet minesweepers had been given to the Russians! Two-week delay in harbor mine clearing would be paid for dearly in arrival of Arctic cold, Red Chinese horde, and subsequent American blood and suffering. Americans should know this specific pro-Soviet Roosevelt legacy.

STALIN IN, CHIANG KAI-SHEK OUT

Behind the scenes, the Tehran meeting marked a great switch in Roosevelt's relations with Stalin and Chiang Kai-shek. Stalin became the object of the president's attentions, Chiang now the poor relation. The Chinese Nationalist Government would never regain its relatively high standing with Washington and favorable media depiction.

David Dallin described the "attitude of the US Government, more influential in China than any other, ... veering in the direction prompted by Moscow."[31] US shift to the left destroyed the old China policy. Now Roosevelt pitched a Chinese "United Front," a foot-in-the-door Nationalist-Communist coalition. In Communist ideology, proven in many East European nations, coalition governments are mere precursors to complete Red control. The American public had no idea of the influence exercised by Moscow in US foreign affairs, especially regarding Chinese relations. Kremlin-desired "Dual Power" flourished in Washington, straight from the words and writings of Lenin and Trotsky, and actions of Stalin. The subject will be detailed shortly.

Chapter 13: Communist Friends in American News Media

"Journalism is considered the best cover for an intelligence officer."[1]

- Retired KGB agent Alexander Vassiliev.

Most newspapers, magazines, and radio outlets quickly endorsed the anti-isolationist Washington call for Allied unity. Propaganda pitch emphasized the exact opposite of truth. As documented by William Neumann and Fordham University President Father Robert Gannon, the public relations program for Soviet respectability began early in 1941, *before* the June German invasion of Russia, preceding US entry into World War II by almost a year. Obviously, the decision had long been made for America to join the fray, so its people must be amply softened up.

Popular *Life* magazine (September 1941) now painted "a new image of Stalin: Whatever the politics of this stocky little dictator, he is the man who has so far come nearest to stopping the German Wehrmacht." Stalin was described as possessing a "great deal of charm and a magnetic personality."[2] By March 1943, *Life* had taken the full plunge – Russians were "one hell of a people" who "look like Americans, dress like Americans and think like Americans."[2] The stereotypical American view of Soviet Russia as a murderous dictatorship began a steady, significant change under the double-barreled propaganda barrage.

Soviet police-state mass murder now didn't matter. *Life* described the fearsome NKVD secret police, the KGB predecessor, as merely "a national police similar to the FBI."[2] News stories featured glowing accounts of Red victories over Germany, the Russian people "brave and patriotic[,] with an acceptable political system."[3]

American pro-Communists fell over each other in farcically praising the Motherland. The politically correct Ambassador to the Soviet Union, Joseph Davies, likened Stalin to philosopher Roman Emperor Marcus Aurelius in humanitarianism and thoughtfulness. Beset by traitors, enemies, and harsh conditions, benevolent tyrant Stalin gallantly adopted necessary measures, including Moscow's notorious 1937-39 "show trials" mocking Western judicial proceedings.

Thinking, reflective Americans did not buy the crooked pitch. A May 1942 letter from Secretary of the Navy Frank Knox to his wife reported, "Our own interests [now] dictate we shall suppress a disposition to denounce Communism in behalf of national security. I hate to think of the unholy mess that awaits assembling of the peace delegates when peace comes[,] if Russia is still an ally."[4] Fellow realists William Bullitt and George Kennan, personally knowledgeable in Soviet ways, knew "winning the peace after this war would be as hard as winning military victory."

CHINA BECOMES AMERICAN PROPAGANDA TARGET

Stalin hit a 1944 home run as Roosevelt approved official US presence at Chinese Communist headquarters in Yen'an Province. Now a host of American "writers and Far East specialists began a domestic campaign in favor of Chinese Communism and against Chiang Kai-shek."[5] Press reports idolized Mao, Zhou, and associated ideas of "popular justice" and "agrarian reform." Negative aspects of the movement, such as burying opponents alive by the thousands and cutting beating hearts out of Christian-mission grammar school students, didn't matter.

Here is a sampling of biased commentary by key figures in the Moscow-ordered US propaganda campaign:

> Owen Lattimore, of Johns Hopkins University, State Department advisor, in describing the Red Chinese election system: "... the most positive step yet taken in China by any party away from dictatorship and toward democracy;"

> Lattimore, on Soviet popularity: "Among the Asian peoples, the Soviet Union has a great power of attraction.... It stands for democracy!"[6]

> Edgar Snow, author of *Red Star Over China* (1939): "The Soviet Union cannot have any expansionist tendencies;"[7]

Theodore H. White, *Time* magazine China correspondent, and Annalee Jacoby: "American backing of the Kuomintang [Nationalist China] regime convinced the Communists of American disregard for democracy in China;"[7]

Harrison Forman: "Today the Chinese Communists are no more Communists than we Americans are;"[7]

The journal *Amerasia,* published in New York by the Red front organization, the Institute of Pacific Relations, December 15, 1944, edited by Philip Jaffe: "Soviet postwar objectives in Asia are likely to coincide fully with those of the United States."[8]

American journalist Agnes Smedley proved a long-time effective Moscow agent. Having spent considerable time in Soviet Russia and China, she happily pronounced Mao's Communists as "saviors of China."[9] Smedley's books, *China's Red Army* (1934), and *Battle Hymn of China* (1943), served as important propaganda weapons. Her pro-Mao American campaign began in 1941 and never ended until her 1950 death. Douglas MacArthur's Army Far East Command intelligence chief Maj. Gen. Charles Willoughby reported in 1949 on Smedley's service as an important spy for the legendary Soviet Asian-based Richard Sorge organization. She served as an effective talent-spotter and recruiter for Moscow-directed espionage.[10]

Historians Harvey Klehr, John Haynes, and F.I. Firsov noted documentation of Smedley's ardent treason in Soviet Comintern (Communist International) archives briefly opened in the early 1990s. The Comintern served as Moscow's umbrella body for world-wide revolutionary efforts. While living in China in 1927-28, Kansas-born American Communist Party leader Earl Browder headed the Red front group, "Pan-Pacific Trade Union Secretariat."[10] With help from Browder and the CPUSA, Smedley worked for the apparatus in China, encouraging the start of an "English language anti-imperialist newspaper" in Shanghai, and "delivering financing for trade union, party work, and student groups."[9]

Atomic traitor Rudy Baker also worked in the Pan-Pacific Secretariat and taught Chinese affairs at a CPUSA school. He went on to lead the "Brother-Son" network, the American Communist Party's "direct connection to Soviet atomic espionage in America."[9] Klehr et al. cited an "August

1939 memo from the CPUSA to Comintern Moscow" that explained Red work in China as "an international struggle for peace and against fascism."[11]

American Pulitzer Prize-winning reporter Edmund Stevens is another of the era's journalistic Red stars. During World War II, while in America, he lavished praise on Stalin, describing Soviet governing structure as "a form of democracy ... more genuine and pure within its scope than any American institution except the town meeting."[12] Stevens wrote about the "large degree of inner-Party democracy" displayed by Soviet Communism.

In 1946, Stevens went back to Russia as *Christian Science Monitor* newspaper resident reporter. New-found Soviet world power impressed him, and he wound up retiring to Moscow. Red propaganda considered the Soviet Union "the one bright, shining star of humankind ... a heaven ... brought to earth in Russia."[13]

It turned out that since 1938, Stevens had belonged to the Young Communist League and CPUSA. Party membership remained hidden throughout his press career. As for Soviet heavenly nature, esteemed historian Arthur Schlesinger Jr. brought gushers down to earth in advising, "Despite the lofty words, in fact the Soviet Union more resembled a living hell."

As observed by James Forrestal, William Bullitt, authors Haynes, Klehr, Firsov, and a number of colleagues, radical leftist influence strongly extended into the public American press. All described the "Considerable ability of the CPUSA and its friends in the US to generate newspaper stories and press coverage about causes it supported."[14] The phenomenon then saturated television and is mostly unchanged to this day. Fawning mainstream press coverage of Sen. Bernie Sanders' 'straight-from-the-Kremlin' 2016 presidential campaign proves the connection. Anti-Communism and anti-Communists "must be neutralized" at any cost, using news media to destroy "fanatical, Fascist" opponents.

Newfound Red Chinese influence in Washington Far East policy did not end with Roosevelt's death. Dallin told the extent of Soviet victory in Truman-led American policy-making: "Long after the military alliance of the US and Soviet Union had ended and all motives for appeasement of the Soviet Union had ceased to operate, the policy of the US in China *continued to labor under the impact of the propaganda campaign of 1944-45.* Seldom has the Soviet government been more successful than in this case in attaining its goals by a really brilliant maneuver" (italics added).[8]

Chapter 14: Russian Zenith, American Nadir

"The high opinion people have of the great and mighty is so blind, and their interest in their gestures, features and manners so general, that if the mighty were only good, the devotion of the people to them would amount to worship."[1]

- Jean de La Bruyere (1645-1696), On Men and Manners.

The infamous February 1945 Yalta Conference brought Red influence in America to full flower. The press trumpeted Yalta as a brilliant example of international cooperation. After reality set in, many thought its pro-Soviet results a combination of Roosevelt's sickness and "susceptibility to Stalin's charm," the latter quite an unexpected outcome for the charm-master president. CPUSA Chairman Earl Browder wrote in the *Daily Worker* of high Red political influence and national acceptability following Roosevelt's Red-assisted November 1944 fourth-term victory, and culmination of all Red efforts in the Yalta result.[2]

Conference conclusion brought a whopper from Roosevelt and alter ego Harry Hopkins: "The Russians had proved that they could be reasonable and farseeing and there wasn't any doubt … that we could live with them and get along with them peacefully for as far into the future as any of us could imagine."[3] How convenient for Roosevelt to skate by realities of deep ideological differences, opposed value systems, and Red proclivity for revolution and mass murder that destroyed peaceful relations immediately after the Yalta meeting. Of course Nazi danger no longer exercised a cohesive effect on the alliance. Wishful future vision did not last out the week! Unsurprisingly, and to lasting regret, Americans found unappeasable Soviets not swayed by silly public or private presidential commentary.

Stalin's actual contempt for supposed American partners strongly carried over to Truman's presidency. At the July 1945 Potsdam Big Three meeting the Generalissimo observed, "Chinese Communists were not real Communists at all."[4] Stalin could depend on American ignorance and his hidden hand to create artificial reality and stand truth on its head. Nothing could beat dogged determination and dopey Americans.

ENGLISH WISDOM

In contrast, Winston Churchill realized the moral gulf separating Russia from the West, expecting a difficult course in securing world peace, political stability, and economic rebirth. He knew the potent global Russian influence and confrontation awaiting war's end. Churchill bemoaned the outcome of total World War as "tragedy." The sixth volume of his comprehensive World War II history, *Triumph and Tragedy*, clearly described the post-war global disaster encouraged by Roosevelt.

Foreseeing trouble two years before war's end, the Prime Minister told his Foreign Secretary Anthony Eden at Tehran, "There might be a more bloody war in the future."[5] Ingrained Red revolutionary zeal must have outlets, Russia had no strong neighboring states in opposition, either in Europe or the Far East. Western-style freedom stood in deep jeopardy. Philip Selznick reminded the world of Bolshevik Leon Trotsky's warning: "As for us, we were never concerned with the ... prattle about the 'sacredness of human life.' We were revolutionaries in opposition, and have remained revolutionaries in power.... We must destroy the social order ...."[6,7]

In a pre-Yalta display of exceptional vision, Foreign Secretary Eden advised Churchill to be wary of Russian political requirements attending Roosevelt's quest for Red Army intervention in China and Manchuria. Eden predicted "A most difficult issue likely to arise over Manchuria and Korea." Soviet Far Eastern political needs would "only be satisfied at the expense of incessant friction with the [Nationalist] Chinese ...."[8] Eden summarized Roosevelt's Far East plans as *"A potential cauldron of international dispute,"* foretelling Russian (1944) and then US (1944-49) sell-out of Nationalist China, the Korean War, and everlasting presence of Communist China and North Korea (italics added).

Although Roosevelt blatantly lied to the American people and Congress in stating "Asian matters were not discussed at Yalta," his Conference meeting with Stalin in Churchill's absence cemented the deal. Uncharacteristic of a self-believed political genius, at Stalin's insistence Roosevelt consented to putting all Soviet Far East provisions in writing. Rarely if ever had the President put on such fetters. There was no way out.

Within three months of German surrender, 1.6 million Soviet troops would crush the Japanese puppet Manchukuo government and its depleted Kwantung Army in China, Manchuria, and Korea. Communist influence and raw power now smothered the Far East, a seemingly high price, but consideration must be given the hundreds of thousands of American lives supposedly saved. Stalin received territorial rights in all three regions as partial and "reasonable" payment, plus ports and islands taken by Japan in the 1904 Russo-Japanese War.

"Big Three" chiefs met the day after Yalta's Roosevelt-Stalin Pacific War side-deal. Eden openly called the secret pact "a discreditable byproduct of the Conference."[9] Nonetheless, accustomed to playing second fiddle in the Atlantic Alliance, Churchill ignored his Foreign Secretary and agreed to Roosevelt's plan.

Roosevelt's former Undersecretary of State Sumner Welles knew free China's hopeless prognosis, as did Secretary of the Navy James Forrestal. Welles condemned Roosevelt for the predictable result of Yalta concessions: demise of Nationalist China and Red succession. Forrestal appreciated that, "The most important military element in the Far East favorable to the United States is a unified China, including Manchuria, friendly to the US. This is the best assurance against turmoil and outbreak of war in the Far East. *If Manchuria is to pass to Soviet control, Russia will have achieved in the Far East approximately the objectives Japan initially set out to accomplish. This would have grave impact on the US* (italics added)."[10]

Gen. Douglas MacArthur called America's China policy "suicidal," and Communist victory in China the worst possible outcome, one that would prove costly "for the next 100 years."[11] We are 67 years into the General's prediction. Powerful China, expected to soon displace the US as the world's largest economy, is a major and growing military power, engaged in muscle-flexing in the Yellow and South China seas, bent on projecting influence far offshore while limiting that of the US Navy. The "new and rich" brashly confronts the "old and debt-ridden."

In 1947, Truman, Acheson, and Joint Chiefs worried about the fall of Greece and Turkey to the Soviets – but nary a word in public discourse or future memoirs on the vital importance of a friendly China to Asian stability and peace. To accept their spoken and written words would mean no significance to America of Communist control of China.

Incredibly, Chiefs considered a Communist China no military threat to America and the Far East. Perhaps pro-Communist propaganda barrage had mesmerized leaders and press about the impact of hostility from the world's most populous nation, let alone prospect of Sino-Soviet alliance controlling one-quarter of the world's people.

REALITY OF ROOSEVELT PUBLIC DECEPTION

A few weeks after Yalta, only five weeks before his death, Roosevelt held a White House meeting with pro-Communist author Edgar Snow. Writers Jung Chang and Jon Halliday related Roosevelt's strong preference for personal sources in foreign matters, including China, and distrust and avoidance of the State Department. Snow was part of the President's "private network" on China that included ardently pro-Red US Marine officer Evans Carlson and important White House assistant and Soviet agent Lauchlin Currie. Snow's book *Red Star Rising* quickly became a key element in the new line.[12]

Roosevelt advised Snow the Soviets were "going to do things in their own way in areas they occupy."[13] This included the pending Red earthquake in vast Far Eastern reaches. The admission rendered meaningless all major conference agreements between the Big Three, especially Stalin's promise to always work in concert with Chiang Kai-shek and promptly hand back to him "all territory the Soviet army occupied."[14]

Meetings of Roosevelt, Stalin, and Churchill, media-portrayed as profoundly important accomplishments paving the way for world peace, were in reality public relations exercises meant to show greatness of presidential leadership. When it came to all-important promotion of US postwar interests, heavy press coverage and pretentious White House announcements added to nothing.

William Neumann summed up FDR's last international conference: "In the United States, the word 'Yalta' was to become like 'Munich,' a pejorative word that connoted betrayal. Roosevelt is charged with failure to defend the interests of the United States and its Polish and Chinese friends."[15]

Shortly before dying, Roosevelt revealed his frame of mind to Snow: "The Russians are now fully satisfied and we can work out everything together. I am convinced we are going to get along."[13] These words represented a superficial, fantasy view of reality. Soviet-American agreement had already fallen apart. Since Yalta's end, news came daily about Soviet intransigence in matters great and small. Roosevelt's simplistic prophecy lay shattered. Young Americans were set for Asian slaughter.

Destruction of mutual enemy Nazi Germany melted the glue binding opposites – advent of peace "exposed the underlying antagonisms between East and West," an ideological rift impossible to paper over.[16] All the charm expended on achieving "full Soviet satisfaction" melted like Spring snow. Self-described Russian-Georgian peasant Stalin had made a complete fool of the great patrician.[17] Most importantly, misguided one-man-act diplomacy caused a great American war effort, politically, to fall flat on its face. Americans got a raw deal in presidential leadership. Roosevelt never answered publicly for his show of incompetence and disloyalty, nor did Truman.

Roosevelt's war conference mischief outlived him. To Truman's surprise and dismay, other secret Soviet deals came to light after Roosevelt's death that must be honored. Reds needed ports on the Baltic and Pacific, full control of Poland, and a large swatch of German territory conquered by the American Army. At the Potsdam Conference, Soviet Foreign Minister Molotov and boss Stalin cited Roosevelt's secret promises chapter and verse with unfailing memories.

Then it was Truman's turn to play buffoon. George Kennan detailed absurd Potsdam agreements to Soviet participation in establishment of "democratic" elections in Germany, her major role in creating just tribunals to prosecute Nazi war criminals, and help in providing "democratic" input in the educational systems of occupied nations![18] Notwithstanding systematic murder beginning with great Lenin and persisting until Stalin's 1953 death, and a network of deadly "corrective labor" camps, the Gulag system, Truman's public proclamations attested to the Soviet Union as a shining world example of democracy and justice.[19]

MOSCOW INVADES FAR EAST – BIG TROUBLE FOR UNITED STATES

As per script, America stood aside as the Roosevelt-ordained Red tide engulfed Japan's Far East conquests. The day of Nagasaki's atomic bombing, August 9, 1945, witnessed a mass, three-pronged Soviet ground attack on North China, Manchuria, and shortly, Korea. Russian forces met little or no resistance. Within days, vast Japanese-held reaches of these territories came under Soviet dominion. Key Manchurian railroads knew Soviet control, as did naval bases at Port Arthur (Lushun) and Dairen (Dalian) (MAP 2). Only then did word finally leak out to the people about Roosevelt's backhanded dealings.

Immensity of new Soviet Asian conquest and sphere of influence is hard to appreciate. The Japanese battle front of northern China comprised over 1,000 miles east to west. Manchuria's north-south and lateral extents are each over 900 miles. Over a million square miles holding 250 million people fell to the Soviets (MAP 1).

The second day of Russia's Far East war, crusty Soviet Foreign Minister Molotov advised US Ambassador to the USSR Averell Harriman of Moscow's desire, after Japanese surrender, to share command of allied occupation headquarters in Tokyo with Gen. MacArthur, plus become part of the occupying force.[20] Reds insisted on troop presence in main-island Japan and equal say in Japanese governance. Red Army Gen. Vasilevsky was Moscow-designated co-leader.

To his credit, and that of Japan, America, and all free nations, Truman did not accept the bait as Roosevelt likely would have. MacArthur vigorously protested Russian occupation of Japan, adding to his "incorrect," high-target status with press Reds and Internationalists. Similar mutual control schemes in Poland, Romania, Bulgaria, Czechoslovakia, and Hungary quickly led to Red domination. But refusing Stalin on Japan meant hell to pay for America and the Far East.

With no heavy fighting, Japan laid down arms August 14, the *sixth day* after Russian invasion.[19] After surrender, Chang and Halliday reported, "Russians pressed on for several weeks. The area Russian troops moved into in northern China was larger than the entire territory they occupied in Eastern [and Central] Europe."[20]

Countervailing Japanese armed force removed, strong Russian army presence destroyed any semblance of Far Eastern balance of power. Divided Korea, and Communist revolution destined to conquer all China, proved a volatile combination. The US military's pitiful state under Truman helped explode the charge.

For years to come, Soviet propaganda held Russian armies as playing the decisive role in Japan's surrender. According to the Communist press, the atomic bomb meant nothing to Japanese capitulation. Signing of formal surrender papers took place September 2, 1945, aboard the battleship USS *Missouri,* in a ceremony chaired by MacArthur.[21]

TIPPING THE SCALE TOWARD COMMUNIST CHINA

For Mao's Communists, heavens now rained gold – time of destiny had come, the "long-awaited moment for which Chinese Communists had groomed themselves all these years."[22] Strong Soviet presence meant Japanese-occupied Chinese cities and provinces, previously unreachable by Communists, would automatically shift to Russian control, or better yet, directly to Red Chinese. Dallin described the "electrifying effect" on Chinese Reds of Soviet declaration of war on Japan and Japanese surrender. One of few historians appreciating and openly stating Chinese Communism's great fortune at this time, Dallin told of "a move of tremendous importance being staged" from August to December 1945 as Reds engulfed the mainland Japanese Empire "without conflicts with Chiang's forces."[22] Stuck in South China with no quick means of reaching the north, the Nationalist Army could hardly interfere with the momentous transition.

Moscow's gift held other beautiful Red facets. Japanese armories came into Soviet and then Chinese People's Army hands, a welcome replenishment. Surrendering puppet Manchukuo troops, formerly controlled by Japan but consisting mostly of Chinese, were mass conscripted into the Red People's Army. Mao's forces swelled from 75,000 to 300,000 in a few months. Now the Great Chairman's maxim, "Political power grows from the barrel of the gun," would be put to maximum test.

Naturally, Japanese Reds sponsored street demonstrations and labor strikes aimed at overthrowing the postwar, US-friendly Yoshida government. A planned January 1947 general strike by over a million government workers was frustrated by orders of occupation leader MacArthur.[23] But aside from the Japanese Communist Party and the usual cadre of spies, Japan remained beyond direct Soviet control. With Roosevelt, Moscow never had to contend with American refusal.

MacArthur appreciated the likelihood of Communist infiltration of Tokyo Supreme Command headquarters. He told George Kennan, "We have probably got some of them. The War Department has some. So does the State Department." The General didn't think these Reds represented danger to Allied control in Japan.[24]

Moscow easily ignored the fact that America had been at bloody war with Japan for three years and nine months, the Red Army for six days. Neither did American largesse in providing Russia uranium, a host of other nuclear weapon components, and whole atomic bomb-related factories, faze Soviets in the least. For the next five years, American slap in the face over Japan remained a source of intense irritation in Soviet dealings with Washington.

Many American leftists also remembered MacArthur daring to stand in the way of Red progress. Far East historian David Dallin and distinguished diplomat George Kennan are among the few who recognized the causative link between Stalin's Korean War approval and material support, and slammed door in postwar Japanese affairs.[25,26]

In the short run, Kremlin leaders would have to be satisfied with nine months of full military control in Manchuria. Long-time State Department China expert Edmund Clubb called the huge province the "Cockpit of Asia." For Moscow, this meant plundering large deposits of coal, iron, and gold, and whole industries for shipment back to the Soviet Union.

In the important realm of industrial capacity, Japan had "ravaged and devastated" Chinese factories, in David Dallin's estimation controlling 90% of Chinese industry.[26] With Japanese occupation bringing modernized factories, Manchuria alone held 70% of Chinese heavy industry.[18] This underscored the province's key role in any Nationalist Chinese economic recovery.

As today's People's Republic of China knows, and America should appreciate, industrial strength makes for economic muscle and national military power. As Dwight Eisenhower knew, "National security could not be measured in terms of military strength alone. The relationship between military and economic strength is intimate and indivisible."[27] Abundant fertile grasslands, prime forests, a population equaling that of France, and hydroelectric power completed the picture of Manchurian importance.

Through Roosevelt's senseless largess, Moscow now exercised great influence on the political future of Manchuria and China, "steering both into the Chinese Communist orbit."[20,28] The same held for the northern half of Korea. Nationalist China received a mortal blow to prospects for economic and military recovery. Fuse burned to Korean War.

Chapter 15: Ill Wind – Communist Triumph in China

Within a brief six weeks of Russian Far East invasion, the Asian balance of power underwent drastic change. In vast reaches of North China, Manchuria, and Korea, including naval bases at Port Arthur (Lushun) and Dairen (Dalian), Communist power replaced that of Japan (MAPS 1, 2). Soviet troops now faced Americans at the 38th Parallel Korean dividing line.[1] Roosevelt sacrificed all to Communism, while Truman stood helplessly as Red military and political occupation engulfed the Far East mainland and filled the vacuum created by Japanese defeat.

For the first time in centuries, Russia's immense Eurasian land mass did not border another great power. The Soviet Union held one-sixth the world's land area. Compliant satellites, akin to client kingdoms of ancient Rome, ringed its entire perimeter. When China joined the Communist realm, the fulcrum of Asian mainland power rested firmly on Moscow and Beijing.

Truman appeared to lack a firm policy for China and Korea, directing his attention to saving Western Europe from economic collapse and Soviet armed threat. David Dallin called the inattention, "A sad picture of US statesmanship – a picture well known in Moscow in all its details."[2]

Historian Jonathan Spence appreciated the great significance of land-, natural resource-, and industry-rich Manchuria to Communist victory in China's civil war. The province's 50-million people represented an important military and economic asset to Beijing. Geography hugely favored the Reds – their main base in Yen'an stood far closer to Manchuria than the Nationalist military center in South China and capital at Chungking (Chongqing) (MAP 2). Chiang had no ready means to move large numbers of troops into the vast province. From 1932 Japanese attack on Shanghai to conquest of Manchuria and great reaches of North China, the Nationalist Guomindang (Kuomintang) army suffered heavy battle losses. Spence described "immense" Nationalist killed in "protracted fighting around Shanghai" and "along the Yangtze River."[3]

Despite false, pro-Communist reporting by America's press, Chiang's government shouldered the overwhelming *continental* burden of fighting Japan, its contribution, according to famed author Ernest Hemingway, "100 times greater than that of the Communists."[4] But "thanks to the Reds' excellent publicity, America has an exaggerated idea of the part Communists played in the war against Japan."[4]

While Chiang had to wait for American help to move divisions north, Soviets controlled major rail lines in North China and Manchuria courtesy of Roosevelt's Yalta agreement. Plus, Soviet-dominated territories of Siberia, Mongolia, and the northern half of Korea curved around Manchuria, granting ready land and sea access[5] (MAP 2). Later, Mao referred to Manchuria as his secure and "comfortable armchair, with Russia as the solid back to lean on, and North Korea and Outer Mongolia on each side on which to rest his arms."[6]

OLDER BROTHER STALIN'S PRICELESS GIFT

In a decisive show of military, logistical, and political support, the Russian Red Army transported "100,000 Communist Chinese soldiers and 50,000 political workers into southern Manchuria."[7] Soviet empowerment of the Chinese Communist Party took place "in maximum secrecy, in stark violation of the [Sino-Soviet] treaty signed with Chiang."[8] *Americans never knew about the dangerous Red collaboration.* Yet these same Americans would be called on to spill blood when Roosevelt's deal turned sour and war came to Korea.

Russian forces left Manchuria May 3, 1946, nine months after entry.[9] Natural anti-Japanese sentiment of Manchurian and north China peoples proved quite favorable to Chinese Communist recruitment efforts.[10] Some parts of China endured 13 years of war with Japan; extensive enemy occupation created over 95 million Chinese refugees. Red political commissars routinely sent soldiers to help peasants in their farm fields and gave strict orders prohibiting stealing of anything from the people. Spence noted the Communist Party's "powerfully effective techniques of mass mobilization in rural settings and genuine skill at manipulation of belief through well-conceptualized propaganda."[11] The same talents flourish in today's New Red America.

Literally and figuratively, fields were favorable to Chinese Red expansion. The "cult of Mao" steadily grew. Wisely, the Party Chairman ordered military commanders to destroy enemy armies and seize weapons before worrying about occupying more territory.[12] Personal possession of guns was strictly prohibited, their relation to political power a key Communist tenet. Common infractions of Chinese Red law drew punishments that included turning over guns and ammunition to the Party. Guns were preferred to money in paying fines. Always pushing "class struggle," complete domination of all Chinese, and free use of "spies, secret police, threats, force, and violence," Chairman Mao Zedong gained "absolute power over one-quarter of the world's population[!]"[13]

Truman memoirs reveal a passive mindset regarding post-World War II China. He seemed to share the State Department contention, voiced by Kennan, that Japanese occupation and pro-West stance more than balanced loss of China to Communism.[14] Though ravaged by war, Japan had great industrial potential, her economy poised to spring forward; China leaned backward in all respects, her problems so great as to defy solution.

Great Chinese demographic strength did not appear to matter to Roosevelt and Truman. Yet, combined populations of China and the USSR should have commanded American leadership attention. It took no deep thought to appreciate the strength and predictability of Sino-Soviet alliance – likewise, the absence of vision regarding China's industrial potential, a disturbingly familiar phenomenon of 20th- and 21st-century America. With Euro-centrism the order of the day, few US leaders cared much about Far East Asia, except for government agents of Communism. Saving Greece and Turkey from Reds and invigorating European economies occupied leader minds.

US WORLD WAR II PACIFIC FIGHTING AND VICTORY – FOR NAUGHT

As attested by Gen. George Marshall and James Forrestal, America fought the Pacific War to prevent one nation, Japan, from controlling China.[15] But now the Truman Administration told of helplessness in face of Red onslaught there. Dean Acheson believed in China's inevitable fall to Communism. Forrestal and Marshall believed Red control of Manchuria meant "Russia will have achieved in the Far East … the objectives Japan initially set out to accomplish. This presents a grave impact on the US."[15]

Unsurprisingly, this hugely significant fact is nowhere found in Truman and Acheson memoirs, nor in the latter's thousand-page "China White Paper" public explanatory. With few exceptions, birth of another titanic Red regime appeared not to bother American civilian and military leadership.

Soviet and Chinese Communists naturally demanded prompt removal of all US forces from China. Hence, American Communists and sympathizers, including Internationalists, backed the identical policy. The circle is completed with Truman's February 1946 statement, "We must clear our hands [militarily in China] as quickly as possible in order to avoid the inevitable Russian recriminations similar to those today regarding British troops in Greece. We must terminate the 'China theater of operations' and in its place quickly develop the military advisory group. We must move all the Marines out of China …. The embarrassment of the presence of American combat troops …" must end.[16] The pronouncement's backdrop included Communist rebels firing on and killing US Marines guarding Nationalist rail lines.

Truman apparently did not appreciate the inherent nature of Russian and Red Chinese antagonism that would not be stilled by any American action. Even his 1948 suggested elimination of the US Marine Corps would not be enough. Exhausted Joint Chiefs roosters convinced Truman that nuclear weapons relegated large amphibious operations to obsolescence. Marines could "go" – in Truman's words, uttered just before Inchon invasion, they were just "the Navy's police force."[17] Plus, this would eliminate another defense expenditure, in satisfaction of Truman's quest to cut US military size and expense, regardless of rising world threat.

In remembrance of their Commander-in-Chief's slight, Marine tanks in Korean War action sometimes sported the painted letters "MP" (military police) on their hulls.

At a time of increasing global troubles from Communism, the US decided to disarm. It made no sense. Did Truman intend American disarmament to be an example to nations? Soviet Russia and Communist China obviously disagreed, along with the prior-mentioned April 1950 National Security Council Paper 68. Acheson memoirs referred to this 1946-1950 period of presidential leadership incompetence as "Truman's time of retrenchment," where military "means came out of any relation to ends."[18] The President seemed to have completely missed the big picture.

Far East authority David Dallin referenced Washington belief of "Stalin [as] the gravedigger of Chinese Communism" a "ridiculous assumption" and prime example of wishful, unrealistic thinking.[19] Dallin joined Churchill in bemoaning "lack of effective American leadership, foresight, and orientation in world affairs."[20,21]

ANOTHER RIDE ON THE 'COALITION GOVERNMENT' HORSE

The "military advisory group" mentioned for China must be weighed with the reality of Gen. George Marshall's presence there December 1945 – July 1946. President Truman's instructional letter to highly-respected Marshall spelled out the herculean mission: arrange a cease-fire between warring Chiang Kai-shek and Communists, and "unify China by peaceful democratic methods ... as soon as possible."[22]

No matter the price, coalition government must be established. Stalin liked the idea of Chinese coalition as a means of inserting a big Communist foot in Chiang's door which would facilitate full control. The President advised Marshall that success in this effort would allow the US to evacuate larger numbers of Japanese troops from North China, and "subsequent withdrawal of our own armed forces. A China disunited and torn by civil strife could not be realistically considered a proper place for American assistance ...."[23] No attention appeared given to who, or what, would fill the vacuum created by US departure from China. Truman washed his hands of a great World War II ally. Again, US policy mirrored Moscow's wish.

As attested by China specialist Donald Nelson's talks with Soviet Foreign Minister Molotov, Moscow first turned against the Nationalists November 1944. By then, the Soviets simply didn't need help from China, which now became expendable. Washington then made the identical shift. The Kremlin originated, the world followed. Implants of Two Governments carried the Dual Power revolutionary standard.

Surprisingly, given Soviet help and American stand-off, by March 1946 the Chinese People's Army had yielded most Manchurian cities to Chiang's Guomindang forces. Mao sensed a time of Nationalist strength and ordered a "switch to guerrilla warfare on a long-term basis."[24] Chinese Reds were on the ropes. They were rescued – by the Americans. The pattern would be repeated five years later in Korea.

Authors Chang and Halliday told of a Marshall-performed "monumental service to Mao." With Red backs to the wall, and

> "Mao's Dunkirk looming late Spring 1946, Marshall put heavy and decisive pressure on Chiang to stop pursuing Communists into northern Manchuria. Chiang gave in, agreeing to a 15-day ceasefire. Marshall's diktat was probably the single most important decision affecting the civil war outcome. Reds who experienced that period, from Lin Biao to army veterans, concurred in private that Chiang made a fatal mistake in accepting Marshall's truce. Had Nationalists pressed on, at the least they may have prevented Reds from establishing a large and secure Manchurian base on the Soviet border, with rail links to Russia, over which huge amounts of heavy artillery moved."[25]

Things worsened for Chiang Kai-shek. Marshall insisted on extending the cease-fire to almost four months for all of Manchuria, and permitting Communists to hold the vital Russian rail connection in northern Manchuria. Chinese Reds gained territory there "far bigger than Germany."[25]

As revealed in the book *The Enemy Within,* by Father Raymond De Jaegher and Irene Kuhn,

American-educated Chinese citizen Ching Nu-Chi served as Marshall's personal secretary and translator on his 1945-46 visit, doing double duty as an agent of Mao and Zhou En-lai. Working in Marshall's Beijing offices, Ching Nu-Chi gained full American confidence and knowledge of secret documents generated by Marshall and US Army Gen. Albert Wedemeyer, on-scene military advisor. After Marshall returned home, Ching maintained close contact with American diplomats in China until start of the Korean War. He naturally became privy to all US communications received and sent in Beijing, which soon reached Red leadership in Yenan.

Marshall met with Zhou and learned of continuing Soviet arms support for the People's Army. This did not prevent Truman from ordering a seven-month arms embargo on Nationalists as added pressure to form coalition government, nor stop Marshall from later acknowledging "the tragic consequences of Communist control of all China … and Manchuria that would result in *defeat or loss of the major purpose of the Pacific War*" (italics added). America spent much blood preventing one nation from dominating China, yet allowed that outcome for the Communists, the same incredible path taken in much of Europe. Obviously, Americans were ripe for the taking.

Truman and Acheson memoirs are silent about national and world security threats inherent in Communist control of China and Sino-Soviet collaboration. Nor is attending Far East Asian instability mentioned. Ample comments are found about the security threat posed by Russian armies in Central and Eastern Europe. Identical deficiency holds for almost all historical coverage. Truly, a firewall protects Democratic presidents from responsibility for American contention with two Red behemoth nations. Americans must be shielded from the consequences of "leading from weakness."

As Barbara Tuchman sadly related, "In the end, China went her own way, as if the Americans had never come."[26] In reality the wrong kind of Americans came and left their marks in helping birth a powerful opponent of true democratic government: Lauchlin Currie, Alger Hiss, Henry Morgenthau Jr, Harry Dexter White, Michael Greenberg, Nathan Gregory Silvermaster, Edgar

Snow, Agnes Smedley, Owen Lattimore, Joan Chase Hinton, John Stewart Service, John Paton Davies, John Carter Vincent, Frank Coe, Solomon Adler, Lawrence Rosinger, and Dean Acheson.

Chapter 16: Politics Rules – Truth of Global Threat Kept from People

"Bred on imperatives, the military temperament is astonished by the number of pretenses in which the statesman has to indulge. The terrible simplicities of war are in strong contrast to the devious methods demanded by the art of government."[1]

- Charles de Gaulle (1890-1970), French general and president.

MISTREATMENT OF CHINESE PEOPLES

The most accurate explanation for Chinese Communist hatred of America came from historian Tuchman: "We were now reaping what foreigners had always sown, *failure to treat Chinese as equals*" (italics added). Unique among historians, Tuchman perceived the "profound underlying anti-white temper of China so seldom appreciated or acknowledged by the West."[2] Unfortunately, lack of appreciation extended to Secretary of State Acheson and his pro-Red China specialists Vincent, Davies, Service, and Rosinger.

Tuchman summarized the price of US and Western inhumanity: "The Chinese had every right to feel cheated and betrayed."[3] Protracted personal or national abuse begets anger and desire for vengeance. The backdrop greatly contributed to Communist China's decision to wage war in Korea against traditional tormentors.

During the Korean War, negative images of the Chinese people continued to plague Western thinking. US Army Lt. Gen. Edward "Ned" Almond, MacArthur's Tokyo Chief of Staff and Tenth Corps Commander, stupidly told 7th Division, 1st Battalion of the 32nd Regiment troops at the Chosin Reservoir, "not to let a bunch of Chinese laundrymen" defeat them.[4] By then, hard-pressed and freezing American soldiers well knew the reality of People's Army "will and toughness." Tuchman related Chinese "innate dignity and self-respect," their "humor and stamina."[4] She reported the strong belief of World War II China-Burma theater commander, US Army Lt. Gen. Joseph Stilwell, that "the Chinese soldier, properly armed, trained, and led, was the equal of any in the world."[5]

The same deficiency of racial chauvinism plagued post-Second World War US occupation of South Korea. Koreans sensed an attitude of superiority among Americans and many clearly resented their presence. David Dallin cited an opinion poll taken in Seoul before the Korean War revealing half the people "considered former Japanese rule preferable to American!"[6]

Meanwhile, most North Korean leaders had spent time in Russia and attended Soviet schools. Dallin noted increasing North Korean connection with "its neighbors, the Soviet Maritime Province and Communist Manchuria," and cold-shoulder toward the South.[7]

Post-world-war political reality crashed quickly on Washington. Stalin threw down the gauntlet in a major Red Square speech February 10, 1946, declaring, "Peace is impossible under the present capitalist development of the world economy." Clarion call to global revolution came just six months after World War II and a year after Roosevelt's post-Yalta proclamation of everlasting peace and goodwill. As George Kennan observed after two years of Truman presidency, "Wishful thinking is still a potent force in the conduct of our relations with the USSR."[8] Despite urgings by James Forrestal and Kennan, Truman took that long to come clean with the American people regarding Soviet world threat.

SHIELDING THE GREAT RED CAMPAIGN

Reason for delay is clear: truth is often politically devastating. Early public admission of dangerous conflict between erstwhile allies of democracy and Communism would tarnish Franklin Roosevelt's 24-karat political reputation. Such grotesquely false public esteem is the prime driving force in American liberal politics, the legitimacy cloaking the Red-Socialist-Internationalist campaign of destruction. Oliver Wendell Holmes, Jr. biographer Catherine Bowen wrote of the destructive process in its early years, circa 1915-1925; Fordham University President Father Robert Gannon described the issue during the 1930s and 40s. Now, a hundred-year experience proves the validity and reality of Two Governments and Dual Power, core tenets of Marxism-Leninism deeply established in America.

While coming pages detail Red Revolutionary features, the over-arching domestic political requirement is clear: the left's godly inner sanctum of power must never be disturbed. The American public may only see Franklin Roosevelt through a narrow, heavily invested and crafted political lens. Acknowledgment of truth would be the ultimate act of political incorrectness.

Imagine President Truman's early 1946 admission that the great and costly world war, in relation to American and Western interests and a billion people living under Communist tyranny, had been fought in vain. The US defeated German Nazism only to confront larger Soviet Russian totalitarianism. Should we discern a difference between a police-state Soviet empire from the Ural Mountains to the North Sea, and murderous Nazism from North Sea to the Urals? A few years later Imperial Japan's Far East Asian dominance yielded to that of Communist China.

According to Truman writings, threat of world war loomed larger than ever and far worse in destructive potential. With fair press and historical reporting, *Roosevelt's war policy would be seen by all reasonable people as a resounding failure.* Winston Churchill clearly saw it that way. The discovery required no great intellectual powers, merely appreciation of what actually happened after the war. Continued socialist inroads meant banishing of greatly disturbing war facts from public understanding.

The following comment from Douglas MacArthur's autobiography, *Reminiscences*, illustrates a prime example of historical censorship: "The panorama of events which contributed so decisively to the downfall of our Second World War ally, the Republic of China, has never been told to the American people. The authorities made little effort to present the true and full picture of events in the Far East to the public."[9]

As Stalin, Roosevelt, and Truman knew, truth must be destroyed for the sake of political power. Today, the disturbing concept forms the first law of power brokers. The American ruling class decreed building a firewall between Roosevelt's terrible leadership and the worsening global clash of Communism and Capitalism. Lies were told, repeated a thousand times, false reality created to make a bumbling, power-drunk, intellectually-shallow, and ego-maniacal president a war hero to his people and the world.

To this day, Roosevelt and Truman are protected from any responsibility for Korean War causation and 54,262 dead Americans, in fact their undeniable progeny. Identical connection holds for the Vietnam War. Their combined leadership provided the most damaging display of foreign affairs disloyalty and incompetence in American history. They treated the American people with supreme paternalism and a "politics-first, it's all about power" mentality. Leadership of Federal Government was, and is, about weaving a tale for public consumption that supplants traditional American values with a wholly alien, anti-American variety. Only under this program of false reality could President Truman and Secretary Acheson get away with failure to publicly mention the great danger to America inherent in Communist control of China.

On August 14, 1950, with Korea at war seven weeks, George Kennan penned an assessment of Truman Administration foreign affairs performance:

> "I could find no comfort in what I could observe of the general conduct of foreign policy by our government in that hectic summer. Never before has there been such utter confusion in the public mind with respect to US foreign policy. The President doesn't understand it; Congress doesn't understand it; nor does the public, nor does the press. They all wander around in a labyrinth of ignorance and error and conjecture, in which truth is intermingled with fiction at a hundred points ...."[10]

A handful of unknown historians recognized the causative links between Roosevelt's Far East concessions, dividing of previously united peoples, massive Soviet military presence, and Korean War outbreak. William Bullitt, Jan Ciechanowski, David Dallin, Edwin Hoyt, and Anthony Kubek saw through political deception, documented the truth, and earned banishment from public awareness. Truth is dangerous to clandestine control.

Chapter 17: Stalin's Englishmen – Gentlemen Traitors
Beyond Suspicion

Since the valiant British Commonwealth Brigade fought as part of Eighth Army, all messages between MacArthur and Pentagon were copied to London. These communications went from the British Embassy in Washington to the American Department in Whitehall. Usually unmentioned in Korean War accounts, but historically factual, was presence in these facilities of three very active, high-ranking British diplomats doubling as agents of the Soviet Union, well positioned to pass military secrets to Moscow, which shared them with Beijing.

In the key Korean month of November 1950, Donald Maclean headed the American Department at the British Foreign Office in London, after spending four productive years (1944-48) on assignment in Washington.[1] Maclean served in the US as British Embassy First Secretary, and London representative on the joint US-Canada-Great Britain atomic energy board. Both positions were very important. The nuclear post brought unsupervised clearance to all US Atomic Energy Commission facilities and first-hand knowledge of nuclear weapon-related secrets.

Maclean's close colleague, British Secret Intelligence Service (MI6) officer, prim and proper H.R. "Kim" Philby, came to Washington in Fall 1950 as Korean War raged.[2] Philby served as chief liaison between British intelligence and the CIA and frequently visited National Security Agency facilities to keep Moscow posted on American knowledge of Soviet espionage. Philby regularly met with CIA Deputy Director Allen Dulles (CIA Director under presidents Eisenhower and Kennedy), future CIA Counter-Intelligence chief James Jesus Angleton, and worked closely with the FBI.[3] Naturally, at London's MI6 foreign intelligence service, he headed the Soviet Counter-intelligence desk![4]

The other trio actor, Guy Burgess, held the position of Washington British Embassy Second Secretary in early 1951, joining Philby on the Inter-Allied Board that shared military developments with London.

Authors Barrie Penrose and Simon Freeman summarized the American-British intelligence debacle: before and during the Korean War, ideologically devoted "Soviet agents worked in the heart of the British diplomatic and intelligence establishment in the US."[5] These fanatical devotees of Soviet Communism effected the most damaging acts on American and British peoples.

Documents declassified in 1981 under Britain's "30-Year Rule" revealed Burgess's regular access to Korean military intelligence reports and messages to and from MacArthur's Tokyo headquarters.[6] Burgess "leaked plans to the Soviets of the October-November 1950 US/ROK push to the Yalu and disposition of UN forces." As the traitor put it, "Everyone knew about US plans."[7,8] This obviously included Red Chinese leadership.

Moscow and Beijing also became privy to top-secret Anglo-American reports on Chinese army strength in Korea.[3] Devoted Marxist and heavy drinker Burgess readily voiced hatred for America to anyone who would listen, including impromptu audiences at public bars. No one in Washington or London seemed to notice or care.

Penrose and Freeman accused Burgess of costing American lives in Korea. British troops also fought on deadly east and west Korean fronts at the time, so British traitors also brought death and injury to countrymen. Including comrade spies Anthony Blunt and John Cairncross, these devoted traitors, known in history as the "Cambridge Five," also exposed to Moscow intelligence "scores of agents operating for the West within the Soviet Union."[9] This meant sure torture and death and profound harm to truly free countries.

Perverse thinking may attempt to rationalize treason to one's country. Maclean, Philby, and Burgess, never arrested for grievously hurting Great Britain and the US, professed honorable motives – they did it "to make England a better nation, to save their homeland from Fascism." The real driving force, of course, was loyalty to Stalin and Communism. These spies held deep ideological devotion to Soviet Communism, the most important requisite for individual and group espionage excellence.

Writers Christopher Andrew and retired KGB agent Oleg Gordievsky related the great impact of Cambridge University-originated Communists on the Korean War. The gang knew everything about US/UN military plans, and so did Moscow and Beijing. Maclean's American Department deputy, Robert Cecil, believed, "The Kremlin found the documents provided to be of *inestimable value in advising the Chinese and North Koreans on UN strategy and negotiating positions* (italics added)."[10]

COMMUNIST CHINESE WAR BONANZA

Knowledge that America would not use nuclear weapons against the Chinese, no matter the provocation, surely proved of great comfort to Stalin and Mao. Rand Institute analyst Bernard Brodie related that the entire 300-bomb US arsenal (another author, Fred Charles Iklé, used the figure of 350) was dedicated to defending Western Europe from the Russians. Likewise, Chinese territory would enjoy immunity from American conventional air attack, meaning People's Army reinforcements and materiel could concentrate right at war's door without fear of disturbance. Clearly, Europe represented the major focus of American military concern, the Far East a poor sister. Plus, the US military wallowed in Truman-ordered budget cuts that sapped conventional strength.

Mao must have reveled in his good fortune; the more secrets flowing in, the greater the prospects for Chinese military success in Korea and the lesser risk of unexpected problems and failure. His new nation could attack at will but hold immunity from counter-attack, an unheard-of war concession. "Volunteer" troops could be tightly concentrated along the North Korean-

Manchurian border, organized and equipped for attack, sent across the Yalu in perfect order, completely safe! China could not lose such a one-sided war. The US would fight with one arm, and a good part of its brain, tied behind its back.

Traitors helped remove the dominant element of surprise from the war equation. Who had such credible guarantees in war? For Mao, Zhou, and the Chinese Communist Party Central Committee, the fix was in.

TOKYO TO WASHINGTON, MOSCOW, BEIJING, AND PYONGYANG

According to historian William Manchester, British spies were not the only Communist sources providing Korean War military plans to the Soviet Union, People's Republic of China, and Democratic People's Republic of (North) Korea. By Fall 1950, Gen. MacArthur claimed his "strategic movements were being betrayed to the Communists. That there was some leak in intelligence was evident to everyone. [Gen.] Walker continuously complained to me that his operations were known to the enemy in advance through sources in Washington."[11]

Little did MacArthur know his Supreme Command of Allied Powers (SCAP) office in Tokyo was one of dozens of allied agencies penetrated by Soviet spies.[12] Soviet espionage authority and noted author Dallin revealed the traitorous accomplishment. North Korean and Chinese armies greatly benefitted from this additional source of classified information on UN ground battle plans. Now dual-sourced materials could be cross-checked for credibility.

Author John Costello identified one Tokyo traitor as yet another Cambridge-vintage Red, Egerton Herbert Norman, from Canada's Ministry of External Affairs. Norman served on MacArthur's SCAP staff.[13] One of his favored contacts was Chi Ch'ao-Ting, Moscow-trained Soviet agent and secret Zhou En-lai protégé. During World War II, Dr. Chi led a "Far East group of Communists operating from the US East Coast."[14] Among Dr. Chi's close confidantes was long-time Red agent, US Treasury official, and six-year Truman appointee as International Monetary Fund (IMF) secretary, Virginius Frank Coe.

Norman's treason joined that of many Canada-based Red agents. As revealed by September 1945 defector Igor Gouzenko, Ottawa Soviet Embassy code clerk, *10* rings infested Canada, only one of which Gouzenko exposed. Following the major exploitation demanded by Moscow Center and so skillfully practiced in the US and Great Britain, every major Canadian government department held Red spies, including parliament and armed forces.

To illustrate the all-encompassing reach of Soviet espionage, Penrose and Freeman noted Oxford University's near-completely ignored 1930s budding spy cell, contemporary with the Cambridge operation. Based on America's Venona Project deciphering of Moscow-New York-Washington World War II Soviet cable traffic, a tiny sample of heavy back-and-forth messaging, the "10% Rule" surely applied: only 1 in 10 Red spy cell operations, and operatives, have been exposed and identified. Conservatively, hundreds of code names remain unmatched with real people. For Reds, unexposed treachery represents the best kind.

Venona discovered over 1,200 "cryptonyms" within the traffic, over 800 of which "were assessed as recruited Soviet agents."[15] At least five of these had White House access, including one operative who "travelled in Ambassador [to the Soviet Union] Averell Harriman's private airplane back from Moscow to the USA[,]" after attending the Yalta meeting. The best suspect for this traitor was Alger Hiss.[15] Retired British senior Intelligence Officer Peter Wright wrote that "The most enduring legacy of Venona was the glimpse it gave us of the vast KGB machine, with networks all across the West, ready for the Cold War as the West prepared for peace."[16]

The Rote Kapelle, or Red Orchestra, served as the most important pre-World War II-originated Russian spy ring in Europe. Soviet military intelligence, the GRU, ran the massive operation. Apparatus activity increased as Nazi Germany occupied much of Europe. Stalin told the Politburo the USSR would attempt to find an opportune time to enter the war after capitalist powers had destroyed each other. Hitler's sneak attack relieved Stalin of that responsibility.

Peter Wright told that in the 1950s, fellow British MI5 officer Michael Hanley identified and listed "every known agent of the Rote Kapelle. There were more than 5,000 names in all."[17]

MAKING FOOLS OF THEIR HOMELANDS

True colors came to light as Burgess and Maclean fled to the Soviet Union in 1951. Philby, made a Soviet intelligence general, waited until 1963 to call Moscow home. The epitome of British gentlemanliness most skillfully utilized "McCarthyist hysteria" to shield himself from discovery.

British counter-intelligence complacency, if not complicity, is obvious. The untouchable trio had friends in high places in British government. It took months for London to acknowledge embarrassing comrade-spy escapes.

After careful study, Wright also alleged that his boss, esteemed Sir Roger Hollis, former Director of British intelligence agency MI5, a domestic-centered body somewhat akin to the FBI, was a Soviet spy. As former intelligence agent Wright related in his excellent book, *Spy Catcher*, "Every man is defined by his friends. I began to draw up a picture of those to whom Hollis was close in the vital years of the late 1920s and 1930s. I wanted to find some evidence of a secret life, a careless friend, a sign of overt political activity."[18]

Two people of interest surfaced during Hollis's time at Oxford, left-wingers Claud Cockburn and Maurice Richardson. Wright found Cockburn's MI5 file, held by Hollis throughout World War II, the intelligence chief neglecting to divulge previous Cockburn associations in a file notation, as required by "Service custom." Did Hollis "have a reason to hide his relationship with Cockburn, a man with extensive Comintern contacts?"

Examining the 1930s Hollis record in China revealed "a similar pattern. China was a hotbed of political activity, and ... an active recruiting ground for the Comintern." Wright discovered a British Army colonel who well-remembered Hollis in China, describing him as "left-wing because he mixed with people like Agnes Smedley, the Communist journalist and Comintern talent-spotter, as well as another man called Arthur Ewert, ... an international socialist."[19]

Shortly before Hollis retired, he denied being a spy in a face-to-face meeting with Wright, who mentioned revelations from defected Ottawa-based Soviet spy clerk Igor Gouzenko as one route of implication. Gouzenko told of a highly-placed Moscow agent code-named "Elli," embedded in British Intelligence since at least 1942. Former Red spy Anatoli Golitsin then exposed continuous KGB London intelligence penetration into the 1960s.

New MI5 Director-General Martin F. Jones came down hard on Wright in defending Hollis, ridiculing any chance of high-level Soviet placement as "grotesque, unacceptable, outrageous." MI5 would be "the laughing stock of the world intelligence community" should word of the suspicion leak out. Burgess, Maclean, and Philby escapes surely had blazed that path, along with 1963 discovery of Russian-implanted microphones in Britain's Moscow Embassy cipher room ceiling, believed to date from *1942*. So the matter officially ended.[19]

Wright characterized Cambridge group deception as "the greatest treachery of the 20th century," castigating the 1950s British Intelligence Service for avoiding "the most obvious counterespionage problem facing Britain – the results of 1930s Soviet infiltrations of the British Establishment."[20] Reds slickly "capitalized on widespread intellectual disillusionment among well-born British intellectuals … and succeeded in recruiting important agents in major government offices and bureaus …."[21] This same Establishment rushed to blame low-level embassy workers if leakage of secrets was suspected – the high-browed and richly-credentialed, exemplified by dapper Philby, stood beyond suspicion.[22]

Without question, the same phenomenon, along identical time lines, infected American Government, media, education, industry, politics, and law.

Wright observed the legal challenge posed by treason: "Unlike any other crime, espionage leaves no trace, and proof is virtually impossible unless a spy either confesses or is caught in the act."[23] He emphasized the tendency "to regard spies as 'rotten apples,' aberrations, rather than as part of a *wider-ranging conspiracy* born of the special circumstances of the 1930s" (italics added).[24]

American Treasury Department traitors Coe and Solomon Adler took early-1950s refuge in beloved Communist China, where the former translated Mao's writings into English. Manhatten Project scientist Joan Chase Hinton preceded Coe and Solomon by five years, happy to make Korean War radio broadcasts from Beijing calling for surrender of US troops. American soldiers called her "Peking Joan." Hinton enriched Red Chinese nuclear bomb development through a suitcase of classified documents, and personal experience working with atomic scientist Enrico Fermi. Her brother, William Hinton, a former Office of War Information (OWI) worker in China, also spent Korean War years in the beloved People's Republic. All made complete fools of American and British governments while exposing great and prevalent Red sympathy, and influence, for all who would see.

Part IV:

War with Red China, November 1950 – May 1951:

US Defeat and Victory

Chapter 18: Communist China Enters the War

The People's Army soldier must have eyes that see in the dark, iron feet to endure long marches, and a stomach satisfied with meager rations.[1]

- Father Raymond De Jaegher, Irene Kuhn, The Enemy Within.

Unfortunately for both sides, no diplomatic relations or official communications existed between the US and PRC before and during the Korean War. In late September 1950, PRC Foreign Minister Zhou En-lai warned Indian ambassador K.M. Panikkar in Beijing that Communist China "would not stand idly by" as North Korea fell: "If American troops crossed the 38th Parallel, China would enter the war."[2] Zhou knew the message would be quickly reported to Western powers.

In retrospect, the Chinese perceived US advance as a dire threat to their security. An historical fact apparently lost on Washington, Japan used the Korean peninsula 18 years earlier, "both as a continental base and as a *corridor of conquest* by which to accomplish seizure of Manchuria and attack on China (italics added)."[3] Significant and nearby American armed presence triggered unpleasant memories in Beijing. Coupled with US "advisors" in Taiwan and 7th Fleet elements in the Taiwan Strait, Mao and Zhou believed the US would find easy pretext for invading China itself.

Building Chinese socialism inherently meant "fighting American imperialism to the death."[4] Now US forces in North Korea stood a mere 500 air miles from Beijing, and if reaching the city of Sinuiju at the Yalu's mouth, only 425 miles, by Chinese standards too close for comfort[5] (MAP 2). But MacArthur discounted likelihood of Chinese entry into the war at the October 14 Wake Island meeting with Truman. If they did enter, the General predicted "the greatest slaughter." The assessment necessitated ignoring reliable intelligence, much of it gathered first hand in upper reaches of North Korea and Manchuria, indicating heavy Chinese troop presence ready to cross the Yalu. In fact, en masse Chinese entry into North Korea began October 8, 1950

(MAP 8). MacArthur had missed the boat.

Events shortly proved the reverse wisdom of MacArthur's words to President Truman. The General correctly predicted the slaughter part – but fared poorly on who stood at the receiving end.

Another equally arrogant leader followed the same mistaken path. Secretary of State Acheson completely misread Foreign Minister Zhou's pronouncements threatening Chinese intervention in Korea. In memoirs, Acheson referred to Zhou's words "as a warning, not to be disregarded, but, on the other hand, not an authoritative statement of policy."[6] Incredulous war analyst Bernard Brodie later asked, "What, indeed, would have been an authoritative statement of policy?" Calling the Chinese threat "non-authoritative" flew in the face of Zhou's importance as Mao's right hand and second-most powerful man in the People's Republic. The threat would never have been spoken without Mao's blessing. From personal observation, State Department China hands John Service, John Davies, John Vincent, and Edmund Clubb well knew Zhou's importance in the Chinese Communist Party hierarchy. This information assuredly passed to Department leadership.

Secretary Acheson also did not trust Indian ambassador Panikkar.[7] "An elitist to the core" and famously correct, Acheson's great mistake in ignoring Zhou's warning was seasoned with a heavy dose of racial chauvinism and ethnocentrism. In four years as Truman's secretary of state, Acheson visited Europe 11 times, Far East Asia not once.

Veteran State Department China specialist Clubb knew the Chinese Communists as well as anyone. On three occasions between July and October 1950, Clubb notified Assistant Secretary of State for Far Eastern Affairs Dean Rusk of high likelihood China would intervene in the Korean War.[8] Field-wise Clubb believed US crossing of the 38th Parallel would trigger Chinese reaction in kind over the Yalu. The savvy Sinologist put it with diplomatic bluntness: "The theoretical alternative of the Chinese Communists remaining passive may be arbitrarily ruled out."[8] Acheson excused a host of deficiencies and deceptions in later admitting, "None of us, myself included, served President Truman at this time as he deserved to be served."

By October 24, 1950, a 300,000-strong Communist Chinese Third and Fourth Field Army counter-attacking force lay concealed in steep mountains south of the Yalu. Laterally, the enemy host extended 150 miles through North Korea's upper reaches (MAP 8). In testament to unequaled marching discipline, two massive armies had accomplished what many narrow-minded American generals would consider impossible: entry onto a terrain-challenging field of battle with horse cavalry, pack animals, machine guns, mortars, and artillery, without detection by the US enemy possessed of air, naval, and ground intelligence capability, rife with motor vehicles of all types.

Ignoring reliable advice and failing to heed Red Chinese warning revealed profound disregard of reality by MacArthur and the Truman administration. So easily were almost 200,000 American lives placed at risk, and the worst disaster in national military history visited on US armed forces.

US/UN INVADE NORTH KOREA

Although Washington's order to cross the 38th Parallel restricted Yalu River access to South Korean units, Secretary of Defense Gen. George Marshall messaged MacArthur September 29, 1950, "We want you to feel unhampered tactically or strategically to proceed north of the 38th Parallel."[9] MacArthur took this as a force-wide green light to the Yalu.

It is known that the crack 3rd and 4th People's Liberation field armies, holding 40 divisions, began the march from central and northern China to Manchuria early July 1950. A stream of Yalu crossings-in-force began October 8, as US/UN forces traversed the 38th Parallel. Edmund Clubb had been dead-on-target. Mao decided to envelop, counterattack, and defeat advancing American, ROK, and allied armies in a surprise deluge of 300,000 "volunteers" in steep, knife-ridged North Korean mountains and narrow valleys below the Yalu (MAP 8).

The first invasion goal was destruction of the 6th, 7th, and 8th ROK divisions, prelude to the ultimate objective of "wiping out the US troops in Korea."[10] Mao ordered every blow east and west to be backed by superior numbers. The assault intended to easily provide the Chinese a 3-to-1 fighting front manpower advantage over their opponents, sometimes more. In one sector on the east front, three CCF divisions holding 27,000 troops attacked two regiments totaling 7,000 US Marines. While disaster beckoned, MacArthur announced on October 23 in Tokyo, "The war is very definitely coming to an end shortly."[10]

Massive, undiscovered Chinese invasion of North Korea, and subsequent overwhelming counterattack against US and UN forces, represented another giant US *leadership* and intelligence failure. Historians assign most of the blame to intelligence sources and agencies, and a fair amount to MacArthur and other Tokyo officers and civilians. Assuredly, failure of top military and civilian leaders to believe repeated and reliable reports of huge Chinese troop presence in North Korea and adjacent areas of Manchuria ranks as the primary error.

Prisoners of war taken October 26, 1950 by UN forces near Wonsan provided an example of official disregard. These were the first POWs identified as organized Chinese troops in North Korea. Prisoners reported crossing the Yalu October 16, two days after "MacArthur assured Truman at the Wake Island meeting" no such thing could happen.[11]

MacArthur deserves a large portion of blame. By October 20 his intelligence chief Maj. Gen. Charles Willoughby received confirmed reports of a "tremendous Red force already across the Yalu."[12] Navy Lieutenant Eugene Clark bravely infiltrated an ROK undercover patrol along the northwest coast of North Korea, several of whom told of heavy Chinese formations in Sinuiju near the mouth of the Yalu (MAP 8). Natives reported Chinese comments on putting 300,000 soldiers across the Yalu, the river "literally alive with the movement of troops and equipment." Lt. Clark repeatedly told these findings to superiors.[13]

Tenth Corps Army First Lieutenant Alexander Haig, attached to Corps headquarters and later a four-star General and Secretary of State under President Reagan, related the fact of over 1,500 warning messages about North Korean intervention passed from Willoughby to MacArthur since June 1949.[14] The theater commander admitted knowledge of increasing Chinese troop presence in Manchuria and along the Yalu. Still, MacArthur ignored reality and believed only a fraction of these troops could threaten the advance. Eighth Army and Tenth Corps intelligence chiefs appeared to share the illusion.

Should air reconnaissance have demonstrated large enemy formations, then those responsible for reviewing photographs and pilot evidence share blame. Successive 1946-1950 Air Force budget cuts markedly reduced US aerial surveillance and analysis personnel and equipment.[15] Secretary of Defense Louis Johnson and Truman himself brought that sad state. At least one US Air Force reconnaissance report of heavy Chinese troop concentrations just north of the Yalu was ignored. Continual rejection of timely, reputable, and repeated intelligence findings on reality of Chinese threat, dumped in the laps of military and civilian chain-of-command leadership, severely indicts the quality of that leadership.

Should insufficient efforts, encouraged by personnel and equipment shortage, have characterized Korea-theater intelligence gathering, this too speaks of leader incompetence. Otherwise, staggering dereliction of duty must be assigned to military air reconnaissance over Korea, aerial spying (if any) over mainland China and Manchuria, CIA and State Department intelligence, Far East Command intelligence, and ground agent operations in North and South Korea. The author holds MacArthur, Joint Chiefs, major intelligence organization directors, Acheson, and Truman as culprits in failure.

Invasion of Chinese Communist Forces (CCF) over Yalu bridges went largely unobserved, unreported, or unappreciated until November 6, when MacArthur alarmed Joint Chiefs with news of "... men and materiel pouring across all bridges over the Yalu from Manchuria. This movement ... threatens the ultimate destruction of forces under my command."[16,17] MacArthur emphasized the danger in another JCS message that day announcing, "a new and fresh army backed up by large reserves and adequate supplies," which meant all Yalu bridges must be bombed forthwith. Yet destroying Yalu bridges would not solve the problem of People's Army "Volunteer" infiltration into North Korea.

Stimulus for new-found appreciation of Chinese threat obviously came from the brief but annihilating CCF First Phase Offensive (October 28 - November 6). Advance American and ROK units north of the Chongchon River were smashed, push to the Yalu stopped cold (MAP 8). Now, PRC intervention moved from theory to harsh reality.

Very soon, bitter cold temperatures, already besetting Korean battle, would freeze the Yalu River and provide limitless points of Communist troop entry. Adding insult to injury, Chiefs would only permit MacArthur to bomb the southern half of bridges, then Truman forbade air bombing within five miles of the Yalu. Given these ominous signs, MacArthur still refused to abandon the drive for total occupation of North Korea.

Chapter 19: CCF Potent Foe –   Old Defeats New

In addition to US leadership flop, a number of factors preserved the element of surprise for Red China and allowed a great non-mechanized army with pack animal transport, lacking air support, to set upon and defeat a so-called modern, high-firepower, motorized force with air cover.

Of great importance, Red Chinese traveled by night, rested by day, and were camouflage masters. The horde, including human carriers and animals, "melted into the forbidding mountains" of upper North Korea.[1] Each soldier carried a small square of white cloth as cover while sleeping in snowy terrain. Tree branches extensively served to mask unit movements in non-snow conditions; one air observer described a marching Chinese regiment as "a moving forest."

Robust CCF nocturnal combat operations featured "tactics of rapid infiltration and bypassing," or encircling, of US, South Korean, and allied formations. Heavy frontal and flanking attacks often achieved complete surprise and destroyed Eighth Army infantry companies and battalions scattered above the Chongchon River in northwestern North Korea. Panicked flight often ensued.

Above all, the Chinese People's Army was proud, highly disciplined, battle-seasoned, physically fit, and able to perform its mission with a fraction of the materials and supplies needed by American units. In the mid-1930s, Communists endured the 6,000-mile Long March, by Barbara Tuchman's estimation "The sturdiest walkers of any army in the world. They had an eye for the country."[2] High, rough mountain terrain did not intimidate them. For 17 years the Red People's Army fought Nationalists and Japanese, lost a few key battles, but like the ancient Roman Republican army, never lost a war.

Party and Army leaders did not fear American military strength, seeing great firepower balanced in their minds by the American soldier's "fear of death." Mao considered US tactics "dull and mechanical, over-reliant on firepower and equipment," an estimation he may have regretted by May 1951.[3] But Red Chinese could march and attack in and across mountains and not depend on well-defined roads. And pack animals proved *superior* to motor vehicles in traversing narrow, winding and steep mountain paths.

MOSCOW-BEIJING RELATIONSHIP

The concept of "monolithic Communism" has long been degraded in historical scholarship. After the Korean War, authors began to emphasize Chinese Communism's independence from Moscow. In fact, from 1944-49, the prevalent CPUSA line featured "agrarian reform" as the essence of Chinese Communism, "not really Communism at all." In the 1940s and early 1950s, Soviet specialists George Kennan and David Dallin held the countervailing belief of Moscow as tightly controlling all foreign Communist parties, an understanding widely shared in official circles during the Korean War. Today's popular writers are likely to consign such belief to a simplistic and inaccurate world view of Communism.

While Beijing and Moscow indeed had a serious falling out starting in 1960, from the 1921 foundation of Chinese Communism to the Korean War, Soviet Communism held the status of "wise, elder brother." Traditionally, the Chinese Communist Party (CCP) venerated and imitated their Russian kin. A host of institutional Russian words and phrases worked their way into Chinese Red organizations. As modeled by Soviet Russia, a small-in-number but powerful committee, the "Politburo," headed the CCP (the blood-stained group was once referred to as "The Twelve Apostles of Evil"). The Chinese called their People's Army a "Red" army. Regions under Communist rule were known as "Soviet" territories. Communist Chinese secret police carried the title of "GPU." Newspaper and magazine names came from Russia: "Red Star," "Truth," "Struggle," "Soviet China."[4] Large portraits of Marx, Engels, Lenin, and Stalin joined those of Mao in public squares.

Furthermore, as with the Soviet military, all People's Army sections contained important military commissars, while "Revolutionary War Councils" directed every field army, and People's soldiers wore the five-pointed Soviet star insignia on their soft caps. Military schools held the same huge images of heroic peoples' leaders.

Regardless of so-called enlightenment displayed by today's historical experts, Chinese Communist revolution modeled itself on Soviet forebears. Both shared the philosophical heart of destruction of all social pillars and machinery of government.[5] On a personal level, Red Chinese added the necessity of "washing one's brain," *hsi nao chin*, which meant elimination of all previously held beliefs.[6] *Ideas* always held first place in the Red pecking order, the mass of people seen as lacking intrinsic value or significance. Nonetheless, Communists fervently held this perverse system as destined to inherit the earth.

"NORTH TO YALU" MEETS CCF FIRST-PHASE

Until the last week of October 1950, both Eighth Army and X Corps made fairly rapid progress north. A patrol of the 7th Regiment, 6th ROK Division, actually reached the Yalu hamlet of Chosan, in Eighth Army's sector, on October 26. So did the US 7th Infantry Division spearhead Task Force Cooper, a bit later (Nov. 23), at the village of Hyesanjin on the eastern front[7] (MAP 8).

Two events then caused the bottom to drop out of US/UN Korean unification: brutally cold weather, and springing to action of 300,000 Chinese "Peoples Volunteers." October's end brought harsh Siberian winds, snow, ice, and temperatures dropping to minus 25 degrees F. Arctic conditions persisted throughout November and December. Weather now "proved as much an adversary as enemy soldiers."[8] Lacking cold-weather boots, clothing, and sleeping bags, thousands of US and ROK troops suffered frostbite and weapons malfunction. Many froze to death. Bolts on rifles would not move, gun barrels split, gasoline turned to jelly, engine and gun oil congealed.

Red Chinese were tough warriors, but simple quilt uniforms, sneaker-like, rubber-soled canvas footwear, and Red Star-emblazoned cloth hats (CCF did not wear helmets), could not protect against bitter cold and winds.[8,9] Harsh weather proved indiscriminate as many thousands of Chinese suffered frostbite and death.

Given conditions, and reflecting his leader MacArthur's wishes, Gen. Almond unwisely urged commanders to proceed with haste toward the Yalu, despite taking of fresh Chinese prisoners who readily admitted presence of huge People's forces. Alone among division chiefs, Marine Gen. Smith resisted pell-mell northern rush, fearing his division's over-extension. Contact between regiments must be maintained, isolation avoided. This basic tenet of combat advance reflected a marked difference in Eighth Army/Tenth Corps and First Marine Division leadership and performance in the coming Chinese onslaught. On a personal level, Tenth Corps Commander Almond and Division Commander Smith felt mutual antagonism.

North Korean geography now worked against MacArthur. As peninsula joins continent, North Korea markedly widens from east to west, similar to the Italian peninsula joining continental Europe (Map 2). The 120-mile "narrow waist" between Pyongyang and Wonsan becomes a near 400-mile expanse at the Yalu. Factoring in the river's zig-zag nature, true border length is over double the map measurement. So especially for the western Eighth Army, and somewhat for eastern Tenth Corps, forces were spread thin, adjacent units often out of contact by as much as 20 to 25 miles.[10]

The second shoe dropped the last week of October: unexpected Chinese Red *nighttime* ground attacks in force, with full shock and violence, falling on west and east American, ROK, and allied salients, the fore-mentioned First Phase Offensive. The counter-attack destroyed United Nations point units at Onjong and Unsan, including the US 8th Cavalry Regiment's 3rd Battalion, while others fled back to the line (MAP 8). Saber-wielding, bugle-blaring Chinese horse cavalry slaughtered panic-stricken US troopers. The *New York Times* carried a brief November 2 report on an American battalion's "Indian-style massacre" by saber-wielding, bugle-blowing Chinese.[11] Near Ipsok, a 3rd Battalion remnant of 200 retreating troops decided to split up and try to make it to safety in small groups. As author Edwin Hoyt reported, "Most were killed or captured. Of the thousand-man battalion, 60% had been lost."[12]

After five days of brutal action, Red attacks ceased and the enemy appeared to withdraw. While field commanders worried about what lay ahead, the surprising setback made no lasting impression on MacArthur. Attack north to the Yalu must continue. Highly-concerned Eighth Army Commander Lt. Gen. Walker sensed the danger but dare not oppose his powerful boss.

A favored Chinese tactic engaged US and ROK line units with rapid night frontal assault, while troops infiltrated around flanks and then the rear to envelop the position. Numerical advantage permitted generous "volunteer" postings. Main Supply Routes (MSRs) were routinely blocked. South Korean formations received special attention as objects of attack, took regular and terrible beatings, and quickly came to fear the Chinese. ROKs were often routed early in the attack, exposing unprotected flanks of adjacent American or allied units, which then sought to fall back, sometimes in order, often in disarray. Mao believed if ROK forces could be wiped out and US troops forced to fight alone, America would abandon Korea altogether.[13]

The Korean War had just witnessed the Chinese People's Liberation Army "First-Phase Offensive," a field test of tactics, deployments, night operations, terrain familiarity, US/ROK defensive capabilities and firepower, and prelude to total war. Red China also become privy to Soviet intelligence on US infantry rifle and machinegun strength and tactics; artillery, mortar, and tank dispositions; and need to avoid daylight air harassment and interdiction. Courtesy of Cambridge and Tokyo headquarters traitors, and MacArthur's unwise pronouncements on UN battle plans, Reds knew the timing and locations of coming US/UN troop movements toward the Yalu.

Chapter 20: The Night the Chinese Came

"Mao Zedong once expressed his strategy of war in just 16 words: 'Enemy advances, we retreat; enemy halts, we harass; enemy tires, we attack; enemy retreats, we pursue.'"[1]

- Dwight Eisenhower, Mandate for Change

The US/UN received a three-week break from reality, then on Thanksgiving evening, November 24, 1950, bore the full-brunt Chinese Second Phase Offensive. Red counter-attack came as devastating surprise. In the west, CCF fell on Eighth Army above the Chongchon River, paralleling the Yalu (MAP 9). CCF came very close to trapping tens of thousands of US 2nd Division, ROK, and allied forces.

Fortunately for the UN, Reds did not succeed in destroying Eighth Army as a fighting force. East sector attacks around and below the Chosin (Changjin) Reservoir sought to encircle and destroy 1st Marine and Army 7th division regiments. CCF succeeded brilliantly in the encircling mission, modestly in the destructive part.

East and west fronts erupted in shrill bugles, popping flares, and screaming Chinese hordes. Many carried bayonet-tipped lances or sabers instead of guns, instructed to take rifles and ammunition from dead and wounded Americans, South Koreans, British and Turks. Some Chinese fired American-made Thompson .45 caliber submachine guns, taken from Chiang's Nationalist troops, others Russian-made submachine "burp" guns with high-capacity drum magazines. Both were deadly at close range.[2] Wreaking the havoc of unexpected heavy attack, successful war's most important element, CCF stopped northern advance of now-bewildered foes squarely in their tracks, then in heavy, unrelenting assaults enveloped Americans and allies and lit the deadly fire of panic.

Many Americans believe a "free press" provides true accounts of combat outcomes. The belief is unfounded. During and after Red China's invasion of North Korea, the American people were subjected to heavy censorship to hide embarrassment of military rout. False press depictions of

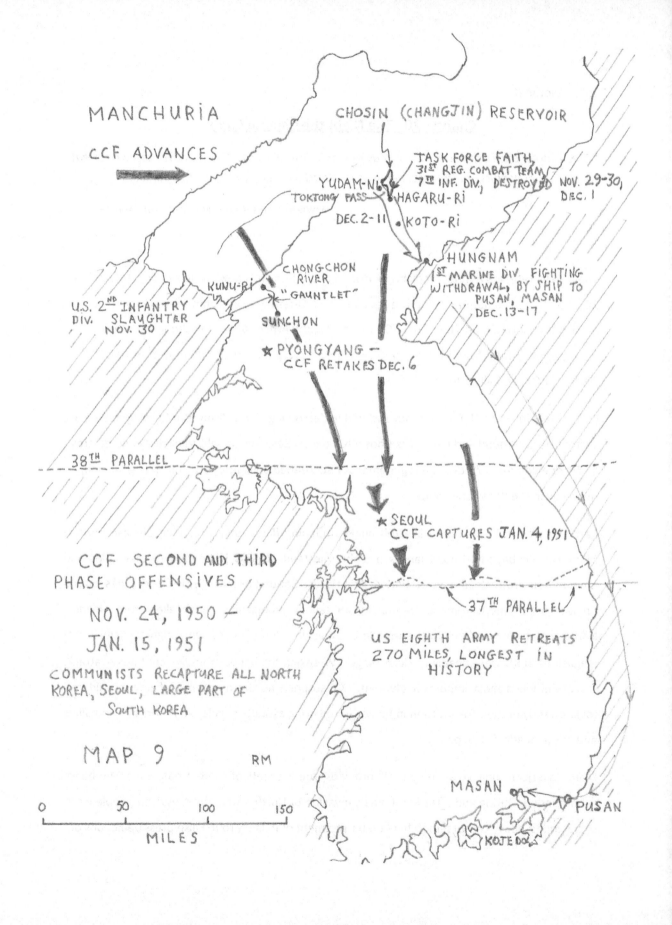

MANCHURIA

CCF ADVANCES →

CHOSIN (CHANGJIN) RESERVOIR

TASK FORCE FAITH,
31ST REG. COMBAT TEAM
7TH INF. DIV., DESTROYED NOV. 29-30,
DEC. 1

YUDAM-NI
TOKTONG PASS   HAGARU-RI
DEC. 2-11   • KOTO-RI

CHONG-CHON
RIVER
KUNU-RI   "GAUNTLET"

HUNGNAM
1ST MARINE DIV. FIGHTING
WITHDRAWAL, BY SHIP TO
PUSAN, MASAN
DEC. 13-17

U.S. 2ND INFANTRY
DIV. SLAUGHTER
NOV. 30

SUNCHON

★ PYONGYANG —
CCF RETAKES DEC. 6

38TH PARALLEL

★ SEOUL
CCF CAPTURES JAN. 4, 1951

CCF SECOND AND THIRD
PHASE OFFENSIVES

NOV. 24, 1950 —

JAN. 15, 1951

COMMUNISTS RECAPTURE ALL NORTH
KOREA, SEOUL, LARGE PART OF
SOUTH KOREA

37TH PARALLEL

US EIGHTH ARMY RETREATS
270 MILES, LONGEST IN
HISTORY

MAP 9   RM

0   50   100   150

MILES

MASAN
PUSAN
KOJE DO

"brave resistance" and "heavy Chinese casualties" covered reality of US, ROK, and allied massacre and "cut and run." The US Army reverted to the early days of Task Force Smith in pell-mell retreat.

ANCIENT BESTS MODERN

The unthinkable now happened with regularity. Chinese *horse* cavalry, armed only with swords, not only defeated but annihilated heavily-armed US Army battalions, even a *tank* battalion, through instillation of panic. En masse, screaming hordes and rumbling gallops caused crews to abandon tanks and literally be cut to pieces by horsemen. The highly successful Chinese First-Phase Offensive established the fright-driven pattern.

We borrow words of Winston Churchill from an 1898 horse cavalry-infantry battle in Sudan to describe the outcome: "Ancient and modern had confronted one another," the former with "weapons, methods, and fanaticism of the Middle Ages," and ancients had won![3] Churchill told of age-old horror now visited on the American Army. The scene revealed "An enormous carnage, men who strewed the ground in heaps … like snowdrifts, the whole mass … dissolved into fragments and particles.[4] A succession of grisly apparitions …, men staggering on foot, men bleeding from terrible wounds, spears stuck right through them, arms and faces cut to pieces, bowels protruding, men gasping, crying, collapsing, expiring."[5]

On a modern but equally disastrous level, Marine regimental commander Col. Puller related seeing "50 shot-up Army battalions, and I mean 50."[6] One road-ambushed Army artillery battalion left some 530 bodies of young boys on the ground. The Colonel described them as "about a third white-Americans, a third Negro-Americans, and a third South Korean." The surprised, wiped-out battalion gave evidence of very little return fire. Red Chinese rout in November-December 1950 equated to at least 25,000 US troops killed, wounded, captured, or destroyed as fighting forces. But censorship ruled the day – Americans never learned the truth about the horrible defeat suffered in Korea. Interests of common people always come last.

So began *"the largest and most bitter retreat in US Army history"*[7] (Italics added, MAP 9). No thought given to fighting its way out, US Eighth Army broke contact and ran so fast from the Chinese that neither side could fire on the other. As US Air Force historian Robert Futrell told, "For more than three weeks of December 1950 UN air forces posed the only opposition to the enemy's forward progress."[8] Ten miles yielded to 20, then 50, then 100. Recently-captured Pyongyang quickly fell, then all North Korea. Reds re-crossed the 38th Parallel and on January 4, 1951, Seoul again surrendered to the Communists. The South's capital, or what was left of it, changed hands three times in six months. Still, the US/UN fled south in hell-bent retreat, falling back deep in South Korea, 270 miles from their North Korean high-water mark (MAP 9).

REDS SLAUGHTER MUCH OF US 2ND DIVISION

The US 2nd Infantry Division, destroyed as a fighting force in upper North Korea, abandoned 90% of its artillery, mortars, tanks, trucks, jeeps, and all manner of personal weapons, ammunition, gear, and supplies. Red China could easily outfit 40,000 troops with the booty.

Noted Army historian SLA Marshall described the Division's most tragic incident, the early-December retreat through the "Gauntlet," a seven-mile valley passage below the Chongchon River from Kunuri to Sunchon[9] (MAP 9). Division Commander Maj. Gen. Laurence Keiser selected this route over a more western road that turned out to allow safer passage for other southbound units. The 2nd would not reform "on the next line of hills to the south, [as] Keiser decided that nothing but a long jump could save the division from the meat grinder."[10]

The division formed into a long, narrow column of marchers and vehicles at the head of a true "terrain corridor." Multiple Chinese roadblocks and control of adjacent hills made a veritable shooting gallery for Red machine guns. Once lead vehicles had to stop, the entire train did likewise. US tanks could often barrel through blocked passages, but less powerful vehicles could not and everything behind became sitting broadside targets.

Bereft of leadership or communication, the column quickly descended into "every man for himself." Roadside ditches held a thousand wounded, dead, and traumatized, bottlenecks jammed with wrecked vehicles, hoods and roofs of anything still moving piled with other wounded and dead. Freshly dead were thrown out to make room for still-living. Vehicles routinely rolled over bodies in the single-lane road.

Daytime air bombing and strafing only briefly suppressed CCF machineguns and at this time could not operate at night. The US Air Force in Korea was a small, "shoestring" force (classified words of Air Force Chief of Staff Gen. Hoyt Vandenberg in 1951 Senate testimony), deficient in bases, planes, parts, and crews and unable to provide continuous fire support. Small trucks and half-track vehicles outfitted with four .50 caliber Browning machine guns, the Army "quad-50s" designed for anti-air use, might have quieted Chinese automatic fire but were not organized for suppressing action.

Spirited and minimally-wounded non-commissioned officers and lieutenants attempted to rally counter-fire at various points along the Gauntlet, and knocked out a handful of CCF automatic weapons and mortars. But too many survived and continued to rain bullets and shells on the shattered column. The Chinese massacred the 2nd Division, a sad spectacle for American arms.

Truth proved too terrible to divulge for Truman and Pentagon. Instead, lies came forth to prevent damaging of politically-revered presidential reputations and those of surrender-minded chief executive and generals. Popular interests could be characterized as "missing in action."

MARINE RESPONSE: "WE HAVE CONTACT ON ALL FOUR SIDES!"

Eighth Army debacle contrasted with concurrent Marine 1st Division performance against similar Chinese onslaught in the east, that according to Neil Sheehan, "brought glory to Corps history."[11] Panic did not beset Marines, one of whom matter-of-factly wrote his wife, "We are now surrounded on all four sides." Col. Puller told his men, and newspaper reporters visiting his Koto-ri base, "Now we've got them just where we want them. We're surrounded. That simplifies our problem of getting to these people and killing them."[12]

At Gen. Smith's insistence, regiments enjoyed relatively close relation, not spread dangerously thin as on the western Eighth Army side. More concerned about his men's safety, Division Commander Smith, alone among American field commanders, subtly refused MacArthur-ordered blind-rush to the Yalu. Tenth Corps Commander Gen. Almond could not oppose his boss. At this stage of the War it was very difficult for Chinese Communist Forces (CCF) to isolate and destroy Marine units.

Marines also made good use of hastily-built forward landing strips near the MSR at Hagaru-ri and Koto-ri, for logistical support, reinforcements, and evacuation of dead and wounded. Combat engineers earned great credit for speedily-built, functional, durable, and vitally important works. Multiple daily flights kept the lifeline open. From December 2 – 6, C-47 aircraft carried 4,060 wounded from Hagaru-ri to rear medical facilities or hospitals in Japan.[13]

Marines vigorously defended bases against Communist attack. Ringed by numerically-superior Chinese at the Chosin Reservoir and MSR, they held lines and composure, fighting back with concentrated rifle and automatic weapon fire. Artillery and mortar batteries also maintained integrity and fired effectively, along with the tank component.[14]

For all the intense action, Gen. Smith knew heavy battle losses and vicious weather compromised Chinese logistics and fighting ability.[13] Smith also noticed something strange about CCF battle tactics. At Yudam-ni, the most northwest point of Marine advance, Chinese attacked vigorously November 28, then gave nothing the following day. Battles at Toktong Pass, Hagaru-ri, and Koto-ri revealed the same on-off pattern[15] (MAP 9).

Ordered to withdraw back to the coast by Gen. Almond, a true "fighting retreat" ensued. Marines maintained good discipline, laying down heavy fire. Almost all weapons, supplies, and wheels accompanied them.[16] Combat engineers again performed yeoman's duty in keeping the MSR open. A blown bridge at a high mountain pass south of Koto-ri necessitated quick air dropping of multiple, 2,500-pound "Treadway" bridge sections, including an extra section "just in case." One section fell on enemy territory, but combat engineers quickly put the others in place. One of the first vehicles using the new bridge, an earth-moving machine, greatly damaged it. Engineers made quick repairs and the Division got under way. The marching column and all manner of tracked and wheeled vehicles used the makeshift span. Large trucks had only 2.5 inches to spare on either side to avoid a thousand-foot drop.

A host of North Korean civilians joined Tenth Corps in seeking evacuation. Red soldiers commonly infiltrated accompanying civilian columns, seeing opportunities for small surprise attacks. Col. Puller admitted to "firing over the heads of the civilians almost every day for a week or more. There were a few times, I'm sorry to say, when I had to fire right into them, and killed a number. It was gruesome, but I knew what would happen if I let them in on us – it would have been the end of our outfit."[17]

A KINDER FACE OF WAR

In a near-miraculous display of ground, sea, and air defense against pressing Chinese, a flotilla of over 190 ships evacuated 105,000 troops from Hungnam south to Pusan, plus 98,000 *northern* civilians to Pusan and the island of Koje-do. Saving the refugee host, the North Korean regime's elderly men, women, mothers, children, and peasant farmers carrying meager possessions on their backs in bone-chilling weather, is a remarkable testament to personal endurance and American humanity. Author Bill Gilbert referred to the refugee evacuation as "the greatest single act of human salvation in wartime history."[18] Chapter 22 is devoted to this remarkable accomplishment.

TASK FORCE FAITH

Before evacuation, disaster befell Tenth Corps at the Chosin's eastern shore. Numerically superior Chinese mass-attacked the 7th Division's Regimental Combat Team (RCT) 31 under command of Lt. Col. Don Faith (MAP 9). Task Force Faith bravely fought off a continuous 80-hour assault in numbing cold, snow, and ice. Low on ammunition and medical supplies, its final stand took place only six miles northeast of the Marine base at Hagaru-ri. Of the original 2,500 officers and men, 1,500 perished, including Lt. Col. Faith. Dead and wounded totaled 80% of the original force. The remainder survived by walking or crawling to the frozen reservoir and reaching the Hagaru-ri Marine perimeter over the ice.[19] Evidently, Marines could not spare a rescue team given their own straits. Author Edwin Hoyt called it "The worst-yet debacle for Americans in the Korean War."[20]

Author Clifton La Bree stated horrible reality: "The 31st RCT bled to death, buying time with its sacrifice. In those critical days at the end of November and early December, encircled Marines guarding the Hagaru-ri airfield and First Marine Division Command Post did not have to contend with Chinese divisions busy attacking from the eastern side of the Chosin Reservoir."[21]

First Marine Division advance and withdrawal inflicted severe damage on at least six and possibly 10 Chinese divisions.[22,23] As Futrell related, "Because of effective Marine counter attacks, and the toll taken by frigid weather, the [Chinese] Third Field Army … required extensive reorganization and replenishment."[24] Nonetheless, for the only time in Corps history, a landing force had to retreat from battle and be extracted from shore. Legendary Col. Puller described the Korean experience: "There was no need to save face - our face had been blown off. People should know the beating we took in Korea" at Chinese hands.[25] Hoyt related "Marine losses from October 26 to December 15 [of] 4,418 battle casualties, 3,500 of them wounded, and 7,300 non-battle casualties, most of them from frostbite."[26]

One censored event was improvised burial of 117 Marines at Koto-ri prior to abandonment. Stiff bodies were ground into frozen earth by tanks whose treads crushed grotesquely protruding frozen limbs. A military cameraman filmed the burial, never shown to the American people.[27]

Tenth Corps evacuees enjoyed hot food and showers aboard ship, debarked at Pusan, and deployed outside Masan for needed rest, nourishment, and regrouping. Rebuilding of 2nd Division also started. Fresh soldiers and Marines replaced dead and badly wounded. Lesser wounded went back to combat units after medical care. Gen. Smith remarked of his Marines: "No division commander has ever been privileged to command a finer body of men."[28]

Chapter 21: Comparing US Army and Marine War Performance

November – December 1950

Few men are born brave; many become so through training and force of discipline.[1]

- Vegetius, De Re Militari, iii.

Evaluation of inter-service combat performance is a sensitive issue. Intra-service comparisons offer similar challenge. Ego, pride, use of positive and negative labels, historical implications, inherent unit and service rivalries, and varying conditions of battle play into analysis and complicate assessment. Objective data and fact may be hard to obtain.

Based on numerous credible Korean War accounts, Marines appeared to have a much better performance record than Army units in heavy combat with CCF the latter part of 1950. Under apparently similar battle conditions, Marines are said to have resisted panic during heavy Chinese attack, and maintained unit integrity while vigorously returning fire and inflicting substantial casualties upon the enemy. Based on performance of Task Force Smith, the first month of Korean action, and response to mass Chinese counter-attack, Army units repeatedly abandoned positions, weapons, equipment, supplies, and vehicles in rush to panicky retreat. Marines appeared to act far more professionally than Army infantry under stress of these particular examples of high-intensity warfare.

Fair accounting of the marked difference requires attention to numerous potentially causative factors. Perhaps Marines had prior combat experience Army troops didn't have. As a volunteer force, did Marines attract better-educated and more behaviorally-sound recruits than the Army? Perhaps superior training made for better, battle-ready warriors. Officer and non-commissioned officer leadership quality is another necessary comparison. Let us examine these and other battle-related variables between the two service branches to make a fair, "apples-to-apples" comparison.

On the western sector in November 1950, US Army regiments fought side-by-side with South Korean divisions. ROK units often covered the flanks, or lateral borders, of American infantry battalions and companies. At this time, ROKs were not usually integrated into American formations, but fought mostly on their own. It is known CCF directed special attention to defeating and humiliating South Korean forces. Chinese leaders believed ROK destruction would bring prompt US withdrawal from Korea.

Clearly, at the time, American commanders had minimal confidence in ROK fighting ability. Multiple references attest to ROK breaking at CCF onslaught, leaving American unit flanks exposed. If ROK troop performance could be called inferior to that of Americans, Eighth Army was much compromised in *its* performance as a result. Later in the war, US policy changed to favoring vast increases in ROK manpower and firepower, along with regular inclusion of Korean cadres in American Army (and Marine) companies and battalions for logistical support and freeing of GIs for combat duties. These were known as "Koreans Attached to the US Army," or KATUSAs.

In the Tenth Corps-manned eastern sector, ROKs did not extensively share the main line, as with Eighth Army. Tenth Corps ROK divisions often fought alone, or at least with greater independence, and functioned well in low-intensity actions along east and northeast coasts of North Korea. Advancing inland, north of Wonsan and Hungnam, Marines fought alongside British and other allied detachments but had dominant presence on the MSR and battlefront.

Local and general pre-war environments of combat troops are necessary areas of comparative evaluation. Surely US Japanese occupation troops knew soft lives compared to combat-ready brothers. The phenomenon is well-noted in Edward Gibbon's classic *Decline and Fall of the Roman Empire.* The less the regional threat of war, the more lax the individual and group military discipline. According to Gibbon (1737 – 1794), legions manning hostile Rhine and Danube frontiers could not afford the luxuries and "laziness" of more quiet Eastern posts.

Also, greater troop contact with civilians while at forward bases equated to diminished combat readiness. Relatively few Marines served occupation duty in Japan, while all initial Army Korean combat units came directly from Japan. From the standpoint of troop environment, the Army appeared to suffer a combat readiness disadvantage relative to Marines.

Obviously, the role of basic and advanced military training and education is to develop reflexive individual response to the shock of battle that indoctrinates effective unit response. As great Army warrior David Hackworth stressed, "He who hesitates pretty quickly gets blasted away."[2] For almost all soldiers, field actions consistent with unit success are learned responses. Personal behaviors that define small and large unit success are learned through soldier-receptiveness to clear leader communication, constant repetition, developing sense of esprit-de-corps, and improved individual and group performance prompted by leader feedback. As with all professional learning, leadership example in combat-realistic field exercises is essential to professional development. The more combat-realistic to individual physical and mental senses, the better prepared the new soldier for high-intensity fighting. Effective soldierly responses to combat are reflexive, spirited, and learned.

To accomplish realistic soldier acclimation to battle, budding soldiers must be familiar with the sights, sounds, and general stresses of shooting war. This precept comes straight from antiquity. Ancient Jewish historian Flavius Josephus observed that "effusion of blood was the only circumstance which distinguished a [Roman] field of battle from a field of exercise."[3] Requirement of intense, high-pressure combat training is a key tenet of strict soldierly discipline, given emphasis by centurions of the Roman Republican Army. As Gibbon remarked, "It was a maxim of Roman Army discipline that the soldier should fear his officers far more than he feared his enemy."[4]

Ideally, there would be no surprises on the battlefield, the highly- and properly-trained soldier prepared for any scenario. Realistically, the unexpected is always part of war, and sometimes the decisive element. In every field of education and training, it is impossible to prepare students and trainees for every possible exigency – potential for complication is limitless.

Soundly conducted professional education and training, coupled with broad practice experience (combat or its closest simulation for soldiers and leaders), enables a defined routine or method to respond competently to, and develop solutions to, *uncertainty and surprise.* In health professions, such practice is called, "Judgment in the face of uncertainty." This ability is a hallmark of the master clinician – and the master warrior. Ability to act with utmost professionalism in meeting unplanned scenarios characterizes not only the master combat soldier, but true professionals in any field.

Leader, and individual, *thinking*, and adaptive response (judgment) based on experience and preparation, followed by rapid and clear communication and necessary action, allow success in the face of uncertainty and surprise. Then comes the warning of combat professional Hackworth: "In battle at least 10% never get the word."[5] This is a frighteningly high percentage for a combat unit, one that could easily predispose to defeat in battle. If the Colonel is correct, too much deadwood attended Army operations in Korea. Romans of old would describe one-in-ten failure as *decimation*. Then the question: did Marines in Korea function under a lower percentage of personal non-communication and function? Since the author has not encountered Marine-related literature on percentage of individual *or group* communication failure and related combat ineffectiveness, the answer is a guarded "yes."

Undoubtedly, high combat group cohesion, or unity of purpose, is also a function of the unit's *esprit de corps*. High morale and unit member sense of co-dependence, born of difficult, shared training experiences, act to reduce or near-eliminate sub-functioning soldiers.

Actions and words of high civilian and military leadership surely impact feelings and behaviors of those lower on the totem pole. Drastic Truman cuts in US defense expenditures from 1946 – 1950 may have disproportionately impacted Army effectiveness. Respected World War II combat leaders Eisenhower and Bradley, and former Army Chief of Staff General George

Marshall, bemoaned gutting of Army fighting strength. With far smaller forces and costs, effect on Marines may not have been so compromising. It should be appreciated that President Truman considered eliminating the Marine Corps in the late 1940s – "modern war made amphibious landings unnecessary, Marines were only the Navy's police force." Korean War Marines remembered the slight, painting vehicle sides with "Truman's Police" and other pithy epithets.[6]

Another comparison is made in US combatant prisoners of war taken by Chinese and North Koreans. While making up about 25% of US Korean fighting troops, Marines comprised only 10% of the 3,600 American Korean War POWs. Far higher percentages of Army personnel surrendered to the enemy. As Hackworth explained, "If we had hardened, well-trained, well-led soldiers in Korea we wouldn't have had all those POWs to begin with. The Marine Corps had very few."[7] Quality of training and leadership are directly implicated in soldierly proneness to capture in combat.

Regarding the issue of prior combat experience, Korean War historian and combat veteran T.R. Fehrenbach, *Army* 2nd Division platoon leader and company commander there, surprisingly reported, "As war broke, somewhat less than 10% of the small United States Marine Corps had seen combat. But fortunately for the Corps, the percentage was highly concentrated within officer and key NCO [Non-Commissioned Officer] grades; most of the Marine troop leaders knew what war was like."[8] As Fehrenbach stated, volunteer Marines "escaped the damaging reforms instituted within the United States Army at the end of World War II. Public pressure simply never developed against them." As a result, by 1950, "a Marine Corps officer was still an officer, and a sergeant behaved the way good sergeants had behaved since the time of Caesar, expecting no nonsense, allowing none. And Marine leaders had never lost sight of their primary – their only – mission, which was to fight."[8]

CLOSEST THING AMERICA HAD TO LEGIONS

Regarding rigorous and realistic basic training, Fehrenbach acknowledged the necessary recruit pain and suffering involved, and at times, risk of death. "But there is no other way to prepare them for the immensely greater horror of combat. In 1950 the Marines, both active and reserve, were better prepared to die on the field of battle than the Army."[9]

Reflecting the important attribute of esprit-de-corps, Fehrenbach observed Marines "walked with a certain confidence and swagger. They were only young men like those about them in Korea, but they were conscious of a standard to live up to, because they had had good training, and it had been impressed upon them that they were United States Marines."[9] Author of "This Kind of War," a comprehensive Korean War history, Fehrenbach offered martial wisdom only gained through personal experience:

> "Men fight well only because of pride and training – pride in themselves, their unit, and their service, [and] enough training to absorb the rough blows of war and to know what to do. They would not lightly let their comrades down.[10] It is this final, basic pride – *what will my buddies think?* – that keeps most soldiers carrying on.[11] And they had discipline, which in essence is the ability not to question orders but to carry them out as intelligently as possible."[10]

As for getting better raw recruits than the Army, Fehrenbach saw "Marine human material … not one whit better than that of the human society from which it came. But it had been hammered into form in a different forge, hardened with a different fire. The Marines were the closest thing to legions the nation had."[10]

Based on above factors, US Marines in November-December 1950 Korean action outperformed Army counterparts. More demanding and realistic Marine training resulting in better combat-prepared fighters accounted for much of performance discrepancy. Perhaps smaller Marine numbers allowed a more focused, intense training experience. With pejorative comments of top Army brass on budget cuts (an *administrative* rather than combat force, *disintegration* instead of demobilization), officer corps and GI esprit-de-corps likely suffered.

Marine combat performance against high-intensity Chinese assaults reflected deep trust within and among grunts, non-commissioned and commissioned officers, and correspondingly high personal and unit spirit. Corps *leaders* are credited with foresight and sense-of-mission in mandating intense training and encouraging realistic preparation for battle to meet defined elements of combat performance excellence. They also wisely stressed Marine history and traditions fostering a sense of martial uniqueness. The time's Army training chain of command did not insist on the same, so new soldiers followed suit. As author and Korean combat veteran Lee Ballenger observed, "It is a soldier's axiom that combat is endurable when compared with training."[12]

Another Marine leadership advantage appears relative to the Army. First Division leadership, in the person of Maj. Gen. Oliver P. Smith, did not strictly follow MacArthur's dictum to rush the Yalu. Smith insisted on strict adherence to standard marching protocols in advance through hostile territory. Regiment and division cohesion mattered greatly to Smith. In this, he mirrored the natural conservatism, caution, and risk-sensitivity of the Roman legionary commander. Unquestioning acceptance of Tenth Corps chief Gen. Almond's order to proceed post-haste to the Yalu, reflecting MacArthur's unwavering mandate, did not sit well with Smith.

Given Almond's superior rank and access to MacArthur, this took considerable personal courage on Smith's part (it also represented a departure from the Roman Army standard of following orders without exception, even with foreknowledge the order was wrong and would cause a negative result). Army division and corps leaders, even 8th Army Commander Gen. Walker, appeared too ready to accept MacArthur's northern charge and overly disperse regiments and battalions.

In prior mention, Army advance through "terrain corridors," valley roads surrounded by substantial hills, was not always accompanied by control of those hills. Troops then became targets of convenience for enemy gunners. Reluctance to confront a five-star General of the Army is understandable given MacArthur's huge post-World War II stature and perceived post-Inchon invincibility, to which Joint Chiefs concurred, albeit with trepidation.

Finally, Marines kept war materiel intact in November-December 1950, while the Army abandoned all manner of vehicles and equipment, plus personal arms and crew-served guns and mortars. Col. Puller could never accept considerable numbers of undamaged Army jeeps and trucks left on the North Korean Main Supply Route with keys still in ignitions. These were signs of military amateurism.

In severely stressful battle situations, Marines held their lines and fought effectively. For the period in question, Marine combat professionalism far exceeded that of the Army.

Chapter 22: "Greatest Sea Rescue in History of Mankind"

In the general misery inflicted on people of both Koreas by war, one refreshing, special incidence of humanitarianism lights the dark path. As human calamity unfolded with Tenth Corps taking ship out of North Korea, the United States Navy and Merchant Marine performed exceptional acts of salvation. The story typically receives brief mention in War accounts – "civilians 'saved' through evacuation by ship out of Hungnam," their fate then dropped like a lead weight, along with acts of heroism by unsung merchant seamen.

Fortunately, curiosity about the fate of almost 100,000 North Korean refugees led to an excellent account of their rescue by well-published author Bill Gilbert. The story begins with MacArthur's ordering of Tenth Corps retreat south to the port of Hungnam, for shipment back to Pusan (MAP 9). Hungnam stood 135 miles deep in North Korea, with Tenth Corps positioned in the North's eastern half. For easily 50 miles of the ground withdrawal, North Korean residents wishing to flee a repressive regime, victims of back-and-forth combat, swarmed from all sides toward the military column. These were the enemy's elderly men, and women and children of all ages. Many were peasant farmers, Christians, and shopkeepers, routinely persecuted by Communist leaders.

Gilbert cited a 1975 report by historian Stanley Bolin describing refugees and their families as "... belong[ing] to a group not welcomed by the leftist revolutionary movement in the North." They included "anti-Communist political activists, land owners, and educators."[1] The mass carried on their backs, dragged, or wheeled the few worldly possessions salvaged from homes.

Refugee entry along the MSR toward Hungnam made passage of US, ROK, and allied forces more difficult and dangerous. A good number of Red soldiers infiltrated the civilian horde, seeking opportunities for exploding hidden grenades or firing small arms into their enemy. Refugees believed Chinese Communists would kill the entire bunch if they could. As the civilian- military mass descended on the port of Hungnam, a hastily improvised fleet of 193 ships

Figure 44. World War II-vintage "Victory" and "Liberty" cargo ships built in American shipyards to supply European and Asian theaters. Taken from "mothball" fleet for Korean War duty, 200-foot ships such as Merchant Marine *SS Meredith Victory* (above, at launch) displaced about 10,000 tons. *National Archives.*

Figure 45. *Meredith Victory* open deck packed with North Korean civilian refugees brought aboard at Hungnam, Dec. 22-23, 1950. *National Archives.*

Figure 46. *Meredith Victory* refugees shoulder-to-shoulder, above and below decks. 14,000 women, mothers (5 babies born during 4-day voyage), children and older men made it on board. No heat on any decks, bitter cold temperatures. Great many despised Communist treatment in North Korea. *National Archives.*

Figure 47. *Meredith* Merchant Marine Capt. Leonard LaRue of Philadelphia oversaw ship's massive loading, later joined Catholic Benedictine order as Brother Marinus, living at abbey in Newton, NJ. "God's own hand was at the helm of our ship." *National Archives.*

Figure 48. Deck rail of *Meredith Victory* jammed with refugees.
Ship also held cargo of jet fuel drums. Most evacuees
had no food or water for 3 days, until stop-over in Pusan.
National Archives.

Figure 49. Tenth Corps Commander Army Maj. Gen. Edward (Ned) Almond (center) gave
approval for unprecedented sea rescue effort. "We got them all (98,100 souls)."
Young, newly promoted Capt. Alexander Haig (left) observed rescue; later 4-star
general and US Secretary of State under President Reagan. Almond's unnamed
pilot on right. Wonju airstrip, Jan. 25, 1951. *Worldtribune.com*

gathered just offshore Hungnam's limited docking facilities. Only seven 200-foot ships could fit in port at one time.

For vessels, danger lurked in waters surrounding Hungnam, which contained a deadly concentration of ship-destroying mines. Communists had laid many types of sea-borne ship-killers around the port. A number of US minesweepers had sunk attempting to clear lanes of entry into port. Ships entering the vicinity and then seeking to dock in the modest-sized harbor wisely accepted minesweeper escort. Readers recall US Pacific Fleet shortage of these ships owing to Franklin Roosevelt's gift of 60 toward building Soviet Far East naval strength.

Meanwhile, CCF pressed ever closer to the Hungnam beachhead. Their gunfire permeated the air, along with counter-barrages from aircraft operating from four attack carriers, plus fearsome 16-inch guns blasting from the battleship *Missouri*, and fire from "two cruisers and 22 destroyers."[2] The Army Third Division provided ground defense from a shrinking perimeter.

Early Siberian winter greatly added to suffering. By December 10, large numbers of refugees began to surround Hungnam docks. No shelter awaited, no break from bone-chilling cold, no provision of food or water. Any thought of escaping North Korea by ship had to wait. Soldiers had priority in boarding vessels.

Loading day and night, 105,000 Tenth Corps troops took ship at Hungnam, a most welcome respite from two-month grimy battle, miserable weather, cold rations, and dearth of sanitary facilities. Fresh change of clothing and hot food followed hot showers. Some had to take multiple showers to remove layers of dirt. Third Infantry Division warrant officer John Middlemas, Second World War veteran who also served in Vietnam, related that, "When we got ready to shower on board ship, we saw that our hands and faces were black, but the rest of our body [sic] was lily white. We hadn't taken our clothes off in a month."[3] For Marines and Army 7th Division doughfeet, it was about two months.

Military evacuation by sea from Hungnam proved a daunting accomplishment for the US Navy and Merchant Marine. Three days journey brought disembarkment at the much larger port of

Pusan, and much needed rest, rebuilding, and regrouping. But equal or greater challenge remained: what to do with nearly 100,000 starving and freezing North Korean civilians packed into the Hungnam beachhead, pressing toward the harbor as troops loaded and departed. Should American lives be risked bringing enemy refugees to safety?

To everlasting and mostly unknown credit, US military and civilian leadership quickly decided on the solution. South Korean physician Dr. Bong Hak Hyun repeatedly pleaded with Gen. Almond for permission to save the civilian horde. Marine Col. Edward Forney, Almond's deputy chief of staff in charge of evacuation efforts, lent his credible voice. Dr. Hyun and Tenth Corps Catholic chaplain Father Patrick Cleary went so far as to secure two LSTs, "Landing Ship – Tanks," from South Korea to help evacuate equipment and free docks for human cargoes.[4] To the extent of human and material capabilities, all refugees would board ships and be brought to safety far to the South Korea rear. Despite domestic leftist revolutionary rantings about inherent evilness, American values could permit no other course. Communist values would allow all to suffer and die, traitors to the revolution.

By December 18, three other LSTs arrived at port courtesy of the South Korean Navy, followed by six cargo ships from Japan. Civilians began loading December 19. Designed to carry 1,000 troops, over 5,000 refugees were packed into each LST. Then came the 10,000-ton US Merchant Marine freighter SS *Meredith Victory*, captained by 37-year-old Master Leonard LaRue of Philadelphia. Built in US shipyards to provide a large fleet of World War II "Liberty" and "Victory" supply ships, then mothballed, vessels such as the *Meredith Victory* had recently been re-activated for Korean service. Master LaRue served as a Merchant sailor in dangerous waters during the great war. At time of Hungnam rescue, the ship carried a heavy load of jet fuel in 50-gallon drums. There had not been time to offload cargo at Pusan, *Meredith Victory* so desperately needed at Hungnam.

Army First Lt. Alexander Haig, attached to Gen. Almond's staff, flew over Hungnam harbor in a light plane, observing "thousands of civilians wading through the freezing surf toward American ships lying at anchor."[5] Sailors threw cargo nets over sides to allow the desperate group to climb aboard. In April 2000, retired four-star General Haig described the scene: "The trauma of it was in watching these refugees in that bitter, bitter cold standing in water up to their waists, waiting for someone to pick them up."[6]

When *Meredith Victory* reached its mooring, winches carried wooden platforms stuffed with North Koreans from dock to ship for unloading, then back for more. Staff Officer J. Robert Lunney reported, "Refugees were loaded like cargo … placed in every cargo hold and between decks. We had no food or water for them. No doctors, no interpreters. The temperature was well below freezing, but the holds were not heated or lighted. There were no sanitary facilities for them. Children carried children, mothers breast-fed babies with another child strapped to their backs, old men carried children …. I saw terror in their faces."[7]

Incredibly, by morning of December 23, 14,000 refugees had been brought aboard the *Meredith Victory*. Captain LaRue later wrote, "It was impossible, and yet they were there. There *couldn't* be that much room – yet there was (emphasis in original)." Open decks of all evacuation ships were jammed shoulder-to-shoulder, fore and aft. Distinguished Korean War historian Lt. Col. Roy E. Appleman noted in his book, *Escaping the Trap*, "Those who saw the thousands of refugees jammed and packed into the LSTs [and freighters] exposed on open decks to freezing weather for three or four days did not forget the sight. These refugees had to be desperate to take such physical torment and punishment. It was part of the war and should be recorded as such." The port of Pusan, the presumed destination, lay "450 sea miles away."[8]

By last rescue ship's departure, not a single refugee remained on land. The US saved them all. Final tally of rescued North Korean souls reached 98,100.[9] In an exceptional performance, the Navy and Merchant Marine rose mightily to the occasion. Gilbert quoted words of author Glenn C. Cowart: "The Hungnam evacuation was a miracle of the first magnitude."[9]

Now came sea journey and expected landing at Pusan. The Third Infantry Division shortened and closed the Hungnam perimeter, while demolition teams set off strong charges to destroy anything of use to the enemy. Warship cannons added a finishing touch.

Five babies were born on the three-day trip to Pusan. No one died or suffered serious injury in loading and transporting phases. Refugee stoicism and courage impressed Captain LaRue and *Meredith Victory* crew. Crew members shared small amounts of food and water with limited numbers of passengers, but most had no water during the three day voyage.

Bodily functions had to be performed "where is," which meant within holds and on deck. Some passengers relieved themselves over the sides. Potent stench engulfed ships. Even after human cargoes were delivered and ships washed down, smell remained.

In addition to human rescue, Hungnam evacuation included 17,500 vehicles and 350,000 tons of equipment and supplies.

One dangerous incident occurred at sea in a *Meredith Victory* cargo hold. A few refugee groups built small charcoal fires for warmth, unfortunately on top of jet fuel drums. Cargo holds contained hundreds of these drums. A crewmember spotted the fires and made frantic arm and hand signals to Koreans that they must be put out as a grave danger and never lit again. Ignition of a single drum would likely cause disastrous explosions that would sink the ship and kill most or all aboard, in Gilbert's words, resulting in "History's worst sea disaster."[10]

Another disturbing event saw a Red agent among the horde, dressed as a South Korean military policeman, trying to spread rumors of American plans to throw the whole mass overboard far out in the Sea of Japan, and of US-intended atomic bombing of the ship. The trouble-maker quickly lost his fake identity and was chained to a steel post for the duration. Calm prevailed.

Another surprise awaited *Meredith Victory*. On arrival at Pusan Christmas Eve, Captain LaRue was told all docks were occupied and port facilities jammed to overflowing. The city already held over a million displaced Koreans. Pusan disembarkment at could not be permitted. The Captain was ordered to steam to the island of Koje-do, another 50 miles southwest, an infamous site for other reasons later in the War (MAP 9). "A few interpreters and military police" joined the ship for the final leg, and most importantly, large amounts of rice were brought aboard and fed to the starving people, "in the hatches and on deck."[11,12] The feeding operation took nearly eight hours.

Back at sea, the *Meredith Victory* crew walked among the North Koreans, handing out "their own extra clothing."[12] Christmas Day, as the ship approached the beach at Koje-do, Captain Raymond Fosse and officers of the nearby transport *Sgt. Truman Kimbro* could not believe their eyes. "When we first saw that victory ship, we couldn't figure out what in the world it had on deck. From a distance, it was simply a dark, solid mass. As the ship came nearer, we could see it was human beings. And there wasn't a sound from them. They just stood there, silently waiting."[12]

Befitting rigors of passage, *Meredith Victory* had no place to dock in the small, crowded Koje-do harbor. In fact, no port facilities existed at that time, just bare beaches. So another night at sea, Christmas night, must be endured by all. Then came the challenge of unloading human cargo. The 10,000-ton freighter could not make landfall, so LSTs were needed to finish the job. With heaving seas complicating the transfer, winches carried two square platforms holding 16 refugees each onto two adjacent LSTs. As these filled and withdrew to shore, the ordeal was repeated. As Captain LaRue observed, "Each person had to climb the rail of the *Victory* and be lowered into the LST."[13] Refugee transfer began 9:15AM (0915 military time), December 26, and ended 2:55PM (1445 hours).[14] About every 45 seconds of that time, 32 refugees made it to LSTs.

Most of the 14,000 rescued by *Meredith Victory* stayed on Koje-do island for one year. Families spread out in the countryside, seeking sticks, branches, pieces of wood and metal to build shelters. Those on other ships who managed to land at Pusan did the same. Food could be given out by the military and International Red Cross, but means did not exist to shelter the masses. Military-related transportation and housing needs took precedence over civilian. Korean people throughout the peninsula had been ravaged by up-and-down marches of enemy armies.

Gradually, hundreds of South Korean cities, towns, and villages took in their brethren. Jobs were gained, small businesses started, schools attended. Refugees made the suffering transition.[15] Living in freedom proved the ultimate reward. Koreans had always been one people, at least until Russians and Americans arrived.

On August 24, 1960, at the National Press Club in Washington, Leonard LaRue, now Catholic Benedictine monk Brother Marinus, received the Merchant Marine Meritorious Service Medal, the highest award bestowed by that service. Each crewmember received a citation of meritorious achievement and accompanying ribbon. A special act of Congress named *Meredith Victory* a "Gallant Ship." The Captain had chosen the religious life, living at St. Paul's Abbey in Newton, New Jersey.

Brother Marinus never forgot the "heartbreaking" news as his ship left Pusan for Koje-do: "The message of Christmas, the message of kindness and goodwill, had come to this woe-laden ship, to these people aboard who, like the Holy Family many centuries before, were themselves refugees from a tyrannical force. I thought as I watched, 'There was no room for them, no room in their native land.' God's own hand was at the helm of my ship."[11]

In 2001, six Korean Benedictine monks came to live at St. Paul's Abbey, which had experienced a decline in religious numbers. Their presence is said to have re-invigorated the holy community.[16] Having spent 44 years at the Abbey, Brother Marinus passed away October 14 that year, at age 87. In 2010, a program sponsored by Seoul-based media, including the Voice of America, marked the rescue's 60th-anniversary, a milestone of special significance to Asians.

The US Maritime Administration described the achievement of SS *Meredith Victory* captain and crew as, "The greatest rescue operation by a single ship in the history of mankind."[17]

Chapter 23: Shell-Shocked Washington Weighs Surrender

"I think, therefore I am. I might take it as a general rule that the things which we conceive very clearly and very distinctly are all true."[1]

- René Descartes (1596-1650), Discourse on Method. A Rule of Life.

Chinese invasion and brutal aftermath sent shivers down Truman, Acheson, Joint Chiefs, and MacArthur's Far East Command. From negative statements by MacArthur to Joint Chiefs, it seemed all might be lost in Korea. Eighth Army had not yet stabilized its hasty retreat, with Tenth Corps evacuated to the Pusan area. As 1951 dawned, Eighth Army's 180,000 troops still might be trapped and destroyed by the Chinese, a disaster of epic proportions. This horror must be prevented by *almost* any means (nuclear attack on Red China and CCF in Korea had been ruled out). At the least, UN forces would be likely to abandon Korea and seek refuge in Japan. These were very bleak days for national leaders and soldiers. General refrain of "Home by Christmas" had turned into nightmare.

At an early December 1950 press conference, President Truman mentioned consideration of "using all weapons at our disposal" in Korea against the Chinese. Truman clearly meant nuclear weapons. There was no misunderstanding the threat. British Prime Minister Clement Attlee took the statement to heart and hastily flew to Washington to calm Truman and emphasize need to concentrate on European defense against Soviet Russia. The US mustn't go overboard on this Korean business. Security of Britain and other Western European nations represented more important fish to fry.

As always, obsession with Europe and the huge Red Army staring at the West across Churchill's Iron Curtain ruled the day. No memories or references could be allowed to 1945 pronouncements by Roosevelt and Harry Hopkins about "Getting along with the Russians for as far into the future as we could see." Political correctness allowed Truman to state, "Europe is still the key to world peace." It was not a good time to be an American fighting man, or patriotic citizen.

British-American meetings brought agreement on a plan that might provide Korean cease-fire and save Eighth Army legions. Stripped to essentials, *it was a diplomatic drive to arrange surrender of UN armies in Korea, "regardless of the consequences."*[2] US/UN forces would lay down arms in return for safe passage off the peninsula, and Communist Chinese would occupy the entirety of North and South Korea. In reality, there would be no South – Korea would be unified under Communism. The proposal included granting Red China a UN seat, and the pitiful statement that the US/UN reserved the right to conduct *diplomatic* efforts to globally condemn China's takeover of Korea. Condemnation would of course not carry over into the Communist half of the world. Truman and Acheson had again changed war objectives, abandoning the idea of North Korean conquest and peninsular unification in favor of "any port in a storm."

Even after the UN regained offensive initiative in later months, American leaders still stood willing to accept any settlement approximating the status quo ante bellum.[3] Propaganda pitch emphasized Truman the statesman and grand humanitarian, putting forth the best solution for world peace and security, not the struggling political leader and nation. In reality, the hoped-for deal represented abject, disastrous American surrender.

Of course the American people would be lied to on a monstrous scale, but this was a routinely-paid political price. Sixty-six years later, this particular Washington-London Red kow-tow is not part of Korean War historical or public discussion, nor has it ever been. Truman's political reputation, the "bold, no-nonsense, give-em-hell Harry" so appreciated by later historians, demanded, and still demands, full protection.

Dictator Stalin's words aptly apply: "We ourselves will determine what is true and what is not." Americans do wise to leaven "freedom of the press" with a large measure of salt. These were darker days than our nation could ever believe.

JOINT CHIEFS PUPPETS DRESSED FOR PUBLIC SHOW

Importantly, and sadly in light of American military tradition, on December 3, 1950, US Joint Chiefs of Staff approved the request for a cease-fire from the Chinese Communists, *"with all its implications of surrender and withdrawal"* (italics added).[4] Nothing could get Truman to again use nuclear weapons, or seriously and distinctly threaten their use. Great and proud victors of World War II would instead grovel before the freshly-birthed People's Republic of China. Leadership surely failed to reflect "the home of the brave."

Politicians routinely bend truth to fit any scenario, but consideration of surrender was an incredible stab-in-the-back to American and British peoples that if implemented and publicized, may have resulted in Truman's deserved impeachment. Such are the lying, devious ways of politicians. People simply cannot believe war-related presidential statements. A leftist press always works hard to protect sacred leftist power. Who cares about people?

On their part, Joint Chiefs proved correctness of the adage, "Councils of war breed timidity and defeatism," attributed to Douglas MacArthur's father and Civil War Medal of Honor recipient Gen. Arthur MacArthur. Crisp, decoration-bedecked Chiefs' parade uniforms made for impressive public effects. Reality underlying deception meant full generals, political appointees all, functioned as striking, talking window manikins meant to confer legitimacy and credibility on non-professional military actions. The public should think, "Look at those rows of ribbons, the bright line of generals' stars, these were America's absolute best, inheritors of martial glory, cream of military wisdom and courage." The parade could not fail to convince. Staged performance worked as intended, and does to this day – march out the glistening brass for all to see and admire! Duplicitous political brilliance is boundless.

H.R. McMaster's startling book *Dereliction of Duty* detailed the disastrous effects of political domination of American military leadership. Although dealing with the Vietnam War and President Lyndon Johnson's huge mistakes, McMaster described the identical, fixed-in-concrete plight of Joint Chiefs of Staff during the Korean War. All Johnson war decisions, like those of

Truman,

> "betrayed his penchant for taking actions disconnected from military realities and without full appreciation of their consequences. The experience underlined what Lyndon Johnson [and Harry Truman] *wanted and expected from 'principal military advisers': the credibility lent his policy by their uniforms rather than their opinions* (italics added)."[5]

In a fitting Epilogue footnote, McMaster told that, "By 1967, some of the more junior officers in the Pentagon had begun to refer to the Joint Chiefs of Staff as the 'Five Silent Men.'"[6]

INSIDE VIEW OF MILITARY SITUATION DURING DECEMBER 1950 CHINESE CRISIS

Gen. J. Lawton Collins served as Army Chief of Staff during the terrible Chinese counter-assault against the American Eighth Army, allied units, and South Korean divisions. His book *War in Peacetime – the History and Lessons of Korea*, provides a first-hand look at the function and attitudes of Joint Chiefs during the Korean War.

For most of December 1950, Red Chinese attack rolled in full swing. On the west, the US-South Korean-allied Eighth Army front above the Chongchon River had crumbled. One after another, 500- to 1,000-strong US Army battalions were eaten whole by the Chinese, a decisive enemy victory in progress. The US 2nd Infantry Division stood in danger of annihilation. The eastern, Tenth Corps front, mostly manned by Marines, knew savage fighting and heavy American and Chinese losses. We learned of its early-December evacuation by ship to Pusan. At the same time, Eighth Army began a 270-mile headlong ground retreat into South Korea. Commanders worried that vast numbers of soldiers could still be trapped, killed, or captured by the Chinese. Except for the superb Marine "fighting withdrawal" (retreat), rout was complete.

The above did not stop Joint Chiefs from concurring with Truman that reprisal by the United States against Chinese territory *might cause war* with China.[7] One believes an American soldier rising to the top Army position would have keen powers of observation. How could Collins deny clearly-existing major war between Communist China and America? All elements of war – large moving armies, shooting, dead and wounded in abundance, were there to see and appreciate. If not war, what else could the situation represent? Joint Chiefs words, like those of Truman, were of course senselessly repeated political drivel. If Collins represented the thinking of other chiefs of service, which was likely, collective evaluation and conclusion defied common sense. Americans must then look upon shiny rows of stars as cheap political reflections.

Loyalty to Commander-in-Chief dictated Collins could not speak truth: Truman's military meltdown had turned into first-class national disaster with the Korean War's new phase. In truth, America was not equipped to fight *anywhere* with dominant presence. The principal US fighting force in Korea, Eighth Army, had been hastily pieced together from small units around the world and was "never fully up to strength or fully armed and equipped ...."[8] But Collins and other Chiefs dared not assign blame and offend their political patron.

Like his president a bit late on the draw, Collins now advocated a crash program of military strengthening, plus industrial mobilization to prepare for meeting *NATO*, not Korean, material commitments. Even the mildly inquisitive might ask, Where were Joint Chiefs' concerns about military weakness *before* Korean War? The answer is clear: missing in action, only voiced *ex post facto*. There is no record of sitting Chiefs standing up and demanding US military reconstitution, as the civilian National Security Council secretly did in April 1950.

Actions of "great" generals in denying substantial Korean reinforcements of men and weapons proved their disregard for fighting troops supposedly in their care. Chiefs appeared to care more for retaining exalted ranks and titles and keeping pensions intact. The record of JCS leadership at this time is pathetic. Framers of the 1947 and 1949 US defense reorganization had well achieved their goal of puppetizing military leadership.

Even five stars could not run against the tide. Wind had long since gone out of JCS Chairman Gen. Bradley's sails. He frankly admitted European security came first, even in the face of thousands of American boys bleeding and dying each week of the China crisis. Bradley recommended the "Korean Conflict" be "kept within its present scope, that we hold to a minimum the forces we must commit and tie down" in Korea. "Above all, we did not want war in Korea to spread into war with Communist China or with Far Eastern Soviet forces.[9] Every infantryman, round of ammo or aircraft that went to Korea meant delay in the far more important task of arming NATO to defend Western Europe."[10] Bradley called the fight "the wrong war, at the wrong time, in the wrong place, against the wrong enemy," a description that gained great traction with historians (He never specified what would constitute the "right" war, time, place, and enemy).

Fighting men would be more than a little unhappy with this approach. Families of fighting men killed and wounded would be enraged. Joint Chiefs appeared to disregard the needs, and suffering, of American servicemen. *Fear* represented the operant JCS theme. Unquenchable Korean War combat-veteran bitterness toward their leaders is understandable.

Truman declared "a state of national emergency" December 15, 1950, but not general military mobilization. In the face of severe Chinese military pressure, political posturing took precedence over decisive war action, a timidity not lost on Beijing, Moscow, or Pyongyang. The president finally admitted "the need for rapid expansion of our armed forces to meet this great danger," and five years after the fact, acknowledged unrelenting Communist Chinese hostility toward the United States.[11] Four National Guard divisions were activated, along with build-up of Navy and Air Force strength. These came none too soon, as US Army morale in Korea sank to a new low with Chinese onslaught and full American retreat. Reflecting Washington mindset, the four Guard divisions, when ready in April 1951, were deployed to Europe, not Korea. Spanking new US Air Force B-47 jet bombers never made it to war-time Korea, and Red MiG-15- antidote F-86 Sabrejets were only minimally committed, as with spare parts and maintenance personnel.

Minimally-aware leadership would have recognized grave Far Eastern danger since the Soviet Army tide flooded China, Manchuria, and Korea in August 1945. Truman waited a long time to respond to the threat, the critical impetus finally provided by North Korea. *He only addressed the danger when politically, he had no other choice.* With Sen. Joseph McCarthy pounding home treason in Government, Republicans crying about Democratic softness on Communism, China gone Red, and Moscow nuclear weapons, Democrats would commit political suicide in losing South Korea. Lyndon Johnson and John F. Kennedy knew this reality, as did Truman.

COLLINS AND CHIEFS TAKE A STANCE, SORT OF

Years after the fact, Gen. Collins indirectly blamed Truman and Acheson for failing to provide much-needed political war guidance to Chiefs and State Department.[12] Without mentioning names, the muted indictment implied deficient presidential leadership. Collins noted that he, Gen. Marshall, and Gen. Bradley referenced absence of White House leadership at the crucial time of Chinese onslaught. The same vacuum held from February to April 1951, when the US had gained the military upper hand over Chinese Communists and again needed sound executive direction.[11,12] When Truman finally lit the political path in May, it led backwards to military draw instead of victory.

Clearly, in matters of necessary Korean War political guidance and strategic direction, Secretary of State Acheson and Truman ruled Secretary of Defense Marshall and Joint Chiefs. With the 1947 National Defense Act, military incompetence of powerful civilian leaders gained free rein, to detriment of military leadership, fighting men in Korea, and the American people. Marshall and Chiefs knew, as a matter of martial common sense, the US should not tip its hand to Reds on willingness to accept the 38th Parallel as the permanent Korean dividing line. Yet Acheson did just that. Marshall and Chiefs appreciated that prohibiting major mobile offensive action starting June 1951 would give Reds what they most needed, a break from crushing US/UN action and massive casualties, and chance to get back on their feet. Acheson advised Truman to accept the disastrous restriction. Secretary Marshall and Chairman Bradley did not press the issue.

The question arises: why didn't Acheson know the foolishness of these decisions? It did not take a military mastermind to foretell the consequences. Could Joint Chiefs block or delay decisions they believed would hurt America's cause in Korea and help CCF get back in the fight? Only if willing to sacrifice professional careers. The law clearly defined the new chain of command, the reality of strict civilian dominance. There is no doubt Chiefs gave loyalty to their president, and *themselves*, far over duty to country and Constitution. Accepting as military professionals obvious and great American Korean War mistakes spoke poorly of Chiefs and the US defense establishment. The system plainly stunk to high heaven.

Thanks to Truman and Acheson, in Summer 1951 Red China and North Korea would have an open field for practicing their delaying brand of negotiations, which brought precious opportunity for military rebuilding. Poor presidential leadership complicated an already tough job for American and South Korean peace delegates. Even compliant Gen. Collins admitted that Truman Administration negotiation instructions were "vacillating, lacked firmness, and distressed our negotiators, men accustomed to sticking to decisions once made."[13] Two years of truce talks featuring 186 formal delegate sessions and many more working group meetings proved a bloody exercise in American wishful thinking and over-eagerness.

It must have personally pained Truman to publicly declare full commitment and support for US fighting men, knowing this was far from truth. Such was the state of military and political affairs as Lt. Gen. Matthew Ridgway took Eighth Army command December 24, 1950, during US/UN sea rescue of the North Korean civilian host. American leaders and people knew good fortune indeed in the person of Gen. Ridgway, just the right leader at a time of desperation. Surely the people had enough of caution, prudence, timidity, and fear.

Chapter 24: Field Command Hand of Fate –

Savior Ridgway

"There were no reserve forces that might be deployed to help, no higher authority to bring in new strength from another theater. All that I had was … already at hand. There would be no more."[1]

- Gen. Matthew B. Ridgway, Commander, US Eighth Army. The Korean War.

A December 23, 1950 jeep accident in South Korea claimed the life of Eighth Army Commander Gen. Walker. On MacArthur's advice, Gen. Matthew Ridgway replaced him. The new commander had served as a distinguished World War II airborne combat leader. Eighth Army now stood 100 miles south of the 38th Parallel, in fact at the *37th* Parallel, still out of contact with CCF. While the enemy took a breather, a major Chinese offensive loomed within a week.

Out of step with the prevailing defeatist attitude, Ridgway soon asked MacArthur's permission to conduct offensive action against the Chinese. MacArthur replied, "The Eighth Army is yours, Matt. Do what you think best."[2]

Gen. Ridgway's five months of Eighth Army field leadership proved the great and decisive difference one person can make in an organization. He exuded confidence, energy, and dedication. Personal inspections revealed a prevalent "all is lost" mentality among enlisted men and officers. Most dispirited of all was Eighth Army headquarters, which surrendered battlefield initiative to the enemy and had no desire to regain it.[3] Through example, exhortation, effective communication, and prompt dismissal of hopelessly negative company, battalion, regiment, and division leaders, Army morale quickly turned around. Ridgway proved the infectiousness of professionally-expressed optimism in overcoming deep pessimism and panic.

Ridgway insisted UN troops not be "road bound" or limited in mobility. D. Clayton James and Anne Wells realized that "Seemingly enormous advantage in mechanization and motorization was offset by dependence on roads, which at best were barely adequate and often little more than trails."[4] The Army must "take to the hills" as needed. Chinese surely did. Ridgway knew Eighth Army's great firepower superiority and control of the skies.

And if success in battle meant fighting at night, so be it. Entrenched Army "dawn-to-dusk" mindset did not meet reality of Korean ground combat. Hackworth lamented great difficulty in getting the Army to utilize night-operations training. Chinese fought nocturnally in large measure to avoid US air attack, and to strike fear in Americans, South Koreans, and allies.

With Red Chinese well-established in South Korea and determined to either annihilate UN forces or throw them into the sea, the heretofore impregnable foe revealed an Achilles heel: logistics. Gen. Smith was right: lacking sea and air supply, depending on ground-based transport through the length of North Korea and deep into the South, CCF appeared to run out of gas after about two weeks of intense fighting. Food and ammunition then became scarce, along with ability to medically tend their wounded. Ridgway ordered re-establishment of contact with Chinese forces in central South Korea. There would be no more major retreat.

RELIANCE ON HEAVY ARTILLERY

US artillery fire markedly increased in the new order. Rugged mountain terrain proved a challenge to artillery placement, which required relatively flat ground. Nonetheless, four 3-gun batteries of 105-millimeter (four-inch) or 155-millimeter (six-inch) cannons might rain down over 10,000 rounds in one day. At this stage, enemy guns could not match such performance.

Tellingly, relative advantage of UN big gun firepower decreased as war entered its second and third years. Communist logistics improved with heavy use of Soviet-supplied trucks, plus continued reliance on pack animals and human carriers, and multiple night routes mostly evading air interdiction efforts. Despite increased UN attempts at cutting supply lines through air attack, including the major 1951 campaign, "Operation Strangle," Reds managed to get growing amounts of heavy cannon, mortar, and munition shipments, plus ample automatic weapons and ammunition, to the main line. Chinese and North Korean artillery, mortar, and machine gun fire then severely pounded UN formations. A single battle site, during two or three days in 1952 or 1953, could be inundated with over 30,000 Red cannon rounds, hosts of mortar shells, and sheets of automatic fire. Having invented mortars, Chinese proved deadly accurate in their use.[5]

CCF used mortar fire as an integral part of infantry warfare. As Marine Korean combat veteran Lee Ballenger disclosed, "Any Marine who fought the Korean War will attest, 'The Chinese could drop a mortar round in your pocket.' They zeroed in on all approaches to their positions, and their ability to switch mortar targets with accuracy was phenomenal," along with "walking mortar rounds to a target. For men inside a fixed target, such as a machine-gun bunker or a tank, watching mortar rounds fall methodically closer and closer, one after the other, could create feelings of helplessness bordering on terror."[6] Abundant Russian-made 120-millimeter mortar fire, a very powerful round, proved especially fearsome.

Chinese often sited mortars deep underground, with only a small, camouflaged, difficult-to-spot opening. Sometimes mortar sites were spaced within tunnel systems, and moved about continually to avoid enemy targeting. Pretty slick for "laundrymen!"

While UN airpower targeted traditional logistical choke points such as North Korean rail tunnels, bridges, narrow passes, and marshalling yards, Communists pre-positioned well-manned repair teams at these sites, plus fresh rails, ties, and other needed supplies. Either later in the day of attack or next day, hundreds or even thousands of workers began moving earth and effecting repairs. As the saying went, "Reds could repair 100 bomb-crater sites in the time it took to repair one." Sometimes parts of bridges were removed and left hidden in nearby brush during daylight, to give air pilots the appearance of destruction, only to be quickly assembled for night use. Tens of thousands of North Koreans and Chinese participated in these work details. Communists used what they had: abundant manpower, and endless material supply from

Soviet Russia. The phenomenon repeated to equal effect in Vietnam.

Like the ancient Roman Army, Red soldiers were relentless diggers, adept at hiding artillery pieces in twisting mountainside caves, sometimes on tracks. Cannons would be rolled out to fire, then brought back into strong cover, making elimination by US/UN air exceedingly difficult.[7,8] Aerial bombing could not yet achieve pin-point accuracy. Communists routinely used oxen and other pack animals to pull artillery and carry mortars, a practice even resorted to by US and ROK heavy gun units. As mentioned, animals did better than motor vehicles or motorized guns in steep, narrow-trail terrain.

RIDGWAY TURNS TIDE – RETREAT PHASE OVER

Three weeks into Eighth Army command, with Reds suffering a combat lull due to logistics shortfall, Ridgway ordered multi-battalion-strength forward attacks to help discourage enemy plans for UN destruction. Operation Killer, a limited offensive, actually a reconnaissance-in-force, marked the mid-January 1951 end of US retreat phase and restart of northward movement against the Communists. The next four weeks brought larger operations that reclaimed lost ground north of the 37th Parallel, around Wonju in central South Korea (MAP 10). Fighting confidence returned to Eighth Army. CCF responded with fresh attacks-in-force starting late January and continuing well into February (3rd - and 4th- Phase Offensives), forcing the US, UN, and allies back 15 to 20 miles in spots but unsuccessful in destroying Eighth Army or its morale.

When Red wave petered out, Ridgway promptly ordered new division-strength offensives that recaptured recently lost territory and pushed the enemy close to the 38th Parallel. Chinese and North Korean units suffered very heavy losses in this resurgence. Interestingly, some State Department and White House officials grouched at the names given US offensive operations, such as "Killer," "Ripper," and others. They preferred more humane-sounding titles, grisly reality of war lost on their sensitive natures.

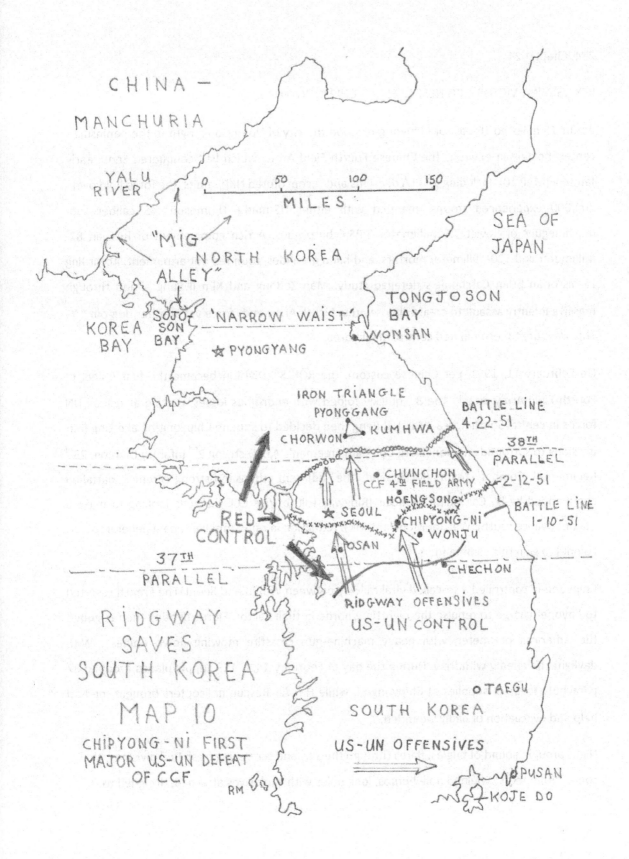

CHINA —
MANCHURIA

YALU
RIVER

0   50   100   150
MILES

SEA OF
JAPAN

"MIG
ALLEY"

NORTH KOREA

SOJO
SON BAY   'NARROW WAIST'

KOREA
BAY

TONGJOSON
BAY

WONSAN

★ PYONGYANG

IRON TRIANGLE
PYONGGANG

BATTLE LINE
4-22-51

CHORWON   KUMHWA

38TH
PARALLEL

CHUNCHON
CCF 4TH FIELD ARMY   2-12-51

RED
CONTROL

★ SEOUL   HOENGSONG

CHIPYONG-NI
WONJU

BATTLE LINE
1-10-51

37TH
PARALLEL

OSAN

CHECHON

RIDGWAY OFFENSIVES
US-UN CONTROL

RIDGWAY
SAVES
SOUTH KOREA

MAP 10

CHIPYONG-NI FIRST
MAJOR US-UN DEFEAT
OF CCF

RM

OTAEGU

SOUTH KOREA

US-UN OFFENSIVES

PUSAN

KOJE DO

KEY US ARMY VICTORY, CHINESE DEFEAT – CHIPYONG-NI

About 15 miles north-east of Chipyong-ni stood the city of Hoengsong, right in the peninsula's center, holding in environs the Chinese Fourth Field Army, which had conquered Seoul early January (MAP 10). Including 18 PLA divisions and reconstituted NKPA units, the force held over 200,000 experienced troops, manned with either US-made Thompson .45 caliber sub-machineguns or Soviet 7.6 millimeter 'PPSh' burp guns. A rich complement of Russian 82-millimeter and 120-millimeter mortars, and hand grenades, rounded out armament. According to historian Brian Catchpole's detailed study, Mao Zedong and Kim Il Sung aimed through massive infantry assault to create chaos within Eighth Army and "force yet another bug-out."[9] This was sure to result in Red control of all Korea.

On February 11, 1951, per Chinese custom, the ROK 8th Division became the first object of Fourth Field Army attack. The 8th quickly folded with enormous losses, putting at risk all UN forces in central South Korea. Marshal Peng then decided to subdue Chipyong-ni, allotting four divisions to surround and annihilate Col. Paul Freeman's 4,000-strong 2nd Infantry Division, 23rd Regimental Combat Team (RCT), and the adjacent thousand-strong French battalion commanded by Lt. Col. Ralph Monclar (Ridgway told of *five* CCF divisions looking to make a major advance south). Warrior Monclar took a reduction in rank from lieutenant general to colonel to gain this command.

Chipyong-ni controlled a so-called vital railway between Wonju and Seoul. The French resorted to bayonet charge to repulse the nighttime horde in their sector. Fierce fighting then engulfed the American perimeter, with heavy machine-gun crossfire mowing down Chinese. With daylight the enemy withdrew. During the day of February 14, C-119 supply planes dropped 87 parachute loads of supplies at Chipyong-ni, while H-5 Air Rescue helicopters brought medical help and evacuation of badly wounded.[10]

Night brought sound of bugles, flares through the sky, and screaming fresh Red divisions. Now some "Volunteers" wielded pole bombs, long poles with explosives attached, designed to destroy UN foxholes and men at the Regimental perimeter, and disable tanks. American planes began dropping parachute flares to illuminate the battlefield. US 155-millimeter (six-inch) artillery wreaked havoc on Chinese formations. Nonetheless, author Catchpole reported entire US platoons wiped out in savage fighting. Wounded Col. Freeman sent all his reserves to the front – it was a time of desperation. He also refused medical evacuation.

The siege and battle of Chipyong-ni, February 13 – 15, 1951, proved a key Korean War turning point[11] (MAP 10). The battle-seasoned 23rd RCT had fought at Taegu, the Chongchon River, and Kunu-ri. Now, at the railroad "Twin Tunnels," Chinese hordes repeatedly charged the regimental perimeter in attempting its destruction. The 23rd "smashed all Red attacks, inflicting some 2,000 enemy killed."

A US 5th Cavalry Regiment, 1st Cavalry Division tank column under command of Col. Marcel Crombez approached at maximum speed from the south to help decide the issue. Using a narrow road and having to bypass a destroyed bridge, the company of sturdy M-46 Patton tanks firing deadly 90-millimeter cannons, and some more lightly-armored Shermans, carried a complement of well-armed infantry to fend off enemy sappers. Continual Chinese small-arms barrage assaulted troopers for most of the ride. The Crombez relief force "crashed through Chinese lines and entered Chipyong-ni a few minutes before sunset to join the 23rd and seal UN victory. Of the 165 infantrymen who had ridden on the tanks …, only 23 had survived that harrowing journey."[12]

Ridgway wrote of the Army's heroic January 31- February 18, 1951 action,

> "The 2nd Division performed in the finest traditions of its service in both World Wars. Among the many tough engagements fought in those three weeks, none was conducted with greater skill, gallantry, and tenacity than that fought by the 23rd RCT …. I believe the troops shared my conviction that this time the enemy attack was going nowhere."[13]

A new day dawned on American, UN, and reversely, Chinese forces. As Catchpole explained,

"The siege had proved the capacity of United Nations forces, outnumbered by 18 to 1, to defeat a Chinese Field Army and to hold a position of crucial strategic importance. The victory at Chipyong-ni was one of the most significant defensive battles fought in the Korean War …. The Chinese had deployed 90,000 men and suffered well over 10,000 casualties … in their first major defeat."[14]

By mid-February 1951, Ridgway's Operation Killer pushed north, with full CCF and NKPA retreat. Reds were now forced to leave "all their positions south of the Han River"[15] (MAP 11).

Communist fall-back continued throughout February. A March 7 Ridgway offensive, Operation Ripper, succeeded in inflicting further heavy Red losses. During Ripper, the ROK Army's 1st Battalion of the 2nd Regiment tasted the rare treat of smashing victory over a Red battalion. Surprise attack accounted for 231 enemy dead, counted in the field, with not a single ROK casualty.[16] Reds retreated north across the entire front, except for a far western swatch of Ridgway-described "useless," marshy coastal land south of the 38th Parallel left to Communists. They hold it to this day.

UN northern advance continued against token resistance. Now evidence surfaced of the beating inflicted on Chinese armies by harsh winter and American firepower. Robert Leckie described "hills littered with their dead; shallow mass graves uncovered everywhere around Wonju and Chechon" in central South Korea[15] (MAP 10). The "fresh and strong and close to home People's Volunteers who attacked" and defeated Eighth Army in the hills below the Yalu had been savaged by brutal weather, a grossly insufficient supply line "running back 260 miles to the Yalu," and massive American firepower. Hunger and lack of medical care added to woes, costing many Red lives.[15]

By early April, Eighth Army took CCF-abandoned Seoul, the capital's 4th and final change of hands. Except for Red-held far westward marshy areas, by month's end the UN occupied the rest of the 38th Parallel eastward across the peninsula. December's bleak prospects vanished as fortunes of war swung boldly to the US/UN.

Marine Gen. Smith credited Gen. Ridgway's "display of a high degree of personal leadership [that] changed Army thinking, stopped Army withdrawal," and caused it to "move forward again."[17] Smith related Ridgway's comments to field commanders about "complete confidence regarding the outcome in Korea. He wanted less looking back toward the MSR, stating that when parachutists landed their MSR was always cut."[18] A dose of courage went a long way.

No substitute exists for military leadership excellence.

Tragically for America, Joint Chiefs Chairman Gen. Bradley and Army Chief of Staff Gen. Collins did not share Matthew Ridgway's confidence. Nor did Secretary Acheson or President Truman.

Chapter 25: Truman Sacks MaArthur, Chinese Do-or-Die

"A party in Richmond, Virginia celebrated Marine Lewis B. 'Chesty' Puller's February 1951 promotion to Brigadier General. One guest was Dr. Douglas S. Freeman, eminent Civil War historian and biographer of George Washington and Robert E. Lee. Puller asked the distinguished scholar, 'Why don't you write a history of the Korean War, Dr. Freeman?' The historian replied, 'General, the true history of a war cannot be written for at least 85 years afterward.' A surprised Puller then asked a logical question: 'Where would you go to find out the truth about the war in Korea, 85 years from now?' Dr. Freeman said, "Why, to the archives of the United States – to the official records.' A grin came across Puller's rugged face. 'That's exactly where you'd never find the truth, Doctor. The truth about battle, by its very nature, can't get into the records – and the truth about Korea has yet to come out anywhere.'"[1]

- Burke Davis, Marine! The Life of Chesty Puller.

On April 11, 1951, US Far East military leadership suffered a jolt as President Truman fired Gen. MacArthur for insubordination. Despite 52 years of distinguished service, MacArthur learned of his dismissal from a Tokyo radio broadcast, instead of personal message. Dean Acheson attributed the insult to break-down in cable communication.

The Far East Commander's March 23 statement telling Red China it faced "imminent collapse" should the US wish to launch mainland naval and air bombardment, along with a call for China's commanding general to meet him in the field to discuss peace, proved the last straw. Truman and close advisors knew MacArthur strongly disagreed with politically-imposed war restrictions that made defeat of Red China exceedingly difficult. They also appreciated the embarrassment caused by the great General's public statements about necessity of inflicting severe defeat on China. Unwavering military belligerency did not fit leftist political mandates of collective security, close regard for the United Nations, and prohibition on US military muscle-flexing.

Dean Acheson gathered liberal minions at his Georgetown home to plan MacArthur's demise. Such challenge to leftist revolutionary mandate, and President Truman, could not be tolerated by elite rulers. There could be no doubt Internationalism ran the show.

The General's worst offense was speaking truth. Truth could not be permitted to interfere with grand plans for peace and preservation of most dear Red China. MacArthur disagreed with Truman's prohibition of attack on Red Chinese territory, wished to accept Chiang Kai-shek's offer of 40,000 or more Nationalist troops for Korea "to save American lives," and refused to clear all public communications with the White House. He very much wanted to *win* the Korean War and severely punish the People's Republic of China for her humiliating counter-attack.

But throughout the world, including America, huge forces had been put in play to achieve Communist government in China. Major steps toward this goal commenced in 1944, during Franklin Roosevelt's presidency. A clever domestic propaganda campaign created the false reality of Red Chinese grand humanitarianism. Mao and company were touted as true democratic "agrarian reformers" dedicated to improving the common Chinese lot. Nationalist Chinese leader Chiang was castigated as a brutal, feudal tyrant. The same pro-Communist political actors remained active during Truman's presidency, encouraging a "hands-off" US policy toward Communist victory in China. Efforts proved highly successful. Never would such a hard-fought gain be abandoned to traditional American whim, exemplified in the shenanigans of an "over-the-hill, reflexively patriotic" warrior truly hated by American leftists. "Progressive" revolutionists Acheson, Frankfurter, Lilienthal, and cohorts wielded great power in Washington.

MASTERS TAKE OFFENSE – NO INTERFERENCE ALLOWED

Of profound significance, MacArthur stood in the way of secret privileged class mandate for Korean War settlement: yielding of Formosa to Red China, despite its huge strategic importance to America's Far East island-chain Pacific perimeter; and seating the People's Republic in the United Nations. Therein stood the basis of Internationalist solution, the "price for peace in Korea."[2] Specifically prohibited to Truman and his administration was military victory over Communist China, according to MacArthur and many others an outcome readily at hand. Elites found it most acceptable to needlessly shed the blood of America's sons as a cost of keeping

Red China intact. MacArthur's opposition, and that of Congress and people, meant *nothing*. New Order would have its way. People were so *dumb,* and destined to be ever more so. What a perfect weapon, propaganda! What perfect media, radio and television. Truth proved no match.

MacArthur clearly saw the long-term consequences of unchecked Chinese power. In comparison, Truman and Acheson seemed bereft of such vision. With Red China in the fight, they didn't want to win the war, just stop it. American military tradition of winning, of employing overwhelming force to achieve victory over an enemy, especially one who attacked the US in surprise and force, evaporated under Truman. America must join the pack, abandon the heights, get in line. It was proper to fear atomic holocaust, Russian intentions, Chinese manpower, and potential fall of the People's Republic that might enrage Moscow.

Strong leftist political backlash was another worry. There could be no deviation from the policy of collective security, satisfying the wishes of the UN General Assembly, and devotion to the UN cause. And with secure leftist control of the Atomic Energy Commission, and its physical possession of all nuclear weapons, America could not threaten, let alone employ in war, retaliation by nuclear means.

US interests, including lives of servicemen, must take a back seat to history's fate: one central authority ruling all, preventing world war, preserving sacred mandarin wealth and dominions.

Without doubt, Communist China, and Communism in general, had many friends in America. These included legal and illegal agents of Soviet Russia, underground operatives, CPUSA members, and legions of Red sympathizers in and out of government. Equally assured is the group's virulent anti-Americanism. For over 30 years, proletarian revolution held the hearts and minds of American Internationalists. To those who would see, of course, Soviet Communism miserably failed to live up to the teachings of Marx, Engels, and Lenin. Dictatorship *over* the proletariat described Soviet reality.

China, that great land, held the chance of creating a true workers' paradise without Russian mayhem and murder. China became the precious child of revolution that must be nurtured to maturity. Generations of political labor in vile, alien America could not be wasted or abandoned because of insignificant war in Korea. Great leftist influence in American foreign policy could never be forsaken. China must and will be saved. Let strangers, fools, the crude, common pack, spill their blood. Sino-Soviet coalition will surely overwhelm America and its alliances, the final story of Capitalist oppression will be written, the world's peoples soon to know true justice. Reviled, fascist-aberrant Americanism must yield to destiny's rushing tide.

US FAR EAST COMMAND SHUFFLE

Gen. Ridgway received MacArthur's Tokyo-based Far East Command slot, while noted Second World War European combat leader Army Lt. Gen. James Van Fleet replaced him as Eighth Army commander. MacArthur returned to America, greeted by record crowds in San Francisco, New York, and Washington.

Van Fleet would be severely combat-tested less than a week later. His immediate superior, Ridgway, could be described as a team-playing "good soldier," at almost all times readily accepting plans he thought wrong imposed on Joint Chiefs by Acheson and Truman. With one major exception, once personal objections were clearly voiced to Chiefs, Ridgway carried out distasteful orders. That was the military way. What choice did a general or admiral have? Only MacArthur felt the political boat could and should be rocked. Upon leaving Far East command, Ridgway became NATO commander, then Army Chief of Staff.

Meanwhile, CCF commander Peng Teh-Huai continually radioed and telegrammed Mao in Beijing about the strategic situation. Both agreed that February-through-mid-April reverses at US hands meant China must be prepared for a drawn-out struggle. Yet another two-part massive offensive would soon aim to either destroy the US Eighth Army or force its complete evacuation from Korea.

Chinese leadership had all bases covered. Rear areas stood immune from US attack, maximum advantage must be taken of the stupid gift. In their estimation, key Soviet support would continue unabated. Substantial human loss meant nothing.

For war's entirety, Peng faithfully obeyed all orders of Chairman Mao. There could be no other course. The carefully-crafted cult of Supreme Mao, all-wise and knowing, never wrong, had taken strong root in Chinese minds. Brain-washing created fertile fields for planting. Marshal Peng ascended to PRC Defense Minister in the mid-1950s.

TABLES TURNED ON COMMUNIST CHINESE FORCES

For over three months (mid-January through April) Eighth Army rolled north, regaining most of lost South Korean territory (MAP 10). The Communist Chinese now gambled all in strong one-two punches, the two-part "Fifth-Phase" or "Spring Offensive" designed to annihilate Americans and occupy the entire Korean peninsula.

Hackworth reported "a wall of fresh, good-looking and well-equipped Chinese troops with plenty of ammo and lots of fighting spirit, [and] fierce enemy artillery, mortar, and self-propelled cannon fire."[3] In the center the Chinese fielded 21 divisions and used 9 North Korean divisions to hold both flanks.[4] April 23 brought night attack by Chinese tanks. For five days UN lines gave way in central and eastern sectors, but held firm five miles above Seoul.

Gen. Van Fleet expressed total confidence in ability of Seoul perimeter troops and defensive fortifications to withstand any CCF attack. Hackworth described the Seoul defense as "right out of World War I, with deep trenches, bunkers, and heavy field fortifications protected by minefields and barbed wire. With a well-overextended logistics tail, the Chinese couldn't make a dent in it."[5] CCF offensive "ran out of punch" in the all-out effort to take Seoul. Generals Ridgway and Van Fleet served as young First World War officers.

Overwhelming US firepower crushed the PLA's first part Fifth Phase drive and inflicted 70,000 casualties.[5] Chinese energy spent in the usual two-week-and-bust onslaught, Van Fleet organized counter-attack across a 140-mile front that took Reds by surprise and pushed the UN back to the 38th Parallel (except for the far western coastal line that remained 10 miles below). The line extended in a northeastern direction with center and eastern parts 10 to 30 miles above the Parallel.

Reds tried another mass assault, the concluding Fifth-Phase effort, only to suffer continual "stacks of dead, four to five feet high, in front of US platoon positions."[6] Chairman Mao and the great People's Republic had most unwisely spent their load. By May 3, 1951, "the enemy was on their knees." Hackworth related, "Not only had we chopped up a force three times our size, but we stood ready to do it again."[7] The two Red attacks cost Peng 175,000 casualties and over 10,000 prisoners of war.[8] Heavy, concentrated American firepower stood in full bloom.

Defeatist Army Chief of Staff Gen. Collins' writings never mentioned the 3-to-1 Chinese manpower advantage so readily neutralized by the US at this time, nor the excellent condition and strength enjoyed by American forces after Chinese massacre. Indeed, Eighth Army appeared "ready to do it again."

May brought more good news from the front: Chinese resistance appeared to have vanished. According to frank-speaking and personally knowledgeable Hackworth, "The Chinese were nowhere in sight – if ever there was a time to keep moving, this was it …. There was no question in my mind that the Chinese were on their last legs, sick and hungry, [with] little will to fight."[9]

At this time of maximum UN success, Gen. Van Fleet asked Ridgway's permission to conduct a "combined amphibious and overland operation towards Wonsan on the east coast, which he was confident the enemy could not stop. The attack would pinch off and destroy a large fraction of Chinese and North Korean forces."[4] This would constitute evening of the score for the Chinese-inflicted Winter 1950-51 US/UN debacle.

Van Fleet later wrote, "In June 1951, we had the enemy whipped. They were definitely gone …, in awful shape."[4] But following a Truman- and Acheson-mandated JCS directive prohibiting major mobile offensive action, Ridgway turned down the request. Politicians ruled the military roost.

Acheson wrote deceptively that for the first time in the Korean War, civilian and military leadership stood in total agreement politically, strategically, and tactically.[10] The Secretary of State did not mention the early-May 1951 Truman decision, behind military backs, to *abandon* highly successful forward mobile warfare in exchange for a defensive-oriented, fixed front across the peninsula. Impact of this 180-degree change in US war policy proved disastrous, bloody, and bereft of common sense.

DISLOYALTY TO THE CONSTITUTION

Regardless of political tripe thrown on the table by Washington, at this critical Korean War juncture, Chinese Communist interests were placed above those of America. For over 30 years Reds had strove to create two American governments. "Dual Power" represented a key planned outcome of Communist infestation and revolution. Bolshevik writings clearly emphasized necessity of Dual Power in the revolutionary scheme, possessing "its own lines of communication and chain of command.[11] All opportunities for power must be seized, even if this means working for the bourgeois state."[12] A prime revolutionary goal was to "create a state within a state."[13]

Unrelenting invasive pressure proved successful – Red shadow government came to fruition in Washington, woven into the Constitutional structure. Roosevelt and Truman looked the other way, politically beholden to leftist money and votes. With adoring press cover, the strong covert arm effectively steered US policy toward Soviet and Red Chinese ends. Point-person Acheson ran the Korean show until the January 1953 Eisenhower inauguration.

Acheson-professed leadership "harmony" brought two years of stalemated war (1951-1953) and much *needless* spilling of American blood, but reality did not matter. Ridgway later wrote, "gaining more real estate" wasn't worth expenditure of American lives.[14] But sound defeat of Red China on the battlefield would provide powerful incentive for Communists to seek peace in

Korea. This *was* worthy of ultimate sacrifice. Instead, the US intentionally gave the battered enemy time to recover, create heavy fortifications, and get back in the battle. Americans by tens of thousands needlessly gave life and limb in two grinding, fixed-war years, because of terribly wrong and dishonest leadership. To paraphrase Gen. Bradley, we accurately describe such senselessness as "The worst decision, at the worst time, in the worst place." Americans deserved so much better of their leaders. The time's key message bears repeating: *anti-Americans ran America.*

Ridgway messaged Chiefs May 30, "The enemy has suffered a severe major defeat. Estimates of enemy killed in action submitted by field commanders total so high that I cannot accept it [sic]. Nevertheless, there has been inflicted a major personnel loss far exceeding ... the loss suffered by the enemy in the April 21 offensive."[15] Strangely, John Toland reported the true Chinese body count as 17,000 dead (far less than other sources) and 10,000 captured. Ridgway ended by advising superiors, "All three US corps commanders reported a noticeable deterioration in the fighting spirit of CCF."[15]

TIME TO WIN THE WAR

On May 28, 1951, Platoon Sergeant Earle Edson, with the Army 13th Engineers, wrote his wife and two children,

> "We have the Chinks [a common slur indicating racial chauvinism] on a wild retreat …. We caught a bunch of Chinese in the open here … and it certainly is a mess. Over a hundred vehicles, plenty of cannons, uncounted dead horses and of course, Chinese. It really was a slaughter. No exaggeration this – we can't turn around without sighting dead men or horses …. I'm sick of the stench of the dead and dying and seeing torn bodies scattered like waste paper on a windy day."[16]

As Eisenhower said, "War is grisly business."

Besides the human toll, "great numbers of Red ammo dumps, mortars, machine guns, and automatic personal weapons had been abandoned," a reflection of CCF and NKPA disintegration.

Despite straight up and down terrain and scarcity of decent roads, the UN continued attacking north through the Kumwha Valley. ROK divisions advanced 60 miles along North Korea's east coast. Much of the North Korean rail and road hub "Iron Triangle" of Chorwon, *Pyonggang*, and Kumwha lay in Allied hands (MAP 11). The North's 120-mile Wonsan-*Pyongyang* narrow waist appeared ripe for taking and would cut North Korea in two.

Time had come to actually win the War. Incredibly, it would never be. In Washington, fear, or worse, ruled the day. In profound consequence to future generations, President Truman, his most influential advisor Dean Acheson, and Joint Chiefs of Staff under Gen. Omar Bradley, had no stomach for dismembering North Korea. The order went out to stop the highly successful offensive in its tracks. China and North Korea would be saved by *Washington* from the jaws of crushing defeat! War strategist Bernard Brodie called the act, "A decision without precedent."[17] Such is the perverted outcome when politicians run wars.

VICTORY BUCK STOPS WITH TRUMAN

President Truman famously displayed a sign on his Oval Office desk: "The buck stops here." The words became a media icon for his portrayal as bold and decisive leader. Image aside, Truman much feared Soviets and Chinese, and not only knew but supervised depletion of US conventional ground and air strength. The President also bears responsibility for 1946-48 American nuclear force gutting. Following illogical Internationalist mandate, Washington leadership "deliberately disarmed in the face of threatening Communism."[18]

Truman admitted in memoirs, "China was prepared for general war, America was not," that MacArthur dared risk wider war with China, a bet Truman would not take.[19] The "no-nonsense" President dared not press war with year-old Red China to a battlefield decision. Former Secretary of State Henry Kissinger bemoaned concurrent US over-estimation of Russian military

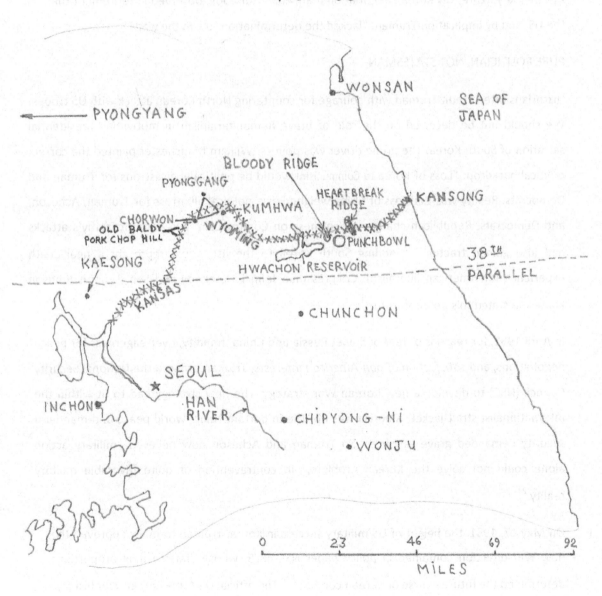

MAP 11

BATTLE-LINE EARLY JULY 1951

AREAS OF HEAVY FIGHTING,
1951-53

WONSAN

SEA OF
JAPAN

PYONGYANG

BLOODY RIDGE

PYONGGANG

HEARTBREAK
RIDGE

KANSONG

KUMHWA

CHORWON
OLD BALDY
PORK CHOP HILL

WYOMING

PUNCHBOWL

KAESONG

38TH
PARALLEL

HWACHON RESERVOIR

KANSAS

CHUNCHON

SEOUL

HAN
RIVER

INCHON

CHIPYONG-NI

WONJU

0   23   46   69   92

MILES

strength that endowed invincibility on the Red Army and equivalence to its five-bomb nuclear arsenal.[20] He described American Korean War-era "near-monopoly" in nuclear weapons, at least a 60-to-1 advantage over Soviets. But Truman had made up his mind – the US would not win the Korean War. US military custom would be stood on its head.

Another key figure, UN Korean negotiation team chief Adm. Joy, observed in retirement that the US, and by implication Truman, "lacked the determination to win the war."[21]

PURE POLITICIAN, NOT STATESMAN

Historians often credit Truman with courage for countering North Korean attack with US troops. We should not be deceived on the role of brave humanitarianism in motivating presidential salvation of South Korea. The prime driver was politics. William Manchester painted the correct political backdrop: "Loss of Korea to Communism+ would be politically disastrous for Truman and Democrats. Reality was that loss of China weighed as a political albatross for Truman, Acheson, and Democrats. Republican charges of 'softness on Communism' and Sen. McCarthy's attacks had also gained traction."[22] Adding South Korea to the list would represent a near-death experience for American liberalism. Congressman John F. Kennedy and Sen. Lyndon Johnson knew and stated this political truth.[23]

In April 1951, for reasons of fear of Soviet Russia and China, timidity, over-eagerness for peace negotiations, and *satisfaction of non-American interests*, Truman ordered the National Security Council (NSC) to develop a new Korean War strategy. The new strategy had to fit within the Internationalist strait-jacket. America was not the important thing; world peace and mandarin security demanded grave sacrifices. So Truman and Acheson now believed "military action alone could not solve the Korean problem," in contravention of quite favorable military reality.[24]

On May 17, 1951, the height of US military success in Korea, Truman formally approved the new War direction contained in policy paper NSC-48/5, whose "far-reaching proportions determined the future course of Korean combat."[24] The official US Army Korean War history assigned "significance of this blueprint for American action in Asia [that] can hardly be overstated .... *It implied no hope of military victory in Korea."[25] Army Chief of Staff Gen. Collins puppeted the astonishing conclusion, "No question but that a military stalemate had been reached."[26] This was an outright lie. Collins made quite a reach equating US crushing of CCF Fifth Phase Offensive as drawn battle. For all who would see, he made a complete fool of himself, showing the backbone of a wet rag.

As desired by Truman and Acheson, Chiefs had thrown in the towel, proving themselves a committee of elder Pompeys in passivity and political complicity. Should a similar Joint Chiefs have existed during the Revolutionary War, there is no doubt the United States would have died an early death at British hands or would never have been born. One can imagine strident cries of despair: "Their navy is so powerful, their reserves so great, the British foe the strongest military power on earth, what purpose is gained by resistance?"

Whatever his personal feelings, new United Nations Command (UNC) head and US Far East Commander Ridgway closely toed Truman's new policy. A good soldier obeyed his Commander in Chief. A better soldier gave first allegiance to the US Constitution and oath of military office mandating its protection and defense. We recall Ridgway's rapid selection of James Van Fleet to command Eighth Army, and the latter's suggestion of large UN amphibious and land attack northeast of the Hwachon Reservoir toward Wonsan, its goal to kill and capture large numbers of Communist troops (MAP 11). Ridgway squelched the operation: casualties could be high, Reds were better able to expend lives, why take the risk? Here Ridgway simply acceded to political supremacy. But thought of inflicting severe defeat on the PRC no longer existed for Truman and Acheson, if it ever did.

Flawed, wishful thinking, fear, and paltry vision characterized American leadership. Actively anti-American hidden government drove nails in America's Korean War coffin and doomed any chance of military victory, or at least a quicker, less human-costly outcome than the one ordained.

DIVORCED FROM COMBAT REALITY

It became acceptable for 30,000 American young men to die and 60,000 be maimed in wasted static war, but 5% of that price was too high to achieve People's Liberation Army humiliation and North Korean dismemberment. At all costs, Internationalist interests must be served. So Truman was led by the nose to abandon reality of US and UN battlefield triumph, along with common sense war leadership leading to military victory, to needlessly sacrifice his own people.

Could American presidents themselves be puppets? It appeared so. Twenty-six months of grueling, meaningless war ensued, six of them under President Eisenhower, a "die-for-tie," war of attrition bloodbath, only ending after Reds milked every drop of advantage from negotiations.[27] Today's America pays the Far Eastern and world price for terribly incompetent presidential leadership, and will continue to for generations to come.

At a May 29, 1951 meeting of Joint Chiefs and the State Department Policy Planning Staff, Adm. Sherman broke the mold of complacency by requesting continued northern battlefront advancement. But the die of stalemate had been cast. Assistant Secretary of State Dean Rusk, no doubt parroting Acheson, told that "he, Paul Nitze, and Averell Harriman were afraid of advancing too far north and provoking the Soviets."[28] George Kennan believed any action near Vladivostok (150 miles north of Wonsan) would bring Soviet countermeasures (MAP 2). Except for Adm. Sherman, recent military success seemed not to matter, nor the deterrent effect of a vastly superior nuclear arsenal.

Washington's new policy directive stood "divorced from combat reality."[29] General political leadership consensus appeared to be, "Get out while the getting's good." The enemy did not fear America. And America did not "get out" of Korean fighting for 26 months, and never got out of Korean troop presence and severe international threat.

Clearly, Truman and Acheson *chose* stalemate as the military outcome in Korea. Red China and Soviet Russia did not militarily impose a drawn result in May-June 1951. Both sides observed unofficial restrictions on offensive capabilities: the US gave sanctuary to huge troop, air, and supply concentrations in Manchuria and areas of China proper, while Reds would not use their potent air power to bomb South Korean UN supply ports and bases, especially at Pusan. Soviet submarine forces were also prohibited from attacking allied ships in the Sea of Japan and Yellow Sea. Both camps seemed to favor confining the War to the Korean peninsula. With coming global US air and naval superiority, Brodie believed Reds got the better of the bargain – our strong points were neutralized, Red numerical advantage enhanced.

The Korean War student wisely embraces a driving point: Washington Euro-centrism meant reservation of preponderant American military strength, including nuclear forces, to Western European defense against the Soviet Red Army. So America fought in Korea as a one-armed, weaker-armed, nation.

Much embarrassment would attend public dissection of this non-professional war policy. Popular revulsion must include blaming Truman and his administration for bungling the chance at victory. So the issue could never reach broad public understanding. Truth would be too terrible, too costly, Truman, Acheson, and Democrats open to political massacre. Better to keep truth under wraps and emphasize ridiculous words of memoirs as "authoritative" statements of "fact" and points of view. Official Army historical records contained damaging information best avoided publically, such as May-June 1951 enemy weakness that placed Chinese and North Korean forces at risk of destruction. Deceptive political narrative must be preserved: Democrats, especially Democrat presidents, are saviors of the people. Leftist power must be safe.

Chapter 26: Acheson's Explanation for Going on the Defensive

"Sound decisions will not be reached through automatic overruling of the preponderant recommendations of the nation's senior military advisors by their civilian superiors. A failure to seek, hear, and weigh the counsel of our experienced military advisors is to court disaster."[1]

- Gen. Ridgway, The Korean War.

Eighteen years after the 1950-51 Korean War strategic debacle, Dean Acheson published his Pulitzer Prize-winning memoirs, "Present at the Creation." Acheson wrote about the American strategic change from combat victory to negotiations as the final answer to ending the War, there being "no sensible alternative."[2] Biographer Robert Beisner accurately described the aristocratic Secretary as "State's leading progressive."[3] During Kennedy and Johnson administrations, Acheson served as "elder statesman" of sorts, his advice sought, incredibly, on the 1962 Cuban missile situation and Vietnam War.

By time of autobiography, Acheson had survived a storm of Republican criticisms over recommendations to Truman that largely determined the course of Korean War. From standpoints of popular opinion and administration credibility, the War had savaged US civilian leadership and gravely wounded the Truman team. Acheson writings evidence attempt at countering negative comments of historians, military brass, and as he derisively put it, "armchair generals and academicians."[4,5]

Acheson went out of his way to describe a state of so-called "shared responsibility" between White House and State and Defense departments in Korean decision-making. He avoided any idea of personal imposition of views or special presidential influence. In the Secretary's telling, all parties were equal. The largely sympathetic Beisner biography acknowledged Truman's "gifts of trust and autonomy greatly expanding Acheson's reach."[6] D. Clayton James and Anne Wells also clearly refuted equality of influence, emphasizing Korean command decisions as largely reflecting policies developed by the Department of State, with

> "Secretary Acheson and his brain-trust Policy Planning Staff the most important deciders. Their input on military matters dominated that of Defense Secretary [Louis Johnson, then George Marshall and Robert Lovett] and Joint Chiefs. Acheson enjoyed Truman's complete trust and exercised by far the most influence over presidential decision-making of any cabinet or military officer. Military policy, strategy, and operations lay in his purview."[7]

Acheson admitted the same in May 1951 Senate testimony, giving the lie to ex-post-facto "shared" decision-making.

During initial US planning of Korean military intervention June 26 – 30, 1950, so called "Blair House Meetings," top military officials Secretary Johnson and Joint Chiefs Chairman Bradley dared not challenge forceful and shrewd Acheson on strategic matters.[8] The pattern held for War's remainder. In the 1960s, the situation repeated with Secretary of Defense Robert McNamara acting the same role of incompetent military martinet during John Kennedy-Lyndon Johnson Vietnam decision-making, with identical bloody and disastrous results.

James and Wells summarized Korean War leadership reality: "From the first week of the war through the end of truce talks, Acheson had been the *principal architect* of the administration's chief positions on direction of the war, as well as on America's relations with its coalition and with the United Nations" (italics added).[9] Put in political terms, devoted leftist point-person and staunch Internationalist Acheson ran the Korean War.

This realistic view on Truman's wielding of executive power is very politically incorrect. It reveals not a decisive president but one bereft of foreign policy experience and expertise, and overly dependent on Acheson. The progressive revolutionary movement does not tolerate running against the grain of carefully cultivated but false public opinion. To this day, Truman's embarrassing war leadership is not part of public understanding. Reds have no masters when it comes to propaganda.

Reds also had friends in the highest places. Hard work, dedication, and persistence paid huge dividends. Acheson talked out of one side of his mouth about importance of peace talks to ending the War, while from the other, allowing the State Department to arm the enemy with fore-knowledge of UN negotiating strategy. The Truman Administration pitched the War both as "localized," not worthy of full mobilization, merely a "police action," while holding it "key to the survival or downfall of the Communist Chinese regime."[10] In this political world, white equaled black, right-and-wrong and objective truth didn't exist, battle history must be stood on its head.

A dictator's words echo, the Kremlin mantra: "We ourselves will determine what is true and what is not." And so people will eat what they are fed, the Internationalist-created new reality. Pity American and Korean peoples. It is no wonder Korean combat and its aftermath turned out so poorly for America and engendered such popular bitterness.

CHANGE IN WIND FOR OFFICIAL KOREAN POLICY

Acheson told of a December 26, 1950 White House meeting, at Chinese crisis depth, with Generals Marshall, Bradley, and Treasury Secretary Snyder, at which he "proposed a rewriting and clarification of General MacArthur's directives."[11] Importantly, the decision to change high Korean policy appeared to come only from Acheson. According to the account, everyone agreed with him. Again, change of course beckoned in Korea. Pathetic overtures to Communist China, encouraged by Clement Attlee, had yielded nothing. Mao smelled blood and would not be deterred from anything but mass American slaughter.

On December 29, *Acheson* sent MacArthur the finalized draft containing key instructions. The submission in no way came from the military chain of command, but told the theater Commander the US should attempt to resist, with present combat strength, at "some point in Korea without incurring serious losses." Stopping Chinese onslaught was of "great importance to US national interests to deflate the military and political prestige of the Chinese Communists." Another item emphasized "increased threat of general war" that would not allow Joint Chiefs to "commit additional US ground forces in Korea. Major war should not be fought in Korea." MacArthur's "directive now is to defend in successive positions," with "safety of your troops as your primary consideration," while "inflicting as much damage to hostile forces in Korea as possible." Finally, if need be, Chiefs would decide "ahead of time" on "the last reasonable opportunity for orderly evacuation" from Korea.[11]

Foretelling the Korean War's next 27 months, Acheson's new US policy now mentioned reliance on peace negotiations to end fighting with Communists, a core Internationalist belief.

In detailed setting of US/UN War policies in Korea, the Secretary of State revealed overwhelming personal military powers. Acheson, evidently with Truman authorization, had ruled out US military victory and accepted the prospect of humiliating defeat, surrender, and ejection from Korea at Chinese Communist hands. Directives spoke clearly of acceptable US submission to Asian Communism.

Acheson related MacArthur's reaction to the new policy: "*It+ seemed to indicate a loss of 'will to win' in Korea; it was unrealistic because it offered no reinforcements – [and] especially fantastic in expecting Eighth Army to be responsible for defending Japan."[13] On January 9, 1951, Chiefs told MacArthur, at Acheson's direction, that "he was authorized to withdraw to Japan" if inability to hold a Korean line placed Eighth Army in danger of destruction. MacArthur shot back, "Under the extraordinary limitations and conditions imposed upon the command in Korea, … the Army can hold, if overriding political considerations so dictate, for any length of time up to its complete destruction. Your clarification is requested."[13]

Acheson thought the General's comments a "posterity paper" meant to deflect blame toward Washington should the worst happen – and as pressure to accept MacArthur-recommended "bombing of Chinese targets and coastal blockade, use of Nationalist forces in Korea, and encouraging Formosa to strike the Chinese mainland." To Acheson and Truman, MacArthur wanted to "widen the war against China," while new official policy favored negotiated settlement over victory.[13]

Chiefs told MacArthur in reply, "It would be to the interest of the US and UN to gain some further time for military and diplomatic consultation before beginning evacuation," and for the US to "inflict maximum practicable punishment on the enemy" and not evacuate Korea "unless actually forced by military considerations."[14] It seemed quite a balancing act for any military commander. Fortunately, wonders worked by Gen. Ridgway now came to the fore. But fear-obsessed, pathetic Washington revealed readiness to accept humiliating withdrawal from Korea rather than resort to threats of, or actual attack on, Communist China.

RISING WAR TIDE

By January 17, 1951, "Joint Chiefs generals Hoyt Vandenberg [Air Force] and J. Lawton Collins [Army], had returned from Korea and reported a wholly changed situation[:] the Chinese were now having their own difficulties." Truman sent MacArthur a personal letter "setting out our national and international purposes in Korea." Still, the General complained of the enemy's "unprecedented military advantage of sanctuary protection for his military potential against our counterattack on Chinese soil."[15] With relief, Acheson reported continued Washington "refusal to permit attack on Chinese territory."

One strains to imagine US granting of sanctuary to Japanese and German targets after Pearl Harbor. But things had drastically changed in Washington. War reality could never displace political imperative. A strait-jacket now smothered traditional national war strategy. American interests would take a decided back seat.

WHEN LOYALTIES CLASH

This book emphasizes timely Red knowledge of all changes in American Korean strategy. We recall major War operational plans copied to the British, whose spies faithfully passed the word to Moscow and Beijing. Yet bad actors were not limited to Washington- and London-based British spies and Red presence in MacArthur's Tokyo Supreme Command Allied Powers staff.

American Reds and sympathizers throughout US Government played key roles not only in keeping Communist governments informed of American plans, but in helping draft those plans in the first place, the whole point underlying Red espionage assault. As mandated by Bolshevik revolutionary operating principles, Dual Power existed and functioned in America. A second, clandestine government operated independently of formal government and popular will, as mandated in Lenin- and Trotsky-espoused doctrine. Important State Department China officers Vincent, Davies, Service, and Rosinger joined Treasury-IMF comrades Coe and Adler in pitching Red revolution. Acheson and political heavyweight David Lilienthal carried the ball passed by justices Brandeis, Holmes, Frankfurter, and Douglas. Walter Lippman, Theodore H. White, Edmund Stevens, and cohorts helped assure leftist press sympathies. Robert Oppenheimer, Joseph Woodrow Weinberg, Martin Kamen, and Ted Hall loyally contributed from the scientific end. Progressives Alan Cranston and Claude Pepper worked with scores of Congressional colleague-sympathizers. President Truman protected the irresistible political legacy, and stood as a prime beneficiary. Chapters 43 through 45 relate the details. America fought the Korean War under severe leftist political constraints.

Gen. MacArthur's wide public support and many influential political friends made him anathema to Dual Power adherents. He had the effrontery to speak reviled truth. Returning to America after his firing, the General expressed "amazement and deep concern" over *the extent to which the orientation of our foreign policy was now largely influenced, if not indeed in some instances dictated from[,] abroad ...."* (italics added).[12] To MacArthur, "High moral principle and the courage to decide great issues on the spiritual level of what is right and what is wrong" had yielded to "moral trepidation" and paying "tribute in the blood of our sons to the doubtful belief that the hand of a blustering enemy may in some way be ... stayed." No punches were pulled in castigating Truman Administration "practice of a new and dangerous ... appeasement on the battlefield where-under we soften our blows, withhold our power, and surrender military advantages ...."[12] Leftist revolution's Internationalist arm demanded no less.

WHAT PRICE POWER?

While supposed Truman-Acheson obsession with avoiding World War III is an accepted and key historical theme excusing disgraceful leadership, neither leader linked Korean attack by 300,000 Red Chinese on US forces to world war precipitation. The same is true for Joint Chiefs. Only America knew this heavy responsibility. Mao could do what he wished in Korea without fear of global consequence.

To apply Bernard Brodie's warning about perils of limited war, the US cut itself down to size in Korea and made the PRC its military equal. Destroying Fascism and Nazism represented pristine political correctness to the American left – destroying Communism in Korea and China unthinkably incorrect. An American president chose to discount his nation's nuclear arsenal and virtual nuclear weapon monopoly – it didn't matter one bit to Washington or America's enemies. Atomic strength conferred no special influence on the American people. Higher cause must be served, Internationalist constraints obeyed. Our true rulers decreed passive American war behavior. That was that.

A vital military truth held no consequence: "In all history[,] passive defense has never won a war – a doctrine … responsible for more military disaster than all other reasons combined."[16] Communist China enjoyed quite a deal in Korea. Excepting authors MacArthur (in Pratt), William Bullitt, Neil Sheehan, and Edwin Hoyt, shame of this debacle has never been publicly visited on President Truman.

MacArthur obviously saw the broad picture of indecisive Korean war and long-term consequences. He willingly sacrificed military command and career to a higher cause: the good of his nation. But while confronting his Commander in Chief with unpleasant war reality and helping stir up considerable opposition to appeasement-based peace negotiations, MacArthur failed in his mission of achieving *decisive war with Red China*. The President got his way, which was the American way. But two major issues came to light because of MacArthur's challenge, both deeply significant to the government-citizen relationship.

The General clearly appreciated continual centralization of political power in Washington, a trend underlying Franklin Roosevelt's philosophy of government, unabated with Truman, or any other successor.[17] For both political parties, vast expansion of federal departments and bureaucracies acted as irresistible magnets, drawing concentrations of people and money and creating powerful interest groups and political levers. Individual freedom must suffer under this process. In time, Washington would control all aspects of American life. For ruling class security this was fine – centralization promoted rapid concentration of power in relatively few hands. This of course is totalitarianism's prime tenet. Any group or process blocking achievement of this goal, including the Constitution and religious influence, must be subjected to relentless attack and ultimate elimination.

HIDDEN HAND TAKES LEVERS

It didn't take genius to diagnose alien control in metastatic Federal Fovernment. MacArthur reasoned that the American people should fear loss of freedom not from recognized *external* foreign threat, but from "insidious forces working from within."[18] He appreciated existence of a "campaign to pervert the truth and shape or confuse the public mind," not fully attributable to Moscow-directed world revolution. Revolutionary allies based in America, passing as patriotic citizens consumed by humanitarian zeal but in reality grotesquely inhumane,

> "ardently support[ed] the general Communist aims while reacting violently to the mere suggestion that they do so. Human freedom always finds ostentatious vocal support from those most bent upon its suppression."[18] Alien power, an "atheistic predatory force which seeks to destroy the spirituality of the human mind, buttressed by the scourge of imperialistic Communism, has infiltrated into positions of public trust and responsibility – into journalism, the press, ... and the schools. It seeks through covert manipulation of the civil power and the media of public information and education to pervert the truth, impair respect for moral values, suppress human freedom and representative government, and, in the end, destroy our faith in religious teachings."[19,20]

Internationalists closely fit this bill, seeking to make government "an instrument of despotic power," while binding the nation to collective security and one-world, united.[21] So too the Democrat Party, a welcoming shield of respectability and legitimacy. As clearly attested by Robert Beisner, Dean Acheson reviled "nationalism" and "nationalist economies" as world war precipitators that must be stamped out. America should quickly enter World War II to assure demise of deadly nationalism. The same globalist penchant blossomed after great War's end and strongly operates today. Obviously, popularly elected congresses, majority-passed public referenda, and public opinion, do not matter in this system.[22] The judicial system acts as leftist enforcer. Elites must rule in the name of all humanity.

Natural progression brings collectivism in property and business enterprise – today's "redistributive justice." Acheson believed "America should take the lead in creating a *new international order*, abandoning protectionism and other policies that stifled an open-world economy (italics added). It was essential to avert the chains of economic smashup that led to totalitarianism and war."[23] He apparently beheld Western parliamentary governments as forces of evil subject to destruction. While the Fascist-Nazi scourge must vanish from the earth, equally-evil Communism should remain, largely as a counter to America. Surely, the successful, late-20th-century push for "free trade" helped encourage the desired "open world economy" while destroying millions of American jobs.

With Dual Power firmly entrenched from 1940 on, full Communism stood right around the corner, covered in flag, universal freedom, social justice, and Democrat Party. No hammer and sickle, or unpleasant throwbacks to Soviet Russia, allowed. MacArthur believed "progress" toward attainment of a totalitarian state took place with

> "dreadful certainty, as though the leaders of the Kremlin themselves were charting our course …, implementing the blueprints of Marx and Lenin with unerring accuracy. Soviet propaganda completely dominates American foreign policy. The pressure of alien doctrines strongly influences the orientation of foreign and domestic policy."[21,24]

In MacArthur's estimation, everything boiled down to a core fact: "Truly representative government based on truth had yielded to *invisible government based on propaganda* (italics added). Suppress the truth, curtail free expression and you destroy the basis of all freedoms."[25] The General believed the people should "renounce undue alien interference in the shaping of

American public policy."[26] Readers note the 65-year-old diagnosis.

The 1947 Defense Reorganization Act, amended in 1949, served as a vital tool in the push to centralized authority. Soviet-style leadership and management does not countenance independence of thought or decision. People must be force-fed from the top. Ruler security demands that uncertainty of control be quickly removed. So MacArthur warned of

> "a new and heretofore unknown and dangerous concept that the members of our armed forces owe primary allegiance and loyalty to those who temporarily exercise the authority of the executive branch of government, rather than to the country and its [C]onstitution which they are to defend (italics added)."[27]

MacArthur held blind soldierly dedication to a president akin to ancient Rome's Pretorian Guard, "owing sole allegiance to the political master of the hour." While American culture scorns visiting of murderous wartime barbarity under the common and despicable German Nazi practice of "just following orders," it looks the other way as military brass cave to immoral political demands costing young lives. Imperial presidents may then wage war at personal whim, or more likely, at demand of higher-ups.

Under this system, Chiefs of military services, including the Joint Chiefs Chairman, are in reality highly-bedecked puppets, making supposedly impressive and authoritative appearances at press conferences and Congressional hearings, alongside secretaries of defense. Under such deception, America endured wars in Korea and Vietnam, extended fighting in Iraq and Afghanistan, and a state of "perpetual war for perpetual peace."

The United States obviously ignored MacArthur's advice to "charge to our allies the main responsibility for ground operations in defense of their own spheres of territorial interest ...."[28]

Perhaps reflecting personal experience, MacArthur cited "inordinate executive power" as subjecting "members of the armed services ...to the most arbitrary and ruthless treatment for daring to speak the truth in accordance with conviction and conscience."[27] Interestingly, in stark contradistinction to American practice to date, Rome's Pretorians often exercised supreme government power, appointing and deposing a host of emperors, an uncontrollable, dangerous politico-military force. No longer did Rome have an army of and by the people.

We allow MacArthur a parting shot at Dean Acheson's "only reasonable choice" of passive defense in Korean fighting. Stopping major mobile action assured

> "indefinite continuance of the indecisive stalemate with its compounding losses, in the vain hope that the enemy will ultimately tire and end his aggression. Could anything be more naïve, more unrealistic, more callous of our mounting dead? The defenders of the existing policy are the same who, suddenly and without slightest ... consideration of the military and political potentialities, threw us into the conflict. These are the very men who, in the face of mounting peril, deliberately demobilized us at the peak of our military strength, and then at the lowest point of our disarmament, plunged us into a war which they now seem afraid to win."[29]

USELESS SACRIFCE OF LIFE AND LIMB

In Acheson's words, "While Gen. MacArthur was fighting the Pentagon, Gen. Ridgway was fighting the enemy."[4] From this point in *Present at the Creation* Korean commentary, contradiction occupies an increasing role. We are told, "Ridgway's mission was not to recover territory but to destroy enemy forces," then promptly advised, "Relentlessly the [US] Army moved north ...." Acheson mentioned a second time, "Gen. Ridgway pushing the Communists north" in another apparent violation of his mission. The US/UN accomplished most Chinese push-back by mid-May 1951 (MAP 11). Ridgway's May 9 complaint to Chiefs about "impossibility of his mission to destroy Communist forces" given prohibition on major offensives severely challenged the "all is well, everyone in agreement" picture painted in Washington.

Acheson held truth to be "the exact reverse of criticisms made at the time and later by partisan political sources as well as by academicians. It has been charged both that the State Department dominated or tried to dominate the military conduct of the war and that the Chiefs of Staff did the same in the diplomatic and political field." The latter defense is absurdly false, the former amply documented by reputable historians James and Wells, Brodie, Sheehan, Tuchman, and McMaster. Acheson's book stands alone in pitching the notion of Joint Chiefs trying to, or able to, dominate *anything* – "pathetic" and "hapless" are their true descriptors. Truman's utter dependence on Acheson in foreign affairs made for unmatched presidential influence.

But nothing could deter the former Secretary's complaint, "Both charges were wrong and the truth was quite the opposite." Acheson cited State memoranda about needed input from the Defense Department, supposedly proving "great deference to Chiefs in assumption of [military] responsibility." His autobiography did not contain the referenced documents.

Unquestionably, from 1947 on, the deck was stacked against military brass. Minutes of Truman's brain-trust meetings at Blair House right after June 25, 1950 North Korean invasion prove Acheson's "alpha male" status in war planning and execution. His bold statement to President Johnson after a Vietnam advisory meeting revealed unchanging colors: "The Joint Chiefs don't know what they are talking about."

LEFTIST REVISIONIST HISTORY

Inconsistency continued in the Secretary's declaration, "Despite illusions to the contrary, UN and US war aims had not included unification of Korea by armed force against all comers. Chinese intervention had now removed this as a practical possibility. The aim was to repulse aggression ...."[4] Acheson assigned finality to Red Chinese actions that rendered them cast in stone, as if to say, "The Chinese intervened in Korea – let the world tremble and stand aside."

As documented in Chapter 10, page 130, Truman signed National Security Council Paper 81/1 September 11, 1950, which "authorized military action north of the 38th [P]arallel ... and urged political unification of all Korea by free elections." Gen. Bradley confirmed Acheson's "... full agreement on these fundamental policies."[30] While US policy now centered on repelling aggression, a somewhat vague task, Red Chinese policy emphasized destruction of the US Army in Korea – no mistaking *that* mission. It provided justification enough for strongly taking the war to Chinese soil.

Acheson recommended that "The ultimate political aim – a Korea united by peaceful means – though clearly remote, should be retained. The line to be sought and held should be north of the [P]arallel and chosen for its tactical defensive possibilities and practicality of attainment."[4] Again, truth and falsity are mashed, Acheson wishing a line somewhere "north" while professing "no interest in gaining territory." Occupying major parts of North Korea was not a war crime but necessary to chastising Communist China and a big step toward achieving three vital ends: military victory, Chinese motivation to conclude a peace agreement, and end to fighting.

The Secretary's contradictions now came full gallop: "As April [1951] opened, Gen. Ridgway entered the area over which he was to fight for two years, *continually weakening and bleeding the enemy without risking his Army,* a mission regarding which he and his Government were in complete accord" (italics added).[31]

The statement is outrageously false. Combat troops and grieving families at home would be surprised to learn the US Army, Marine Corps, Air Force, and Navy were not at risk from July 1951 to July 1953. Frequency and intensity of this period's fighting, and associated killed and wounded, are amply documented and will be shortly discussed. CCF developed heavy artillery and mortar capability in this phase, inflicting severe losses on American, Korean, and allied units.

Acheson and Truman *chose* to fight a two-year static war, instead of driving 100-plus miles to the peninsular Wonsan – Pyongyang "neck" and cutting the North in two. Ridgway's May 9, 1951 protest to Joint Chiefs was anything but an example of full accord and bears repetition: "The mission to destroy North Korean and Chinese forces in Korea was *impossible* so long as he could make no advance with major forces beyond the lines Kansas-Wyoming" (italics added, MAP 11); the Kansas-Wyoming Line ran from the west at Munsan, in a northeast direction to

Kojin-ni (near Kansong) on the Sea of Japan. Acheson's thesis of static warfare and negotiation dependence *is* destroyed, along with future prospect of massive Communist losses, as inflicted during their Fifth Phase Offensive.[32] Pretense of Achesonian military strategic expertise is likewise shattered. Towering ego could not hide first-magnitude martial ignorance.

WHAT WERE TRUMAN AND ACHESON THINKING?

David Hackworth pounded home a point of pure common sense: "Any army that did not intend to attack obviously had no hope of winning."[33] If the Korean War was not important enough to win, it should not have been fought. Poor war leaders Acheson and Truman mistakenly deflated US combat abilities and strong points to Chinese People's Army level. Any help provided by the new and misguided policy of blind rush to peace negotiations went solely to Communists.

Washington unwillingness to add new US divisions to Eighth Army helped ordain drawn Korean outcome and Communist negotiation intransigence. Besides Gen. Van Fleet, a number of top officers believed America could have won battlefield victory purely with conventional arms. Adm. Joy held that "all-out effort to achieve military victory between July 1951 and the armistice ... would have been neither impossible nor unusually difficult. Such decisive action probably would have meant fewer American casualties than were actually suffered during the stalemate period."[34] Joy went on to note deaths of many United Nations Command prisoners of war during the two-year truce talks, with author Brian Catchpole reporting "some 1,600 UN prisoners of war had died in 1951" alone.[35] Gen. MacArthur's 1964 book *Reminiscences* related "firm belief that UNC could have attained victory in conventional warfare and with much less casualties than actually occurred under protracted negotiations."[36]

In Fall 1952, Ridgway successor as Far East Commander, Gen. Mark Clark, pushed for an "all-out offensive to win the war, provided Washington could furnish ... the additional infantry divisions and air and naval support required."[36] Gen. Edward "Ned" Almond accurately told the Army chief of military history in 1969 that Gen. Ridgway's opposition to major offensive action to win the war reflected a "strategic philosophy compromised by politics."[36]

James and Wells added the opinion of Bernard Brodie, "a giant among post-1945 strategic intellectuals," as "the most powerful voice raised in ex post facto protest" of misguided American strategy. It was not a question of gaining more territory, Acheson's favored excuse against major offensive action, but of providing strong Communist "incentive to come to terms."[37] American leaders totally failed in that mission. Top civilian and military officials admitted the reality of the anti-major offensive, pro-truce talks line at May-June 1951 Senate hearings on MacArthur's dismissal. These included Secretary of Defense Marshall, Joint Chiefs Chairman Bradley, and Chiefs Collins (Army), Sherman (Navy), and Vandenberg (Air Force).[37]

Korean War combat reality further shreds Acheson's words. As stated by the time's combat veterans David Hackworth, Lee Ballenger, and T.R. Fehrenbach, Communist forces grew *stronger, not weaker,* as war dragged on. American soldiers shed blood and died in major numbers during this time – Catchpole related "Casualties on both sides higher in the so-called static war than in the war of movement during 1950."[38]

No national leader should be allowed to brush off heavy US losses in any war, let alone Korea. Yes, CCF paid a high price in blood for its efforts, but it still made no sense to engage in a war of attrition with a system devoid of human valuation possessing millions of troops. Successful war policy of annihilation should never have yielded to the enemy game. Truman trampled on World War II military legacy and totality of American war history. Accepted practice translated into, "Don't push too hard on the Chinese Communists."

Despite exalted Washington status and polished language, lies are still lies. US soldiers risked *lives* every day of that stupid, senseless, meaningless carnage, while vaunted peace talks became a cesspool of obstinacy and stagnation. How willingly reality is abandoned for political survival and satisfaction of Internationalist interests. Nothing better demonstrates supremacy of politics over human life.

267, Chapter 26

MACARTHUR DARES PRESS THE ISSUE

On March 7, 1951, MacArthur foretold War outcome: Unless enemy war potential [Manchurian troop and supply marshalling areas] was opened to counterattack, battle lines would in time "reach a point of theoretical military stalemate." Self-styled war genius Acheson accused MacArthur of inability and unwillingness to understand Gen. Ridgway's mission "to establish such a battle line at an advantageous and defensible point as the first step in ending the aggression and the war."[31] Instead of fighting for annihilating enemy defeat, US strategy would focus on establishing a strong *defensive* line and then seek to slug it out to a battlefield draw while negotiators sooner or later ended the war.

To that point, no other war in American history placed diplomacy before victory. The new policy reeked of insanity and the hidden hand. Study of this policy can bring no other conclusion, so the decision must be banished from public discussion. Acheson memoirs do not come close to covering the gaping deficiency posed by the defensive line thesis as key to achieving peace.

A week later, MacArthur dug his hole deeper in telling Hugh Baillie, president of the United Press, of American mistake in stopping Eighth Army advance at the 38th Parallel, or short of "accomplishment of our mission in the unification of Korea."[31] To Acheson and fellow Internationalists, the General "sabotaged a Government operation," the behind-the-scenes effort to create peace talks, a most grievous sin. But perhaps MacArthur had tried to upset the leadership applecart, soon to roll over military minions, before it abandoned decisive war with Red China.

Acheson revealed, "For some time we had been discussing within the Government and with our allies *an idea strongly held in the General Assembly* that *further diplomatic efforts toward settlement should be made before major forces moved north of the [P]arallel*" (italics added).[31] What a break for the PRC! Acheson spilled the beans on necessity for curbing the successful military offensive and saving the Chinese People's Army, and possibly the People's Republic.

The idea crystallized in favor of a presidential statement on UNC behalf: "There was a basis for peace in Korea – the UN Command was prepared to enter into arrangement for a cease-fire to open the way for a broader settlement."[31] Was ever a modern battle victor so gracious to an enemy? MacArthur was right – the US/UN did not want to win victory in Korea.

Clearly, satisfying the UN General Assembly and its powerful backers, such as the Rockefeller brothers, took precedence over US military and political necessity. Soldiers became cannon fodder for Internationalism. The whole process took place behind backs of Congress, American people, and press. Illusion of Communist desire for peace must be created in public minds, to cover the novel and uncomfortable mid-War reality of American preference for talks instead of fighting to victory. Washington had taken the first steps toward opening talks, not the enemy. Communism could then be preserved in China and North Korea. Truman's leadership team asked for continuation of "people's rule" there, blind or uncaring about consequences to future generations.

The prior-mentioned MacArthur March 24 public announcement harshly opposing "diplomacy first" proved the topper. Now he had to go. The great General "denigrated the enemy," telling of China's "exaggerated and vaunted military power [that] lacked the necessary industrial base for modern war."[39] Acheson wrote of "outrage" over the insult, a view shared by Deputy Secretary of Defense Robert Lovett. Unfortunately for the American people, not enough top US officials felt rage over American boys needlessly killed and maimed by Communist Chinese and North Koreans. Acheson reported President Truman as "perfectly calm" over MacArthur's provocations, but in a state of "controlled fury," a typical inconsistency.

Another coffin nail historically popularized was the General's letter to Republican Congressman Joseph Martin, containing the famous words, "In war, there is no substitute for victory." Martin publicized the missive and created more embarrassment for Truman and company. MacArthur did his best to make his Commander in Chief look bad.

The General may have sniffed sell-out in the wind and sought a counterstroke. Dual Power based on dual loyalties again came into play – two separate governmental realities were about to clash. Civilians comprised both power bases, one promoting American interests, the other, Moscow's.

On April 5, 1951, as Chinese Communists prepared to launch the "decisive" Fifth Phase or Spring Offensive, JCS submitted a report to Secretary of Defense Marshall bound for the National Security Council. Chiefs "conceded for the first time that the Korean problem cannot be resolved in a manner satisfactory to the US by military action alone." Gen. Collins admitted "Joint Chiefs … limitation on any general advance north beyond the Kansas-Wyoming line. As fighting in Korea ebbed back and forth in Spring 1951, it became evident neither side would win decisive military victory."[40] Top brass obviously joined new politico-military false reality – describing Spring 1951 US/UN rout of CCF as slow-moving, back and forth fighting represented a true political "180." For all who wished to see, Collins stained his military reputation.

Over three months of convincing CCF defeat at American hands simply didn't matter. *US military leadership gave up winning the Korean War as US forces were in process of winning the War.* Of course, Joint Chiefs merely did as told. The same holds for the NSC. There is more than a tinge of disloyalty here to country and fellow men-at-arms. Military oath called for "protecting and defending the Constitution." The two groups joined the president in dishonoring oath and nation.

PULLING RUG FROM VICTORY

American forces not only learned how to fight CCF, they became quite proficient at administering sound beatings. CCF's worst pounding stood right around the corner. Timing of American loss of will to win is so embarrassing to all parties that only full press cover-up could protect proponents from widespread scorn and ridicule. The left obligingly served up a hefty dose of "don't think." Truth of pending US/UN victory in Korea is publically unknown.

Based on outcomes, a strong case is made for the People's Republic of China enjoying special status in Washington. Why the protective attitude toward China? The answer is found in an uncomfortable fact: part of US Government existed to serve Communist interests. As MacArthur knew, "The true object of a commander in war is to destroy the forces opposed to him. But this was not the case in Korea. The situation would be ludicrous if men's lives were not involved."[41]

Acheson's pathetic rationalizations merely represented a variation of the "don't think" dictum. The aim is to conduct politically-soothing discussions while ignoring unpleasant truth. Acheson felt comfortable accusing MacArthur and supporters as exemplifying the "extreme Republican right," at a time when "pro-left," let alone "extreme left," did not exist in public usage. Acheson lived an ideological life, as far left as any American secretary of state. Extremist accusation exposes the gulf separating traditional Americanism from progressive revolutionary fervor.

Before MacArthur's firing, Defense Secretary Marshall proposed to Truman and Acheson that the General be summoned to Washington for direct discussions. Acheson admitted to squelching the idea, to "convincing Marshall" not to give MacArthur a political forum to attack the Truman Administration on its Korean policy. Truman's strong right arm never admitted to rolling over military figures, especially a tired and sick Secretary of Defense.

Acheson memoirs predicted and self-confirmed, "The war should 'peter out,' as it eventually did …," again firing far off target.[42] Strong Red Chinese attacks in the war's last four months shattered the prophecy, not to mention carnage at Bloody and Heartbreak ridges, Bunker Hill, the Hook, and vicious fighting at another 130 hills and outposts during peace talks. US Army and Marine blood attested to 1952-53 Chinese offensive ferocity. ROKs fared far worse. "The War bled out time-and-again" would be the accurate description.

In understanding people like Acheson, we look to their daily operating preferences. The tall, impeccably dressed, heavily-connected and articulate lawyer-Harvard graduate excelled in personal intimidation. People were not to be respected for innate worth, but treated as obstacles and challenges to overcome. Acheson then projected universal supreme knowledge. Part of the International elite, he held a "them versus us" mentality, scorning common folk as "primitives." His memoirs contain a chapter entitled, "Attack of the Primitives." To a domination-obsessed man, picking off naturally subservient generals and admirals proved a reliable past-time. His boss, President Truman, shared dislike for military brass (except Gen. George Marshall), so no rank could be pulled from above.

Acheson's government service legacy is tarnished by the blood of Korea. He ordained the course of War events. Truman is blamed for letting Acheson have his way. Both were targets of left and right political pressures, but the left put Truman in the White House and elected him in 1948. One thing is certain in Washington political outcomes, surely exemplified by Acheson – Gen. Collins absurdity: people receive "the correct words," Red insiders and friends "get the decision" – the old "180." Such is the political way.

ACHESON'S MARTIAL UNPROFESSIONALISM – 'UNDREAMED OF GIFT' TO REDS

New US war strategy appeared to mimic the Maginot Line mentality of over-reliance on supposedly impregnable defensive fortifications. According to Acheson, as of June 1951, the plan called for the US/UN to "fight it out on the Kansas-Wyoming line and the Punch Bowl just north of it if it took all summer, or more than two summers. Experience had taught a costly lesson: to push the Chinese back upon their border – their source of reinforcement and supply – only increased their strength …, while decreasing our own as our forces attenuated their lines of supply, became separated, and lost touch with air support as they moved north."[43]

Now the flawed military authority and grand strategist waxed with special farce. Readers will note introduction of the "Chinese invincibility" theme serving the end of "salvation in negotiation." Acheson and Truman senselessly found "invincibility" in Red Chinese loss of some half-million men over eight months of Korean war, plus NKPA near-destruction, and in desperately deficient Communist logistics.

Brodie recognized Washington's need, and failure, "to be responsive to feedback from the fighting front."[44] Had Joint Chiefs possessed gumption, they would jump up and down emphasizing dire enemy straits and propitious time for victory. Instead, in mid-June 1951, Truman, Acheson, and Chiefs halted the "extraordinarily successful" offensive, relieved logistical pressure on Reds, and actually "*saved* existing CCF in Korea from annihilation" (italics added).

At this War juncture, there was no substitute for continuing "maximum pressure on the disintegrating Chinese armies as a means of getting them to conclude peace."[45] Brodie called American leadership incompetence and Red favoritism "an undreamed of gift" in the annals of war.[46]

IGNORE WHAT CAN'T BE EXPLAINED

Also noteworthy is Truman-Acheson failure to address the all-important negotiation issue: what would motivate Red Chinese to "actually conclude a peace agreement?"[45] Nearly 1,500 pages of Truman and Acheson memoirs, plus 2,800 by Bradley, Collins, Beisner, and David McCullough's Truman work, yield not a single word on this most-important consideration! Truman, Acheson, Chiefs, and biographers had obligations to share reasoning behind the tragic belief that Chinese and North Koreans wanted a quickly concluded peace. Much blood would pour out on the issue.

We ask about Communist motivation for favorable response to carefully dropped US/UN peace-talks intention. Given Red military straits at the time, and ruling out humanitarianism, the answer can only be self-interest in forestalling complete destruction of their Korean armies. The slick Secretary of State and his boss "should have known that by suddenly relieving all pressure on the Chinese and granting them ... a chance to recover, we were depriving them of any incentive to agree to our terms .... In deciding to halt we decided ... on continuance of the war."[46]

Ridicule is the left's most potent political weapon.[47] Acheson proved no slouch at denigration, berating "The generals, among them Van Fleet and Mark Clark, who later declared that they had been deprived of their chance for total victory." The leftist icon held misguided thinking of these commanders as representing only "thoughts conceived in tranquility."[48]

Despite mutual antagonism, MacArthur and Acheson shared similar personalities dominated by monumental egos, arrogance, and high skill at crushing other people.

WASHINGTON BROACHES PEACE TALKS, NOT REDS

In fulfilling the Secretary's expressed wishes reflecting Internationalist mandate, America took the first step in seeking Korean War cease-fire through late-April, early-May 1951 peace-talks feelers sent to Moscow and Beijing.[49] Acheson admitted making this initial appeal to Communists for start of talks. This of course corresponded to time of peak US/UN military success.

Reds must have smelled a trick: Americans could not be *that* stupid! The effort did not reach first base. This fact serves to correct the common and mistaken historical belief of Communist initiation of the Korean peace process. The lie greatly eased acceptance of talks by the American people – we should be pleased "the other side had blinked first."

In truth, Washington wanted peace before all. The reader recalls Truman's decision at this time, reached after April 1951 consultation with, and imprimatur from the National Security Council, for negotiations to end the War. Great fear gripped Washington over a "drift to serious trouble" with Russians and Chinese over Korea. One would think the same drift attended Chinese decision to mass-attack American forces in Korea six months earlier, but thanks to Moscow, and Soviet agents in America and Britain, the Chinese knew what they could get away with. A thousand US combat casualties per week did not reach the threshold of serious provocation in Washington. Now, with Chinese attack in shambles, something must be done to bring about talks between warring parties.

Acheson then imposed on veteran Soviet specialist George Kennan to meet informally with Soviet UN chief Jakob Malik to discuss Moscow's interest in negotiations. Naturally, Malik had to consult top Kremlin leaders before making any definitive comment. A May 31 Kennan-Malik meeting was followed by another June 5, at which Malik revealed what Soviet bosses allowed: "The Soviet Government wanted peace and a peaceful solution in Korea as rapidly as possible."[50] The spark of Kennan's informal meetings with Mr. Malik naturally led to the world view of Soviet-originated peace initiative. Reds are masters at gaining propaganda advantage.

Since Long March days, astute Mao preached the wisdom, "When the enemy is strong, negotiate." Revered Lenin advised the same – one must appreciate the back and forth tides of war and revolution and act accordingly. This was such a time. Simon Montefiore reported that none other than Stalin "decided to advise the Chinese and North Koreans to negotiate."[51]

As we know, at the moment of greatest PRC military danger, with US State Department urging, Russia's UN delegation chief Malik obligingly announced in an otherwise vitriolic June 23, 1951 UN radio address that peace talks should be undertaken in Korea. "Big Brother" Moscow would encourage North Koreans and Chinese to agree to a cease-fire conference that would bring a "peaceful solution." Soviets were always a "peace-loving people" obsessed with telling the world their natural pacifism.

Malik's public message advised starting discussions between belligerents "for a cease fire and an armistice providing for the mutual withdrawal of forces from the 38th Parallel."[50] A "small State-Defense group" then drafted instructions and an opening message to be delivered by Gen. Ridgway to Peng Teh-huai, Commander in Chief of Communist Forces in Korea. Ridgway did so in a June 30 Tokyo radio broadcast: "If the Communist commander was prepared to negotiate a cease-fire and armistice, Ridgway was prepared to send a representative to begin discussions."[52] Favorable Communist reply came July 2, with the first meeting of delegations at the small village of Kaesong, south of the 38th Parallel, July 10 (MAP 11).

Very little time had passed since Kennan-Malik talks. In taking the poisoned bait, Truman and Acheson inhaled heady perfume, never pausing for a reality check. Could this represent a new direction for world Communism? Professional American diplomats and foreign policy specialists dealing with Soviet leaders would be extremely wary. Acheson possessed this deep personal experience from extensive Lend-Lease negotiations with Russian officials. The Red top echelon featured only dyed-in-the-wool, fanatical Marxist revolutionaries. But rapidity of these first steps seemed to suggest ardent desire of both parties for quick peace.

Early indication that the picture might not be so rosy came as Communist forces surrounded what had been a neutrally-positioned Kaesong and made "an arrogant and offensive propaganda demonstration, excluding the allied press and behaving in their customary ill-mannered and boorish way."[53] Hope returned with Red agreement on the agenda within a brief two weeks, referred to by Acheson as "a phenomenal feat."[53] As sides settled in for serious agenda discussion, American leaders and delegates had no idea that only the first page had been turned in a very long book. As Acheson related, agreement on just the first agenda item, location of the line of demarcation, took six months.

"WHY, THEY JUST FOOLED THE HECK OUT OF US"

In memoir peace negotiation discussion, Acheson addressed with shallow candor reasons for the two-year war of words. He admitted *US susceptibility to deception and unnecessary entry into "an endless propaganda morass"* (italics added).[53] Gullibility, lack of vision, failure to confront reality, and flat-out ignorance are surely inconsistent with leadership excellence and unworthy of the American people. Who did Acheson think he was dealing with, if not hardened, truth-denying, former bank robbers and active murderers?

The excellent Robert Beisner biography sheds important light on Acheson's rather extensive, and publicly unknown, personal dealings with Soviet Russian officials during 1941-43. This particular State Department work experience should have made Acheson an expert in diagnosing Communist negotiation tactics and strategy.

Starting February 1, 1941, Acheson gained appointment as Assistant Secretary of State for Economic Affairs.[54] An important part of his departmental responsibility was helping "draft legislation for Lend-Lease," Roosevelt's "imaginative plan for sending US aid to putative allies."[54] As Beisner related, the new administrator "had primary responsibility of negotiating the gritty details of lend-lease agreements with both Soviets and British. Three years of haggling with Moscow diplomats … left him with a sour taste for Russians themselves." In Acheson's words relating to his Lend-Lease work, "they [Russians] were clumsy and difficult, trussed by hidebound instructions, and lacked a feel for the possible."[55]

Any case for Acheson surprise at Communist Korean peace talk intransigence is blown away at this revelation. Acheson knew the Red style as well as anyone in Washington. The same holds for post-World War II statements about not knowing the true state of US-Soviet relations until late 1947. The Secretary of State knew the score in both cases – his memoirs are quite disingenuous in these matters.

(Acheson's post-World War II open preference for sharing atomic energy and weapon development information with the Soviets, broad experience with Soviet Lend-Lease, and platinum-status Internationalism, encourage belief in his personal help with Moscow's nuclear bomb program. Beyond question, and quite politically incorrect, Lend-Lease enriched the Soviet Union with bomb-grade uranium-235, other costly, weapon-specific radioactive metals, and bomb production machinery. Such provision closely fits Acheson's super-leftist ideology, and would represent traitorous behavior. Somewhere in Soviet archives lurks the bombshell truth.)

James and Wells blamed "shell-shocked" Truman for taking the negotiation bait, "innocent of the hidden Red agenda of obstruction and deceit."[56] But the colossal blunder of prematurely stopping the broad offensive against the Chinese received only brief mention in Acheson writings, firmly shunted to the realm of non-causation relative to peace-talks duration and war extension. Truman memoirs contain not a word on the subject. The excuse of Acheson innocence in Red dealings does not stand the light of day.

Acheson promptly dismissed criticisms of "both professional and armchair warriors" linking heavy combat pressure with early armistice conclusion. He denied with "certainty" that reduced military pressure on CCF caused needless extension of talks, considering it a "simplistic" explanation. The Secretary reported a sense of relief in Far East Supreme Commander Gen. Ridgway taking "no such callous attitude toward the lives of his men, but … [doing] his best to keep our losses at a minimum …."[57] Ridgway is credited with "perfecting" his lines in what were in actuality senseless, costly battles with the enemy. In truth, the only thing static warfare "perfected" was a machine for killing American, ROK, and allied boys.

Two years of needless bloodshed producing the majority of war killed and wounded could be casually waved off in crass attempt to sugar-coat the inexcusable. It bears repeating that totalitarians worship ideas and anointed figures, holding cheap the remainder of human life.

One envisions Acheson labeling the June 1944 Normandy invasion as "callous." Perhaps the arch-liberal lawyer-Secretary would have advocated rapid Allied creation of a fixed defensive perimeter around the invasion site for the purpose of defeating the German Army. "Gaining French and German real estate" would of course be useless.

When it comes to disregard of American life and national interests, it is hard to match that of Truman and Acheson. The administration appeared hell-bent on bailing out the enemy. Ideologically, the Secretary of State found kindred spirits in Moscow and Beijing. Practically, and indisputably to those who would see, Red Chinese interests clearly trumped those of Red, White, and Blue.

ACHESON: AMERICA'S FAULT FOR DRAGGED-OUT WAR

Credibility for decrying cause-and-effect relation between heavy mobile combat pressure on CCF and Communist incentive to conclude an armistice supposedly came from two contemporary State Department papers. These "confirmed the views of all of us, soldiers and civilians alike, that we were on the *only sound course* …." (italics added).[57] Unfortunately, the "authoritative" documents are not provided in Acheson memoirs, so we are unable to assess any convincing points. Yet Acheson's book regresses to casually and briefly mention "bitter battles and heavy casualties" the last eight months of war.[58] So easily are American deaths and injuries in Korea shunted aside.

Truman and Acheson made the choice – more death for nothing, instead of less death for victory. Values evident at the June 1944 Normandy landings had been trashed. America had to that time spent blood in noble causes, knowing victory always came with a price.

Acheson revealed high deceptive skill in deflecting reality of disastrous decision-making. It is one thing to make mistakes – inherent in all human endeavors, great or otherwise. It is another to needlessly cost the lives of tens of thousands of mostly young citizens and bring heartbreak to parents, spouses, and siblings, plus plant seeds for a 63-year national and world problem. Accepting blame is difficult for the proud and once-mighty.

Instead, in an incredible gush of chutzpah, the Secretary blamed *America* for costly prolongation of war. According to Acheson, American negotiation insistence on a truce line north of the 38th Parallel surprised and disappointed Russians and Chinese. Communists are said to have entered talks with the understanding that both sides would revert to the parallel as the Korean dividing line. Acheson believed the US position represented a "considerable loss of prestige to China and Russia." Despite ample personal experience to the contrary, Acheson seemed to believe the US/UN could reason with Reds, they were good folks.[59] So easily does the great prince reveal ideological sympathies.

In the face of self-described reduced combat action owing to his new "right course," Acheson again admitted to "heavy fighting and severe casualties on both sides" in early Autumn 1951 attacks on "enemy positions ringing the Punchbowl."[60] These included costly battles at Bloody Ridge and Heartbreak Ridge, which fell to Eighth Army mid-October (MAP 11).

Acheson strangely described the War's last 20 months as "neither stopped nor blazed up .... It slumbered like an ominous and infinitely dangerous dragon ...."[61] Given fierceness of action and heavy casualties, the assessment would surprise US fighting men, and prove unbelievable to hard-hit ROK troops.

Contradiction also befouled memoir treatment of the POW issue. UN General Assembly members are said to have believed, "quite erroneously," that prisoner-of-war issues were "holding up an armistice." In the very next page, Acheson tells us, "Bring[ing] about an armistice in Korea centered on the question of the return of POWs."[58,62] Then, Acheson does his best to hide personal dominance in directing negotiation outcomes, telling readers Gen. William K. Harrison, UN chief peace talks delegate after Adm. Joy's departure, suspended meetings the end of September 1952. Harrison had no such authority – he merely relayed instruction issued by the Secretary of State.

Part V:

Disciples of Leftist American Revolution,

1915 - 1952

Chapter 27: America's Masters – The Internationalists

"The cloud of an unwanted socialism seemed to be … appearing on the economic horizon. Only through a free and expanding economy could both our marvelous productivity and political liberty be assuredly sustained ….."[1]

- Dwight D. Eisenhower, Mandate for Change.

" … the American politician has discovered socialism – and embraced it … as a wondrous machine for the purpose of buying votes – buying immense pressure groups with favors, laws and, above all, vast appropriations.

- John T. Flynn, The Roosevelt Myth.

Causation to stop the Winter-Spring 1951 UNC offensive came from another quarter: the pro-Red contingent in the State Department and other Dual Power agencies holding politically savvy and influential "American" Internationalists, who believed Red China must be saved at all costs. This author holds classic Internationalist Acheson a prime example of the Dual Power phenomenon. According to the prescribed line of thinking, the United States could not be allowed to exercise dominant influence in the Far East, especially with China. False reality had to be, and was substituted for the truth of impending US military victory in Korea.

As the time's Ohio Senator Robert A. Taft publicly stated, "The greatest Kremlin asset in our history is the pro-Communist group in the State Department who promote at every opportunity the Communist cause in China."[2] Collapse of Chinese armies in Korea could well presage demise of the revered People's Republic. Moscow officials were reported quite concerned over this prospect and in Truman's thinking likely to intervene in prevention. MacArthur shared the same concern with Ridgway the previous December.

Common sense suggests that Soviet threat of massive Korean and/or Western European intervention may have cowed Truman into eliminating UN northern advance. The 60- or 70-to-1 US nuclear bomb advantage over Russia must be ignored as incorrect truth. Conventionally,

America stood as a relative military weakling. Even after the Korean War, Dwight Eisenhower reported 175 Soviet Army divisions posted to Europe, compared to *five* for the US, out of total American ground strength of 20 divisions.[3] Beyond speculation is action of the Mao-loving contingent at State, Treasury, and the White House (John Paton Davies, Lawrence Rosinger, John Stewart Service, and John Carter Vincent of State; Treasury's V. Frank Coe and Solomon Adler; presidential assistants Lauchlin Currie, Michael Greenberg, David Niles, and Philleo Nash) who worked hard for years to toe Moscow's Far East line and help establish the People's Republic. The most precious child must be nurtured to maturity and strength.

Internationalist money and electoral support put Truman in office in 1944-45 and kept him there in 1948, a source of irresistible political pressure. Powerful labor boss and 100% Socialist Sidney Hillman personally approved Truman's selection as vice-presidential candidate at the 1944 Democrat National Convention in Chicago.[4] Roosevelt waited for Hillman's decision before endorsing Truman. The Missouri Senator-turned-Vice-President directly owed his presidency to Hillman. Massive left-labor, urban-based political machines turned out huge votes for the Roosevelt-Truman ticket, winning many northern industrial states and assuring victory.

A prime example is the 1944 presidential electoral vote in New York State, the largest electoral prize at that time in America. It turned out Republican candidate Thomas Dewey beat Roosevelt by a half-million popular votes in New York on straight Democrat – Republican ballots. Importantly, Roosevelt also carried New York nominations from the Communist-controlled American Labor Party and the half-Red American Liberal Party. These provided Roosevelt another 850,000 popular votes, giving him statewide victory and 44 vital electoral votes. Similar examples could be given for industrial states such as Pennsylvania, New Jersey, Connnecticut, Massachusetts, Illinois, and Michigan.

William Manchester described *"Powerful forces in Washington* opposed [to] American commitments in the Far East on the ground they would weaken the US effort in Europe" (italics added).[5] Of equal importance, the US must not be allowed to restrict Communist activities in China and Far East Asia. China's weight must swing to Moscow. In the progressive view, reviled

America needed a counterweight global competitor, a too-powerful US might prove unmanageable, dear Russia needed a strong ally. Powerful leftist interests, exemplified in the leadership of garment workers union boss Hillman, CPUSA Chairman Earl Browder, and clothing industry magnate and 1948 Truman campaign bankroller Abraham Feinberg, trumped those of the American people, a story that continues to this day.

Most historians dance around the truth of American leftist political clout. As emphasized in this book's Two Governments chapters, Reds used the White House, Congress, State and Treasury departments, Manhattan Project, and strong influence in law, academia, and vehicles of mass communication to further the political agenda of advancing Communism at all costs. If this entailed hurting America and its people, so be it. While enjoying freedom of political activity and economic opportunity, Internationalists felt no compunction about destroying their host. In fact, they felt *obliged* to do so.

KEY PEOPLE AND PRECEPTS

Internationalists are the most politically influential multi-generational destroyers in America, having worked mightily for a century to control most areas of US Government, education, law, politics, and public communication. They are tireless, secularist, bold, and loathe love of country.

Catherine Drinker Bowen's biography of Supreme Court Justice Oliver Wendell Holmes, *Yankee from Olympus*, matter-of-factly detailed circa-1915 beginnings of Internationalist strength in Washington. Her definition and description of American Internationalism is foundational to understanding the phenomenon. Among early figures were Louis Brandeis, Herbert Croly, Felix Frankfurter, Francis Hackett, Walter Lippman, Philip Littell, and Englishman Harold Laski, head of the British Labour Party.[6] The group founded the left's flagship magazine, the *New Republic*. President Woodrow Wilson, whose ill-fated League of Nations proved a magnet for American One-Worlders, would soon nominate openly socialist Brandeis to the Supreme Court, stirring up a hornet's nest of unsuccessful opposition, and indicating leftist political muscle.

The then Harvard president actually led a protest movement to sidetrack the nomination. Brandeis graduated from Harvard Law School in the 1870s, while later Court colleague Frankfurter held a long-standing faculty appointment there, starting in pre-First World War years.[7] The latter selected pending Harvard Law graduates for highly-desired US Supreme Court justice clerkships. Alger Hiss was among Frankfurter's selections, clerking with revered Justice Holmes.

Bowen openly described Internationalism's basic tenet: freely-stated hatred of presently-constituted America, which boiled down to revulsion for the Capitalistic-oppressive Constitution; contempt for, and *need to control*, average, "primitive" Americans; continual denigration of American institutions and traditions, including the wasteful scourge of patriotism; and characterization of Founding Fathers as vile slave owners bent on oppression and profit. Regular and vicious attacks on America's name included crediting the American South with ideological foundation of Nazi Germany, and brutal pounding of Christianity for standing in the way of new world order.[8]

FREEDOM OF SPEECH DOUBLE-STANDARD

While Internationalists could demean traditional living and dead Americans with impunity, and have the trashing considered "non-discriminatory" under the umbrella of protected "free speech," *any other comparisons between groups of people represented "discrimination" and "injustice" and must be banned*. True sons and daughters of the revolutionary hammer and sickle, they considered much of Biblical language, preached from pulpit or not, "hate speech" subject to censorship.

All foundational elements of traditional America came under heavy "liberal" attack. As Supreme Court Justice Brandeis put it in March 1921, America "must recognize which way the world is moving."[9] Proletarian revolution represented "the wave of the future." The agenda closely resembled, or was identical to, Marxist doctrine expressed in the *Communist Manifesto*. Home, church, academia, politics, public and private education, law, and mass communication represented objects of unrelenting attack. Within and without the United States, Internationalists and Communists worked for a common objective: destruction of traditional America. The descriptor "Red" well fits grand Internationalist designs. Hundreds of today's prominent Democrat national politicians are true progeny of Marx, Lenin, and Stalin.

HISTORICAL SPEARHEADS OF NEW WORLD ORDER

During the 1920s and 30s, the movement's favored historians included the influential German, Oswald Spengler, whose aptly-named book "Decline of the West" became a favorite of elite universities and colleges such as Harvard, Berkeley, Princeton, Chicago, and Wisconsin; and Britain's Arnold Toynbee, whose extensive world history series fit the same mold and found equal popularity among liberal academics.[10]

Late Canadian author and literary professor Robertson Davies, surely no raving Capitalist, emphasized importance of the Spengler-Toynbee clarion to champions of proletarian revolution. In essence, Capitalism's time was over, proletarian rule beckoned, Americans must appreciate necessity of radical change to save country and humanity. The Great Depression added to stridency. Precepts closely fit Franklin Roosevelt's centralized political and economic domestic agenda. Only a hundredth of one percent of Americans might hold these revolutionary yearnings, but that was enough. Elites were put on earth to inherit the earth, to rule and control humanity. Great energy and expense were and are expended in managing public awareness and promoting the desired political agenda. Objective truth is frowned on as a needless impediment to power. Public ignorance encourages concentration of power in relatively few hands.

Progressive politics also aims to eliminate personal thinking – it is dangerous and unnecessary. Anything that discourages or prevents thinking is desirable. Group-think is the preferred substitute, akin in safety to grazing of farm animals, always ready for sacrifice and slaughter. All answers and solutions are found in group-think.

The agenda's immediate goal is ever-increasing chaos, facilitating the final reward of complete power, the necessary choke-hold over the American people.

Internationalists are social engineers *par excellence,* unequaled nation- and world-revampers and builders, charged with leveling out differences between peoples and nations. Self-beheld as intellectually superior and destined to rule backward America and the world, any popular resistance must be crushed, including Christianity, Judaism, and the middle class.

Wealth of some Internationalists is beyond most public comprehension. It buys, makes, and owns US presidents, senators, and congressmen. Puppets tremble when strings are pulled. "Free Trade" is a favored concept, along with loss of American jobs to cheap-labor foreign states.

Despite availability of huge Rockefeller, Carnegie, and Ford foundation wealth, a host of 11- and 12-figure family fortunes, and unparalleled political influence, a disease runs rampant in the elite, their only blemish: personal insecurity. Independence of Americans is reviled and feared, a great threat. Part of ruler discomfort stems from keen appreciation of the political potential of massive private gun ownership. Revered Mao Zedong underscored *that* point! All segments of society must come under thumb through an "all-encompassing control apparatus." Nothing else will bring desired absolute security.

HIDDEN HAND REACHES DEEP

Specialists on Soviet espionage in America John Earl Haynes and Harvey Klehr documented deep, very long-standing Communist penetration of American higher education. Academia has a long history of *honoring* "Soviet spies and Stalinist acolytes."[11] New York's Bard College endowed the "Alger Hiss Professorship of History and Literature," initially held by Joel Kovel, who preached "The US as enemy of humanity." Bard fired Kovel in 2009 for alleged anti-Zionist leanings. Jonathan Brent replaced him as Visiting Hiss Professor.[12]

Columbia University Law School created the "Corliss Lamont Chair of Civil Liberties," whose namesake revered "Stalin, Mao, Castro, and Ho Chi Minh." Son of a wealthy business partner of early-20th-century banking magnate J.P. Morgan, Lamont graduated from Harvard and earned a PhD in philosophy from Columbia in 1932. Lamont and wife made a "pilgrimage" to Moscow that year and "loved what they saw, particularly moved by the sight of Vladimir Lenin's preserved corpse." Lamont announced, "The new world of the 20th-century is the Soviet Union."[13]

During the 1937-39 Soviet Great Purge that killed one million Russians, Poles, and Germans, a great many of them Jewish, Lamont "defended the notorious Moscow Trials featuring trumped-up charges and pre-ordained verdicts." He served as American Civil Liberties Union director from 1932-54, and wrote the 1952 book, "The Myth of Soviet Aggression." Lamont donated $1 million in 1982 to establish the endowed chair in his name.[13]

Not to be outdone, the University of Washington founded the "Harry Bridges Center for Labor Studies," and the Harry Bridges Chair, to honor an influential West Coast Communist labor leader.[2] These efforts are housed within the "departments of Political Science and History at Washington." Of course funds for these endeavors came from multi-millionaires happy to milk Capitalism while paying to see it destroyed.

Bridges immigrated to America from Australia, a well-known devout Communist. He founded the west coast International Longshoremen and Warehouse Union and spent over 40 years as its head. Bridges also found time to serve on the CPUSA Central Committee, "directly approved by the Kremlin for this post. Over 1,000 contributors raised the funds necessary to endow the Harry Bridges Chair in 1992." George Lovell now holds the Bridges Chair, with the Center consisting of 53 faculty associates and 31 visiting committee people."[14]

The Center receives support and financing from officials of the International Longshoremen and International Machinists and Aerospace Workers unions, Washington State senators and representatives, the Service Employees International Union, and the Washington State Labor Council of the AFL-CIO.[15]

The words "Communist," "Internationalist," and "Socialist" are not found in the Bridges Center website. In fact, at a 2001 ceremony, former US House Speaker and present San Francisco Democrat Congresswoman Nancy Pelosi heaped unstinting praise on Harry Bridges on the 100th anniversary of his birth.[14,15]

Haynes and Klehr further documented strong Red presence in American Historical Association leadership and like professional groups. For decades, these "revisionists" have blocked publication of anti-Communist-themed articles in major historical journals. Almost all new historical doctoral dissertations must "reflect a benign view of Communism, loathing for anti-Communism, and hostility toward America."[16] Political correctness rules much of American historical literature.

TRUMAN'S RED SHARKS

However blackened by the left as unwarranted hysteria, 1940s and 50s Republican charges of Democratic "softness on communism" had factual basis. Franklin Roosevelt practiced unwavering "concession without reciprocation" toward the Soviet Union, including a "look but don't touch" policy on Soviet spies operating in America. As confessed agent Hede Massing remarked, "It was open-season, the golden age of espionage. America could not have been more accommodating."[17]

Harry Truman inherited the same leftist zealots and associated political debts, in 1946 appointing Assistant Secretary of the Treasury Harry Dexter White and Treasury Division of Monetary Research Director Virginius Frank Coe to important posts at the International Monetary Fund (IMF). Years before, Treasury Secretary Henry Morgenthau Jr. had granted White considerable authority in global financial matters. Treasury big-shot White also worked as a one-man employment agency for government-bound Soviet agents.

Besides ignoring clear and detailed written documentation from FBI Director J. Edgar Hoover about their rich histories as Soviet agents, the President likewise turned a blind eye to *illegal* Atomic Energy Commission shipments of super-secret nuclear hardware to Soviet Russia that continued to 1950. Both cases are anything but "red herring," Truman's farcical 1948 presidential campaign put-down of Red espionage bonanza. His acts can't be defended; they are only explicable as political paybacks.

Heavy Red presence in Federal Government made for active treason before and during the Korean War, right under Truman's nose. Two of his White House assistants, David K. Niles and Philleo Nash, had strong Communist ties. The same disloyalty manifested in November 1951 and after with continuing State Department provision of Korean War negotiation strategy to Communist peace talk delegates. These grievous acts of treason prolonged the war and cost American and allied lives, yet are ignored in popular understanding as dangerous affronts to revered political figures.

<u>Chapter 28: Dual Power – Great National Undoing</u>

Soldiers of Stalin – the Secret World of Betrayal

President Ronald Reagan's Defense Department arms control official Fred Charles Iklé quoted Russian revolutionist Leon Trotsky on the favored Red strategy of *"Dual Power."* The technique addresses necessary "historic preparation" for national revolutionary take-over. Lenin employed the stratagem for 20 years prior to Bolshevik success in the 1917 Russian Revolution. Iklé cited Communist use of Dual Power in gaining footholds in countries from which they might then achieve full control.[1]

Here is Trotsky's thinking on pre-revolutionary essentials:

> "The political mechanism of revolution consists of the transfer of power from one class to the other. The forcible overthrow is usually accomplished in a brief time. But no historic class lifts itself … to a position of rulership suddenly in one night …. The historic preparation of revolution brings about in the pre-revolutionary period a situation in which *the class which is called to realize the new social system, although not yet master of the country, has actually concentrated in its hands a significant share of the state power,* while the official apparatus of the government is still in the hands of the old lords. That is the initial [D]ual [P]ower in every revolution" (italics added).[1]

Iklé summarized the stratagem as simply "implantation of political followers in the incumbent government," in Communism's case hardly a benign process but akin to bodily infection with metastatic cancer cells.[2] Trotsky further emphasized the many years of "preparatory campaign" needed to strengthen "the class called on to realize the new social system." This entailed creating and developing "a political movement and a political party that can win votes." Central to the idea's success is achieving "a strong, *legitimate* foothold in the bourgeois government" (italics added).[2] Red-embracing Franklin and Eleanor Roosevelt, Harry White, Lauchlin Currie, Alger Hiss, Nathan Gregory Silvermaster, Acheson, Coe, and Adler nicely fit the bill.

DEALING WITH TOTALITARIAN MINDS AND CONTROL MANIA

Late British counter-intelligence officer Peter Wright possessed rare knowledge of the theory and operating principles of authoritarian rule. Few if any American leaders dare voice, or are ignorant of, core features of the Bolshevik operating system. The subject is *verboten*, forbidden in American culture and society.

As Red revolutionary history proved, the Soviet Government custom-crafted tools of repression to meet specific demands of, and challenges to, exercise of political power. As Wright explained, "[Vladimir] Lenin understood better than anyone how to gain control of a country and, just as important, how to keep it. Lenin believed that *the political class had to control the men with the guns*, along with the intelligence service, and by these means ensure that neither the Army nor another political class could challenge for power" (italics added).[3]

Bolshevik Felix Dzerzhinsky masterminded the unparalleled 20th-century Soviet intelligence service, creating the NKVD- and KGB-predecessor CHEKA agency. This comprised three heavily manned and financially-supported sections or "directorates" for diagnosing and treating threats to the Soviet political system.[3] Russian leaders *always* felt threatened on three levels: the outside world, domestic society, and their military. Reds didn't need concrete proof of anything – mere fact of human existence outside Communist Party leadership provided ample basis for preparing massive assault against all. As proven by great Lenin's fear of displacement by Trotsky, later assassinated in Mexico, fellow leaders could also be objects of profound distrust, police control, and murder.

Inherent Russian xenophobia and paranoia mandated detection and elimination of foreign conspirators. For this purpose Dzerzhinshky crafted the "First Chief Directorate," to prevent and defeat extra-national plots against the Soviet. Then came internal threat, managed by the Second Chief Directorate, a domestic intelligence agency. The Third Chief Directorate invaded Soviet military structure. Presence of numerous, high-ranking "political commissars" within Soviet, then Chinese, North Korean, and East European armies, assured strict Communist control over armed forces. Any military conspiracy against the ruling class could be discouraged, or if present, nipped in the bud.

Communist doctrine clearly viewed private gun ownership as a distinct power threat. Control of guns meant intact rulership. Citizens were strictly prohibited from owning guns. In a practical sense, no privately held guns meant no private political power that might challenge oligarchs. This is bedrock Red doctrine in today's America.

All three agencies of repression garnered ample resources and represented a major Soviet industry. Wealthy Internationalist backers such as the American millionaire Hammer family happily funded police-state dominion. As intentioned, all three engendered great fear throughout Red society, always ready to "behead the community – to destroy any potential leadership that might organize resistance to Soviet rule."[4]

To their detriment, Americans, British, and other Western peoples never learned the vastness of Soviet suppression instruments, nor appreciated Soviet single-mindedness in infesting and taking over democratic governments. For 70 years, popular media have shunned the subject of Red barbarity, while concentrating on the Nazi variety. Decent people never knew the Red movement's absence of moral boundaries, its fanatical devotion to world revolution, the inherently anti-Jewish and anti-Christian nature of Red oligarchs. These were, and are, intentionally withheld from public knowledge to promote desired control outcomes.

Lenin's famous remark to Dzerzhinsky appropriately described Red revolutionary strategy: "The West are wishful thinkers, we will give them what they want to think."[5] So a "secret world of betrayal" could function within US Government against wishes and interests, and beyond knowledge, of the American people.[6] Global Soviet espionage attack could be launched, "at a time when the Western political leadership was … pursuing a policy of alliance and extending the hand of friendship."[7] KGB networks spread "all across the West, ready for the Cold War as the West prepared for peace."[8] Tragically, "peace had not come in 1945."[7]

Leninist and Trotskyist precepts exposed by authors Iklé, Wright, and Philip Selznick are part of basic Communist thought and practice. Selznick noted Communism's "distinctive competence to turn members of a voluntary association into disciplined and deployable political agents.[9] Expenditure of years of effort in gathering and developing basic cadres are not begrudged.[10] The [hidden] structure of Communist politics is not completely revealed until the system is seen in action."[11]

Suggested Red patterns fit 20th- and 21st-century American experience to a 'T.' Internationalism's pre-First World War Washington invasion, and the similar and concurrent Communist campaign of destruction, reveal the Dual Power template. Two strong leftist revolutionary pincer movements surrounded and sought to crush the US. By the 1930s, Communism became *de rigueur* in American and British intellectual circles, a desirable identification socially and politically. Red radicals Joseph Lash, Abbot Simon, and others, lived for years in the White House as guests of Eleanor Roosevelt.[12] Reds entered Government employment by the thousands in Roosevelt New Deal programs.

After Roosevelt's 1944 presidential victory, CPUSA Chairman Earl Browder boasted about enhanced Communist political clout and broad national acceptability.[13] Three days after the death of world Communism's greatest friend, President Roosevelt, *Daily Worker* editorialist Minister Starobin wrote, "It now becomes possible to consider for the first time on a general scale the transition of many countries toward socialism in a new, and generally peaceful way, through the older state forms .... Yes, the state will control; but it is already and will be a state dominated by a new configuration of classes."[14] Welcome to America!

When Korean War brought domestic unpopularity to "Communist" and "Red" labels, the euphemisms "progressive," "liberal," and "Democrat" provided a comfortable and inclusive umbrella. Super-leftists surely achieved legitimacy over the course of 30 years, sought out and gained high positions from which to bend national policy, and achieved increasing political success with Executive and Legislative branches and in crafting electoral vote majorities. Leftist political power grew to engulf at least 25 states. Judicial undermining and academic clout are special achievements.

As late judge and unsuccessful Supreme Court candidate Robert Bork emphasized, the judiciary functions as leftist revolution's "enforcement arm," neutralizing public majority votes and true representative democracy. Relentless pursuit of revolutionary goals, high energy, and strong class consciousness characterize the effort.

To fully accomplish the mission of destruction, Christianity and Judaism remain to be marginalized, and all basic moral-social guidelines obliterated, including those of family, laws governing criminal behavior, historical understanding of American Constitutional foundation, and traditional thoughts about self-discipline.

Through constant press agitation and brainwashing, the thought gained root with so-called victimized elements of society: "These folks care so much about us. They will do things for us. They will save us. We will vote for them." Franklin Roosevelt's socialist legacy lives on — progressive power demands it.

The over-arching theme could be titled, "How to bring the greatest nation in world history under foot." Details included barrels of money for political purchasing, control of mass media, law, and academia, abundant patience, and a never-give-up will of iron. Great irony attends Red functioning in a system of personal freedom permitting gross abuses aimed at destroying that system.

True leftist revolutionaries always fought against and worked to prohibit "dated" moral standards. Continual heavy attacks must be made on Church, patriotism, family, Founding Fathers, American uniqueness, the Constitution, and *any source of authority*, while censoring information regarding the hidden hand of Internationalist power.[15] People must be kept uninformed and incapable of interference. The goal is always dissolution, disintegration, a hacking away at pillars of "alien" (American) life.

The plan worked to perfection. Very few Americans surmised the Red roots underlying the process controlling daily life. As master diagnostician George Kennan stated, "The more I see of this Internationalist society, the more I understand that it is in the shadow of things, rather than the substance, that control is exercised."[16]

The unparalleled communication tool of television proved a special control lever. Late respected journalist Edward R. Murrow told that in its beginning years, the medium faced a high road and low road in programming, and took the latter. Boston University President Daniel Marsh warned 60 years ago, "If the television craze continues with the present level of programs, we are destined to have a nation of morons."[17] Let the masses be entertained – who cares about truth?

The same techniques and consequences applied to Roosevelt-Truman hawking of "coalition government" to seal national rifts between non-Communist and Communist parties. A favored Roosevelt tactic in "solving" postwar leadership problems in Poland, Romania, Hungary, Bulgaria, and China, "coalition" merely greased the skids of pre-revolutionary phase invasion, assured Dual Power success, and paved the road to rapid Red control.

For example, historian Robert Dallek believed Roosevelt's Far East territorial concessions to the Soviet Union were conditioned on "Russian support of a coalition [government+ in China."[18] Roosevelt mistakenly thought Nationalist-Communist collaboration would offer maximum Chinese military effort against Japan. The point is invalidated in Mao's dictum on Communist emphasis: fighting Japan should consume only 10% of Red effort and obviously didn't matter much to the Chairman.[19]

Roosevelt also likely wished Soviet Russia to become a superpower, and for Communism to dominate China. Truman picked up the banner in sending Gen. Marshall to China to impose a settlement with Chiang Kai-shek preserving and strengthening the Red position. One thing is certain: in China and America, the Dual Power stratagem worked as intended.

MARCHING ORDERS AND SECRET POLICE

Twentieth-century Communist Party discipline was a strict personal responsibility. The same holds today for the People's Republic of China, North Korea, Vietnam, and Cuba. Everyone worked for ends set by Moscow Party leadership. Dedication to promoting Red principles permeated every activity. No deviations could be allowed in defining those ends or in full personal commitment to their achievement. "Morality" meant total adherence to Communist doctrine, nothing else. Reality could be remade into unreality, truth pulverized into polar falsity. Policy lay solely in the domain of Party leadership.

Top-down, centralized rule considered public opinion insignificant. Communist rank-and-file could only be loyal, no other options existed. They worked for the Party, the Party sustained their lives. Behaviors toward "strangers," those not Reds or pro-Reds, were not limited by Judeo-Christian moral standards. Ends were all-important, means unimportant. People didn't count, only totalitarian ideas. The practice of politics was fought as a war. Human life meant soul-less bags of chemicals.

By millions, the system sacrificed people toward "higher" ends. One could overlook sequelae of revolutionary success such as increased poverty, class eradication, family dissolution, endemic minority violence, and failed public education as small prices for power. Chaos is dictatorship's necessary elixir.

The Soviet Union's 1990-91 dissolution meant nothing to plan success. Momentum built up over generations could not be stilled. American leftist power continued to increase with each year, as beloved chaos drew near. A single terrible act such as nuclear terrorism could bring national panic and dysfunction. If such devastation came from within, as a calculated act meant to bring instant dictatorship, all the better. Comrades would dance on American graves in celebration.

MANAGING THE MASSES

Public deception is an art-form to Internationalists, key to gaining and maintaining power. Dual Power public pronouncements are always couched in terms of popular interests. Actors freely wrap themselves in flag and country. Professed ideology is centered on helping the needy achieve social, economic, and health justice. There is never a hint of revolutionary intent, hardly ever open membership in radical, pro-violent organizations. Propaganda is slick and portrays sincerity and credibility. Terms such as "proletarian dictatorship," "class warfare," and "liquidation" of opponents are strictly prohibited. Deception must be preserved at all costs, the press ever-willing to censor bad news.

An example of subtle censorship is found in 20th-century historian Arthur M. Schlesinger, Jr.'s respected book, *The Age of Roosevelt – The Politics of Upheaval*. The otherwise comprehensive work fails to mention "Internationalism," let alone detail its major players and functioning. "Progressivism" is only addressed in passing. While Schlesinger gives leftist-socialist-Communist labor figures their due in influencing Roosevelt administrations, powerful American Internationalist political forces are ignored.

The leftist political chain is unbroken since 1915. Today's progressive leaders, senators Harry Reid, Patrick Leahy, Dick Durbin, and Bernie Sanders, entrenched Congresswoman Pelosi and over 150 others, are true heirs of early 20th- century Internationalists and Communists. Showered with media attention, new Reds symbolize arch-respectability, US House and Senate backdrops and rows of flags attesting love of country. Targets of attack are the young, the truly suffering underclass, and "leaderless activists thirsting to be recognized as an emerging political force."[20] Fred Iklé advised *in 2006* that "illegal Hispanic immigrants" represent a "minority of choice," a specially vulnerable and numerous target of great value in sowing the "despairing, divided society, so easily ruled by a brutal tyrant."[21] Arthur Schlesinger, Jr. accurately described the process as "the disuniting of America."[21]

As with profoundly disrespectful press treatment of former Vice-President Dan Quayle, Alaska Governor and Vice-Presidential candidate Sarah Palin, and 2016 Republican presidential nominee Donald Trump, weapons of character assassination and heaping ridicule are freely used to politically destroy perceived dangerous opposition. Since truth doesn't matter, outrageously false claims are made and endlessly repeated. Political contests are considered wars, ends justifying any means. Public opinion polls are cited as evidence of the opponent's flawed character and public danger. Reputations are destroyed and political careers stopped dead.

Liberal figures such as Hillary and Bill Clinton, Barbara Boxer, and Nancy Pelosi are never subjected to such harsh criticism from mainstream media. The degree of importance assigned to 'reactionary' people or groups (such as the National Rifle Association) is directly proportional to viciousness of smear tactics. Potential heroes of common people are special targets. Reds do not tolerate competing power. Only one line is permissible, a single source of authority.

CREATING THE NEW GESTAPO

A final revolutionary requirement completes the picture and deals with stubborn people or groups left standing. As Dual Power yields to singular leftist power, a national secret police must be created, skilled in physical repression. Dictatorial power requires this lever to guarantee permanence.

Government now works mightily to remake society into a security system, at the expense of political, economic, and social freedom. Already the US Department of Homeland Security is stocking up on automatic weapons and ammunition, far in excess of current needs. Seven-thousand submachine guns are due for 2014-16 delivery, along with tons of ammunition.

National thugs will carry reassuring titles such as "Homeland Public Safety Guardians," "Communities United for Peace," or other soothing labels in diametric opposition to truth.

President Obama will do his best to create this force before leaving office in 2017. Acute national disasters such as nuclear terrorism or biological attack on American cities will move the date up.

Resort to physical punishment and deadly liquidation is necessary to eliminate ever-present 'mad reactionary' threats. Privately-owned guns must be registered with proper authorities as prelude to seizure, as recently happened in Australia. Our rulers are only comfortable with a disarmed middle-class or its remnant. Mao's wisdom is ever in mind: "Political power grows from the barrel of the gun." Potentially anti-government sources of influence are feared and set for extinction. Life doesn't count, only power. After all, great Stalin himself told, "Death solves all problems. No man, no problem."[22]

Part VI:

'Die – For – Tie' War, Peace Negotiations,

and Leadership Realities,

1951 – 53

Chapter 29:   Korean Battle - Fix, PART II

"When either political or economic considerations finally limit purely military requirements,

we ask, if not for stalemate, then for defeat."[1]

- S.L.A. Marshall, Our Mistakes in Korea.

We resume War dialogue at an indisputable point. By mid-May 1951, with Red Chinese armies disintegrating, out of supplies and ammunition, and unable to treat their wounded, US/UN armies stood unopposed in the field. Chairman Mao appreciated the disaster visited upon CCF. Word went out from Beijing: Turn the war into a test of endurance.[2] But first, Reds needed time to regroup, re-arm, and survive this phase of greatest military danger. Now Soviet and Chinese Communists showed their mastery at psychological games.

The negotiation weapon occupied a prominent spot in the Red war toolbox. Communist ideology as applied by Lenin, Stalin, Mao, and later by Vietnam's Ho Chi Minh, appreciated the quest for world domination as up-and-down, give-and-take. Placing this tool on the table simply represented continuation of war by other means.

Unknown at the time, Generalissimo Stalin gave Chinese and North Koreans a push toward negotiations.[3] A prior US peace talks attempt came to nothing. The text has mentioned Dean Acheson's pressure on State colleague George Kennan to talk informally about a peace conference with Soviet UN delegate chief Malik. After Moscow approval, Malik made his radio speech favoring truce negotiations. It was time to bend war reality toward Red ends. Truman and Acheson could not respond fast enough to Soviet overture. *Hint* of Chinese willingness to engage in talks did the trick.

The politically-inspired National Security Council parroted negotiations, not mobile and decisive combat operations, to end the War and avoid World War III. Talks would be life-saving, the common sense approach. Compliant and redundant Joint Chiefs joined the bandwagon.

As author Francis T. Miller knew, "The Soviet olive branch concealed poisoned thorns," and brought "a cleverly devised stall."[4] Soviet and Chinese Communists never acted out of charity to opponents. Nothing could more benefit PRC war effort in Korea than removal of US forward pressure at the North Korean front, exactly the course set as the negotiations door opened July 1951.

Suddenly, *in contravention of battlefield reality*, Chinese were held up as "unbeatable, their troop reserves unlimited and irresistible."[5] A compact program of propaganda emanated from the White House, State Department, and Joint Chiefs, pitching "stalemate" as the mandated operant descriptor for Korean War outcome.

BLITZKRIEG TO SITZKRIEG

In rush to settlement, Truman, Acheson, and Chiefs lost sight of war's purpose: "to strike your enemy, not to sit back and wait for him to strike you.[6] An army not intending to attack obviously had no hope of winning." So, in May-June 1951, for the first time in national history, Truman made America give up on achieving military victory in war. After a year of hard fighting, Eighth Army was forced to dig in on high ground, in central and eastern sectors 20 to 40 miles north of the 38th Parallel (MAP 11).

Jumping at the negotiations balloon, Truman's orders prohibited major offensive operations. Ridgway's May 9 "mission-impossibility" protest to Joint Chiefs followed.[7] Most Iron Triangle and Punchbowl battle sites lay north of the Kansas-Wyoming line (MAP 11). Tragically, this would be the battlefront for the next two years.

Mobile war and high US troop morale now ended in Korea. Bloody two-year static war began, resembling World War I trench warfare. James and Wells chillingly defined this phase as "an indecisive killing ground without meaning."[8] In fact, line-bound battle years meant 30,000 US killed and 60,000 seriously wounded.[9] New Acheson-Truman policy brought unrelenting dribs and drabs of killing — two, four, eight at a time, or whole squads and platoons, instead of battalions.

Yet one standard excuse used by politicians and generals, including Ridgway, for justifying the stupid change from offensive success to defensive stalemate, was the high cost in blood of major offensive operations. Meanwhile, horrendous static war losses meant nothing to successful battle outcome, or even negotiation success.

Even though political wasting of human lives is criminal in all respects, President Truman's leftist-revered political reputation has always trumped the truth of Korean blood-letting. But those who served in Korea could never be fooled, nor many of that time's public. Truman was a very unpopular war-time Chief Executive.

FAILURE OF WILL

Truman and Acheson sent a strong, unmistakable signal to Beijing, Moscow, and Pyongyang: a powerful UN offensive such as the one crippling Third and Fourth Field armies would never again be mounted. Surely, the US could put together needed men and material for such a campaign; the key factor to Communists was US *failure of will.* Reds sensed American leaders sorely, even desperately wanted peace and would bend over backward to end fighting. Mao and cohorts knew the Red hand helping steer America's ship of state. Weakness of Washington leadership must be ruthlessly exploited. The "fix" still operated. Chinese Communists could only read this as a unique opportunity to avoid disaster and regain the offensive edge.

DIE-FOR-TIE WAR – CHOOSING STALEMATE AND CARNAGE

Generals told politicians the freshly dug and "sturdy" Eighth Army static line would completely frustrate Red attack. But "fighters in the trenches knew better."[10] No defensive line was foolproof – as proved by France's vaunted World War II Maginot Line. Warrior Hackworth defined proper "depth" as "good defensive positions behind the main line that were, or could be, occupied by soldiers in a snap."[10]

In reality, UN trenches, bunkers, and observation and command posts were flimsy and shallow compared to the Chinese. They had to be: relative paucity of troops meant excessively long reaches of main line covered by thin numbers. A Scottish officer attached to the British Commonwealth Division told a US Marine colleague, "You dissipate your strength trying to make your basketball courts in the rear safe."[11] Marine Lt. Col. Norman Hicks related the opinion of a battle-experienced officer: "... Frankly, our defense at that time was not sound. The MLR was a continuous line – and a damned thin one ...."[11] More than a few infantry commanders noted that "a wide-fronted linear defense dissipated strength and made strong, mutually supporting fire difficult. Lack of depth did not provide for receiving the shock of an enemy attack or for weakening attackers before their ejection by counterattack."[11] The deficiency exacted a bloody price.

The enemy shrewdly used prospective negotiation-induced May – July 1951 breathing space in a feverish building campaign. Communists reorganized and re-equipped shattered units. They "dug a defensive line ... such as the world had never seen – 10 times the depth of any in World War I. They dug positions that could – and might have to, their leaders reasoned – stand against nuclear explosion."[12]

Red defensive fortifications at and behind the battlefront included a 14-mile system of deep tunnels, trenches, and large, strong bunkers, many hewn from solid rock, resistant to US artillery and air bombardment, and in enemy wish, to atomic attack (such resistance was of course never tested). In mountainous areas, Chinese again burrowed far into rock to create large underground rooms accommodating hundreds.

Thus situated, most enemy forces "could not be dislodged or destroyed" by conventional means.[13] They *could* be destroyed while deployed for night battle outside their shelters, or within by huge, conventional "Tarzon" bombs, 12,000-pounders used in Yalu River bridge bombings, featuring radio-controlled fins helping guide the weapon to its target. The author found no record of Tarzon bomb use against Chinese fortifications.

Forty-kiloton nuclear bombs, twice as powerful as the Nagasaki weapon, would either destroy enemy field works and troops, or seal them off and suffocate life within. But Truman admitted having no stomach for mass Chinese slaughter: "I did not wish to have any part in the killing of millions of innocents ...."[14] Starting an atomic war is totally unthinkable ...."[15]

For the next 40 years, Truman failure to threaten or use US atomic might against Communist China or Soviet Russia meant 40-year-subjection of American people to Red slaughter. Today it means identical threat of destruction from heavily nuclear-armed Russia, Red China, and North Korea. This is Internationalism's preferred course.

Meanwhile in Korea, metastasis of Communist logistical arteries, night movement, and daytime camouflage excellence, assured not only adequate enemy arms and provisions, but often *superior* firepower over the War's last two years.

When heavy and accurate US fire came close to punching holes in the front, fear- or fix-driven United Nations Command directives prohibited strong penetration that might envelop large enemy units. Reds enjoyed a "no-lose" status. Their opponent could not hit back hard. Gen. Van Fleet mentioned one such missed opportunity at the battle of White Horse Mountain, a highly successful South Korean Army performance.[16]

MATERIAL NEEDS OF OPPOSING ARMIES – RED INFANTRY ADVANTAGE 1

The time's grinding warfare better suited Red soldiers and Communism's life-expendable philosophy. War is largely an uncivilized activity, but Americans needed civilized amenities, Communists did not. While Reds could exist and thrive in very primitive conditions, GIs must have relative luxuries, at least in the opinion of top brass. David Hackworth compared Spartan but strong Chinese defense-in-depth to US rear area "depth" rife with volleyball courts, officer and enlisted-men food and drink clubs, post exchanges, and other recreational amenities.

Should Reds have pierced Allied lines, as with April to July 1953 offensives, they had clear sailing deep to the rear. Military leadership is faulted for misplaced battle priorities.

US "ROTATION:" RED INFANTRY ADVANTAGE 2

In the Second World War, American soldiers typically stayed with assigned combat units for multiple years. Korean War featured a "rotation system" that encouraged infantrymen to leave combat altogether after one year and return stateside. Soldiers earning 36 points rotated out of Korea to America. Each month of front-line combat brought four points. Service in the rear, still considered a combat zone, earned three points per month. So GIs at the front would be homeward bound after nine months, those behind the front at 12 months. Being anywhere in Korea meant two points, which got far-from-rear and service troops home in 18 months.[17] "High-point men" within days or weeks of rotation might resist presence in combat patrols as too risky.

With one exception, battle-experienced US officers authoring Korean War books roundly condemn rotation as destroying personal incentive to learn necessities of infantry warfare and survive and succeed in combat. Hackworth observed that doughfoots simply wanted to earn monthly points until time came to go home, paying "more attention to counting days than to fighting Reds."[18] He faulted troopers for failing to learn terrain features that might provide a tactical edge.

Ominously, Communist soldiers lacked any rotation plan. North Korean and Chinese counterparts knew they could only leave the front "if they went out feet-first," giving "a decided advantage in personal motivation for taking the job seriously." As a consequence, enemy infantry intimately knew battlefield topography and fared better than Americans in setting up and carrying off small-unit ambush actions, a prominent and bloody aspect of fighting in the war's last two years.

As T.R. Fehrenbach related, "Rotation had removed too many men who had learned the answers; companies were shot through with new, green men and, worse yet, new green officers."[19] Troopers paid the price at killing fields named Bloody Ridge, Heartbreak Ridge, Outpost Bruce, The Hook, and Bunker Hill.

Gen. Matthew Ridgway stands as a one-man island in praising troop rotation's supposed morale-building effects. He pegged the rotation system as largely responsible for promoting high troop esprit-de-corps during the War's final year, "allow[ing] many a veteran who had served his share of time to make it home to see his family."[20] While it is true rotation sent combat-experienced troops home, the General ignored above-documented negative effects.

Ridgway is also a lone ranger in perceiving high American esprit-de-corps in the latter part of War. No other author described soldier high-spiritedness during the static-defensive phase.

American fighting men left Korean killing grounds not with a sense of paying a necessary price for freedom, but disgusted with meaningless slaughter.

HEAVY US LOSSES AT BLOODY RIDGE AND HEARTBREAK RIDGE

Without exaggeration, Truman and Acheson literally cut the heart out of US/UN military success in Korea. In a battalion officer's words, "The heart to fight, though not gone, was not the bright light it had once been."[21] From July to November 1951, the first five months of truce talks, American forces suffered 22,000 killed and wounded, the ROK and UN 38,000. The carnage represented 1,125 US soldiers lost per week, supposedly to improve UN line defensive capability, but in reality all for naught. There is a good chance that continued major US offensive would have won the war during that period, at far less price. It is criminal to have politicians run wars.

Late August, September and October brought bitter battles for conquest of Bloody Ridge and Heartbreak Ridge, near the Punchbowl, a very steep, sharp-rimmed old volcanic crater about 25 miles inside North Korea, northeast of the Hwachon Reservoir (MAP 11). Fighting at Bloody Ridge took 2,700 US killed in action, most from the 2nd Division's 9th Infantry Regiment; at Heartbreak Ridge, 3,700, the 2nd Division's 23rd Infantry Regiment bearing the brunt.[22]

According to Fehrenbach, the NKPA suffered a staggering 35,000 killed and wounded at the two ridges, the American 23rd Regiment 5,600 just at Heartbreak.[21] Battle names are apt.

Chinese and North Koreans realized their rear areas far behind the main line would never be subject to heavy UN infantry assault. They also learned again the deadly impact of massive American artillery firepower. US artillery at Bloody Ridge fired almost a half-million rounds, at Heartbreak some quarter-million, concentrations unseen in prior localized warfare. Air bombing and artillery could make enemy life near the MLR miserable, but the remainder of Red territory was safe from being overrun. As Fehrenbach observed, "The heartbreak was not for the men who had died, but at what had been accomplished by it all."[23]

Importantly, the Korean combat veteran-author believed "The United Nations Command had learned a great deal from Heartbreak and Bloody ridges. … [T]he new enemy fortifications and newer, greener troops in the Eighth Army [meant] *effective pressure on the enemy could be achieved only at a cost in blood unacceptable to Washington*" (italics added).[24] This appeared to signal greater UN incentive to seek and conclude peace than to human-uncaring Communists, a portent of great danger ahead.

Truman successor Dwight Eisenhower seemed to appreciate that long, bloody, grinding war of attrition proved to Red advantage. Ike's successor Kennedy may have known the precept, but kept pouring "advisers," in reality US fighting troops, into Vietnam. Next-in-line President Johnson undoubtedly failed to grasp the important perception.

Gen. Mark Clark, Far East Commander in Chief the last 14 months of War, explained unpleasant military reality: "The enemy was able to plan his ground operations, along the front line, with relative certainty that our forces inside Korea were inadequate to mount a decisive offensive against him. If the Communists had taken terrain features important to our defense line, we had to counterattack to recapture them. That is where we suffered our heaviest casualties."[25] Clark clearly contradicted Acheson's warped view of stalemated, "petered-out" war.

American leaders had unlimited excuses for not decisively pursuing CCF in North Korea.

Secretary Acheson and Gen. Collins shoved before the people the "waning support of UN allies" for continuing the war into North Korea a second time. The US and South Korea would have to go it alone, not a dismal prospect given smallness of allied troop commitments. But this might shatter the all-important Internationalist mandate of "collective security" and hurt United Nations standing. It would also represent dreaded display of nationalism, the proffered bane of humanity.

Despite Dean Acheson's false words, US/UN blood shed in senseless massacre did nothing to hasten negotiations and end the War, and could have been expended in lesser numbers with continued offensives to decisively defeat Red China and attain military victory for America, South Korea, and allies.

Vicious fighting for the Heartbreak Ridge killing ground, just north of the Punchbowl, finally ended in allied "victory" October 15, 1951.[26] Its occupation meant nothing, thousands wounded and killed in wasted sacrifice. State Department insanity ruled the US military.

Negotiations started and continued with great Red intransigence. From first meetings at the village of Kaesong, below the 38th Parallel, UN delegates suffered barrages of insults from their counterparts and not-so-subtle intimidation by armed Chinese troops (MAP 11). Every conference table act, step, and discussion was calculated to delay, degrade, and frustrate the UN. A US B-26 medium bomber "mistakenly" attacked a Chinese patrol near Kaesong, bringing Communist howls about attempted murder of their delegation and breaking off of talks.

As Bernard Brodie related, Communists had mastered the "studied insult."[27] Acheson forbade UN delegates from suspending talks – it supposedly would give Communists a public relations victory and negotiation advantage. Reds keenly sensed US over-eagerness to meet and close an armistice, an attitude they felt must be exploited.

ANOTHER FAR EAST COMMANDER DEFIES SUPERIORS

To his credit, 1951 Far East Commander in Chief Gen. Ridgway sent Pentagon bosses, including

Army Chief of Staff Gen. Collins, frank messages about what the UN needed to do regarding negotiations. The essence was "more steel and less silk," meaning far heavier military hand and less political-diplomatic interference to gain a quick and favorable cease-fire.[28]

Due to frank Red intimidation, Ridgway insisted in mid-September that talks move to the small settlement of Panmunjom, on the 38th Parallel, a truly neutral site (MAP 12). He then took a bold stance toward Washington superiors. Ignored by most Korean War accounts, Ridgway messaged Joint Chiefs, "If your decision should be to direct me to resume delegation meetings in Kaesong, I shall refrain from doing so."[29,30]

The theater commander so preferable to dreaded MacArthur now proposed to refuse a direct order, a fire-able offense, to be sure. But a second theater commander sacking of a widely respected general so soon after MacArthur's would have brought down on Truman's head whatever house remained. One Pyrrhic victory was plenty. Joint Chiefs Chairman Gen. Bradley scrambled to Tokyo to defuse the crisis – "all was well, State backs you 100%." Ridgway was appeased, and Reds naturally got the word, now proposing the shift to the final discussion site of Panmunjom as their idea.

OPERATION 'LITTLE SWITCH' BREAKS POW IMPASS

Continual bloodshed from give-and-take combat attended drawn-out peace talks. By November 1952, US dead and wounded again reached 1,000 per week, a meaningless carnage given cessation of talks over the issue of Communist POW repatriation.[31] Should Red war prisoners be forced to return to "people's paradise," as America and Britain did with German-held Russian prisoners after World War II, or offered the chance at a better life in South Korea or Taiwan?

Truman is credited with insisting on the latter, one of the few times the UN side held a firm negotiating position regardless of Communist response. As war prisoner disposition represented the last major negotiations stumbling block, yielding on this issue would have allowed armistice signing 18 months or more before actual July 27, 1953 conclusion. A host of military and civilian casualties, more prisoners lost to the Communist side, and continued

MAP 12

KOREAN DEMILITARIZED ZONE –
JULY 27, 1953 ARMISTICE TO PRESENT –
MANY U.S., ROK, U.N. OUTPOSTS LOST TO CCF 1952-53

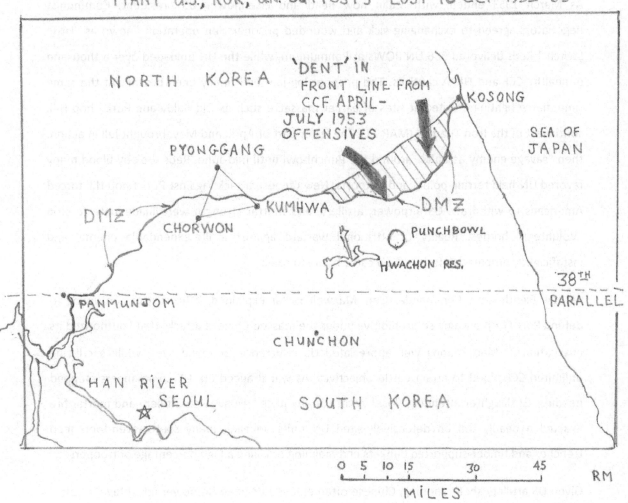

NORTH KOREA

'DENT' IN FRONT LINE FROM CCF APRIL-JULY 1953 OFFENSIVES

KOSONG

SEA OF JAPAN

PYONGGANG

DMZ

KUMHWA

CHORWON

DMZ

PUNCHBOWL

HWACHON RES.

38TH PARALLEL

PANMUNJOM

CHUNCHON

HAN RIVER

SEOUL

SOUTH KOREA

0 5 10 15   30   45   RM
MILES

suffering and death by US and allied POWs attended the decision, causing many military officers and scholars to disagree with Truman's repatriation stance.

After the exhaustive process of individually interviewing 132,000 Red POWs, 70,000 chose to abandon Communism and live in either South Korea or Taiwan. Until Spring 1953, this was unacceptable to Communists.

As March 1953 ended, with Stalin now dead and Eisenhower US president, Communist negotiators agreed to exchanging sick and wounded prisoners, an operation known as "Little Switch." Reds delivered 686 UN POWs at Panmunjom, while the UN unloaded over a thousand unhealthy CCF and NKPA captives. The prisoner log-jam had finally been broken. At the same time, fierce fighting erupted at sites of earlier massacre such as Old Baldy and Pork Chop Hill, southwest of the Iron Triangle (MAP 11). The latter part of April, and May, brought lull in action, then "savage enemy assaults" around the Punchbowl until mid-June. Reds took by blood many favored UN-held terrain points and outposts. New Chinese attacks against Pork Chop Hill forced Americans to withdraw. US airpower, artillery, and mortar strength were inadequate to stop "Volunteer" hordes. Reality of attritional warfare against a life-expendable enemy, and insufficiently prepared defenses, now came home to roost.

As new Eighth Army Commander Gen. Maxwell Taylor explained, "The cost of continuing to defend Pork Chop became so prohibitive under the massed Chinese attacks that I authorized its evacuation."[32] Mao Zedong well appreciated US reluctance to spend lives, while sacrificing unlimited CCF blood to attain battle objectives. As war dragged on, US commanders stopped needless GI slaughter attending "local victory at any price." Heavy Red artillery and mortar fire exacted a deadly toll on defensively-sited UN units, leveling many six-to-seven-foot deep trenches and timber-supported bunkers and maiming or killing a high percentage of troopers.

Given US artillery shell rationing, Chinese often enjoyed decided firepower advantage, a role-reversal from Spring 1951 battle. The potent World War II "Arsenal of Democracy" again failed to supply America's fighters with needed men, guns, ammunition, planes, and leadership courage. Slowly and inexorably, Korean War swung toward Red advantage.

As with a fireworks celebration, Reds saved their best effort for last, an all-out offensive July 13 – 20, 1953, aimed mainly at ROK forces and not seen in Korea since May 1951. A river of blood washed the battlefield: 25,000 Red killed, an estimated 47,000 wounded, heavy ROK losses. Communists made ground gains up to *20 miles* south, the point driven home that America and South Korea had better be satisfied with the new status quo, and the South should forget any ideas of attacking the North and reunifying the peninsula. The large dent made by Reds in the central to eastern main line is readily evident in viewing a present Korean Demilitarized Zone (DMZ) map (MAP 12).

WHEN AMATEURS RUN WARS

As truce talks started July 1951, UN ground forces numbered about 550,000, the Communist side 570,000; by Summer 1952 respective ground strengths increased to 678,000 and 720,000.[33] US leaders had changed their minds and now encouraged and helped train much greater numbers of ROK forces. In the latter year of war South Korea fielded 600,000 men, manned "two-thirds of the Korean line, and [would[take more than two-thirds of the total casualties."[34]

Purposeless loss of life and limb bothered common US sensibilities, but nothing could induce Truman and Acheson to abandon war of attrition. Courtesy of these same leaders, America intentionally fought for a tie, and became caught in a no-win war, precisely the situation to be avoided. If ever the threat and use of nuclear weapons made sense, it was now. But courage could not be found for such a step. Hiroshima and Nagasaki had neutered Truman's nuclear response potential. Eisenhower at least placed these cards on the table, and believed they worked to end the war.

The war of words certainly worked beautifully for Reds. Peace appeared to be just beyond reach, a bitter experience for American and South Korean negotiators and costly in blood for armies and peoples. Astonishingly, the same insanity prevailed 15 years later in Vietnam, the

314, Chapter 29

magic elixirs of peace talks and "body counts" failing to save South Vietnam.[35]

Chapter 30: Horse Power Stops Atomic Power!

Greatly embarrassing to US civilian and military leaders, the CCF Korean War "order of battle" for 1952-53, a roster of active enemy combat units, revealed continued presence of two *horse cavalry* divisions, in addition to "five armies (multiple corps or groups of divisions), four artillery divisions, and two North Korean corps (groups of divisions)."[1] Plus, many Chinese formations used horse-drawn artillery, exemplified in the 58th Division's fierce fighting against Marines at Chosin Reservoir battle-sites Yudam-ni and Hagaru-ri.[2]

Unsurprisingly, retired Army Chief of Staff Gen. J. Lawton Collins' book, *War in Peacetime – History and Lessons of Korea,* failed to include 19th-century-style horse cavalry in listing Red combat assets in Korea. The Army Chief also confusingly used two Red troop strengths in his book, first "750,000," then "450,000." He also referenced the former figure in describing Manchuria-based CCF reserves, the so-called invincible asset ready to descend into Korea by "thousands upon thousands" and engulf friendly armies.[1]

The storyline pitched this unsolvable problem as forcing US acceptance of drawn outcome in Korea. As Collins advised, "Pursuing the enemy beyond the Kansas-Wyoming line was not feasible."[3] Even though Allies had recently won a major victory, Collins believed the "ebb-and-flow" nature of Korean fighting assured "neither side would win decisive military victory."[4] The judgment was surely premature given the sore state of CCF in May 1951. Collins acknowledged Eighth Army success in "crushing" two successive Communist offensives in April and May, but "great uncommitted Chinese war potential in Manchuria surpassed that of the UNC" and caused him to give up any hope of victory.[5] Obviously, the General ignored uncommitted US nuclear weapon potential as a counter to Chinese infantry reserves, a politically-incorrect hot iron not to be touched.

ONE SCARED CHIEF

Collins groped to find reasons for accepting a tie: steep, razor-ridged mountains, poor roads, lack of "communication facilities" – all "prohibited" major UN advance north. Unmentioned are identical terrain and problems encountered by Chinese "volunteers." Like boss Acheson, Collins piled on defeatism, throwing in the old standby, "lengthened supply line dilemma," and associated shortening of same for Chinese.[6] For good measure, Collins also played his ace-of-spades, the fearsome shadow of Soviet hordes. Russian intervention meant, "Head for the hills, it was all over," UN forces in Korea must immediately evacuate to Japan.[7] No thought could be given to a countering American nuclear threat, or reality of massive US nuclear superiority.

Collins was one frightened fellow. Why leave the barracks when things are so dangerous? Possession of hundreds of nuclear bombs meant nothing, never mentioned in the former Chief of Staff's analysis. The Truman crew recognized and feared *two* irresistible Communist powers! Bernard Brodie correctly diagnosed America's self-inflicted military "cutting down to size" to fit Korean War demands. The US should, and did, act as a non-nuclear supplicant power, not as the world's foremost, virtual-nuclear-monopoly power.

Four-star General Collins appeared to be telling a scary bedtime tale to children, in hopes they would quickly fall asleep. All his excuses are absurd, meant to camouflage unwillingness of Truman, Acheson, and compliant Chiefs to pursue victory. With such gutless Army leadership, we are not surprised over US inability to defeat an enemy force still relying on primitively-armed horse cavalry. *Horse-power had intimidated and stopped atomic power in its tracks!* This is the bizarre reality of Korean War, driven by leftist revolutionary leadership in the person of boss Acheson.

Civilian and military leadership, and US military education, never bit the bullet on this martial disgrace. The American press dared not touch the story, its many pro-Communist leaders happy over Chinese Red survival and military chastening of vile America. Red power politics is darkness, the enemy of truth and goodness.

Gen. Collins earned a distinguished World War II European combat command record. But based solely on his "War in Peacetime" writings, Americans may wish he is never held up as a martial model to aspiring soldiers, that his definition of military hopelessness is not part of American military education. Should the Collins precept be accepted, every battle and war should be decided by who fields the largest forces and reserves. American military and technological resources would not count in assessing chances for victory. War fighting should then be unnecessary – let a referee just grant victory to the more numerous host. The People's Republic of China would then quickly rule the world!

At this point in his career, Collins obviously left military pride back in Europe and acted a political role in not rocking the required boat of "negotiation first." In atrophy of courage and will in military career end phase, he exemplified the pathos of ancient Rome's Pompeius Magnus. As active duty Army general second in rank only to five-star Joint Chiefs Chairman Gen. Bradley, Collins succeeded in portraying himself as a martial fool. Before fighting America to a draw, Red Chinese first intimidated the life out of Truman, Acheson, and supple Joint Chiefs. One expected better of a strongly nuclear-armed, formerly world-class military state.

TIME FOR DIRE THREATS

Threat of nuclear attack on China should have been on the table. Otherwise, why even have the weapons? CCF reserve concentrations in Manchuria were openly situated and quite vulnerable to atomic strike, a situation made to order for the US. The same holds in countering the specter of Soviet Russian ground intervention threats in Korea and Europe – but not a peep from scared Chiefs. They bought "no general advance north beyond lines Kansas-Wyoming" hook, line, and sinker.[3] Let Chinese and Soviets be portrayed as supermen.

Gen. Collins' book acknowledged the stance of Truman Administration "political leaders" and key Capitol Hill figures, "strongly in favor of negotiation to end fighting."[5] There is no doubt this group included government and press Internationalists, Communists, and pro-Communists. Yet the General spoke for Joint Chiefs frankly and with contradiction in "not seeing many advantages in armistice." He appreciated that "any negotiation that put an end to the heavy casualties then being inflicted on Chinese forces, and yet permitted them to remain in Korea, would be *greatly to Communist advantage* (italics added)."[4] Regarding actual conduct of peace talks, the Army Chief noted ex post facto, "Instructions from the Truman Administration regarding negotiation policy were vacillating and lacked firmness ...."[8]

To his credit, Collins envisioned necessity of indefinite US troop presence in maintaining long-term South Korean security, along with need for a vigilantly defended Demilitarized Zone (DMZ). Shrewd in politics, the General made reasonable statements about the harm of attempted premature negotiated settlement, while pathetically resorting to staunching the War's "severe drain on national resources" in favoring peace talks over victory.[5]

Of course, in pre-Korean War years President Truman's sparse military budgets suffocated US military strength. In parroting the line of minimal national security investment, Collins mimicked the crassness of "180-degree" politicians. As he admitted, the new defense system brought by "The National Security Act of 1947 and 1949 Amendments greatly strengthened the authority and control of the defense secretary over the Army, Navy, Air Departments and all other agencies of the Department of Defense."[9] Chiefs were now pacifists, under thumbs of president, secretary of defense, civilian service secretaries, National Security Council, and most of all at this time, Secretary of State Acheson.

With the "depleted state of US armed forces" came "unprecedented war-fighting conditions and restraints" on UN command operations. Military professionalism took a decided back seat to politics, along with real-time courage of privately and publically-stated soldier-leader convictions. Truly, amateurs ran the show. So easily did America punt away decided military advantage for two bloody years of foul negotiations.

Winston Churchill's words are appropriate: "Military strength is safety and peace."[10] The US under Truman learned this truth the hard way.

Chapter 31: Air Power's Failure to Isolate the Battlefield

"Air power can't live up to its billing out there. Somebody … has sold the American people a bill of goods as to what air power can do. From what I've seen, one bomb will hit a railroad track and one-hundred bombs will miss, some of them by miles. The Air Force [also] does not understand air support, does not believe in it and has never practiced it. … I'm just stating what I saw in action.

Our officer corps have had far too much schooling and far too little combat experience. Push-button war is as far off as in the days of Julius Caesar. The rifle, hand grenade and bayonet are still the most important weapons. We're going to lose the next war if we don't get back to them …."[1]

- Brig. Gen. Lewis B. 'Chesty' Puller, USMC, 1951. Marine! The Life of Chesty Puller.

With advent of the atomic bomb, and 1947 defense reorganization, the Army Air Corps became a separate service, the US Air Force. No longer would there be Army and Navy departments within a "War" Department. Now a Secretary of Defense held sway over the entire military system, under a Department of Defense umbrella. Armed forces "unification" was the rallying cry, masking civilian power grab. Until 1949 the term "National Military Establishment" described the entire American military.

To an extent the new Air Force enjoyed a favored status relative to other branches. Jet aircraft promised to greatly increase air performance capabilities. Some military "experts" relegated mass infantry and amphibious operations to things of the past. How satisfying to American sensibilities to bomb an enemy into submission without blood and mud of brutal ground campaigns. The Air Force was the place to be.

As the gung-ho Air Force flew into stratospheric importance, a few vital facts never got off the ground. Despite years of intense day and night bombing of German cities and military facilities in World War II, at great cost in blood for friend and foe, German armaments production *increased* every year of the war. Strategic bombing could not reduce the arms pipeline, let alone shut it down.[2] Massive bomb tonnage wreaked destruction far and wide, but accuracy of bomb placement was another matter. Millions of American infantry still had to march from the English Channel to the Third Reich's heart to defeat Germany. Korean War commanders such as then-Marine Col. Puller told of bombs grossly off target, with frequent "friendly fire" incidents hurting the wrong side.

British World War II Air Marshall Harris believed massive, unrelenting aerial bombing could of itself defeat Nazi Germany. Somewhere in Pentagon chambers during that time, a similar thought took hold that hung on for decades: air bombing could "isolate" a battlefield, which meant ability to cut off enemy logistic supply and manpower reinforcement, prevent enemy retreat, and so presage certain enemy defeat. Without supply and mobility, any army's days are numbered.

In the Korean War, air isolation of the battlefield simply did not work. At critical junctures, air interdiction of enemy supply lines and troop concentrations greatly helped the UN cause, especially during the Naktong siege and as preparation for Inchon amphibious assault. Robert Frank Futrell's masterful treatise, "The United States Air Force in Korea 1950-1953," attributed NKPA defeat in South Korea to air bombing, machine gun and small cannon strafing, air-to-ground rocket attacks, and complete UN air dominance over the South.[3] Futrell told of 46,000 North Korean army deaths to effects of air action, almost equal to artillery's destructive toll. NKPA prisoner interviews told of morale-destroying fear of air attack. Futrell's scenario shunts September 15, 1950 Inchon invasion to secondary causation for North Korean collapse, an incorrect conclusion. Yet Eighth Army Commander Gen. Walker acknowledged that without Fifth Air Force support, "we would not have been able to stay in Korea."[4]

The truth is that as War progressed, Communist supply capability markedly *grew*. One US/UN answer, the previously mentioned Operation Strangle air campaign, miserably failed to stem Red manpower and supply reinforcement. The Operation sought to destroy North Korean rail and road facilities and ground traffic in a four-month daily pounding. Bridges, tunnels, rail staging areas, and other "choke points" were targeted, hit, destroyed, and promptly rebuilt by

North Korean work teams containing tens of thousands of prepositioned laborers, arriving on site shortly after bombs stopped falling. Futrell mentioned Reds could repair 100 bomb-craters as easily as one.

Of equal tragedy, the same mistaken belief in decisiveness of air support to battle outcome characterized the Vietnam experience. Despite destructive B-52 carpet bombing and heavy tactical air support of ground operations, the Red lifeline Ho Chi Minh Trail could not be shut down. Enemy supplies continued to flow and will-to-resist remained intact, just as in Korea.

Like Acheson, Secretary of Defense Robert McNamara proved a poor war strategist and tactician, only adept at spilling blood. A mere 11 years after Korean truce, Vietnam air bombing advocates seemed not to have learned anything from Korean experience. Air power's failure to isolate and defeat the enemy is a prominent and predictive Korean War theme.

Prevalence of daytime air strikes encouraged Communist forces to fight at night and take strict camouflage cover during the day. The US attempted night air operations in Korea with limited success. World War II-era B-26 light bombers and jet F-82 fighter-bombers flew 35 to 50 sorties per night, or single attacks by individual planes, against enemy supply routes, truck convoys, and infantry reinforcements. Cargo planes carried loads of parachute-deployed flares to illuminate night skies for attacking aircraft. Low cloud cover, fog, and mountainous terrain hindered these efforts.

Inability to mount powerful, sustained close-infantry-support night air bombing and rocketing campaigns proved a great US weakness in Korea.[5] This was the time CCF left the safety of strong bunkers and could have been seriously mauled.

Adding to US/UN decline, American ground firepower advantage shriveled in two years of static war.[6] Lacking tactical air, barbed wire, or minefield emplacement, Communist logistics improved to enabling *superior* artillery and mortar firepower at many times and places. Reds made great strides in using truck transport (supplied by Soviets) in lieu of animals, especially in replenishing stocks of artillery and mortar rounds. Plus, Reds expended lives without hesitation.

The US experienced periods of ammunition rationing owing to domestic labor strikes and endless Pentagon red tape in processing ammunition orders. Shortages were most acute in mortar and artillery shells.[7]

AIR FORCE GUTTING

It must be remembered the US Air Force in Korea represented a "shoestring" force, gathered in pieces from across the globe, never rich in aircraft, crews, airfields, maintenance capability, and supplies. This revelation came in classified 1951 testimony by Air Force Chief of Staff Gen. Hoyt Vandenberg, who told the Senate the US simply didn't have bomber or fighter fleets necessary for successful attack on Communist China's vast reaches. What we had "would be a drop in the bucket" relative to what was needed.[8]

The F-86 Sabre Jet fighter represented the only American plane able to routinely out-fight the MiG-15. An incredible reality, Vandenberg related that "Our ability to support a second F-86 unit in the Far East Air Force for Korea does not exist."[9] Congressmen should have jumped up and down in protest. The "watchdog" press never spread the word, ably protecting Truman, Acheson, and company from rightful national disgrace.

Futrell issued an appropriate observation:

> "What was happening in the Far East in Summer 1951 was one more indication of the truth … that since World War II the US had become fat and complacent and had dropped its guard. America's superior technology was not yet able to match the Soviet Union's totalitarian economy in quantity production of swept-wing air-superiority fighters."[10]

As Futrell disclosed, in June 1951 "Communist China possessed some 445 modern MiG-15 fighters, while FEAF possessed 89 F-86s in theater inventory," a situation "little short of shameful."[10] Superb speed, high ceiling, and superior climbing ability made MiGs masters of the sky, until Sabre advent. Returning from a Korean visit, Gen. Vandenberg noted, "Communist China has become one of the major air powers in the world almost overnight."[11] By December 1951 US Sabre strength in Korea reached 127, while Reds held some 600 MiGs in Manchurian and Chinese bases.[11]

High-performing jet aircraft also require regular maintenance, another major American shortcoming. In early 1952, "Men of the 4th and 51st Fighter-Interceptor wings experienced bitter frustration" as the Korean "Sabre out-of-commission rate spiraled upward. An average of 45% of Sabres had to be carried as out-of-commission ... for want of parts ... and maintenance."[12]

Far East Bomber Command had its own troubles. The last week of October 1951, World War II-vintage B-29s suffered the "worst losses of the Korean War: five planes [destroyed] from flak or enemy fighters, eight with major damage, 55 crewmen dead or missing, 12 others wounded."[13] Military unpreparedness always exacts a bitter price, along with military-related treason. The Arsenal of Democracy now stood missing in action. The buck stops with Truman.

DISGRACEFUL PRESIDENTIAL LEADERSHIP

President Truman cut World War II air personnel strength of 2.2 million down to 414,000 by 1950. When Korean War began, the entire US Air Force contained about 2,500 functional aircraft. By comparison, the Soviet Air Force easily held 10,000 combat-ready planes. Futrell also wrote of serious deficiencies in air reconnaissance plane numbers, crews, ground support, photograph evaluation experts, and facilities for evaluation. These certainly compromised air-based intelligence before and during Korean War.[14]

There were never more than 150 F-86 Sabre Jet fighters in Korea, the best air combat planes we had; most of slim inventory could not be spared for this secondary theater.[15] As proven above, Korean War B-29 bombers, along with smaller B-26s, were sitting ducks for challenging, high-performing Chinese MiG-15 jets appearing in the Yalu vicinity early November 1950.

Pre-Sabre American jets operating in Korea, the F-80 Shooting Star, F-82, F-84, carrier-based F9F Pantherjets, and World War II-vintage P-51 propeller-driven Mustangs, proved no match for MiGs. Although deployed for duty in 1951, new medium B-47 Stratojet bombers never made it to Korea, nor did massive B-36s. Perennial workhorse B-52s were not yet in production.

The reader does well to appreciate relative combat advantages and disadvantages of piston-driven and jet aircraft. P-51 Mustangs, along with most propeller planes, needed much shorter runways than jet counterparts. Very few Korean airfields had the 6- to 7,000-foot runways needed by jets. And many Korean runways were in rough condition, easier on take-offs and landings for the slower, older planes.

Jets also consumed much more fuel per mile than gasoline-engined craft, meaning propeller planes had significantly longer cruising ranges. Especially when leaving from Japanese airfields, Korea-bound jets often had little "time on target" from which to release weapons and fire guns. Even with wing tanks in place and an extra 150-200 miles of range, jet pilots usually had concern about running out of fuel.

Many American jets "jumped" by MiGs in North Korea's "MiG Alley," between the Yalu and Chongchon rivers in northwest North Korea, could not engage in air-to-air combat because of low fuel. MiGs suffered an even greater limited range problem, which assured that Manchurian-based squadrons could not venture near or beyond the 38th Parallel (MAP 10).

Slower speed of propeller aircraft also allowed easier target identification in close support ground missions. Mustang and Corsair pilots proved adept at dropping munitions on enemy targets very close to friendly troops. To their disadvantage, slower airspeeds made such planes vulnerable to enemy small-arms and machine-gun fire, which exacted a heavy toll in pilots, crews, and equipment.

Futrell reported 1,041 Far East Air Force Korean War planes and crews shot down by enemy fire, along with 945 lost to "non-enemy causes." Air-to-air combat claimed 147 US/UN aircraft, enemy groundfire 816. Seventy-eight planes and crews succumbed to "unknown enemy action." FEAF human toll included "1,144 dead, 306 wounded, 214 prisoners of war repatriated under the armistice agreement, and 35 men whom Reds continued to hold in captivity" until May 1955.[16] The same ground fire vulnerability and lethality manifested in Vietnam.

HELICOPTERS IN KOREA

On July 22, 1950, with Korean War less than a month old, the US Eighth Army Surgeon requested helicopter evacuation of seriously wounded troops from front-line aid stations to Mobile Army Surgical hospitals at Miryang and Pusan. By end of August, helicopters had evacuated 83 soldiers, who according to the Eighth Army Surgeon, "would never have survived a 10- to 14-hour trip by ambulance to a field hospital."[17]

Korea's alternating rice-paddy and mountain terrain well suited helicopter operations. Fixed wing aircraft had difficult-to-impossible times landing in such areas. The small H-5 chopper carried only pilot and technician and was fitted with "external litter capsules" on either side to hold two wounded soldiers. Its radius of operation was 85 miles. By March 1951 larger Sikorsky H-19 helicopters arrived in Korea, capable of internally holding eight litter (stretcher) patients or 10 ambulatory patients, plus pilot and medical technician. H-19s had a 120-mile operational radius.[18]

Slowness of helicopter travel, especially at takeoff and landing, made such venue highly dangerous to pilots, crews, and passengers. Communist small-arms and machinegun fire made for treacherous going.

July 1952 monsoon rains, followed by severe flooding, proved the worth of helicopter evacuation on another level. High waters trapped over 700 UN troops in dangerous forward positions. Helicopters saved them all.[19]

Robert Futrell told that, "1,690 United States Air Force (USAF) airmen went down in enemy territory" during the Korean War. While many crashed and did not survive, the Air Rescue Service, using helicopters and amphibious planes, managed to save 170 pilots and crew from behind enemy lines. Air Rescue also provided aeromedical evacuation of 8,598 wounded ground-fighters, most from front-line positions.[20]

In only the first four months of Korean war, the full airlift effort carried 24,496 patients for prompt treatment. In the face of brutal November-December 1950 Arctic temperatures, twin-engine C-47 cargo planes flew an additional "4,700 wounded or frost-bitten soldiers and Marines from Communist-besieged airstrips at Hagaru-ri and Koto-ri" for care at South Korean or Japanese hospitals.[21]

NURSE HEROES

Army and Air Force flight nurses played crucial roles in caring for airlifted seriously wounded.[22] In the difficult aftermath of 1950 – 51 Chinese invasion and counterattack, C-47 interiors were fitted with litter racks stacked three-high on either side, along most of the fuselage length. The C-47 could transport 26 patients, the larger C-54 held 36 – the huge C-124 Globemaster 127 litter patients or 200 walking wounded.

Nurses and medical technicians manned these flights night and day in all types of challenging weather, shuttling within Korea, from Korea to Japan, and within Japan, commonly flying three round trips per day and "literally working themselves to exhaustion."[23] Unheated cabins, air turbulence, engine noise and vibration, and care demands of wounded made for great nurse stress. These female health professionals earned life-saving hero status in the Korean War.

Time proved of greatest essence for troops suffering head, abdominal, or sucking chest wounds. Rapidity of medical treatment "determined whether these patients would live or die." Remarkably, and owing largely to helicopter evacuation at or near the front, many of these wounded "found themselves in surgery within one hour."[24]

Counting multiple flights experienced by some patients, the USAF's 315th Air Division evacuated

311,673 battle-wounded and sick US servicemen within and from Korea during the War. As Futrell remarked with justifiable satisfaction, "Aeromedical evacuation played a large part in reducing the Korean War death rate of wounded to one-half the rate of World War II, and one-quarter the rate of World War I."[25]

'ARSENAL OF DEMOCRACY' DEMISE

Truman's military austerity program well played into the hands of Communism's global revolutionary ambitions. By the late 1940s, the USSR's yearly combat aircraft production outstripped that of America by 7,000 to 1,200.[26] During and after World War II, scores of secret American aircraft features had either been stolen by the Russians, or purchased from the US Patent Office in Washington for a pittance. Reds bought US patents by the crate. The "Russian way" was to copy the "American way." Judging by troublesome and numerous MiG-15s, Soviet pilots, and ground crews sent to Chinese allies, the plan worked exceedingly well.

The MiG's distinctive, high-performance tail assembly came straight from American drawing boards, courtesy of spy William Perl, college friend of executed traitor Julius Rosenberg and one of relatively few spies tried and convicted in court. As Katherine Sibley related, Perl, a Columbia University PhD, "provided Soviets test reports of advanced aircraft and helicopters." A "US Air Force aerodynamics expert claimed publicly in 1953 that Perl's information was used in development of the USSR's new MiG fighter, alleg[ing] that the unusual MiG tail was specifically a US development along with other features."[27]

MiG threat in Korea gave the lie to protestations of Red military and industrial espionage innocence in America. The Truman political line held Red spying an *external,* not internal, threat.[28] With press cover, Truman Administration leftists created and sustained this patently false and absurd public position. But American pilots and crews died by hundreds because of this treason. Red genius at penetration knew no greater reward.

PUBLIC AWARENESS: WHERE ART THOU?

President Truman's culpability in running down the US military is finely illustrated in comparing Korean War-era Communist and American air forces. Vaunted American industrial potential appeared to have vanished overnight. Frank Futrell documented 1,830 planes in the 1952 Chinese Communist Air Force, including 1,000 high-performance jet fighters. At the same time, Soviet Far East air strength reached another 5,360 aircraft.

By November 1952 Moscow gifted the PRC 100 current-production IL-28 jet bombers, all based in Manchuria. The US had not a single jet bomber serving in Korea! In Futrell's words, *"The Communist air order of battle in the Far East not only dwarfed the United Nations air forces, but the Reds also possessed more modern planes than did the United Nations air forces."*[29]

Reds carried a very big stick in air power. Powerful attacking flights could be unleashed "against United Nations forces at any time."[29] No wonder American leaders balked at attacking Red Chinese territory, or at actually winning the Korean War. Not one American in 10,000 knows the truth of Red air muscle and post-World War II US military weakness. The folks are good enough for dying and maiming, but not for *knowing.* Shame on American media for censoring this vital War truth and covering up Truman incompetence.

The 300/350-bomb US nuclear arsenal might have struck in case Soviets mass-invaded Western Europe, but otherwise America was militarily spent prior to, and during much of, the Korean War. As proven by sparse allocation of state-of-the-art aircraft, even in bloody War Korea remained a poor sister to Washington, never that important to President, Joint Chiefs, and most top leaders.[30]

Per standard practice, the press never jumped on pronounced US Euro-centrism and second-class relegation of Far Eastern peoples. Nor did it pound the issue of disgraceful American military unpreparedness. Not even heavy spilling of blood could bring truth to light. Someone in Washington let his country down in a very big way by neglecting the Constitutional responsibility to provide for the national defense. "Bold and decisive" Commander in Chief Truman received a pass on that one.

WAR ON HARRY'S SHOESTRING

Regarding Korean tactical air support, which meant bomb, rocket, machine gun, and small cannon fire to suppress enemy infantry and armor and assist friendly advance, "the most effective ground-air support was demonstrated by the Marines, whose ground and air units were *accustomed to training together* (italics added)."[31] The same held in the war against Japan.

Marine Korean combat veteran and author Lee Ballenger described delays in close air support of infantry when requests for such help had to be made to a general air operations center. A study of 87 Marine requests for air interdiction in 1952 found 42 resulted in airstrikes, while 45 did not, a 52% no-assistance outcome. Average wait time for successful requests was 3.5 hours.[32] Such delay obviously did not meet necessity for timely help, and just as surely reflected insufficient Korean allocation of air support manpower and equipment.

Again, American troops paid a heavy price in life and limb for leadership failure. Media-favored "Give-'em-hell Harry" characterization boiled down in Korea to presidential timidity and half-heartedness.

Close support air operations commonly featured daytime attacks with napalm canisters, 500-pound bombs, machine gun strafing, and rocket clusters. Unfortunately, for typical 1952 – 53 small-unit actions, flights were usually limited to four attacking aircraft. Numerous reports document delivery of such strikes to enemy fortifications and troop concentrations. US infantry typically attacked on aircraft departure, all too often in the teeth of potent enemy resistance.

Doubling or tripling aircraft numbers might have destroyed more enemy troops and strong points and saved many American lives. There is no doubt the 150-mile MLR generated much more requests for air help than could be accommodated.

Figure 50. President Franklin Roosevelt, 1944. Personal White House physician Dr. McIntyre pronounced President "in excellent health" prior to 1944 presidential campaign. Other insiders knew he was rapidly failing. *National Archives.*

Figure 51. Averell Harriman receives sincere thanks for diplomatic services from President Truman. Secretary of State Acheson (left), Defense Secretary George Marshall. *National Archives.*

Figure 52. Sidney Hillman, president Amalgamated Clothing Workers of America 1914-46. Vice-president Congress of Industrial Organizations (CIO). Made Sen. Harry Truman vice-presidential candidate 1944. One of America"s most powerful men, 100% socialist. Wife Bessie also leftist labor advocate. *aflcio.org.*

Figure 53. CPUSA chairman Earl Browder worked closely with Sidney Hillman turning out big-city and labor vote in Franklin Roosevelt elections. Announced broad American acceptance of Communist principles and people after "consummation of our efforts at Yalta." Served as spy recruiter for Soviet intelligence. *Paul Dorsey/The LIFE Pictures Collection/gettyimages.*

Figure 54. Browder and James Ford in 'farmers-workers unite" pitch. Sowing discord was in their genes. Hammer-sickle Red symbolism out of public favor with Korean War. *Wikipedia.*

Figure 55. President-elect Eisenhower (in parka) reviews top-performing ROK 1ˢᵗ Division, Dec. 1952 Korea visit. *National Archives.*

Figure 56. Ike about to inspect US 2ⁿᵈ Infantry Division, Dec. 1952 Korea. "Small battles on small hills will not end this war." *National Archives.*

Figure 57. President-Elect Eisenhower shares chow with Army Sgt. Virgil Hutcherson, Co. B, 15th Inf. Reg., 3rd Infantry Division, Korea. 'What might this be?' *National Archives.*

Figure 58. Marine warrior Col. Lewis 'Chesty' Puller, commander 1st Regiment Inchon landing, drive to Seoul, Chosin Reservoir campaign, fighting retreat. Carried Caesar"s *Commentaries* in field jacket. "He liked to fight." *National Archives.*

Figure 59. Future California US Sen. Alan Cranston (left), presidential candidate John Kennedy and wife Jackie, Sen. Arthur Clapper. Cranston a wealthy, big-time pro-Red Internationalist. *Wikipedia.*

Figure 60. Winston Churchill held FDR's failure to address World War II political issues, and Roosevelt -Truman transition, global disasters to freedom and peace. Great leader also had keen sense of humor. Lady Astor once told him, "If you were my husband, I would give you poison." Churchill replied, "Madam, if I was your husband, I would take it!" *Wikipedia.*

Figure 61. Whittaker Chambers (center) during Alger Hiss controversy. Suave, Harvard lawyer, prominent State Department official Hiss versus pudgy former Soviet spy in America who told truth about vast Red conspiracy. *National Archives.*

Figure 62. Super-leftist David Lilienthal, first Chairman, US Atomic Energy Commission, circa 1947. Proposed full sharing nuclear secrets and materials with Soviet Russia, joining Dean Acheson and Robert Oppenheimer. Soviet nuclear equality "to provide firmest basis of security." Senseless largess placed American people under continual threat of nuclear/thermonuclear destruction. *Soviet interests clearly came before American.* Wife Red activist. *National Archives.*

Figure 63. Distinguished jurist, Harvard academician, Associate Supreme Court Justice Felix Frankfurter. Leftist champion, patron, political advisor, close friend to Dean Acheson. *National Archives.*

Figure 64. Mao chats with Red propagandist Anna Louise Strong, Israel Epstein (far left), Treasury Deparment's Solomon Adler (far right) and V. Frank Coe (2nd from right). Epstein lived in China, worked for *New York Times* and *United Press*, great friend of Chinese Communist leaders. Remained loyal to Reds even after 5-year imprisonment (1968-73) during Cultural Revolution. Died age 90 in 2005, PRC leadership hailed him as "great, old friend of Chinese people." *Wikipedia.*

Figure 65. Communists Israel Epstein, Solomon Adler, Mao, and Frank Coe. Adler and Coe left US for PRC early 1950s. All showed true loyalty. *Wikipedia.*

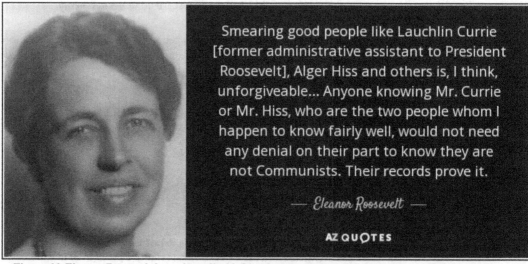

Smearing good people like Lauchlin Currie [former administrative assistant to President Roosevelt], Alger Hiss and others is, I think, unforgiveable... Anyone knowing Mr. Currie or Mr. Hiss, who are the two people whom I happen to know fairly well, would not need any denial on their part to know they are not Communists. Their records prove it.

— *Eleanor Roosevelt* —

AZ QUOTES

Figure 66. Eleanor Roosevelt brought radical leftist-Communist "good folks" to live at White House, backed them at Congressional committee hearings, supported them financially, generally played role of radical-socialist godmother. *Wikipedia.*

Figure 67. President George H.W. Bush presents Medal of Freedom, highest civilian award, to exceptional diplomat, Soviet specialist, and author George Kennan. Barbara Bush looks on. *alamy.com.*

Figure 68. State Department China hand John S. Service, 1960. Great friend of Chinese Communism. *National Archives.*

Figure 69. PRC Foreign Minister Zhou En-lai greets retired Mr. and Mrs. John S. Service. Chinese Communists long-remembered favors done. *National Archives.*

Figure 70. Roosevelt, Stalin at Yalta, Feb. 1945. Stalin cements eastern, central European conquests, massive Soviet Army invasion Japanese-occupied North China, Manchuria, Korea. European and Asian power balances swing toward Moscow-Beijing. *National Archives.*

Figure 71. Soviet Army blankets North China, Manchuria, Korea. Chinese People's Army and political commissars inundate territories. Moscow policy prevails in Washington: China goes Red. (PPSh burp guns shown, deadly at close range in Korea). *National Archives.*

Figure 72. Walter Lippman, Internationalist, very influential Washington media guru with contacts throughout Government. Knew Red power in US foreign policy. *National Archives.*

Figure 73. Harry Hopkins (center-left tall man), power second only to Roosevelt; Stalin and Soviet Field Marshal. Molotov in background. Soviet intelligence held Hopkins '*nash,* one of ours.' Living and working at White House, Hopkins assured Soviets received all atomic bomb secrets, uranium, heavy water, every material for making nuclear weapons. *National Archives.*

Figure 74. Sick Roosevelt reports to Congress and people on Yalta results, March 1, 1945. "No more spheres of interests, balances of power, Asian matters not discussed." This after secretly requesting huge Soviet Army invasion Far East Asian mainland, granting Stalin vital sphere of interest! Roosevelt died April 12. Other secret deals with Soviets then came to light, to President Truman's consternation. *National Archives.*

Figure 75. Joint Chiefs Chairman Gen. Omar Bradley swears in Gen. J. Lawton Collins as Army Chief of Staff. Air Force Chief of Staff Gen. Hoyt Vandenberg to Bradley"s left. Collins: Red Chinese reserves "un-opposable, best US can expect in Korea is military stalemate. We can't win." *TrumanLibrary.org.*

Figure 76. Lt. Gen.Walton Walker, brave Commander Eighth Army start of Korean War until Dec. 23, 1950 vehicle death. *National Archives.*

Figure 77. US Eighth Army Commander Gen. James Van Fleet. "Military victory in Korea attainable, not terribly difficult, without nuclear weapons." Lost son to Korean combat. *pinterest.com.*

Figure 78. Marshal Peng (left), Mao Zedong in Beijing after Korean War end. Peng became PRC Defense Minister (1954-59), falling out with Chairman over 'Great Leap Forward' economic policy. *Wikipedia.*

Figure 79. Marshal Peng brought in chains to Beijing by Red Guards during Cultural Revolution, suffered great humiliation and death. *Wikipedia.*

Figure 80. Father Emil Kapaun of Kansas, Army Chaplain giving great spiritual and material aid to US POWs captured in 1950 PLA First Phase Offensive. Died of barbaric treatment 1951. Posthumously received Medal of Honor from President Obama. *Wikipedia.*

Figure 81. Korean War result: today"s economic-military behemoth People's Republic of China. PLA goose-step precision, while muscle-flexing in South China Sea. *i.telegraph.co.uk.*

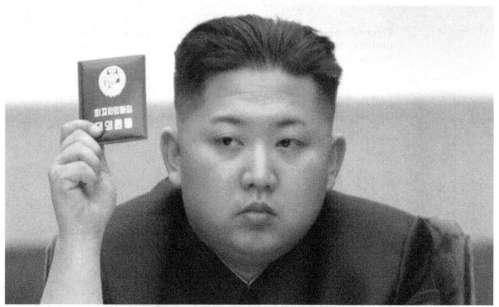

Figure 82. North Korea's Chairman Kim Jong Un, grandson of founding leader Kim Il Sung. Hostile regime's regular threats of nuclear attack on America and South Korea prove a deadly important, lasting Korean War outcome. Today we pay for failure to use available American military power to gain Korean victory. *Wikipedia.*

Lesson: poor US war leadership has disastrous consequences to future security and peace.

Chapter 32: Evaluating Washington War Leadership

"A diplomat's words must have no relation to actions – otherwise what kind of diplomacy is it? Words are one thing, actions another. Good words are a concealment of bad deeds. Sincere diplomacy is no more possible than dry water or iron wood."[1]

– Joseph V. Stalin, quoted in Fehrenbach, This Kind of War.

Leftist revolutionary political decision-making has no regard for popular interests. Concepts are pitched on their usefulness in dragging down the reviled capitalist system. Wise war strategy, however, rests on the central question, "Will this idea work?"

Each war brings a unique set of circumstances that must be factored into a plan's chances for success.[2] With opening of peace negotiations and beginning of static war, stated Truman-Acheson Korean War strategy called for early conclusion of a peace agreement with Communists. In their minds, the public could be convinced this represented the best means of reducing risk of another world war, saving American lives, and cementing liberation of South Korea from Communist rule. Attention could then be refocused on strengthening Western European security. To some influential people in American government, peace talks also represented necessary salvation of Red China.

WASHINGTON PEACE TALKS: RESOUNDING LEADERSHIP FAILURE

As acknowledged in memoirs, Truman knew Communist China's November-December 1950 US Army rout had vastly inflated its prestige in Asia and throughout the world. Proletarian revolutionary arms had nearly destroyed the armed host of hated imperialist and world-oppressing America.

Mao soon gained a tighter grip on China; as dedicated field commander Marshal Peng eventually learned, no Communist leader valuing his life could dare challenge the Great Helmsman. Red revolutionaries in French Indo-China, soon to be Vietnam, felt emboldened. Across the globe, Reds and Internationalists received shots in the arm. Traditionalists in US

Government became dominated by fear of global Communist revolution.

For the sake of long-term Asian stability and American interests throughout the world, the dangerous situation had to be countered. It made political sense to militarily humble Mao's legions. But by May 1, 1951, all pertinent US Government agencies were on board with Truman's latest Korean policy.

Peace talks coupled with prohibition on major offensive warfare made Red Chinese military defeat impossible. American refusal to fight the PRC to a decision would have serious and lasting consequences.

The first war between America and world Communism brought other key factors impacting achievement of early Korean cease-fire. In Communist philosophy, people in general, and soldiers specifically, did not matter. Lives could be expended in battle without limit – only ultimate victory mattered. There would be no Red desire to reach early peace for the sole purpose of saving lives. Humanitarian motivation simply did not exist. This should bring decided advantage to Communist negotiation strategy and comparable UN disadvantage.

No doubt could exist in American leader minds about the above reality and its implications. Tit-for-tat killing, grinding "war of attrition," would heavily play into enemy hands and should be assiduously avoided. Yet this was precisely the game Truman and Acheson chose to play! American leadership seemed bereft of common sense, a very common outcome when politics rules all. Collective Washington leader wisdom in this matter could easily fit on a pin-point.

IGNORING KNOWLEDGABLE DIPLOMATS WHO KNEW BETTER

Before, during, and after World War II, many Americans had gained valuable first-hand experience dealing with Soviets. Unable to travel Moscow streets without official escort, not permitted travel opportunities outside the capital, American diplomats learned realities of police-state life and the frustration of dealing with naturally suspicious and distrusting Russians.

Fruitless, 49-session US-Russian talks on Korea, Red-imposed Berlin blockade, and struggle to keep Greece and Turkey in the Western orbit, reinforced presence of opposite Communist and Western value systems. Finally, the American people were beginning to learn truth about the world contest and trouble to come.

As American diplomats proved time after time, in and out of Soviet Russia, reaching *any* agreement with Reds entailed storm and stress. Communist deliberations featured resistance, hostility, paranoia, and xenophobia.[3] What would take reasonable people a day to agree on would take Reds months of wrangling. This backdrop, added to a Korean battlefield situation requiring time to stabilize, regroup and rearm CCF, should have made clear to Truman and Acheson an upcoming *delay-centered* Red negotiation strategy. This conclusion required no sophisticated thinking. Acheson's years of personal Lend-Lease dealings with Moscow officials alone should have nailed that point home.

BLINDNESS TO PEACE NEGOTIATION REALITY

Since prospect of more combat losses didn't sway Communists, Truman and Acheson had to consider motivating factors tending to induce Reds to seek early peace. Acts of goodwill, such as humanitarian aid to civilians under Red dominion, had to be ruled out – Marxists regarded them as signs of weakness to be exploited. The idea of US material support for China and North Korea in the form of food, medicine, and reconstruction would be politically suicidal should word leak out. Chinese Reds had already expressed disdain for US attempts at trading a United Nations seat for Korean concessions.

Five US diplomats highly experienced in Soviet affairs, former ambassadors to the Soviet Union William Bullitt, Laurence Steinhardt, Adm. William Standley, Averell Harriman and George Kennan, attested to impossibility of banking goodwill with Moscow. Repeated personal encounter made them experts in the naturally contrary nature of Kremlin officials. Their valuable understanding meant nothing to Roosevelt, who ran his own foreign relations show. Except for Harriman, there is no evidence Acheson and Truman consulted the other richly-experienced participants in Communist methodology regarding the wise course in Korea.

Not a single word is found in Truman and Acheson memoirs, works by generals Bradley, Collins, and Ridgway, Robert Beisner's Acheson biography, nor David McCullough's extensive Truman tome, about motivating Reds to accept Korean peace terms. Naturally, given abject Truman Administration failure at concluding peace, the subject was off-limits.

Equally disturbing is Truman's failure to add *political* ends to Korean negotiations, instead seeking only military settlement to end fighting. Neglecting all-important political factors is akin to ignoring malignant cell clusters during cancer treatment.

The president walked the same path as predecessor Roosevelt in not addressing major political differences between combatants. D. Clayton James referred to "This second failure within a decade to link military and nonmilitary objectives [as] one of the key factors that would lead the US into its tragic entanglement in Vietnam."[4]

DEARTH OF COMMON SENSE

Given potent challenges in the realm of Communist diplomacy, success in Korean peace talks meant all US/UN negotiation strengths must be marshaled. Every valuable, useful personal asset should be employed in realistic policy formulation and implementation. To ignore the wisdom of credible and extensive experience invited the worst trouble.

Combat pressure appeared to be the only realistic leverage to encourage Chinese to quickly end fighting. Yet, beyond reason and sound judgment, the President and chief war advisor Acheson elected to drop that lever from their tool kit. What should have been the essence of peace negotiations was, and is, historically unspoken, and non-existent in popular Korean War understanding. It didn't make sense then, nor 65 years later.

FAILURE TO ADEQUATELY SUPPORT US/UN PEACE NEGOTIATORS

Truman and Acheson decided on truce negotiations to end the War, but did not give proper leadership support to the US peace team effort. Vice Adm. C. Turner Joy headed the UN delegation during the first 10 months of talks. He later reported,

> "The greatest handicap under which we negotiated was *the apparent reluctance or inability ... of Washington to give us firm and minimum positions which would be supported by national policy.* In other words, positions which we could carry through to the breaking point of negotiations if necessary" (italics added).[5]

James and Wells delicately acknowledged that "Truman's roles in beginning the truce talks and inadequately supporting Joy and his successor [Gen. Harrison] on the overall American policy picture leave him quite vulnerable to criticism."[5]

Left unsaid is Internationalism's dominant role in shaping US foreign and War policy. Secretary Acheson's political background is completely ignored as a causative factor in Korean War decisions. His firm adherence to globalist ideology equaled that of justices Holmes, Brandeis, Frankfurter, Cardozo, William O. Douglas, and key insiders Lilienthal, Lippman, Archibald MacLeish, the Rockefeller brothers, the Red spy host and the many sympathetic Government operatives. Open and powerful sentiment for giving Soviets atomic bomb secrets and production know-how is not connected to Korean War outbreak, a terrible historical omission.

Assessment of Truman-Acheson war leadership in April-July 1951 must bring a verdict of US over-eagerness for peace, and shallow understanding, if any, of Communist motivation and US need for decisive Chinese defeat. Though six years in office, it is easy to envision Truman lacking war management and foreign policy expertise. He routinely, even reflexively relied on Acheson's supposed wisdom. Could the apparently sharp-thinking, slick, arrogant cabinet official, referred to as a genius by at least one author, be a closet incompetent, especially in military matters? Or, given outlandish war actions and a political history of pro-Soviet sympathies, is there reasonable basis for questioning his loyalty to country?

HISTORICAL OBSERVATIONS ON LEADERSHIP – CLAY VESSELS AND NAKED EMPERORS

Perhaps a deeper historical perspective would offer needed wisdom in judging national leadership competence, and inclination to treason. Superb historian Barbara Tuchman generalized history as "the unfolding of miscalculations."[6] Foreign and war policies of Franklin Roosevelt offer a prime example.

Unwisely envisioning postwar harmony between the West and Soviet Union, Roosevelt staked the outcome of World War II on full satisfaction of Soviet territorial and material ambitions, in his mind assuring Stalin's cooperation in the new world order. Unfortunately for the world, thirty years of Bolshevik history taught the opposite. Charm didn't work on a hardened, murderous dictator and system of government. "Hardheaded common sense" and persistent application of moral law stood a chance, but Roosevelt left these at the door.[7] "Concession without reciprocation" represented unwavering policy toward Russia despite anti-American implications. Roosevelt regularly preached morality to Americans while practicing amorality dealing with Soviets. Horrendous world war did not bring peace and stability but world division into two hostile camps.

Tuchman noted how President Wilson's post-First World War "promises of a just peace and self-determination withered at the touch of hard realities," and the same promises and outcomes 26 years later with Roosevelt, "with even greater consequences."[8] The latter words are lethally radioactive in leftist academia and popular culture. FDR must be an object of unquestionable worship, not rational analysis. Reasoned *thinking* would expose the truth of gross leadership failure and must therefore be avoided.

Roosevelt's mess surely ranks as one of history's greatest leadership miscalculations. William Bullitt, once a close FDR friend, told that "Few errors more disastrous have ever been made by a president of the United States, and those citizens of the US who bamboozled the president into acting as if Stalin was a cross between Abraham Lincoln and Woodrow Wilson deserve a high place on an American role of dishonor."[9]

Grand whitewashing of Roosevelt's debacle by popular media and "correct" academia is unequaled in presidential annals and truly represents "history stood on its head." Free ride in the responsibility realm is capped by endless praise about Roosevelt's war leadership excellence and impressive monuments in Washington and New York City. Nothing could further defy truth. The political "180" is alive and well.

Media deception also lies at the heart of Cold War "contest" for world domination between Capitalism and Communism. There could be no other basis for contest. Who would choose mass murder, the barbaric gulag system, secret police running government, and epidemic paranoia? As attested by James Forrestal, the American press bent over backward for Communism, ever sympathetic and accessible.[10]

Then and now, objective history must yield to political imperative. The control mechanism includes public acceptance of behavioral mores of a truly alien, Soviet culture, imposed on the nation by a small, aggressive, politically-astute "secular-progressive" minority, true ideological heirs of Marx, Lenin, and Stalin.

OVERVALUING NATIONAL LEADERSHIP

Given 20th- century world-war outcomes and the following brief historical review, Americans have every right to cynicism regarding presidential promises, especially those related to war and peace. Bernard Brodie, well-versed on the failings of great people in these realms, shared the words of Swedish statesman Count Axel Oxenstierne (1583-1654) to his son: "Always remember with how little wisdom the world is governed."[11] Renowned Prussian general and military strategist Carl von Clausewitz (1780-1831) "had grown painfully accustomed to seeing stupidity in high places."[12] English political leader Robert Arthur Cecil, known as Lord Salisbury (1830-1903), similarly noted to the Viceroy of India in 1877, "No lesson seems to be so deeply inculcated by the experience of life as that you should never trust in experts."[13] President Truman himself referred to "People who are afraid to learn anything new, because then they wouldn't be experts anymore." Successor President Eisenhower characterized Western national leadership as "too timid, lazy, fearful, and overly concerned about personal careers."[14] Winston Churchill bemoaned failure to confront serious political issues with Soviets *before* end of World War II, while strong American and British armies remained in Europe.[15]

For all the pomp, circumstance, fawning adulation of office, and potent political skills of presidents and cabinet leaders, knowledge of historical precedent and experience in life-and-death foreign relations is often lacking. Constraints imposed by political supporters limit exercise of presidential options. Able to easily manipulate people within our system of government, presidents often fall short in trying to manage Communist and other totalitarian leaders holding opposite world views. Here domestic magic fails.

Franklin Roosevelt, Truman, John Kennedy, Lyndon Johnson, and Richard Nixon naively and unsuccessfully sought to modify Soviet, and war enemy, behaviors. They could not match up with murderous adversaries raised on constant-war mentalities and dominated by revolutionary fervor. Readers do well to appreciate the general Communist perception of inevitable war with Capitalism and barbarous ferocity of Bolshevik-type politics.

Given gross World War II political failures of Roosevelt and Truman, one thing is clear: reading of history was not among their passions. Roosevelt especially proved an intellectual lightweight, placing national interests and global power balances at whims of hunches and personal impulses.[16,17] He completely missed the mark in dealing with Stalin.

Supreme dilettante Roosevelt had no idea his every word and statement about Stalin were promptly relayed to Moscow, by multiple sources, no less. Venona cable traffic decrypters were shocked to discover all top-secret Roosevelt – Churchill messages winding up in the Generalissimo's lap. Stalin was always at least one step ahead. Charm school diplomacy stood no chance. The nation, and world, deserved far better.

INTIMATE RELATION OF WAR AND POLITICS

Our presidents might have learned and practiced the Clausewitz precept: "War is fundamentally a branch of politics."[18] There must be unity of war fighting with the political object(s) of that war. Any war must seek to accomplish defined political objectives, which could mean new governments, firming existing governments, inclusion in, formation of, or dissolution of politico-military alliances, or encouragement of true democracies. American leadership in World War II and the Korean War dismally failed to provide the "supreme war requirement" of timely, appropriate, and decisive *political direction* to combat commanders.[19] US Marine Gen. Victor Krulak emphasized the insufficiency of battlefield victory alone, and concurrent necessity of political and economic victory, to truly successful war outcome.[20]

Churchill knew the serious World War II political shortcomings of Roosevelt and Truman, rightly describing them as "tragic" to the cause of world democracy. The former Prime Minister, booted out of office at war's end, tellingly described the situation:

> "A deadly hiatus existed between the fading of President Roosevelt's strength and the growth of President Truman's grip of the vast world problem. In this melancholy void one president could not act while the other could not know. Indispensable political direction was lacking at the moment when it was most needed. The United States stood on the scene of victory, master of world fortunes, but without a true and coherent design. Thus this climax of apparently measureless success was to me a most unhappy time."[21]

Despite liberal shunning of these words, it is obvious wise Churchill knew the score, the trouble ahead. Few Americans had this appreciation, a state of deficiency conducive to deceptive, incompetent, anti-American leadership. Internationally-beholden presidents are hard-pressed to incorporate basic pro-American necessities and facts into their repertoires of action. Many of their key supporters are anti-American!

Until the Truman-imposed "tie" in Korea, usual presidential practice viewed war as an athletic event to be "won," instead of as deadly business that must achieve highly-defined political and economic ends.

Neglect of these results portends national and international tragedy. Full national commitment and great US military victory in World War II brought half the world under Communist domination, the greatest testament possible to political failure. Authors James and Wells used overly sensitive language to express gaping war leadership deficiency: "The Anglo-American alliance of World War II attained total victory but *dubious postwar political gains*" (italics added).[22] Authors walk on eggshells in timidly describing global calamity.

BEWARE LONGEVITY OF PRESIDENTIAL DECISIONS

A number of important lessons emerge. As proven by today's North Korean dilemma, presidential decisions in matters of war may have very long-lasting effects quite negative to citizen and national safety. Clear public discussions of positive and negative aspects of war decisions are uncommon. Most people are woefully uninformed. Considerations of right and wrong usually yield to political expediency. Presidential leadership may be focused on maintaining political power through frequent and gross lying, not on making decisions that promote national security. Politically-disconnected groups are apt to be placed in positions of danger and suffer the most harm from misguided national leadership.

As top leaders, Truman and Acheson are also strongly indicted for not developing a "back-up plan" given failure of their rapid peace negotiations settlement premise. There had to be strictly-allotted time for conclusion of peace, beyond which a new strategy would be employed. No evidence exists of any "Plan B." The failure smacks of leadership amateurism. Apparently, Eisenhower did bring a Plan B to the table, a coming subject of discussion.

A REQUISITE OF FINE LEADERSHIP

A final Clausewitz observation is in order. Military and civilian leadership excellence entails possession of "instinctive judgment," or judgment in the face of uncertainty. This unique quality of true professionals comes only after broad experience and reflection. Each "war is rich in individual phenomena ... an unexplored sea, full of rocks ... around which the general must steer in dark night."[23] While bright, aggressive, combat-hardened generals such as Ridgway, Van Fleet, and Mark Clark possessed instinctive battlefield judgment, military amateurs such as war-inexperienced secretaries of state and defense cannot develop it and are unfit to dominate military decision-making. The Defense Reorganization Act of 1947 mandating unprecedented civilian control of war-making, so avidly sought by Internationalists as a control lever, came back in Korea and Vietnam to impale the American people on deadly incompetence.

JOINT CHIEFS – MISSING IN ACTION

This book intentionally leaves out US Joint Chiefs of Staff from many discussions on Korean War leadership. Chiefs at that time simply did not exercise true war leadership. Organizationally, the new 1947 defense scheme cut the legs off military leadership. As admitted by Gen. Bradley, the newly-enshrined National Security Council usurped a good degree of JCS policymaking.

Clearly, the main Joint Chiefs function was, and is, to lend congressional and public credibility to executive-level military policies and actions. Then, and today, Chiefs served somewhere between smartly-dressed greeters and star- and ribbon-bedecked messenger boys, going wherever the Truman-Acheson tides sent them.

Only a few years after Korea, junior- and mid-level Pentagon officers, unerringly sensing leadership reality, would characterize Joint Chiefs as "The Five Silent Men."

It is easy to agree with Brodie's contention that true "independence of thinking is always rare in any profession ..., but the military provides some of the most barren soil of all for its nurture – despite frequent assertions to the contrary."[24] Korean-era Chiefs failed to bring any mental intelligence, innovation, or true leadership to the table, functioning as wet rags on handles wielded by their bosses. The esteemed military virtue of courage seemed to have escaped them. If they *had* stepped forward, Acheson would likely have squashed them like bugs. Truman did not like generals and admirals, and also declined to step forward in their defense.

So ranks and pensions remained safe, along with public perception of shiny chiefs as "trusted, wise, seasoned warriors." They looked so impressive!

Exceptional author H.R. McMaster rightly pegged the true JCS role in greasing the skids of public acceptance of Vietnam War national military policy.[25] Nothing had changed since Korea, no lessons learned in Washington. Surely the Korean example provided educational value in highlighting the fifth-wheel military leader status in Washington's political hierarchy.

Students in service academies, officer candidate schools, and military command programs would benefit from knowing the spinelessness of Korean- and Vietnam-era Chiefs. The American people should know the same. Evidence indicates US military leadership dropped the Korean-lessons ball partly due to general embarrassment over Korean War performance best ignored in the classroom. War-related US military education after 1953 will be discussed shortly.

Omar Bradley's replacement as Army Chief of Staff, Gen. Collins, swallowed the nauseous Truman-Acheson line of Chinese unbeatability, groveling in print before his masters at America's great fortune in having an "honorable" war exit. But what is more honorable in war than victory? Washington civilian and military leaders *chose* to ignore "the terrible state to which the erstwhile triumphant Chinese enemy had been reduced."[26] How different than the recent smashing of Germany, Italy, and Japan, a war with full Internationalist backing (only after Hitler attacked the Soviet Union).

Surely it lay upon Ridgway and Chiefs to educate civilian superiors on battlefield reality. As a number of authors stressed, "The US/UN military situation in May-June 1951 could not have been better."[26] Red China's "two best field armies" had their time of heady victory but ended up crushed. Of course, strict US policy granting sanctuary from attack to all Chinese territory allowed unmolested building of numerous People's reserve forces and ready march into Korea.

But sending in new hordes could not be an inviting prospect: risk of failure stood tall, unlike their opening gambit. As shown by Third and Fourth Field army defeat, prospect of new and massive Chinese losses again beckoned. China would strain to even establish a new line in North Korea's middle reaches. Conditions surely favored a 100-mile UN advance to the North's "narrow waist" between Sojoson Bay on the west and the eastern Tongjoson Bay, roughly the Wonsan-Pyongyang line, a "better place to stop"[27] (MAP 10).

Continuation of the UN mobile offensive meant forcing China to "to pay a heavy price for continuing the war. *What we did by halting our offensive was to make that price dirt cheap*" (italics added).[28] Instead of having to create whole new armies to replace the decimated Third and Fourth, Chinese could reinforce whatever structure remained of original forces, a far easier job.[28] Joint Chiefs had to know this reality, along with the unprecedented absurdity of Truman-Acheson war leadership.

We search Korean War literature in vain for evidence of JCS resistance to the new war direction. Chiefs' acceptance of flawed policy meant acquiescence in needless shedding of American blood. Loyalty to Truman trumped Constitutional oath, professional ethics, and personal morality. Chiefs were ultimately loyal to themselves.

The "Five Silent Men" example could not fail to be noted by officers down the chain of command. Author-warrior T.R. Fehrenbach quoted a Korean proverb: "The water downstream will not be clear if the water upstream is muddied."[29] Since organizational standards of performance are set from the top, a clear message had been sent: the "smart" officer thinks of himself before those under him. Military career "success" means playing the same political tricks used by civilians. Institutional military leadership had been heavily politicized. Nothing could be more destructive to professional leadership standards of honesty, loyalty, integrity, and discipline, Sun Tzu's ancient concepts of proper military command.

The US proved very accommodating to the People's Republic. A reeling enemy was allowed back in the game, a contest now of *their* choice – endless negotiation and war of attrition. American interests took a back seat, a common outcome. Truman and Acheson well carried on Roosevelt's pro-Red policy of "concession without reciprocation." For foreign powers, even hostile Communist ones, there was nothing so sweet as having friends in Government.

Chapter 33: Politics, Military Failure, and Treason

"We neglected to plan for contingencies both foreseeable and probable."[1]

- Gen. Matthew B. Ridgway, The Korean War.

An intimate of New Deal government and Harvard-educated lawyer, Dean Acheson served four years under Roosevelt and Truman as Assistant Secretary and Undersecretary of State before appointment and confirmation as Secretary. Close friend, Supreme Court Justice Felix Frankfurter, served as academic and political patron.

Politically, Acheson was an Internationalist; personally, a first-rank elitist. He knew everything better than everyone. He co-authored, with fellow liberal insider David Lilienthal, the 1946-47 US policy paper on control of atomic energy, the "Acheson-Lilienthal Report," favoring sharing of all "secret" information with the Soviet Union as "the firmest basis of security."[2]

Incredibly, the paper pitched Soviet possession of nuclear weapons as favorable to America and the West. A great many Manhattan Project atomic scientists shared this view. They weren't working for the United States, but "for the world." Actually, many such scientists favored Soviet interests over American.

While surely best for Soviet security, the brazenly wrong-headed stance could only mean big trouble for America. Russia's first atomic bomb explosion in August 1949 directly served to bring on Korean War.

A sharing philosophy may have been tenable should opposing global forces and ideologies be amenable to compromise. But Acheson and Lilienthal had to know the antipodal nature of Communism to Judeo-Christian moral principles. Objective reality, truth, right and wrong, and rationality did not exist for Reds. Reasonable assessment of this misguided and highly dangerous policy includes motivation to hurt America while helping Soviets.

Unparalleled Soviet specialist George Kennan believed that, given inherent, unceasing, and readily expressed Communist hatred of Capitalism, encouraging Reds to develop atomic bombs posed great danger to American safety. *Thousands* of Marxist-sympathetic ideologues masquerading as loyal Americans worked within and without US Government to favor Moscow at Washington expense. As Acheson stated in memoirs, Capitalistic nationalism drove world war and must be opposed. Internationalists viewed Communism as a global counter-balance to dreaded American hegemony, so embracing, along with justices Holmes and Brandeis, "proletarian rule, the wave of the future." Today, as judged by legions of professed socialist revolutionaries backing their champion Sen. Sanders, domestic anti-Americanism is culturally and politically more powerful than ever.

Acheson recommended Lilienthal's appointment as first Atomic Energy Commission Chairman, a post held from 1946-50. These years corresponded to lax security at American atomic energy facilities (disturbing continuation of the Manhattan Project's nuclear open-door policy), internal nuclear production atrophy, and left-mandated Russian catch-up. The latter accomplishment depended on putting US nuclear development in neutral gear, just what happened under Truman and Lilienthal.

American nuclear secrets were anathema to Internationalists. How dare the US withhold anything from Soviets after their staggering sacrifices in defeating Nazi Germany? Of course, Moscow-Berlin alliance precipitating World War II should be ignored. Wartime US Ambassador to the USSR Joseph R. Davies told the world Moscow had every right to spy on the Manhattan Project and deserved full benefit of American knowledge, describing what actually happened from 1942-45 and after.

However, it was not enough for Moscow to receive every form of US physical help in building atomic bombs, including provision of uranium, necessary rare metals, and whole factories devoted to nuclear bomb building. A two-pronged approach to nuclear parity meant putting brakes on US atomic weapon development.[3] The powerful left must control the cache and distribute the largess. The US military was not permitted to hold nuclear weapons, only the civilian AEC. This is course made it difficult to train with and use such weapons in a timely manner against the Russian enemy, the whole point. Former Secretary of State Henry Kissinger joined Dwight Eisenhower in believing that only the threat of nuclear response could stop Red invasion of Western Europe. Moscow enjoyed at least a 30-to-1 ground troop advantage there over the West!

In fascinating, matter-of-fact commentary, politically-correct historian Robert Dallek told that, "Roosevelt had known for almost a year since February 1943 that the Russians were aware of American work on a bomb and *were receiving secret information on its development from agents in the United States*" (italics added).[4] Judging by Dallek's assertion and unimpeded Lend-Lease flow of uranium and all nuclear hardware to Russia, Soviet nuclear espionage obviously did not bother the President.

The Acheson-Lilienthal document called for America to build nuclear power plants in the Soviet Union. As it turned out, Reds didn't need them – they built their own. Also, on Truman's watch, and despite formal export restrictions, the FBI documented US shipments of "secret" nuclear hardware to Russia, revealed by sworn Congressional testimony of Special Agent Robert Lamphere.[5] Soviet raiding of Atomic Energy Commission supplies had to take place courtesy of AEC Chairman Lilienthal and friends. To leftists this meant "furthering the cause of America's 'firm security.'" To Reds, facts and objective reality meant nothing. What really counted, of course, was Motherland security.

UNTHINKABLE BUT LOGICAL – ACHESON A BAD GUY

After much consideration of Acheson's Korean War-related actions, rife with mismanagement, military incompetence, and lack of common sense, the author believes a streak of disloyalty hid within his undeniable strong leftist credentials, motivating actions contrary to American interests. Despite limited memoir statements on evils of Marxism, and use of Biblical quotations, Acheson perfectly fit the mold of pro-Communist government insider. Animus to traditional America reflected the elitist, Harvard, US-critical Internationalist philosophy. Self-viewed "head above it all" mentality blended well with frequent display of *chutzpah* and class-distinction-driven social philosophy.

Acheson's autobiography contains a chapter entitled "Attack of the Primitives," his description for the American majority. (In radical leftist ideology, 'primitives' are not to be confused with 'proletarians,' the 'suffering, brutally-oppressed workers and laborers.' Contempt for common folk joined revulsion at Capitalist oppression of labor, a strong leftist theme.) The Secretary and minions stood as perfect American counterparts to the hundreds-if-not-thousands-strong Cambridge cadre of devoted Communists. As in England, many American establishment youth had gone Red.

Given the strong light shined on him as Secretary of State, a contrast to relatively sheltered Assistant- and Undersecretary of State roles, Acheson did what he could for beloved comrades. Besides nuclear largess to America's prime opponent, Acheson helped supervise a strongly pro-Communist State Department stance toward China. His self-serving, monumental 1949 White Paper detailing reasons for China's "unavoidable loss" to Communism brims with selective fact-finding and deceit meant to deflect heat from embarrassing and costly American failure. Highly critical of Nationalist China, the paper served as a lightning rod for accusations of Truman Administration "softness on Communism."[6]

A number of explanations account for Acheson's failure to press for military victory in Korea. Gross incompetence in military affairs is a reasonable conclusion, endorsed by James and Wells' observation of Acheson confidence in military strategy and tactics, while in reality knowing "little about military matters."[7]

Undoubtedly, Acheson had no business steering Korean military strategy, nor did Truman in granting him free rein over the military. While his personal administrative style surely impressed Truman, Acheson completely lacked military leadership experience. Professed absurd judgments based on superficial understanding, such as pitching the pseudo-dilemma "lengthened supply line" catch-phrase or shibboleth, the whole peace negotiations debacle, and massive, worthless bloodshed, prove Acheson far out of his element in making war policy and field operational decisions.

FACTS DON'T MAKE SENSE

On the other hand, Acheson's professed ignorance of Communist negotiation strategy is impossible to accept. Given extensive first-hand experience with Lend-Lease Russian negotiations, he surely knew the score. Only 13 years had elapsed since Munich Conference concessions to Hitler. Totalitarian appeasement still gripped Western minds. Could similar mistakes now be made to again promote police-state interests? It is also possible Acheson possessed sincere desire to make Korean peace at any price, including concessions to a war enemy. He may have felt sympathy for the enemy and sought to stop the killing for the sake of all parties, even if US interests suffered.

Acheson graduated from elite schools, Exeter and Harvard, educators of America's ruling class. His mother's family fortune came from making and selling Canadian alcoholic beverages. His home featured servants and governesses. As with many wealthy liberals, perhaps Acheson felt guilt about proletarian exploitation. Political connections included Supreme Court justices, cabinet officials, even presidents. With help from Justice Frankfurter, he made his way skillfully and shrewdly up the Washington politico-bureaucratic ladder to gain important State Department posts under Roosevelt and Truman. Intellectual astuteness and familiarity with the ways of the world belie the excuse of innocence, of blindsiding by Communist peace talk delegates. So do passing, or permitting others to pass, what should have been closely-guarded UN truce talks strategic points to the Communist side, as attested by US delegates.

One strains to find examples of lawyerly strategic war excellence. The opposite is found in the 9 AD Roman battle disaster in the German Teutoberger Forest, west of the Elbe River. Romans considered the region pacified and no longer a war threat. This may account for lawyer Quinctilius Varus gaining command over three legions and marching them to slaughter at the hands of a German barbarian army headed by Arminius (known in German lore as great martial hero Herman), who also served without loyalty as a Roman Army officer.

Acheson considered himself superior to, and abhorred, crass, publicity-seeking politicians. To him, people were meant to be ruled. Strongly based in liberal ideology, pro-labor but more focused on popular control, he was surely closer to Red than Red, White, and Blue.

ROOSEVELT-TRUMAN POLITICAL ENVIRONMENT

A number of facts conclusively reveal the wide Soviet espionage net cast over United States Government and industry before, during, and after the Second World War. Foremost is the Venona Project's 1995 public revelation. Venona partially or fully decrypted thousands of Soviet war-time spy messages between Washington, New York, and Moscow. Most of these are available for on-line reading.[8,9,10] Moscow Center assigned code names to many US Government officials, some mentioned repeatedly in separate communications (arch-spy Nathan Gregory Silvermaster holds the record, the subject of 64 messages).

While Moscow knew about Venona by the late 1940s, it took US Government almost 50 years to come clean with its people, four years after the Soviet Union's demise!

Other credible confirmation comes from confessed spies, Congressional testimony transcripts, FBI reports, trials of arrested spies, and Soviet files released in the early 1990s. The following information is beyond dispute.

Treason in Federal Government flourished in Roosevelt and Truman administrations. One accurately describes such traitorous incidences as daily occurrences. The White House, and State and Treasury departments, harbored many traitors. So did World War II-era Executive agencies such as the pre-CIA Office of Strategic Services (OSS), Office of War Information, Voice of America radio broadcasting, and US Army Signal Corps. Congressional committees held their share of Red spies, along with US Navy warships. Manhattan Project infestation represented the effort's crown jewel. These important Moscow accomplishments were anything but unplanned outcomes.

Even before 1933 opening of US-USSR diplomatic relations under Roosevelt, Moscow leaders set their sights on *policy control within the US Government.* These leaders were fanatically devoted Red revolutionaries. As detailed by authors Philip Selznick, Herbert Romerstein and Stanislav Levchenko, Edward Van Der Rhoer, and Fred Iklé, unending push toward policy control is embedded in Red genes.[11,12,13] Communists contributed to Roosevelt's 1940 presidential electoral victory, and greatly helped the fourth term win in 1944.[14,15] Left-labor coalition in industrialized eastern and midwestern states, managed by Earl Browder and Sidney Hillman, turned out Roosevelt pluralities in both races.

Meanwhile, White House and State Department Reds and pro-Reds Lauchlin Currie and Alger Hiss steered US policy toward Communist China from 1944-49, helped by Treasury big-shot Harry Dexter White. All continually pumped vital information to Nathan Gregory Silvermaster's high-functioning Washington spy ring.

As mentioned, Truman appointed blatant Communists White and V. Frank Coe to important International Monetary Fund posts despite written warnings about their espionage histories from FBI Director J. Edgar Hoover. Long-time Roosevelt and Truman White House aide David K. Niles played a key role in getting Reds fake passports by the hundreds, facilitating unimpeded international movement. As Whittaker Chambers revealed, false passports were called "boots" in Soviet espionage circles. "The manufacture of boots is a major branch of Soviet espionage. The most successful single operative in this endeavor supplied Soviets with at least 100 fraudulent passports every month." A popular Manhattan Fifth Avenue photographer, arrested in 1938, worked closely with the CPUSA to create the fakes.[16]

Secret US Korean War battle plans flowed to Moscow, then Beijing and Pyongyang, from Gen. MacArthur's Tokyo headquarters. British Red spies posted to Washington and London regularly sent pending War moves to Soviet masters.[17] Reds knew Truman's inability to use nuclear weapons against China, plus sanctuary status of all PRC territory from US/UN attack.

Finally, there is no doubt Red armistice negotiators in Korea received US delegate negotiating positions *before* the US team got them. This particular treason originated in Acheson's State Department. When personally informed of the traitorous acts by former American peace negotiator Adm. Arleigh Burke, Truman did nothing in response.

LOYALTY TO MOSCOW

It is clear anti-Americans played important roles in setting US Government policy during Roosevelt and Truman presidencies, and therefore unsurprising that Korean War decisions often favored the enemy. To anti-Americans, *the US was the enemy*! Romerstein and Levchenko cited a December 13, 1917 Soviet Government decree "assigning two million roubles for the needs of the revolutionary internationalist movement. The Soviet Government considers it necessary to come forth with all aid ... to the assistance of the left, internationalist, wing of the workers movement[s] of all countries ...."[18]

Like other personally forceful cabinet figures, Acheson's prime attribute was ability to dominate fellow officials. His ability to talk-down civilians and military brass should have been put to use confronting Chinese and North Korean peace talk delegates. As mentioned, Acheson's elitist political preferences featured contempt for the American majority, the group fighting and dying in Korea. He held similar sentiment for Congress, successfully advising Truman to bypass Senate and House approval in sending US troops to save South Korea. In senseless war decisions, Truman and Acheson had blood on their hands. So did weak-kneed Joint Chiefs.

Acheson's personal political leanings, and associated leftist political pressure, played important roles in his crafting of war policy. America could only enter Korean fighting under the leftist-popular collective security umbrella. Going-it-alone could not be countenanced. The United Nations must be given its due. Roosevelt had staked the world's fate, and Truman's political life, on his precious UN. It could not fail. Acheson insisted on UN branding for US, ROK, and allied intervention. He also made sure the US didn't hit back too hard against the People's

Republic of China. Mao and cohorts, so favored by State China hands Service, Vincent, Davies, and Rosinger, must be kept in the game at all costs.

Finally, treason must be offered as explanation for illogical war policies and apparent strategic incompetence. To date, no documents have surfaced proving Acheson's complicity in selling out his country. The author predicts future revelation of the Secretary's 1940s and 50s ties to Soviet intelligence. One source will be KGB and GRU (Soviet military intelligence) files only minutely revealed at time of this manuscript. Of course most potential for political explosion will be long dead. But for truth, "Better late than never."

Chapter 34: American Largess to Chinese Communism

"In essence, everything that occurred in Korea after the summer of 1951 was a waste of time and lives. The North Korean military adventure had failed, the UN attempt to impose a military solution had failed, and the Chinese attempt to force the UN out of Korea had failed.

The war entered an entirely new phase. Now it was the turn of the politicians to fail."[1]

- Edwin P. Hoyt, The Bloody Road to Panmunjom.

In June 1951, Beijing's most pressing issue was the "immediate problem of saving their existing force in Korea from annihilation. *This we accomplished for them simply by halting our offensive"* (italics added).[2] More than anything, the US wanted an early War end, but also wished to preserve Mao's Communist Chinese regime. A 30-year Bolshevik effort had paid fantastic dividends – Red hand grasped the tiller of United States Government. Truman eliminated Korean military pressure, the only reliable way of encouraging China to rapidly conclude peace, thereby assuring continuation of war. It is difficult to conceptualize a more misguided or incompetent solution to the problem. Special indeed, the Korean War's leftist constraints.

Wildest dreams of Mao and Marshal Peng could not envision a *second* incredible enemy granting of recovery within the last five years. Immediately, cessation of major front-line offensive action relieved pressure on Chinese lines of supply and gave encouragement to the desperate Chinese battle situation. Likewise, risk of massive Red human and material losses vanished. We harken to Truman sending Gen. Marshall to China December 1945, with orders to arrange a cease-fire between Chiang's then-ascendant Kuomintang army and the Red People's Army. Marshall's effort turned into a months-long reprieve for Communists, who cemented their hold on upper Manchurian reaches and access to adjacent Soviet rail supply. To top it off, Truman ordered a seven-month arms embargo on Nationalists as Moscow continued full-bore CCF arming.

Red Chinese leadership had to be familiar with rank American stupidity, and filled with amazement at senseless American leadership. What a pathetic display of unrequited friendship. Hordes of "People's Volunteers" could be sent to kill and maim Americans, open hostility and vile insult thrown at "imperialist dogs," yet the most precious gifts kept flowing from Washington. Who could understand such fools? American leadership ignored war reality, proved unwilling to press battlefield advantage, and acted with due consideration for the Communist war dilemma.

Chinese Reds were now off the hook. Truman and Acheson took exceptional care of dominant Red interests. No one benefitted from the revised policy except the Communist side. The American/UN side reaped nothing but two more years of worthless bloodshed. This is not hyperbole, but fact.

The lesson could not be lost on Chairman Mao. How powerful the Soviet "elder brother," who could make American presidents and governments dance to their tunes! While happy to take advantage of senseless largess, how could Chinese respect the US Government? Marxist-Leninist rule could not fail to encompass the earth.

Prospect of Red Korean force annihilation, and achievement of UN military and political victory, now stood remote to impossible. For Communists, the situation resembled martial paradise. Americans obviously lacked will to win, let alone killer instinct. Who knew the illogical, crazy American thinking? If the brilliant negotiation ploy was not Communist bait-and-switch, then Red duplicity and American accommodation never existed in Moscow, Beijing, Washington, or London.

From July 1951 onward, fresh attack upon the Red enemy would entail "heavy fighting, not pursuit of a defeated horde." As Bernard Brodie repeatedly emphasized, "The Communists were left without incentive to come to peace terms."[3] That Truman and Acheson could not appreciate, or intentionally ignored, this critical fact, impugns their powers of reason and credibility. Should they have understood the unprecedented gift so obligingly presented and still have acted so illogically, their motives must stand severe criticism and questioning of intent.

Whose interests were paramount to the President? It is hard to believe breathing new life into Chinese infantry would lessen Truman's nightmare of igniting World War III. Or perhaps the frightening dream existed only in Internationalist minds – the political masters and Washington *force majeur*. Distinction between potential war in Europe and actual bloodshed in Korea seemed not to matter in Washington. As Gen. Bradley admitted, "To the Joint Chiefs of Staff, Korea was a comparatively minor irritation."[4]

Truman had unwisely created a new and dangerous war reality: *negotiation without strong mobile offensive combat pressure on the Chinese*. The sensible, pro-American path joined peace talks with further rout of CCF. Did Acheson and Truman hope to impress the enemy with their goodwill?

Authors Brodie, and James and Wells, agree there are no unilateral gratuitous actions in war that bring corresponding gestures from the opponent. Blind faith has no part in war. Brodie's remarks are appropriate:

> "War is not a game in which one makes gentlemanly gestures in hope of getting like treatment in return.[5] The [Chinese] army that was about to be destroyed we accorded gratuitously a chance to recover.[3] Where restraint is applied as a permanent condition regardless of enemy responses, we must be clearly aware that it may be costing us a great deal in military effectiveness – hence also in casualties to our own and friendly troops."[6]

The only correct and realistic course joined peace negotiations with continued strong combat pressure that kept Red armies on their heels. Large sections of North Korea stood ripe for taking, which might later be bargained for early and meaningful Communist concessions. Chinese Red leaders must have scratched their heads in wonder at the pacific, stupid US decision. They would never abandon a powerful, highly successful military offensive until achieving its goals.

Truman, Acheson, and the US/UN now received what they asked for: mockery of co-operative peace discussions through Communist intransigence and contrariness over seemingly simple points such as agendas and conference table shape, let alone matters of difficulty. Reds felt no rush: stalling provided necessary time for military rebuilding.

At the very first peace conference July 11, 1951, US and ROK delegates noted they sat much closer to the floor at the conference table than North Koreans and Chinese Communists. UN chair legs had been cut down so reviled "capitalist dogs" had to look up toward noble people's champions. As worshipped Bolshevik V. I. Lenin put it, "The mark of the muddlehead is to barter concrete advantages for verbal commitments."[7]

In abandoning broad-scale, mobile offensive warfare at its most successful point, America in fact adopted the *pro-Chinese Communist* position! Such largess harkened back to Franklin Roosevelt's innumerable pro-Red actions that hurt American interests and promoted Soviet imperialism. Truman and Acheson had made a huge and intentional "mistake of judgment, *by no means preordained by military circumstances* (italics added)."[8] Left-reviled MacArthur called it, "The worst of all choices, to go on indefinitely, neither to win or lose in that stalemate."[9] Of course "we the people" are not supposed to think such things and make such linkages. The preferred narrative may not be changed. But facts are there for all to see. Truman's leadership can only be characterized as disgraceful. We know who *really* ran Washington.

"MR. PRESIDENT, SOMEBODY IS LEAKING INFORMATION TO THE COMMUNISTS"

The American negotiating team, led by Vice Admiral C. Turner Joy, knew Communist negotiators received highly sensitive Washington policy directives before they did. Delegate Rear Admiral Burke, who left negotiations because of pro-Communist State Department-imposed directives, told President Truman at the White House, "Somebody in this government is leaking information on US positions because I know the Communists got our orders before we did. I can't prove it, but I know it."[10] Burke confidently told fellow delegates the same. While admitting to Burke State Department origination of the directives, Truman didn't know the author(s), nor is there evidence of follow-up investigation to find the culprit(s).

Outspoken Burke mentioned to the President, "Nobody in Washington pays any attention to recommendations made by Gen. Ridgway" on taking and holding proper and firm stances in peace talks. Noting he agreed with Ridgway's proposals (even though they were overridden by Acheson), Truman mentioned a bigger picture that needed to be satisfied beyond Ridgway's combat theater: "We've got to do things that are best for the government as a whole. Ridgway doesn't know the full picture."[11] Was this a roundabout way of admitting constraints on his actions imposed by Internationalists? The latter included the wealth and influence of the Rockefeller, Ford, and Carnegie foundations. The Rockefeller family donated the Manhattan land on which UN headquarters was built.

As attested by J. Edgar Hoover and Eisenhower Attorney General Herbert Brownell, satisfaction of leftist political power well fits Truman's pattern of allowing Communists or pro-Communists to occupy key government posts.[12] Traitors such as Harry Dexter White, Alger Hiss, Virginius Frank Coe, David K. Niles, Niles' White House replacement as presidential assistant, Philleo Nash, plus Solomon Adler, John Vincent, John Service, and John Davies, not only passed secrets to Moscow but helped set policy throughout US Government, a deadly form of treason wasting lives of US servicemen. Left-reviled FBI Director Hoover put it bluntly:

> "The Communist Party and its underground have always regarded infiltration of government service as a top priority project. We in the Bureau have always felt that the Communists in the Federal Government were a threat to the national security. This gives them a chance to engage in espionage, and a chance to influence American policy in ways detrimental to our national interest, and to sabotage the policy set down by the Government if it hurt the Soviet Union."[13]

The US and UN naively behaved as if truce talks would shortly conclude in a meaningful peace agreement. Detailed and well-dispersed writings of Soviet specialist George Kennan should have banished such unfounded optimism. Every iota of concession and obstruction would be squeezed out of talks – it was the Communist way. Neither Acheson or Truman appeared to know a thing about their Chinese, North Korean, and Soviet enemies, or more likely, willingly ignored reality.

The first six weeks of talks told what lay ahead. The initial hurdle, agreeing on an agenda, proved deceptively easy, taking only two weeks. Then came the intractable "line of demarcation" issue. The UN originally wanted the line to be the battle front, while Reds insisted on the 38th Parallel. Control of some 1,600 square miles of land lay in the balance, not much in comparison to Korea's total area of 85,000 square miles. The US/UN had fought for and won this limited prize. But repeatedly, Washington ordered UN negotiators to adopt conciliatory positions toward intransigent Communists, Joint Chiefs caving to State time after time.

For example, Reds issued an ultimatum for control of Kaesong, the original peace talks site, a village south of the 38th Parallel; Ridgway and UN delegates vigorously opposed the concession. Acheson prevailed in ordering fulfillment of Communist wish. Near the South Korean border, today Kaesong is the site of intimidating North Korean ballistic missile launches, salvos fired July 2014 and June 2016.

Ridgway and delegates then argued for a flexible line of demarcation reflecting battle outcomes, while Reds wanted an "agreed-on" fixed line at the 38th Parallel. Acheson backed the Red proposal.[14] Of course when it suited their offensive plans in Spring and Summer 1953, Chinese and North Koreans wantonly violated the agreed-on main line.

If Russian-experienced US diplomatic officials such as Kennan, William Bullitt, Laurence Steinhardt, Adm. William Standley, Averell Harriman, and Loy Henderson knew reams about Soviet negotiation strategy, why didn't the White House and State Department? Classic Communist doctrine regarded peace talks as continuation of warfare in another form with the "imperialist enemy." Notions of personal courtesy and gentlemanly conduct meant nothing, inconsideration and harshness the orders of the day. "To behave otherwise would betray their faith as good Communists and serious revolutionaries."[15]

POLITICAL SCENARIO

Washington mandates confounded negotiators: which side was State on? Civilian-leader behaviors were odd and misplaced, encouraging analysts to fear the worst: ideological sympathy for the enemy, and subsequent actions equating to treason.

Proletarian revolution in the world's most populous country now tottered. New China utterly depended on a well-functioning People's Liberation Army. Internationalists in America joined fellow champions of proletarian dictatorship, the many Reds and pro-Reds within and without US Government, including the Executive Branch, in seeking immediate action to preserve the People's Liberation Army and Mao's Red leadership. They were the only alternative to "corrupt feudalism" in China.

Much hard work had gone into supporting PRC birth. An impressive record of presidential electoral support conferred credibility on Red-Socialist politics and apt White House attention to political pressures. All the effort and dedication could not be wasted. With the host of influential anti-Americans who helped create Communist China still at work, and politics trumping all, the concept of Red Chinese preservation at all costs is not only reasonable, but politically realistic.

Chapter 35: Truth Versus Deception

"Systematic murder started soon after Lenin took power in 1917 and never stopped until Stalin's death [1953]. None were ever tried for these crimes.

As Stalin emphasized, 'One must sometimes correct history. Political necessity is better than mere truth. We ourselves will be able to determine what is true and what is not.[1] '"

- Simon Montefiore, Stalin – The Court of the Red Tsar.

Even with considerable press cover, Truman paid a dear political price for Korean mis-steps. His credibility grievously wounded in MacArthur's removal, the President's public support rightly plummeted during the Korean War. But the theme of disastrous presidential war leadership never made the threshold of popular understanding; it was as if key events and decisions never happened. The left cannot deal with truth.

Americans had no idea of pending December 1950 US surrender to Communist China, imminent May 1951 US military victory, and subsequent abandonment of highly successful mobile war. Likewise, State Department sandbagging of the UN peace negotiation team never crossed public minds. On a broader scale, the people didn't appreciate shocking American military weakness after World War II and consequent difficulty in effectively fighting anywhere. A largely Red-sympathetic liberal press helped perpetuate popular ignorance.

In the world of politics, truth is leper-like, forbidden territory. The whole idea of truth makes progressives especially uncomfortable. We expect grand deception from Red and Socialist leadership as their stock-in-trade, not surprised to behold Chinese troops counter-attacking in North Korea falsely described as "Volunteers," or Manchurian voters 100% in favor of Chinese annexation. But American presidents playing crass politics with blood is especially hurtful. How terribly our leaders treated the people for the sake of power.

One group not fooled are US Korean War combat veterans. To a man, and 63 years after the fact, they ridicule Truman's political War characterization as a "Conflict." They know that in military unpreparedness and the attempt to shield Americans from Korean battle realities, Truman shortchanged his fighting men and their families to satisfy leftist, non-American interests. The People's Republic of China and its army must be shielded from heavy blows. Europe must be protected at all costs, Soviet Russia must be feared. Strong veteran animosity toward their War president is itself a politically-incorrect non-story. Knowledgeable Americans could only conclude that to national leaders, people simply didn't count.

In retirement years, Gen. Ridgway authored a Korean War history implicating lengthened US supply lines in North Korea as a major reason for curtailing large-scale mobile offensive operations. According to the "lengthened supply lines" dilemma, no army could advance very far from its supply base, an obviously disproved thesis throughout history. Brodie pointed out that US sea and air dominance allowed for seizing new North Korean ports and bases, providing the prospect of ample and shorter lines of logistical access.[2] Potent supply capability of US Navy and Merchant Marine ships, many from Japan, made the US war effort possible, and would likewise adequately supply an extensive advance into North Korea. The "lengthened supply-line" pseudo-dilemma also discounts the role of *intense* air supply, exemplified in one instance by the 1948 Berlin Airlift.

Ever the loyal soldier, excepting his Kaesong-Panmunjom holdout, Ridgway's writings admitted the questionable wisdom of "stopping that proud Army in its tracks at the first whisper that Reds might be ready to sue for peace."[2] Of course in truth the US instituted peace talks through Acheson's request to George Kennan for informal discussions with Soviet UN chief delegate Jakob Malik. Then Ridgway excused Truman's gross mistakes by stressing the undesirability of "merely acquiring more North Korean real estate." Surprised at the general's stance given longevity of negotiations and bloodiness of stalemated battle, Bernard Brodie accused Ridgway of completely missing the point on necessity of continued heavy forward pressure on "disintegrating Chinese armies. It had nothing to do with gaining territory but everything to do with forcing Red China to not only start peace negotiations, but actually conclude them! The line they finally settled for two years later, or something like that line, might have been achieved in far less time if we had meanwhile continued the pressure that was disintegrating their armies."[2] Large pieces of North Korea represented valuable bargaining chips.

Ridgway simply ignored the obvious linkage between the two-year talks debacle and failure to keep strong pressure on the enemy. This reality speaks ill of a proud warrior's powers of observation and volumes about susceptibility to political influence. Colleague Gen. Almond, interviewed for the official Army Korean War history, described Ridgway's strategic philosophy as "a compromise with politics." At least Ridgway risked his career once in the name of doing right in Korea. For Chiefs, falling on swords was not an option.

An unpleasant fact, the line represented by the final July 1953 truce agreement was very close to the Spring 1951 front. Toward War's end, Reds battered central and eastern UN lines to advance some 20 miles south in places. Following the prior two-year pattern, much blood had been expended for nothing. If Truman had mustered the political courage in May-June 1951 to continue heavy pressure on reeling Chinese armies and force their "inducement to seek an early end" to fighting, truce settlement might have been achieved far earlier, saving tens of thousands of American lives and perhaps hundreds of thousands of Koreans.

Red China deserved a major military reverse to counter the beating inflicted on the US Army in North Korea. While "Volunteers" by hundreds of thousands gave lives in Korea, especially in the March – May 1951 bloodbath, Reds were saved from catastrophic defeat. After the war, the People's Republic gained a reputation in Asian and world minds as a fearsome military power standing down the once-mighty American Army. Proud standing holds to this day, especially regarding prospect of military confrontation with the US.

Passage of over a half-century offers a firm look at the time's presidential public statements on war and foreign policy. Sadly, in the case of Korea, there is little agreement between public words and private actions. Considerable disjunction between reality and popular understanding engenders profound disappointment in national leadership. Politics is surely the often-despicable practice of grand-scale lying and deception. Magnificent backdrops for subterfuge and trickery, the Capitol, White House, and Supreme Court bedazzle people with greatness and credibility. It is difficult to look beyond shiny actors and brilliant stage and perceive truth, but it is necessary for national salvation.

Late Judge and Supreme Court candidate Robert H. Bork, unsurprisingly a figure of profound leftist vilification, correctly diagnosed and boldly described the campaign of destruction. His assertion bears full consideration:

> "Forces that advance the agenda of modern liberalism are the 'intellectual' class and that class's enforcement arm, the judiciary, headed by the Supreme Court of the United States.[3] To the degree they have already succeeded, democratic government has not survived. As the behavior of modern liberal politicians, the courts, and the bureaucrats demonstrates, they have no intention of relinquishing any of their power to the popular will."[4]

Tyranny well describes today's American political reality.

Chapter 36: National Leadership Theme: Inconsistency

"It was the sort of war that sapped morale. There was no victory. There was only never-ending fighting. And no one could say when or how it was going to end. That is the sort of nightmare the Korean War had turned into by the autumn of 1952.[1]

Even those who backed the Truman war policies could not but be discouraged by the never-ending pressure, the ceaseless casualties, the frustrations and feeling of going nowhere ....."[2]

- Edwin P. Hoyt, The Bloody Road to Panmunjom.

The Korean War era reveals gaping deficiency in US presidential, cabinet-level, and Joint Chiefs of Staff leadership. Through no fault of his own, Harry Truman started his presidency with one foot in a deep hole. Numerous authors, including Dean Acheson, relate Franklin Roosevelt's arm's length treatment of Vice-President Truman that kept him in the dark about vital world events. Acheson knew that as president, Truman "suffered greatly from Roosevelt's failure to keep him adequately informed."[3] Closed door continued despite the fourth-term president's tenuous health. Leadership vacuum had to and did ensue on his death.

Vice-presidential neglect speaks ill of FDR's leadership. So do fore-mentioned prohibitions on note-taking and use of agendas at Cabinet and international meetings. Except for Stalin, no one could get the President to "put it in writing." His war and foreign policies reeked of "Great White Father Knows Best" condescension, with boundless foreign and domestic pro-Communism unlinked to Moscow reciprocity.

While Winston Churchill bemoaned the Roosevelt-Truman transition's terrible state, the Russian side painted another realistic portrait of the new president. American-based TASS (Soviet news agency) journalist Vladimir Pravdin, doubling as a KGB agent, advised Moscow Truman was "notoriously untried and ill-informed on foreign policy."[4]

According to biographer Robert Beisner, Acheson held a surprisingly negative opinion of FDR's leadership ability. Acheson tellingly described frank presidential failure on the postwar geopolitical scene: "I learned how false were our postulates. One powerful ally of the war years had become an enemy in and of the hoped-for new order, which itself was proving an illusion. The first three years after the war brought painful enlightenment …. It was in that period that we fully awakened to the facts of the surrounding world."[5]

Why highly-perceptive Acheson took three years to awaken is unclear. George Kennan spoke with unmistakable authority on Soviet revolutionary intentions, along with William Bullitt, David Dallin, Anthony Kubek, Laurence Steinhardt, Loy Henderson, and US military attaché in Moscow, Maj. Gen. John Deane. The world had split into two opposed and frighteningly powerful camps. Danger was everywhere, not limited to Berlin, Greece, and Turkey. Rival and hostile ideologies stoked unrest above and below the Korean 38th Parallel. Seemingly blind to world reality, Truman chose this three-year period to disarm his nation.

From Second World War's end, as part of the strange, inappropriate response to world danger, the Truman Administration allowed mismatched development of the two Koreas. The North created a strong, Communist-directed, -patterned, and -armed military establishment, while courtesy of America, the South had little to nothing in effective opposition. Roosevelt laid the groundwork, Truman cemented the path to War. From 1947 to 1950, America clearly signaled the world Korea didn't matter.

Shock of North Korean invasion, and appreciation of the political disaster inherent in losing another Asian nation to Communism, brought change of heart. Now Washington wanted to save South Korea. Pre-Korean War US policy toward Korea is accurately described as weak and unsure.

CONTINUOUSLY SHIFTING KOREAN WAR STRATEGY

In the first year of fighting, US strategic War objectives changed every few months. Initially, the War aimed to save South Korea from Communism; then the switch to the misguided plan to free all North Korea from Red rule and unify the peninsula under democracy. Chinese onslaught brought wholesale abandonment of unification in favor of US/UN force survival in or out of South Korea. Acheson let it be known America would happily settle on the status quo ante-bellum, a 38th Parallel cease-fire line.

Communist dangling of truce talks then induced rush to the negotiation table and dependence on peaceful solution in lieu of successful mobile warfare. Saying they wanted to keep maximum military pressure on Reds but doing the exact opposite, the political "one-two," Truman and Acheson imposed a World War I-reminiscent static but violent front. "Die-for-tie" senseless warfare endured two years while armistice talks sputtered, died, and were reborn March 1953 in the Eisenhower Administration. Fear dominated American decision-making down the leadership line, fueled by misunderstanding of enemy reality, potent ethnocentrism and racism, and treasonous influence in Washington.

Indecision continued in the peace talks phase. As Ridgway's Korean book boldly told, "It is a fact that, whether or not we should have entered into any negotiations at all, directives emanating from Washington made the negotiations more difficult and may well have helped delay the final agreement."[6] The Truman Administration often undercut US peace negotiators through restrictions on potentially offensive but appropriate verbal comments at sessions, and frequent and abrupt changes in policy. The US side was not permitted to walk away from talks, despite ample Red provocation. It would give Communists "a public relations advantage." Delegation head Adm. Joy, Far East Naval Commander, found Washington ready to concede points or do the opposite of existing policy, without consulting the negotiation team.

Ridgway cited another "most striking example" of Truman-Acheson interference:

> "After our negotiators had insisted on including in the armistice terms a prohibition against the construction of new [North Korean] airfields and the rehabilitation of old ones, Washington directed the negotiators to concede on this issue. There was at that time not a single combat-effective airfield left in all North Korea …. The Communists … promptly moved their fighter planes down from Manchuria into North Korea, where they could strike deep into South Korea. This order from Washington was bitter medicine."[6]

In another major concession, Washington pushed down delegate throats an early agreement on a "permanent" line of demarcation. UN peace delegates strongly believed this would restrict allied combat effort and give Reds a "no-lose" situation. The agreement did not inhibit Communists from storming 20 miles deep through parts of that line in 1953 offensives, making fools of their opponents. Communist deceit and obstruction provided enough frustration – to have Washington as another source of contention added to woes. As Adm. Joy painfully knew, with exception of Communist POW repatriation, Truman-Acheson War and negotiation leadership could easily be characterized as vacillating and ineffective.

Despite Soviet atomic bomb possession, the US held a huge nuclear advantage in weapons numbers and explosive forces, never exploited by Truman and Acheson. Unknown publicly, but surely known to Washington, and later documented by author Robert Futrell, by Summer 1951 Soviets had inserted close to 500 MiG-15 jets and over 60,000 air support personnel, including pilots, into Manchurian airfields, many of them near the Yalu.[7] Though it could never be publicized, in reality the US and Soviet Union were at war in the air over Korea. Sadly, in numbers of state-of-the-art jet fighters and bombers, Communists left the US in the dust.

WASHINGTON LEADERSHIP DISGRACE

Fear of massive Soviet armed ground response likely helped rule out deep, May-June 1951 advance into North Korea, which would represent crushing and deserved Chinese Communist defeat. Ancillary reasons for US paralysis are only poor excuses, including President Truman's statement, "The public would not tolerate thousands of dead young Americans in a major offensive." Washington could not politically spin the deaths without making itself look incompetent. Ever-flowing dribs and drabs of killing, by ones, twos, and fours, could be smoothed over, its reality covered as the cost of achieving peace. According to Washington propaganda, the US was engaged in an earnest, no-holds-barred, all-out negotiation effort for peace. Hence, for the final two years of war, 30,000 Americans gave all for naught, "died-for-tie," while a far lower price in blood might have achieved decisive rout of Red Chinese and their strong motivation to conclude an acceptable and early peace.

In just over five years, the United States had gone from the heights of Second World War victory to Korean humiliation and disgrace. For this, posterity praises Truman's "bold, no-nonsense" leadership. For Korea, "non-sensible" better fits the facts.

US Army leadership, especially that of generals Bradley and Collins, matched the civilian-superior model. Paralyzing fear ruled the day, an embarrassment to American martial tradition. Nuclear threat in answer to endless Chinese manpower was off the table. The American left strictly prohibited this response. Career safety mandated "getting behind the Commander-in-Chief" no matter the senseless course, the continued immorality of wasting young lives, the righteousness of enveloping much of peninsular North Korea while administering a sound beating to Red armies. Instead, Red China could relax – its emergency was over.

According to Truman, fear of igniting World War III represented the greatest excuse for Korean cold feet, "an ever-present factor in his every decision."[8] But Communist actions in Asia, whatever their severity, could never rise to world war threshold. Only American actions could. Since Truman would never cross the Internationalists, they must have shared this fear and belief. Soviet Russia and Communist China must always stand in opposition to distrusted and reviled imperialist America, which could never be allowed to attain world dominance.

PRC REGIONAL AND GLOBAL POWER

Douglas MacArthur appreciated the lasting consequences of newfound Red Chinese world stature, predicting a century of disaster to US interests. Writings of Truman, Acheson, and Army Joint Chiefs Bradley and Collins never addressed long-term international problems inherent in failure to achieve Korean military victory. A combination of flawed vision (hard to believe for wily Acheson), numbness from pressure of present events, and over-reliance on peace talks encouraged Korean debacle. Civilian and military leadership would fail again in Vietnam in long-term Far Eastern vision, knowledge of enemy capabilities, and blatant practice of racial chauvinism.

A decade before his time of maximum stress, great 20th-century war figure Winston Churchill wrote that holding "the leadership of a party or nation with dignity and authority requires that the leader's qualities and message shall meet not only the need but the mood of both."[9] He knew "those in authority cannot always be relied upon to take enlightened and comprehending views."[10] Before and during the Korean War, Truman frequently failed to satisfy American need and mood. Abandonment of military victory represented politics and leadership at their worst. Such unparalleled blunders fathered a cascade of Asian and world catastrophes.

It fits the state of American political, educational, social, and cultural decline that very few of our youth know of Churchill, including most college students. Fittingly, newly-elected President Obama wasted no time dispatching a bronze Oval Office Churchill bust back to London. His life, accomplishments, and nationalism reek of political incorrectness.

Chapter 37: P.O.W. Problems

More than 132,000 Red soldier-prisoners presented a serious American control and care challenge. The vast majority were captured in the first-year, mobile war phase. Over 100,000 were housed at the huge, hastily-improvised detention facility on the coastal island of Koje-do, site of the December 1950 North Korean refugee horde disembarkment[1] (MAPS 5, 10). Close by, another 100,000 civilian refugees and political prisoners added to management woes.

Red army leadership intentionally allowed certain soldiers to be captured and sent to Koje-do to organize prisoner revolt. In April 1952 Red prisoners succeeded in capturing hapless Camp Commander Army Brig. Gen. Francis Dodd, soon freed by new Commander Brig. Gen. Charles Colson at expense of a signed statement acknowledging widespread prisoner abuse, fueling a strong anti-American propaganda barrage. Both one-stars were busted down to colonel, careers ruined. The incident happened May 11, 1952, just as Gen. Ridgway was about to leave Far East Command to assume NATO leadership.

With crudely fashioned weapons and numerical strength, Reds incited severe violence at Koje-do, requiring insertion of a US Army regiment under command of respected leader Brig. Gen. Haydon "Bull" Boatner. Ordered to promptly establish order, the brigadier got down to business. While new prisoner quarters were under construction in other island bases, a ring of openly-placed .50 caliber heavy machine guns surrounded Communist-controlled barracks, along with fully battle-armed battalions. After prisoners ignored requests to lay down arms, formations stormed rebel headquarters, shot those holding weapons, and broke Red control. One US trooper died, along with 70 Communists. Tens of thousands of prisoners were transferred to new facilities. The camp at Koje-do ceased to be a source of rebellion.

Rebellion posed no possibility in brutally-run Communist prison camps holding American, South Korean, and allied captives. Starting in early July 1950, the first American days of Korean combat, North Koreans took significant numbers of US Army prisoners. Distinguished Army historian Roy E. Appleman reported 36 captured GIs under 2nd Lt. Janson Cox, taken near Osan July 6, and another 72 July 11 in the same area. Pyongyang radio broadcasts trumpeted the captures.[2] Author Richard Whelan told of an official December 1952 Communist report of 11,559 total UN prisoners. Of these, Americans accounted for 3,200, South Koreans 7,100, allied forces 1,200.

Whelan cited an official US figure of "11,230 Americans missing in action; Communist figures meant that over 8,000 Americans had died – one way or another – after capture."[3] Almost 80,000 South Korean troops disappeared, "either murdered or else forced to serve in the NKPA."

Although Whelan uniquely reported "a great wave of revulsion and moral outrage against the [Communist] atrocities" attending post-War publication in the American press, there is little if any indication of retained Korean War crime-awareness by the American public or media. Barbaric Red treatment of war prisoners is not commonly or reflexively associated with what little Korean War knowledge and status exist in American culture. While Nazi barbarity is continually portrayed in popular media, treatment of ample Red counterpart is almost non-existent. Friends of the Soviet system indeed do not relate the truth of that system.

James and Wells accused North Korean soldiers of "ruthlessness that equaled Japanese brutalities against captured soldiers in the Second World War."[4] NKPA prisoner atrocities continued throughout the War, including summary murder of US, allied, and ROK soldiers who wished to surrender, forced marches of military and civilian prisoners on tough mountain trails with regular killing of those who couldn't keep up, and unceasing mental and physical torture often exceeding human endurance. Wounded and disabled prisoners received no consideration. None, except turncoats, received but the barest rations of water and food. UN prisoners did well to stay alive. Those who lost will to live quickly died.

CCF treated POWs more humanely, making legitimate attempts to provide medical care and not resorting to gunshots to the head. In the first months after Chinese invasion, some US captives, especially wounded, were not taken prisoner and told to head back to their lines. On November 29, 1950 at the eastern, Tenth Corps front, attacking Chinese forces took British and American prisoners from Task Force Drysdale, as it attempted to reach Hagaru-ri from Koto-ri. Captured in fittingly-named Hellfire Valley, wounded US Marines, soldiers, and British 41 Commando company troopers received Chinese medical attention and food. The Chinese departed early the following morning, allowing many treated prisoners to escape.[5]

Press coverage of the Korean POW situation showed Red adeptness at gaining public relations advantage. Newspaper front-page pictures of American POWs typically showed them playing various sports and basically enjoying life. Even *Stars and Stripes,* the official US Army newspaper, featured undoubtedly staged photos of leisurely American POW enjoyment.

Paris-based correspondent for the pro-Communist paper *Ce Soir*, Wilfred Burchett, instigated many such photo-ops, which included the highest-ranking US prisoner, Maj. Gen. William Dean, apparently enjoying country-club type amenities. Burchett helped this process through contacts with Red officials, who arranged access for some correspondents to selected North Korean prison camps. Prisoners would be cleaned up and given fresh clothing in preparation for the visits. The most favorable pictures were shared with the regular press.

British leftist author and Red front leader M. Monica Felton, busy conducting press events "proving" American and allied War atrocities, found time to visit Communist prison camps and publicly extol the "fine treatment received by UN POWs." The London *Daily Worker's* Alan Winnington functioned as another Moscow-Beijing Korean War mouthpiece.

We know Franklin Roosevelt encouraged Communist entry into American armed forces by the thousands. These fine folks often gravitated to communication-related military work. We recall Executive-mandated presence of Red radio operators on US Navy warships, Red organizations in every service branch, noteworthy US Army Signal Corps infestation, and pro-Red China domestic propaganda barrage. The entire effort contributed to Communism's positive press portrayal – "These are true patriotic Americans, our best friends ever." The CPUSA even featured a World War II veterans association to prove outstanding citizenship!

Truth has zero significance to totalitarians, who daily invent warped, outrageous versions of reality. Judging by political outcomes, the scam works quite well.

On viewing "POW life is great" photos, enraged Far East Commander Gen. Ridgway ordered immediate firing of the *Stars and Stripes* editor.[6] Postwar prisoner interviews and physical appearances revealed a wholly different reality. According to official records, 73% of American prisoners died in Red camps from starvation, lack of medical care, and physical and mental abuse. The remainder, except for favored turncoats, suffered extreme malnutrition. The American and world press had been "had." Despite prolific viciousness toward prisoners, truth didn't matter – Reds reigned as undisputed propaganda world champions.

Reporters emphasized overcrowding and disorder at UN facilities, especially the sprawling Koje-do camp. It did not help that the International Red Cross and press could regularly visit UN prisons, but aside from the above set-ups, were not permitted to inspect Communist camps in North Korea and Manchuria.[7]

NORTH KOREAN BARBARITY SURFACES

Reports by a band of American War veterans, known as the "Korean War Project," and 1953 testimony before the US Senate Subcommittee on Korean War Atrocities, substantiated the "Death March" of mostly US military and missionary prisoners beginning September 20, 1950, as UN forces fought their way from Inchon to Seoul. Corroboration of facts came from eyewitness affidavits of survivors, participants, perpetrators, and photographs. North Koreans put 376 captives on a 200-mile up-and-down march from Seoul to Pyongyang. The brutal trek took 20 days, with scant food and water. Many made the march in bare, bloody feet. Only 33 survived, some of whom testified to the Senate Korean Atrocities Subcommittee.[8]

John Toland's exceptional book, *In Mortal Combat,* provides a superb account of North Korean

POW abuse. Another, larger "Death March II" is detailed, associated with the October 1950 US/UN advance into North Korea (MAP 7). Seeking to hold on to captured soldiers, civilians, and religious volunteers for their propaganda and leverage value, Red leaders moved POWs north from Pyongyang to camps around and even across the Yalu River.

As reported by US Army Col. James M. Hanley, Eighth Army Chief of the War Crimes Section, North Koreans placed one prisoner group on trains, stopping in the Sunchon Tunnel between Pyongyang and the Yalu. On pretense of feeding the captives, 68 Americans were taken out of cars and summarily shot. The largely unknown event came to be known as the "Sunchon Tunnel Massacre."[9] Destinations included Prison Number 5, at Pyoktang, overlooking the Yalu from the North Korean side, and a POW camp at the Manchurian city of Manpo, 125 air miles upstream from the river's mouth (MAP 7).

South Koreans fared far worse. Col. Hanley revealed their slayings "by tens of thousands."[10] Reds bound long lines of men, women, and children with ropes, then executed them with submachine guns. Many were thrown down mine shafts, or doused in gasoline to be burned to death. Countless hillsides held hundreds of corpses.

Forced-march prisoners included British Salvation Army official Herbert Lord, diplomats from Britain's legation in Seoul, "many Roman Catholic sisters and priests headed by Bishop Byrne, and six men and women from the Methodist Mission in Kaesong, including the Reverend Larry Zellers."[11] Monsignor Quinlan of the Columban Fathers joined Australian Catholic priest Father Philip Crosbie, 82-year-old Father Villemot, and Carmelite nuns in the line.

By October 31, 1950, with weather taking a decided turn to cold, rain, and snow, a North Korean major told captives, "You are now under strict military discipline. We are going to march to Chunggang-jin," over 100 miles from Pyongyang.[12] Injured Sister Mary Clare, blind Sister Marie-Madeleine, and sick Mother Thérèse needed help just to walk.

In Toland's words, "Mr. Lord stepped forward to voice his concerns. 'They will die if they have to march!' The major replied, 'Then let them march till they die. That is a military order.'"[13] The missionary and civilian cohort fell in behind a long line of some 700 American military prisoners, many with bleeding feet. As the column struggled to climb daunting mountains between Pyongyang and the Yalu, many sick and weakened soldier-prisoners fell out, and received gunshots to the head from North Korean guards. The murdered included priests, ministers, and nuns. Each marching day brought fresh massacre of 15, 18, or 20 unfortunate souls who could not keep up. Others froze to death during the night. On occasion fires were lit in rest areas, warmed bodies teeming with lice.

A number of heroes inspired the suffering mass. The particularly brutal North Korean major questioned US Army Lt. Cordus Thornton: "Why did you let those men drop out?" The young Lieutenant answered, "Because they were dying, sir." The major shot back, "Why didn't you obey my orders?", then asked nearby NKPA soldiers, "What should be done to a man who disobeys the People's Army?" Immediately came the response, "Shoot him!" The major then proclaimed, "There, you've had your trial." Lt. Thornton told the major, "In Texas, sir, we would call that a lynching."[14]

Thornton's hands were tied behind him, his face covered with a small towel. "The major cocked his pistol and stepped behind the Lieutenant, while parents tried to cover their children's eyes. The major flipped up the back of Thornton's fur cap, then pulled the trigger. Thornton collapsed to the ground."[14]

Sgt. Henry Leerkamp organized a burial party, soldiers using sticks and fingers to dig the hard, cold ground. "Thornton was laid in the shallow grave and covered with dirt and stones."[15] Minister Zellers thought, "What a privilege to be with such people." Monsignor Quinlan, familiar with this part of North Korea from pre-Communist days, observed to Rev. Zellers of the victims, "The Good Lord will give them a better welcome in heaven than the Communists have ever given them in this unhappy land."

Making 20 miles on some days, the column reached its final destination of Chunggang-jin November 8, 1950. Nearly a hundred dead prisoners dotted the mountains and valleys of upper

North Korea. Survivors endured harsh weather and extreme mental and physical suffering, with much more to come. Another Death March stained Korean War history.

MEDAL OF HONOR RECIPIENT FATHER EMIL J. KAPUAN

During the October 31 – November 8 US POW march, another prisoner ordeal began in North Korea's Chongchon River valley (MAP 8). The Chinese First Phase Offensive enveloped the 3rd Battalion of the US Army's 8th Cavalry Regiment (1st Cavalry Division) at Unsan, a spearhead element in MacArthur's Yalu push. Battalion Catholic Chaplain Captain Emil J. Kapuan, of Pilsen, Kansas, repeatedly braved enemy fire in dragging wounded soldiers from the line, and digging shallow covers to protect other wounded. Father Kapuan refused "several chances to escape, volunteering to stay behind and care for soldiers" who couldn't walk. The Chinese captured him and a host of 3rd Battalion troopers November 2, 1950.[16] CCF also destroyed the ROK 2nd Corps, another MacArthur spearhead formation.

Forced march north followed for several days, Father Kapuan and 3rd Battalion POWs trudging through steep mountains, snow, and bitter cold temperatures. The Catholic priest served as a stretcher-bearer until reaching a Red prison camp. Then, day after day, he went from soldier to soldier, offering a bit of scavenged food, tending the sick, saying prayers and fostering the practice of faith. Communist guards punished Father Kapuan by making him "sit outside in subzero weather" without clothing. This did not deter the Chaplain from disobeying his tormentors by holding an Easter morning sunrise service.

As the official US Army account noted, when Father Kapuan's inevitable physical decline set in, "the Chinese transferred him to a filthy, unheated hospital where he died alone, denied medical treatment.[17] While carried to the hospital, he asked God's forgiveness for his captors, and made fellow prisoners promise to keep their faith. Chaplain Kapuan died in captivity May 23, 1951."[17]

For exceptional service in the face of inhuman conditions, Father Kapuan posthumously received the Medal of Honor, presented to his nephew by President Obama at the White

House, April 11, 2013. The Catholic Church has begun the process of conferring sainthood on the hero priest.

COMMUNIST BRAINWASHING, PROPAGANDA, AND 'PROGRESSIVE' PRISONERS

In respect of rampant US, South Korean, and allied POW misery and death, it is fitting the US Congress held post-Korean War sessions on Red atrocities. Strict Communist Chinese philosophy on seizing power over people and governments included the policy of "washing one's brain," which meant eliminating from personal thought all elements of prior life, such as religious education and practice, patriotism, literature, family traditions, and history that encouraged devotion to non-Communist causes.

UN POWs became familiar with the Chinese "Lenient Policy," which entailed developing friendship with their captors, studying principles of Marxism-Leninism, and adulation of Stalin and Mao.[18] Captives excelling at the task, *"progressive prisoners,"* called by Chinese at one camp "Peace Fighters," enjoyed special privileges: clean clothes, better food, playing sports, ability to write letters to and receive mail from families.

Prisoners hostile to progressive status were subject to immediate punishment, which could mean "many sophisticated varieties of torture."[19] Physical punishment included vicious beating, burning of skin, and hanging from ropes. Brian Catchpole cited "the deaths of many thousands of prisoners, particularly among those Americans who had been captured early on in the war." In 1951 alone, 1,600 UN POW deaths were reported.[20]

After the war, Army Lt. Col. Robert Abbott of Rochester, NY, told Congress,

> "In my camp we were exposed to Communist propaganda materials, much of which came from the US. One of the publications we had most to do with was the *Daily Worker,*" the official newspaper of the Communist Party USA and like its parent body, an absolute Kremlin tool. It "attempted in every way to demoralize POWs. Communist guards gloried in being able to point to articles in the *Daily Worker*. They attempted to show us that the war was very unpopular in America, that we were forgotten men.[8,21] One of the books they continuously pointed out was 'Hidden History of the Korean War'

by [pseudo-American author] I.F. Stone."

Dyed-in-the-wool Stalinist Stone faithfully toed Moscow's line, entirely blaming the US for the Korean mess and absolving Reds of any wrong. Americans sometimes pay a costly price for so-called freedom of communication.

Lt. Col. Abbott concluded 1953 testimony before the Senate Subcommittee on Korean War Atrocities with a perceptive statement: "In my opinion communism seeks to destroy our way of life, that as long as there is one communist in America he constitutes a threat to our way of life, for they have all dedicated themselves to destroying capitalism and democracy .... [T]he end justifies the means for anything he may do ...."[22]

To its shame, a 2008 taxpayer-funded American public television program included multiple comments by a former *Daily Worker* reporter about the 1940s and 50s Brooklyn Dodgers baseball team, of all topics. Producers aimed at "inclusion," treating the reporter as just another member of the US press representing "salt-of-the-earth" Reds, unaware of, or uncaring about, suffering of American POWs in Korea. An unreported small storm of protest hit public television – imagine a Nazi commentator speaking to a national television audience on "sporting activities enjoyed" by death camp captives. Insult to living and dead Korean War veterans is deep and inexcusable. To date (2016), in the author's knowledge, no other Communist reporters have surfaced as eyewitnesses in sports-related national public television programming.

Part VII:

Eisenhower's War, January – July 1953,

Nuclear Weapon Policy in Korea,

and War's End

Chapter 38: Ike's War

"Americans assess the cost of war in terms of human life, the Russians in over-all drain on the nation. Great Communist victories inevitably require huge casualties."[1]

- Dwight D. Eisenhower, Crusade in Europe.

In 1952, President Truman chose not to exercise his unique right to run for a third presidential term. Public opinion polls registered very low approval ratings, even worse than Nixon at the time of Watergate. The President had spent over seven years in the hottest of seats, the last four in bitter wrangling with Republicans. Americans had tired of 20 years of Democratic control; public feeling extended to Truman. Undeniable facts such as Communist rule in China, the Soviet A-bomb, and the Korean War could not be politically hidden. The Korean roller coaster gave a regular pounding, especially in its long, stagnated phase. "Softness on Communism" proved another sticky issue, Secretary Acheson pouring oil on flames in publicly backing convicted perjurer and long-time influential State Department Communist Alger Hiss.

"WE LIKE IKE"

At their October 14, 1950 Wake Island meeting, Truman jokingly (or not) asked Gen. MacArthur about political aspirations. MacArthur replied, "The only general I know who might run for president is named Eisenhower."

Before reaching Supreme Command of allied forces in Europe, Dwight Eisenhower served as staff officer under MacArthur in The Philippines and Washington. Before that, thought of highest Army field command must have been farthest from Eisenhower's mind. He had been stuck in grade at the rank of major for 15 years. Biographer Alden Hatch referred to this period as Eisenhower's "long dry spell."[2] He and wife Mamie also knew personal tragedy, suffering the death of their three-year-old son to scarlet fever January 1921. In 1935, MacArthur advanced him to Lt. Colonel, a promotion Eisenhower feared might never come. As World War II drew near, Ike's hard work, energy, and intelligence impressed Washington high brass.

Political pressure in 1951-52 from Senate and House Republicans and key backers caused "Ike" to resign as Truman-appointed NATO commander to seek presidential nomination. Distinguished Second World War combat leadership bestowed great prestige on likable Eisenhower. His famous and ready grin helped. Controversy over Korea proved a significant factor in a resounding November 1952 win over Democrat candidate Adlai Stevenson.

During the campaign, Eisenhower promised to visit Korea if elected. He did that in December, before inauguration. He made a prior Korean trip in Summer 1946.

Ridgway's replacement as Far East Commander, Gen. Mark Clark, prepared a plan of major attack to break War stalemate, looking forward to personally presenting it during Eisenhower's Korean visit. Clark thought the retired general-of-the-army would relish the prospect. No such luck ensued – Ike wasn't interested in prolonging the ground war and didn't even look at the proposal. The president-elect made trips to the front, talked to many soldiers, including front-line son Lt. John Eisenhower, and came to his own conclusions.

Eisenhower later wrote about his belief that Korean fighting could not continue in its bloody and senseless mode. Peace talks had been recessed two months, and would not reconvene until March 1953, a six-month hiatus. As he asserted, "My conclusion as I left Korea was that we could not stand forever on a static front and continue to accept casualties without any visible results. Small attacks on small hills would not end this war."[3]

Ike looked at nuclear weapons as a necessary element in American global defense against Communism. The US simply could not commit conventional resources necessary to deter ground-strong Soviet Russia from invading Western Europe. The effort would bankrupt America. Atomic strike had to be part of US response.[4] The policy of resorting to broad nuclear attack to counter numerical Red Army superiority, as worked out by Eisenhower and Secretary of State John Foster Dulles, came to be known as "massive retaliation."

Reagan Administration defense and arms control official Fred Iklé revealed that "The idea of using nuclear weapons *first* to respond to an attack with conventional forces – or rather to deter it – lived on as NATO doctrine until the end of the Cold War."[5] Unsurprisingly, according to Iklé, the Moscow-led Warsaw Pact, Red counter to the North Atlantic Treaty Organization, "was more prepared for first use than NATO."[5]

Truman's August 1945 ordering of Hiroshima and Nagasaki nuclear bombings likely had a constraining effect on later willingness to use such weapons. Truman had stated he would not be a party "to killing of millions of innocents."[6] His reluctance carried over to issuance of nuclear threats, and contrasted with President Kennedy's televised warning of "full retaliatory response by the United States on the Soviet Union" during the 1962 Cuban Missile Crisis. Kennedy's clear threat emphasized American resolve in countering nearby nuclear-tipped ballistic missiles aimed at the US. Russian leaders knew that firing nuclear missiles at the United States would bring massive thermonuclear counterattack. We will never know if a similar statement by Truman would have discouraged Chinese entry into the Korean War and possibly saved millions of lives.

OVERCOMING TRUMAN – ACHESON ATOMIC TIMIDITY

Beyond question is failure of US nuclear superiority to prevent Korean War outbreak. Iklé noted Stalin's approval of Kim Il Sung's attack on South Korea despite US possession of some 300 (Bernard Brodie's estimate) to 350 (Iklé's estimate) nuclear bombs and only *five* by Soviets.[7]

The Kremlin possessed keen awareness of Truman's nuclear paralysis. Even American entry into the war on South Korean behalf did not stop Stalin from sending fighter pilots, state of the art fighter jets, and tens of thousands of air support personnel into Manchuria to support the Communist cause, let alone huge quantities of war materiel.[8] Risk-aware and die-hard-realist Stalin knew it was politically impossible for Truman and Acheson to resort to atomic strike. The small army of leftist revolutionaries would be wild with anger and recrimination. Given depletion of conventional military strength, this equated to little or no US deterrent capability.

PLAYING THE "A" CARD

President Eisenhower set about renewing armistice negotiations, aimed at getting Communists to move quickly to conclude an agreement. In January-February 1953, Secretary of State Dulles dropped word to India's ambassador in Washington that should peace talks not produce the desired result, the US would "widen the Korean War beyond its present boundaries and use weapons not yet tried in Korea" to achieve decisive military victory. The word was spread in other diplomatic venues, among them the Taiwan Straits area and at Panmunjom.[9] Thinly veiled threat of atomic bombing of Chinese and North Korean targets could not be missed. Peace negotiations flop and stalemated war represented "intolerable conditions" to Ike. Solution was found in threatening massive US offensive. As he explained, "To keep the attack from becoming overly costly in lives, it was clear that we would have to use atomic weapons."[4]

Eisenhower mentioned Gen. MacArthur's pre-inauguration suggestion to him of nuclear necessity in Korea. Unsurprisingly, the president-elect related "Joint Chiefs of Staff pessimism about the feasibility of using tactical atomic weapons on front-line positions, in view of Red China's extensive underground fortifications …; but nuclear weapons would obviously be effective for strategic targets in North Korea, Manchuria, and on the Chinese coast."[4]

A momentous event then took place in a dacha outside Moscow, further encouraging Korean peace prospects: Generalissimo Stalin died March 6, 1953. New Soviet Premier Malenkov shortly announced, "All problems between the Soviet Union and the West, including the United States, could be solved peacefully."

Panmunjom talks restarted that March, with signals from Beijing that time had come for peace. China accepted Gen. Clark's February 22, 1953 proposal for exchange of badly sick and wounded prisoners. Subsequent Operation Little Switch saw return of 684 UN prisoners by Reds and 6,670 Communist troops by the UN. China soon accepted the principle of POW-decided repatriation for the vast body of remaining captives.

To show unhappiness with half of Korea in Communist hands, President Rhee ordered immediate release of 25,000 Red POWs, causing uproar among Communist delegates and angst in Washington. Could America restrain its key ally, prevent it from striking out on its own against the North? Emergency diplomacy smoothed Rhee's feathers and brought US "guarantee" of South Korean defense, continued military and economic support, and lasting troop presence.

To discourage South Korean dreams of reunification, CCF launched heavy April 1953 offensives against mostly ROK units in central and eastern front sectors. These continued until a few days before the July 27 armistice signing. ROKs took quite a beating. By giving the South a "bloody nose," China emphasized the reality of military power in Korea. The South could never fight CCF alone.

UNSTATED EISENHOWER PERCEPTION: US LOSING KOREAN WAR

Due consideration must be given a previously unappreciated reality – the US entered 1953 with the distinct prospect of *losing* the Korean War. Many facts and American statements, including those of Eisenhower, clearly support this conclusion. Attritional nature of fighting began to grate at American civilian and military sensibilities. Time appeared to stand on the Red side. As monster Stalin once told Zhou En-lai, North Koreans and Chinese could keep fighting indefinitely because they "lose nothing, *except for their men*" (emphasis in original).[10] It is likely that war-astute Ike added up Korean War negatives and came to a politically-incorrect, un-publishable conclusion: from 1952-53, tide of battle had turned most unfavorably against the US/UN and toward Communists.

By War's last year, US front-line troops disturbingly realized the Chinese could take any MLR position they wanted, only because they would expend whatever the lives needed. UN forces would not make this trade. Military historian SLA Marshall summed up reality: "The contest of attrition is all in favor of the side that values human life less." Then, as attested by Hackworth,

Ballenger, and Marshall, US combat performance declined in 1952-53 owing to the rotation policy and depressing static-war mentality.[11,12,13,14]

As "Slam" Marshall explained, "Troop rotation is a killer of men rather than a saver. There are never enough experienced men to fill rugged assignments and let new hands break in gradually. In scouting quality, diversification of maneuver, and catlike caution, GIs are rarely a match for the Chinese. [Courtesy of Truman and Acheson,] the US fought the type of war the Chinese wanted, not what was best for America."[14]

Absence of major mobile UN attack and a stagnant main line equated to reduced troop morale. Hackworth warned that a force not attacking had no hope of winning. In Ballenger's words, "Even the Marines noticed the keen combat edge had eroded."[12] US artillery supremacy likewise melted over War's last half. Massive, accurate, and concentrated Chinese cannon and mortar fire proved deadly to soldiers and Marines sheltered in pseudo-impregnable trenches and bunkers, which crumbled under People's Army barrages. Now Red fortifications superiority provided huge advantage – it was far more difficult for US heavy guns and even close-support aircraft to destroy opposing troop formations than for the enemy.

Adding to US insult, artillery shell and hand-grenade shortages beset Army and Marines, forcing *rationing* of rounds, with strict limits on daily firings. Ammunition frugality corresponded to exceptionally strong CCF shelling. As one Marine artillery officer stated, "We fired by the hundreds, the Chinese responded by the thousands."[15] Welcome to America, the former "Arsenal of Democracy," now the land of "Not Enough." Truman should have paid a heavy political price for disgraceful leadership causing needless GI killing and wounding. The press was missing-in-action, unwilling to launch politically-incorrect attack on a leftist-favored son.

The US surrendered at least a half-dozen outposts to 1952 enemy combat. Intense October fighting at "The Hook" resulted by month's end in CCF controlling over a mile of UN MLR trench.[16] While Reds were ultimately thrown off The Hook by bloody Marine counterattacks, the omen was anything but promising. The number of abandoned US outposts markedly increased in the April 1953 Chinese mass assault. Many of these lost positions had initially been won at high cost in American life and limb. In a huge CCF June assault, the Associated Press reported, "The ROK 5th and 8th Divisions today buckled under a crushing attack by great waves of Chinese troops who rolled back the Korean line of demarcation as much as two miles … along a blazing 30-mile stretch of the East Central Front. Censorship was tightened at US 8th Army Headquarters."[17]

New Eighth Army Commander Gen. Maxwell Taylor let the Chinese keep what had been hard-won American gains: "It did not make sense to spend the lives necessary to recapture lost positions."[17] *Conventional US ground, air, and artillery striking at present levels could not stop these Red victories.* Also, given lack of true UN defensive depth, Chinese breakthroughs could, and did in 1953, quickly result in deep and dangerous penetrations.

HANDWRITING CLEARLY SEEN FOR US/UN

Eisenhower's comment after visiting Korea December 1952, "We could not continue this war in its present course," may now be viewed in a new light.[18] Korean War combat was not working out for America, let alone dependence on peace talks to end fighting.[19] Negotiations were recessed from October 1952 to March 1953. The American people would not support vast ground war enlargement. Eisenhower concluded that threat of nuclear response had to be made, albeit three years late, to avoid defeat in Korea. Essentially, Ike put MacArthur's plan for nuclear bombing of Communist China and Manchuria on the table.[20,21] Already saddled with heavy nuclear baggage, Truman could not do this.

Stalin's early-March 1953 death proved at least of equal importance in motivating the PRC to accept prisoner-decided repatriation and armistice conclusion. China could not fight the war without massive Soviet support. In time of need, the wise man heeds his elder brother.

Chapter 39: Nuclear Explosives and Korean War

"Was failure to respond to Chinese intervention with the full use of our atomic bomb a tragic backing down for which future generations will have to pay?"[1]

- Gen. Matthew Ridgway, The Korean War.

Chairman Mao Zedong did not hesitate to take on great World War II 'victor' and nuclear weapon pioneer America. He knew of Dual Power inroads in Washington, and Red ideology's US political clout. The Great Helmsman also knew "the fix was in," as Red traitors gave ever-flowing information on highest War-related policy decisions, including Truman's nuclear reticence and US field force shortcomings. The year-old PRC shortly humiliated unprepared America.

PAPER TIGER WITH NUCLEAR TEETH

Eisenhower's book, *Mandate for Change*, written after leaving office in 1961, related belief that nuclear threat helped conclude an acceptable Korean peace.[2] He did not divulge presidential order for Atomic Energy Commission release of multiple atomic bombs to America's island base at Guam, to be in position for Far East air dropping. The threat had teeth. Furthermore, Far East Commander Gen. Mark Clark's combat autobiography, *From the Danube to the Yalu,* reported his May 23, 1953 authorization to "carry on the war in new ways never yet tried in Korea," should Communists reject the final UN peace proposal.[3,4] Although Clark's book did not specify what "new ways" meant, Eisenhower left no doubt about willingness to resort to nuclear weapons.

Winston Churchill imposed on good friend Ike to refrain from public commentary about use of atomic bombs in Korea. He felt such language drove an even deeper wedge between East and West. Churchill worried that London, most of England, and the heart of British civilization could be wiped off the map in one Russian stroke. Ike deeply respected his world war colleague and avoided open mention.

Regarding Washington anticipation of CCF's April 1951 Fifth Phase Offensive, author Tong Zhao of the Georgia Institute of Technology recently related Truman's supposed secret March decision agreeing to a JCS – Ridgway request for nuclear bomb pre-positioning on Guam. Zhao reported a flight of B-29 bombers with operational A-bombs under Air Force custody arriving there in April.[6,7] Surprisingly, this appeared to indicate Truman consideration of nuclear use should US forces be routed in Fifth Phase mass attack, with prospect of convincing Communist Chinese Korean victory. Public unawareness of apparent Truman pro-nuclear action signaled lack of desire to convey strong open warnings to Beijing about consequences of Eighth Army Korean demise. Of course, resounding US/UN Fifth Phase victory made nuclear intervention unnecessary at that point.

If Dr. Zhao is correct, 1951 Guam A-bombs must have been few in number, or shipped back to America before Eisenhower took office. Ike either added to a meager Guam stockpile, or ordered a new host of weapons.

Two facts are assured: Moscow promptly discovered US Guam-based nuclear arms plans, and China did not change massive Fifth Phase attack plans. American bomb-shuffling surely did not intimidate Red revolutionaries.

Should Communist negotiation intransigence continue, Eisenhower credibility hinged on carrying through nuclear attack on North Korea and China. US Fifth Phase defeat would put Truman on the nuclear spot, but would he order atomic attack in the face of leftist political dictates? The answer is clear: *only* if defeat-driven domestic political disaster beckoned. In no other Korean instance did Truman favor his military over political realities.

Not only Joint Chiefs of Staff negatively viewed atomic weapons value in Korea. Some US military and think-tank "experts" held nuclear bombs to be ineffective there, believing heavy mountain terrain would blunt and restrict vast explosive force ("blast effect") and prevent widespread enemy destruction. Enemy soldiers on a mountain's "far" side might be shielded from blast on the near side. The time's US atomic bomb stockpile contained a host of 40 kiloton-yield weapons, about twice the Nagasaki plutonium bomb's destructive power that killed over 50,000 Japanese ("kiloton" refers to the *equivalence* of a thousand tons, or two million pounds, of the explosive TNT).[8]

Some strategists recommended "airburst" explosion thousands of feet above ground. Others believed nuclear bombs were ideally suited to destroy deep Chinese defensive works through ground-level detonation, and especially useful in night attack, given CCF nocturnal battle preference. If it wished, the US could turn night into day for the Chinese and provide a striking example of superior power. It is clear that opening of sufficiently wide channels through deep Chinese lines would entail use of multiple, perhaps six to 10, or more, atomic bombs.

Effect of heavy radiation spewed from nuclear weapons on *friendly* troops had to be considered. Some 15-18% of blast energy is released as X-rays, gamma rays, and other types of radiation. UN force proximity to explosions, wind direction, cloud cover, and presence of snow on the ground help determine radiation exposure. UN forces could suffer heavy casualties and might have to withdraw 10 to 20 miles from blast sites, or prior to explosion be placed in protective structures.

Tong Zhao's 2009 paper told of 12,000 US troops subjected in 1951 to nearby nuclear explosion in a Nevada war-simulation exercise.[6] Post-nuclear reality in Hiroshima and Nagasaki suggested habitability of blast-site and adjacent areas within months after explosion, albeit with increased risk of radiation sickness and genetic defects.

Another daunting Truman-Eisenhower-era fact is the thermonuclear or hydrogen bomb, a fusion device packing anywhere from 10 to 1,000 times the blast energy and radioactivity of nuclear fission forebears. A small hydrogen bomb releases a 400-kiloton blast force, equal to 20 Nagasaki bombs; a large one 20 *megatons*, a fearsome thousand times the destructive force expended at Nagasaki ("megaton" refers to the equivalence of a *million* tons, or an incomprehensible two billion pounds, of TNT). A single 20-megaton H-bomb would release a nightmarish *twenty million* times the explosive force of the Second World War's most powerful conventional bomb.[9] This bomb would eradicate life and buildings from a 40-mile diameter circle, vaporize whole mountains, cause fires 100 miles away, and contaminate tens of thousands of square miles with deadly radioactive fallout. Such weapons are in reality civilization-enders.

Nine months after the first US hydrogen bomb explosion November 1952, Soviets did likewise. Russian thermonuclear explosion closely followed end of Korean fighting. Viewing the test firsthand, future Soviet Chairman Nikita Khruschev, by his own admission "up to his elbows in blood," realized unleashing such horrendous weapons would utterly destroy human civilization and should never be used. Most people never got as close as Khruschev and didn't understand the vastness of impact.

The US hydrogen bomb tested March 1, 1954 at the western Pacific Bikini Atoll yielded 15 megatons of energy, spreading radiation over the ocean *"that would have been fatal to unprotected people within an area of some 7,000 square miles"* (italics added), equal to a land tract 140 by 50 miles.[9] Such a blast would completely destroy the New York City metropolitan area, or the Washington-Baltimore-Philadelphia hub, easily killing tens of millions. This same bomb carved a 50-foot deep crater in coral rock in erasing the surrounding island and adjacent reefs.

In a letter, Churchill told Eisenhower,

> "Human minds recoil from the realization of such facts. The people, including the well-informed, can only gape and console themselves with the reflection that death comes to all anyhow. This merciful numbness can not be enjoyed by the few men upon whom the supreme responsibility falls. They have to drive their minds forward into these hideous and deadly spheres of thought."[10]

US invention of atomic artillery shells during the Korean War, so-called "tactical" nuclear weapons, represented another technological "advance." These possessed 1- or 2-kiloton charges, powerful enough to destroy people and structures within a one-mile diameter circle. Gen. Clark unsuccessfully requested Washington permission to use these to eliminate especially resistant enemy points. Later, the US and USSR even built back-packable nuclear bombs the size of five-gallon buckets. They were impractical, at least for America – the carrier could not escape the blast site by foot within a reasonable time after setting the bomb trigger, and was doomed to death or serious injury. Of course, such a mission's suicidal nature would not deter Islamic radicals.

Other compact Russian atomic bombs could fit within regular travel luggage, hence the name "suitcase bombs." In the early 1990s, Russian Army Gen. Ledbedev told the US Congress that 100 such miniature bombs had been produced, and half were missing![11] In the realm of Mutually Assured Destruction (MAD), contemporary American nuclear scientists Thomas Reed and Danny Stillman reported US creation of "man-portable 20-kiloton weapons," an incredibly dangerous development. If stolen or bought by terrorists and stealthily placed, these would completely destroy any American city center, along with a half- to one-million people.

Reality suggests that nuclear weapons are sinister devices to both enemies and creators. The US developed a miniaturized "W-88" hydrogen-bomb warhead, to enhance strategic delivery of "Multiple Independently-targeted Reentry Vehicles," or MIRVs. A ballistic-missile-firing submarine may carry 16, 24, or more intercontinental-range rockets, *each* carrying 14 MIRV warheads.

Unfortunately, the PRC stole the miniaturized M-88 design from America, and today is highly-likely manufacturing and deploying such Armageddon-producers (*for over 70 years, the US has miserably failed in the nuclear security realm*). The deadly warheads are a mere one-foot in diameter and four-feet long. Should a deranged enemy somehow get hold of one and use it against America, the Constitution-based United States will disappear that day into long-standing chaos and dictatorship. No nation could remain intact after such a blow.

IKE'S "ATOMS FOR PEACE" – GOOD INTENTIONS, BAD ENDINGS

Unknown outside the nuclear arms community, President Eisenhower, Secretary of State John Foster Dulles, and then-AEC Chairman Lewis Strauss bear heavy responsibility for worldwide spread of nuclear weapons, including into North Korea. Unintended disaster befell Eisenhower's plan to supply nuclear reactors to nations across the globe, ostensibly for "research" and provision of electric power. Fred Iklé believed

> "No other US policy, no multilateral policy, no United Nations activity has done more harm than Eisenhower's Atoms for Peace program in hastening and expanding … nuclear know-how for building bombs. And once the United States had legitimized the worldwide transfer of nuclear reactors, England, Canada, France, Germany, Japan, and the Soviet Union began to compete with American-exported reactors."[11]

Atoms for Peace soon evolved into "Atomic Weapons for War." A book by Henry Sokolski, *Best of Intentions*, details the American tragedy.[12]

Most unwisely through Atoms for Peace, the US Government provided over 20 countries with highly-enriched uranium (HEU) reactor fuel, U-235, "the ideal material for making bombs," truly "the stuff of atomic bombs."[13] Only in the past 15 years has the US made an effort to take back this bomb-grade uranium, at "a maddeningly slow pace."[13]

The principle of profound, long-lasting effect of American presidential decisions is no better illustrated than in the list of nations receiving atomic materials and bomb-building knowledge through gifted nuclear reactors. After America blazed the trail, North Korea received its first reactor from the USSR. Various countries followed suit in supplying nuclear plants to India, "Iraq, Iran, Vietnam, Yugoslavia, the Congo, and Laos."[11] Such folly proves the clay feet and serious negligence of many US presidential administrations and prominent national leaders and bodies.

Another unpopular subject is missing uranium and plutonium. Over the decades the US

Government managed to lose some three metric *tons* of plutonium, "enough to build several hundred atomic weapons of the 1945 design."[14] What is worse, "the know-how and wherewithal to make atomic bombs is ... likely to spread beyond the control of national governments" to include terrorist groups such as Al-Qaeda and the Islamic State of Iraq and Al-Sham (ISIS). Dissolution of the Soviet Union brought awareness of numerous minimally-guarded and unprotected uranium and plutonium stockpiles that could arm terrorists for decades. Securing these dangerous sites has been jointly pursued for over 20 years by US and Russian teams.

An August 25, 2005 *New York Times* article carried a statement by Pakistani President Pervez Musharraf on nuclear scientist A.Q. Khan providing North Korea with key centrifuge machines for manufacturing weapons-grade uranium. The People's Republic of China had already enabled Pakistani nuclear weapon development. Acquiring sufficient quantities of highly enriched uranium or plutonium is the major challenge in developing atomic bombs.

In the last 10 years, North Korea proudly announced its ability to reprocess spent nuclear reactor fuel rods into bomb-grade plutonium, and has exploded five nuclear bombs, the first in 2006, the last two in 2016. The North is likely armed with at least 10 fission or atomic weapons – aassuredly, thermonuclear bomb (H-Bomb) development is underway.

A May 10, 2015 Associated Press article by Matthew Pennington, carried in *The Palm Beach Post*, reported American "experts forecast that North Korea could increase its nuclear arsenal ... to between 20 and 100 weapons by 2020." The same piece told that "North Korea successfully test-fired a newly developed ballistic missile from a submarine," and launched "three anti-ship cruise missiles."[15] In the words of "[f]ormer senior US official Victor Cha ..., North Korea's missile capabilities are advancing at a clip that is concerning, if not alarming."[15]

Beyond doubt, North Korea will soon perfect land- and sea-based intercontinental ballistic missiles carrying nuclear or thermonuclear warheads. North Korea has important friends, the United States, South Korea, Japan, and allies some very frightening problems.

One thing is certain. American global promotion, via war or peace, of political freedom, economic development, and "free trade" has failed to stem threat of nuclear proliferation and attack. As Fred Iklé advised, "Few … grasp the dimensions of the storm awaiting us. Fewer still are mindful of its historic evolution."[16]

POST WORLD WAR US NUCLEAR POWER: DEAD-IN-WATER

Discussion of nuclear weapons and Korea is especially apt in reference to War's causation. Unknown publicly, an American atomic calamity existed after World War II. As attested by personal observations of Manhattan Project scientist Dr. Robert Bacher and AEC chief David Lilienthal at the Los Alamos, New Mexico bomb production plant, no A-bomb manufacture occurred there in the year 1946.

The following year, radioactive bomb trigger mechanisms were found to have decayed, disabling the few weapons in the "nuclear arsenal."[17] In fact, there was no nuclear arsenal! Factoring in Robert Oppenheimer's December 1947 letter to President Truman mentioning the same deplorable state, it is safe to assume the US had not a single functional atomic bomb from 1946-48. Plus, no uranium stockpile existed from which to make bombs.

According to an amazed Bernard Brodie, AEC Chairman Lilienthal did not want America to amass a uranium stockpile – doing so would drive up world uranium prices and make it prohibitively expensive to build nuclear bombs. Brodie pointed out the argument's absurdity: fissile material U-235 or plutonium comprised a very small part of an atomic bomb's cost. Delivery systems represented the major outlay.[19] The author does not hesitate to ask the question: Whose side was Lilienthal on? America had clearly shifted its nuclear program to neutral gear.

Thanks to British spy Donald Maclean and a score of Red Americans, Soviets knew every detail of the deficiency. The 1948 Berlin blockade now made sense, along with feebleness of US response. Internationalists made sure the Soviet Union caught up with the United States in nuclear weapon capability. Important American government officials placed a choke-hold on America's Manhattan Project and following nuclear weapon developments. Moscow had great friends in Atomic Energy Commission Chairman Lilienthal and Secretary of State Acheson.

AEC SLEIGHT-OF-HAND

Legislation creating the Atomic Energy Commission represented a major Moscow coup. Now nuclear arms would be physically taken from the military and placed under control of leftist politicians. Devoted progressive ideologue Acheson called the shots at State and Defense, while colleague Lilienthal ran the A-bomb show. No greater testament existed of unceasing, powerful, Red-directed pressure on vital US political levers, resulting in monumental decisions favoring Soviet interests at expense of American. No other conclusion can be reached: the left wielded immense political power. US Government had been hijacked.

Public announcement of Atomic Energy Act provisions included presumed welcome news of FBI supervision of AEC personnel evaluation and hiring. As recalled, Army officers handled what passed for Manhattan Project security, so FBI presence should ramp-up prospects for nuclear secrecy. Law makers and the new law could enjoy great credibility in parroting this "fact."

What never made it to public awareness was a law provision "allowing AEC employment of any former Manhattan Project employee *without* FBI review." Thanks to dutiful Congressmen and law-writing staffers, Reds and pro-Reds had clear sailing into the AEC! No better example proves leftist revolutionary power in America – the old "political 180" had again been pulled on trusting people. Who actually read the entire law text? Surely not public and press. The rule of politics remained unchanged: "People get the words, insiders get the decisions."

ANOTHER LOYAL RED FRIEND

Truman's second memoirs volume noted the above-referenced December 31, 1947 letter from J. Robert Oppenheimer, Manhattan Project scientific chief and head of the AEC's General

Advisory Committee. In it, Oppenheimer observed, "In none of the technical areas vital to the common defense and security ... was the state of [nuclear] development adequate. Our atomic armament was inadequate, both quantitatively and qualitatively, and the tempo of progress was throughout dangerously slow."[20] Abject nuclear neglect had been the rule for over two years, as Cold War worsened and hot war beckoned.

Oppenheimer's letter blamed "secrecy" for the "misunderstanding and error" threatening the "common defense and security." Importantly, Oppenheimer joined many nuclear scientists in holding a no-secrets philosophy regarding atomic energy, an enduring position throughout the Manhattan Project and his AEC advisory role. Commission Chairman Lilienthal and Acheson strongly shared the philosophy. Oppenheimer's statement to Truman is revealing: "The [Atomic Energy] Commission has inherited from the Manhattan District, and has maintained, an essentially enlightened policy."[21] This meant readiness to share atomic bomb knowledge, materials, and production facilities with the Soviet Union, precisely what happened under Roosevelt, Harry Hopkins, Oppenheimer, and Truman.

Given today's knowledge of vast Soviet espionage attack on America and senseless Washington largess, Russia's first atomic explosion in August 1949 came as no surprise. Truman publicly danced around reality in suggesting the nuclear event may not have been a bomb. In fact, the Red weapon, and the next three, proved exact copies of the first American bomb.

In gifting of key processes, scarce radioactive materials, even whole nuclear production factories, the US had supported Moscow's nuclear development effort for seven years. This chilling fact should have made headlines and stirred the American people to political action, but to this day remains unreported and publicly unknown. Anti-American largess simply represented great Soviet political influence in America. Oppenheimer proved another loyal Moscow subject and press darling.

Except for later emergence of truth-based radio and television, nothing has changed for mainstream news – incorrect truth must be ignored and untouched, as lies prevail.

The above facts contradict Truman's memoir statement of "uncompromising opposition to sharing or yielding of atomic military secrets to any other government."[21] So does the US-sponsored, HD Smyth-written booklet, *Atomic Energy for Military Purposes*, rushed to publication at time of Hiroshima and Nagasaki A-bombings.[22] Many nuclear scientists insisted America share atomic secrets with the world, no doubt in part to assuage their consciences, and equally to give the Soviet bomb program a boost. Non-Americans comprised 70% of Manhattan Project scientists. Obviously, the "secret" has been known to the world for over 70 years. College students have designed plans for workable atomic bombs.

Today, one can order the Smyth booklet from Amazon.com for about $45. Not one to dwell on Soviet espionage, AEC's David Lilienthal believed the Smyth Report an important source of global nuclear weapon proliferation. Political statements are typically at 180-degree variance from truth.

Great public controversy swirled about Oppenheimer in 1954 with a loyalty investigation headed by Gordon Gray. The government proposed to lift the scientist's security clearance, which would sever all relations with the AEC and be a public insult. Since Second World War's end, the press portrayed Oppenheimer as an all-knowledgeable hero figure, revulsed by atomic bomb destructiveness, and against US development of the more deadly hydrogen bomb. The scientist believed the US should limit itself to an arsenal of fission bombs, and allow Soviets to develop the greatly more powerful fusion or hydrogen weapons.

In that case, a single multiple-megaton Red H-bomb would yield far more destructive power than all American atomic or fission bombs. A host of hydrogen weapons would overwhelm any fission-based atomic stockpile. "Mutual Assured Destruction" would yield to assured US destruction.

It is fair to characterize Oppenheimer as a "peace-loving, liberal-minded elite," a true Internationalist.[23] His pre-Manhattan Project, West Coast Communist ties are well documented, along with statements of retired KGB officers about personal comfort in having Moscow learn all nuclear secrets.[24,25] The very politically-incorrect details of Oppenheimer's complicity in Soviet nuclear espionage are spelled out in the Jerrold and Leona Schecter book, *Sacred Secrets: How Soviet Intelligence Operations Changed American History."*

The 1954 Gray Board learned of a Manhattan Project-era statement by US Army security officer Capt. Peer DaSilva: "J.R. Oppenheimer is playing a key part in attempts of the Soviet Union to secure, by espionage, highly secret information vital to the security of the United States. Oppenheimer allowed a tight clique of known communists or communist sympathizers to grow up around him throughout the Manhattan Project."[26] These represented "a significant proportion of the key personnel in whose hands the success and secrecy of the project is entrusted."[26]

Among significant Oppenheimer personal conversations uncovered are those with San Francisco Soviet Consul General Gregory Kheifetz, a top North American KGB *legal* officer, which cemented Oppenheimer "becoming a willing source for the Soviet Union of classified military secrets, and his obedience to Soviet intelligence in separating himself as an open member of the American Communist Party to become an unlisted member from 1942-44."[27]

As the Soviet Union teetered and fell in 1990-91, retired high-ranking KGB officer Pavel Sudoplatov came out with his book, *Special Tasks: The Memoirs of an Unwanted Witness – A Soviet Spymaster.* Sudoplatov confirmed the invaluable contributions of Western scientists, not limited to Oppenheimer but including Nils Bohr and many others, to Red nuclear bomb development. Moscow researchers and selected American authors then discovered *"a memorandum from Soviet archives reporting that Oppenheimer had agreed to cooperate in a subtle form of espionage.* He never handed documents to any Soviet courier but knowingly facilitated 'sharing' of atomic secrets (italics added)."[28] The Schecters put it succinctly: "Through documents in the Russian presidential and intelligence archives, Oppenheimer's cooperation [was] unmasked."[29]

Of course the leftist US press could never allow permanent defilement of a great revolutionary warrior. Prominent liberal columnists Walter Lippman, James Reston, and Marquis Childs, ardent advocates for Alger Hiss's innocence, now stepped up for colleague Oppenheimer. A decade later, showing the firm but rarely-surfacing Internationalist hand controlling the White House, President Lyndon Johnson was impelled to bestow on Oppenheimer America's highest civilian award, the Medal of Freedom. Rulers stuffed it right down the throats of president and people.

Grains of truth had never been allowed to grow and develop in American understanding: far from a hero, this particular Stalin disciple helped bring about Korean War and 54,262 dead Americans. There were far more important concerns than interests of dumb American "primitives."

Interestingly, according to Fred Iklé, Oppenheimer's "great and ethical" mind held a streak of genocide. Revealed only in 2006, Oppenheimer wished to release a rain of highly radioactive and carcinogenic Strontium-90 over Germany. Manhattan Project scientist Joseph Rotblatt related Oppenheimer's 1943 letter to nuclear pioneer Enrico Fermi urging production of "enough Sr-90 to kill half a million people."[30]

ATOMIC TRAITOR GEORGE KOVAL

Bringing matters to the 21st-century, the Schecters cited the June 3, 2000, Kremlin meeting of presidents Vladimir Putin and Bill Clinton, during which "Putin had words of praise for American scientists who willingly helped the USSR develop its own A-bomb. They were not traitors to their country, Putin said. Rather, they were serving the cause of international peace."[31,32] In fact, Red atomic bombs rapidly led to war in Korea. Truth-denying Red ideology always took precedence over reality.

Gradually, information emerges about Moscow's nuclear hand. The 2009 book, *The Nuclear Express*, by American scientists Reed and Stillman, relates the story of hitherto unknown atomic spy Zhorzh (George) Koval. The name came to light October 27, 2007, when Russian Federation President Putin posthumously awarded Koval the top honor of "Hero of the Russian Federation." The ceremony took place "22 months after that agent's death in Moscow at age 92." The award emphasized the important work of "Koval and associates [in] successfully penetrating American factories and laboratories turning out the plutonium, enriched uranium, and polonium needed for production of the American A-bomb."

The Koval clique was cited for "collecting and transferring descriptions of those materials, the technology needed to produce them, and the quantities being turned out." It is apparent George Koval was a major Russian spy in America.

Koval came from classic spy roots. Born 1913 in Sioux City, Iowa, of Russian immigrant parents, by age 15 he graduated high school with honors. The family moved back to Russia in 1932, George earning a Moscow degree in chemical technology. He then joined military intelligence, the GRU, and returned to America October, 1940, arriving via tanker ship in San Francisco. Lacking a US passport, Koval simply "... walked out through the control point together with the captain, his wife and little daughter, who sailed together with him."

The chemist, assigned the code-name "Delmar," journeyed to the GRU New York City station, "... under the cover of the Raven Electric Company, a supplier to General Electric and other US firms." Successfully reinserted into American life, Koval managed to get himself drafted into the US Army in 1943, then to a post at the massive Oak Ridge, Tennessee, Manhattan Project plant. There, he "hit pay-dirt."

Like the James Bond "007" agent, Koval gained the position of "health physics officer," tracking "radiation levels throughout the sprawling facility." The job "gave him top-secret clearance, ... one of the few people who had access to the entire program ...." He also had charge of Oak Ridge's polonium stock, a rare element essential to initiating bomb-grade plutonium chain reaction.

Not quite a year later, Koval received June 1945 Manhattan Project orders to join the top-secret Dayton, Ohio nuclear installation, again as health officer with full visiting privileges in all buildings. The spy now had keys to yet another kingdom. What he knew, Russians knew. The Ohio plant produced the *polonium* initiator, or trigger, for the plutonium bomb, successfully tested July 16, 1945 at Alamogordo, New Mexico, and dropped with devastating effect on the city of Nagasaki, August 9.

One more hurdle surmounted in the nuclear bomb quest, Soviets surprised the world by exploding their first atomic bomb August 29, 1949, a plutonium-based weapon. It took the 2007 Russian Federation "Hero" ceremony for the truth about Koval's espionage to finally surface: the plutonium chain reaction initiator (trigger) mechanism for Russia's first A-bomb was "prepared to the 'recipe' provided by military intelligence agent Delmar – Zhorzh Abramovich Koval."

Sufficient damage to America done, in 1948 Koval returned to Russia to stay. Author Michael Walsh stated that the spy "used his real name throughout," and wondered why the US didn't discover his treachery until "the horses were in the next county and the barn had burned down." Walsh offers as explanations the Soviet ally status in World War II, Manhattan Project Director Gen. Groves' reliance on Army security officers to perform background checks to FBI exclusion, and intentional overlooking of suspicious backgrounds in the presence of scientific ability. Unmentioned is total dedication of Red revolutionaries to hero Stalin and beloved Soviet Russia, and utter contempt for evil America.

Scientists Reed and Stillman also divulged "… presence of at least two GRU agents within Manhattan Engineering District headquarters. As of 2009, one is still alive, living in Moscow."[32] Perhaps the spy's name will emerge in another "Hero" award. As with scientific nuclear espionage, Manhattan Project chief Gen. Groves, and Americans, had not a clue about Soviet penetration of his headquarters.

RED NUKES BRING KOREAN WAR

Loss of American nuclear monopoly meant wars of revolution received Stalin's full support, without fear of atomic retaliation. For America, the atomic bomb lost any restraining effect on Soviet behavior, if indeed any existed given postwar American nuclear bungling and Stalin's knowledge of US leadership stupidity. Door to Korean War now stood wide open.

Under Truman's watch, America put brakes on nuclear weapon development, allowing Soviets to catch up, precisely the state of affairs Moscow desired. America also disarmed its conventional force, another great Red advantage.

For 17 years prior to war in Korea, and not by accident, Washington gave primacy to Soviet Russian interests. As Mao reminded the world, the US was truly a "paper tiger," albeit as Khruschev reminded, "with nuclear teeth," when it chose to bare them.

As MacArthur and many top American military officers knew, "For a brief window of time in the early 1950s, the United States possessed the unmatched atomic capability to take on and defeat the Communist powers. Sooner or later, they believed, it was the destiny of the United States … to fight the Communists. Better now, surely, when the nation possessed the means to achieve victory at minimal risk to the American continent, than a generation hence …."[33]

<u>Chapter 40: War's End</u>

"Anyone who believes that the last months of the Korean War – the 'stalemate' – were inactive has not read history."[1]

- Korean combat veteran Lee Ballenger, *US Marines in Korea, Vol. 1: 1952.*

The United States fought the Korean War "from a position of decided military weakness that caused severe compromises in military and political objectives."[2] President Truman's timid leadership, manifested in failure to capitalize on China's time of military distress, plus politically-mandated Euro-centrism, assured drawn-out battle and outcome. Loyal FDR successor Truman sacrificed American military strength to New Deal/Fair Deal domestic programs and provision of "collective security and economic aid abroad."[3] Truman's domestic agenda was "always more important to him personally than the outcome on the Korean peninsula."[4] America's postwar strategy centered on containing Soviet Communism in Europe.[5] Necessity of preventing Red takeover of all Europe is clearly part of Roosevelt's tragic war legacy, a rogue bull elephant kept from public view.

The Korean War's last two years are often called the "stalemate" period, but blood flowed all-too-freely on each side. The US/UN set up scores of outposts fronting the main line, which served to invite Chinese attack and UN counter-attack. Both sides employed tactics of "daily patrols, ambushes, raids, and constant artillery barrages."[6] Massive daily Chinese artillery and mortar bombardment wreaked havoc on UN fortifications and caused a great many dead and wounded. Outposts Hook, Bunker Hill, and Pork Chop Hill became scenes of back-and-forth close combat, with Chinese evicting Americans, who then paid a high price retaking the hills. The PRC might make four, six, or eight attempts at storming UN positions, mindless of human toll. Reds also simultaneously assaulted several different outposts, counting on "sheer weight of numbers" to carry the day.[7]

The US/UN inflicted four or five times more casualties than it took, but the trade-off still favored the side uncaring about life. As Ballenger emphasized, "China could afford the human loss, the US, South Korea, and allies could not."[8] From the UN standpoint, the last two years of war represented a senseless war of attrition.

Reds continually dug trenches and bunkers closer and closer to the UN MLR. More shallow UN diggings were commonly reduced to rubble from Red artillery and mortar pastings, which flattened Army and Marine six-foot deep trenches and integrated bunkers.

US ammunition rationing, especially of artillery rounds, meant Chinese cannon fire often outperformed that of American. Shell shortages prevented US artillery from stopping Communist build-up of men and fortifications and permitted full-brunt heavy Red gun fire without comparable or heavier counter-fire. With "overwhelming firepower the only [*usable*] method in the American arsenal to neutralize Chinese numbers," markedly reduced artillery fire immediately cut the legs off basic UN strategy (italics added).[9]

SIXTY DEAD AND WOUNDED GIs PER DAY

For the Korean War's last two years, America suffered an average of 1,800 killed and wounded per month.[10] In just the fighting for Outpost Bruce, a single 51-hour ordeal, Marines had to replace the original 40-strong platoon many times. "Each group of 40 men fought off assaults by the hundreds."[11] Twenty-eight Marines gave lives, with 70 wounded. At Bunker Hill in August 1952, Marines suffered "144 KIA, 15 missing, 1,237 wounded."[12] This in one month, at just one part of a long Main Line of Resistance! The carnage meant nothing toward concluding a peace agreement – "the enemy was mentally, emotionally, and numerically equipped to wait it out ...."[13]

Regarding the above, American leaders grossly misused the Marine Corps in Korea. A branch of service trained and experienced in offensive warfare, employing amphibious assault to take and seize enemy positions while inflicting heavy casualties, was forced to fight defensively. Digging in and awaiting enemy attack over a long period of time, a form of siege warfare, "was the antithesis of Marine Corps philosophy."[14] The same huge mistake carried over into Vietnam.

SECOND WORLD WAR'S DEADLY LEGACY

Three years of Korean fighting produced staggering human and material destruction. According to John Toland, over two million North and South Korean civilians died, while homeless in South Korea alone numbered 3.7 million.[15] US/UN forces killed some half-million Chinese "volunteers," with equal carnage of wounded. PLA Korean combat losses amounted to 10 times those incurred in over 10 years of Chinese civil war and fighting Japan. British historian Max Hastings estimated 415,000 ROK soldiers killed and 429,000 wounded.[16]

Of the 1,319,000 Americans serving in the Korean War, 54,262 did not return alive. A staggering 13,000 had been reported missing-in-action or captured. Most of the missing are unaccounted for and presumed dead, likely victims of POW atrocities.

Armistice-agreed Operation Big Switch began August 5, 1953, and within a month saw 3,597 American and 7,862 South Korean Communist-held prisoners returned within the Demilitarized Zone. The UN sent almost 76,000 Red prisoners who accepted repatriation back to North Korea or the PRC, while bringing 22,600 to the DMZ-housed Neutral Nations Repatriation Commission. All but 137 of these decided on life in South Korea or Formosa. They could thank President Truman's unyielding position on prisoner repatriation for new leases on life. (South Korean President Rhee had released some 25,000 Red prisoners months before in a show of pique at UN failure to unify Korea.)

Army personnel comprised most of American prisoners; Marines lost relatively few. Twenty-one US POWs chose to remain behind, taken within the PRC as apparently indoctrinated Reds. They were never accepted within Communist Chinese society or by its leadership and gradually made their way back to America.[17] Today, as North Korea permits, US searches continue for graves of the missing.

WAR AND VISIONARY MISMANAGEMENT

Korean War consequences are powerfully felt to this day and show no signs of receding. Few if any post-World War II American leaders envisioned mainland China's latent economic and military power and potential regional and world influence. Truman's decision to conduct peace talks and stop forward combat pressure against Reds represented one of the greatest and far-reaching military blunders in American history, allowing a beaten Chinese army to be reconstituted and resume wholesale killing of Americans, Koreans, and allies for another two years.

Truman permitted Mao Zedong to stand down, in part with horse cavalry and animal-drawn artillery, what had recently been the world's greatest military power and emerge from armistice negotiations as a military equal. Communist prestige in Asia soared. Vietnamese revolutionary Ho Chi Minh felt great encouragement in his struggle against the French. North Korean hostility never abated, while its prime supporter, the People's Republic of China, grew into an economic and military giant. Today's PRC muscle-flexing in the South China Sea, including harassment of American ships and reconnaissance aircraft, claims to neighboring-nation islands, and building of military bases thereon, is an unfortunate and dangerous legacy.

Generals Van Fleet and Clark, author Brodie, and James and Wells, believed the US/UN did not have to accept a draw in Korea.[18] A large portion of North Korea could have been taken in May-June 1951, up to the relatively narrow Pyongyang-Wonsan "waist" or "neck," while severely punishing the Chinese People's Army (MAP 10). An enemy motivated to respect American military power would be receptive to early truce agreement. For Red China, fighting the "champ" to a draw represented notable victory for a new-born nation.

Senior American decision-making at key War junctures proved so harmful to GI welfare and national interests that the question arises whether US strategy had been turned over to the enemy. This is not far-fetched – Acheson stood as a supreme Internationalist, backed by a host of Dual Power Reds in the White House, State and Treasury departments, and many other Federal Government agencies. From 1944 – 49, these America-haters parroted Moscow's anti-Nationalist line in China while taking every opportunity to praise and promote Chinese Communism.[19] The same period witnessed US support of Soviet Russia's nuclear bomb program through the Lend-Lease program, Manhattan Project, Atomic Energy Commission, and concurrent demise of American nuclear strength. Red scripts emanating from Moscow were meant to be followed.

Interestingly, the popular 1977 movie "MacArthur" showed many Truman discussions with key advisors, but did not use Acheson's name. The character was simply referred to as "The Secretary." Protection of Truman's reputation as bold decision-maker may have prompted omitting the name of the President's controversial right arm. There may also be negative connotation to mentioning Acheson in the context of "soft on Communism."

Biographer David McCullough praised Truman for preventing the Korean War from becoming a world war. Truman memoirs repeatedly emphasized fixation on "preventing World War III." Yet a media/academic/cultural firewall holds back any connection between Truman's Korean mishandling, war in Vietnam, and today's problems with nuclear-armed North Korean and PRC police states. Truman is off the hook regarding public awareness of his unfinished business in Korea, leading directly to a 63-years-and-counting festering national sore.

HIDING US WEAKNESS

Truman appeared to believe only the United States could prevent world war. US policy must "avoid all-out military action against China … because it is a gigantic booby trap."[20] Truman and Acheson wanted to negotiate with and appease Red China, even if she had thrown the US/UN off the Korean peninsula.

Truly, Truman uniquely defined "total war." The PRC attacked US armies in force and came close to annihilating American, South Korean, and allied forces, but according to Truman did not cross the threshold of "war" against America. US retaliation on China for its attack on US troops *would* represent an act of war likely to precipitate World War III, so Chinese territory enjoyed sacrosanctity. It seemed an illogical double standard.

According to Truman, acceptance of MacArthur's advice to bomb Manchurian army and air bases meant the US "would have been openly at war with Red China and probably Russia."[21] But what was Korean fighting against Red China if not "open war?"

Obsession with Europe helped prevent wise action in Korea. A huge Red Army stared at the West across Churchill's Iron Curtain. Truman always held Europe "the key to world peace." The tainted-goods quality of memoirs is highlighted by his outrageous statement, "It should never be forgotten that America had yet to prove to Europeans that defense of Europe was something we would take seriously."[22] Two world wars, 500,000 dead Americans, the Marshall Plan, and NATO shred the ridiculous words.

Patient reading of Truman musings brings out truth: the US had nothing militarily and hence backed down from full Chinese confrontation. Truman had gutted the armed forces. And leftist politics demanded US moderation in war with China. The buck stopped with the Commander in Chief. What kind of world did he envision with that senseless response to Communist world realities?

MYTH – GREAT LEADER TRUMAN

In war, Truman belied the image of bold decision-maker portrayed in sympathetic press, biographies, and movies. In a 1949 speech, Congressman and fellow Democrat John F. Kennedy noted "… the tragic story of China, whose freedom we once fought to preserve. What our young men saved, our diplomats and our President have frittered away."[23]

Lack of friendship between the Kennedys and Truman was understandable. So too, the reality of presidential dependence on knowledgeable advisors for sound development and execution of policy.

With disastrous Korean War outcomes and undisturbed Red influence in Government, the President's national leadership ability must receive low marks. While Truman may have been "bold" in bringing NATO and the Marshall Plan to life, he acted with incompetence at the Potsdam Conference, in shielding the American people from reality of postwar Communist world threat, in Korean War management, and in covering Dual Power reality with the "red herring" canard. Truman unawareness of US shipment of classified atomic bomb hardware to Russia under his watch defies belief.

With exception of Franklin Roosevelt's public portrayal, and that of President Obama, no more glaring example of leftist press bias exists than Harry Truman's undeserved mythological-hero status.

TOP BRASS UNLOAD FRUSTRATIONS

Ignorance or disregard of Communist tactics, added to obsessive fear and heavy Internationalist political pressure, allowed Truman and Acheson to ignore vital truth: "The enemy's real intention was to fuel the peace flame only to gain time to rebuild its forces."[24] Advent of peace negotiations made the "Conflict" into "Truman's War." As Bernard Brodie appreciated, "Nothing was clearer, perhaps too clear for the opponent, than the President's desire to terminate that war."[25] Truman's misguided War direction allowed Communists to "come back from imminent collapse and defeat … and be able to sign the armistice as established equals."[26]

Then-Lt. Gen. Maxwell Taylor, later a favorite of President Kennedy and Defense Secretary McNamara, replaced James Van Fleet as Eighth Army Commander February 11, 1953. Van Fleet served 22 months in the challenging post, far longer than other UN field commanders, and had a son killed in 1952 Korean action (Mao Zedong also lost a son to Korean combat). The Army gave Van Fleet a fourth star before retirement in testament to fine leadership under trying limitations.

Perhaps filial sacrifice encouraged Van Fleet to publicize strongly-held war opinions at career's end. He wrote a two-part *Life* magazine article shortly after, pulling no punches in describing personal bitterness at having the rug pulled from victory in Spring 1951. Van Fleet had no doubt his soldiers could have decisively beaten CCF, unique in viewing Korea as "… so much more a favorable battleground for us than for them. I kept seeing favorable opportunities to destroy the armies of the Chinese Reds."

Van Fleet mentioned the April 22, 1951 attack by 630,000 Chinese, the first element of the Fifth Phase offensive, followed May 16 by the concluding mass assault. Overwhelming US firepower beat back both Red efforts, at huge enemy cost. He also related Acheson State Department undercutting of Korean military and armistice efforts through pre-negotiation comments to Reds on UN willingness to accept the 38th Parallel as the demarcation line. Communist China simply could not be allowed to lose the Korean War.

We recall the September 1951 personal message from Ridgway to Army Chief of Staff Gen. Collins complaining that in truce talks, "The Joint Chiefs always acceded to Communist demands."[27] Truman and Acheson sold out the American fighting man behind his back, while inept Joint Chiefs lay as doormats. The American people, and especially Korean War fighting men living and dead and their families, suffered great disservice. Adverse political considerations mandated press and popular cultural ignorance of incorrect reality. The Roosevelt-Truman leftist power foundation and associated lies could not be disturbed.

Admiral Joy, the first Senior Delegate for UN truce negotiations, wrote the respected book, "How Communists Negotiate," after leaving truce talks. Joy's commentary supported the unparalleled study of culturally-opposite Soviet methods made by George Kennan. At his final Panmunjom session, Joy told North Koreans and Chinese, "You impute to the United Nations the same suspicion, greed and deviousness which are your stock in trade." Kennan would readily agree with this assessment of basic Soviet Communist qualities.[28]

At Acheson's direction, Joy turned over the "unenviable job" to Army Maj. Gen. William K. Harrison, who stayed on to finish and sign the armistice July 27, 1953. In recognition of a lifetime of stellar leadership, the US Navy named a new combat ship after Joy, which participated in the alleged 1964 Tonkin Gulf attack by North Vietnam, directly bringing Vietnam War.

Before leaving Far East Command for NATO, Gen. Ridgway observed, "There should be no doubt in the minds of our people as to the methods which the leaders of Communism are willing to use, and actually do use, in their efforts to destroy free peoples and the principles for which they stand."[29]

Far East Commander Gen. Clark necessarily added his name to armistice documents. Years later, he related

> "Personal disappointment that my government did not find it expedient to whip the Communists thoroughly in our first shooting war with them. There was no use continuing the frustrating stalemate where we were going no place, and suffering 30,000 American casualties a year. I would be less than truthful if I failed to record that I put my signature on that document with a heavy heart."[30]

WELCOME TO LIMITED WAR

Hardened US combat commanders like Clark and Van Fleet, accustomed to *winning* wars, felt deeply betrayed over the drawn Korean outcome. Frustrated David Hackworth acknowledged, "We hadn't even tried to win after the first year."[31]

A new vista dawned on the American people and military – *limited war*, undertaken by presidential directive without Congressional input, let alone declaration. Now military non-professionals, more accurately military amateurs such as secretaries of state and defense and National Security Council civilians, all working for the president, dictated strategies, plans, and even field operations to weak military chiefs of staff.

In sum, to mortal detriment of GIs, political appointees made, and continue to make, military decisions far beyond their knowledge and capability. The names of Acheson, Kennedy-Johnson defense chief Robert McNamara, and George W. Bush's Defense Secretary Donald Rumsfeld come to mind: forceful men used to beating opponents into submission to get their way, and their war. Joint Chiefs functioned as political pawns, along with the entirety of US military services. Any fighting officers and men in Korea who thought about American decisions and related them to the combat situation had to know soldiers were meaningless Washington puppets. Only politics could account for the senselessness, stupidity, even insanity. Politics and a compliant press could also contain the deadly fact of treason.

PROBLEMS OF LIMITED WAR

Bernard Brodie raised vital points about limited war unaddressed by any other Korean War author, and unmentioned in 60-plus years of national debate. What American civilian and military leadership consider limited war, "limited in terms of emotional and material commitments, may be *total* war to our opponents and to one or more of our allies" (italics added).[32] In this scenario, while the US is partially in the fight, the enemy may be "all-in," and their "resolve may well exceed ours."

Brodie also perceived limited-in-scope American war-fighting as "automatically cutting itself down to a size that the opponent may be able to cope with ...." This appears to be true in Korea, Vietnam, and Iraq and Afghanistan wars. In addition, astute war enemies recognize and take advantage of internal American political opposition in encouraging dilution of national war support.

Euphemism supports continual politico-military sleight-of-hand. The term "limited war" is not only a misnomer, but a deceiver to boot. Brodie appreciated the deadliness and long duration of limited wars, citing 844,000 South Korean war casualties, plus over 3,000 Allied killed in action and 12,500 wounded.[32] Later wars in Vietnam, Iraq, and Afghanistan each lasted over 10 years. Brodie held American public capacity to support limited war as itself limited and "likely to be precarious ... and not to be counted on if that war be prolonged."[32]

A reasonable and life-saving conclusion to the limited war dilemma is abandonment of prospective national combat action in face of partial emotional and material commitment. Lives may only be spent in presence of full national will and backing. "All-in" is the requirement for war. "Half-in" means half-baked outcome and terrible waste of young blood. Yet in today's war against Islamic terrorism, the latter policy appears all-too-common in American quest to minimize civilian casualties in air and ground attack and act only in concert with, and approval of, "coalition partners."

TOP-DOWN CONTROL – THE POLITICAL MODEL

Increased civilian control of the military became a vital and popularly ignored Second World War outcome. The 1947 Defense Reorganization Act and 1949 revision facilitated civilian power grab. Power-mad politicians and wealthy supporters drove the process. They could not tolerate any degree of military independence and needed tight control to satisfy political agendas, including the mandate of America as world policeman under UN aegis.

Proof lies not only in Washington's absurd Korean battlefield decision-making, but in reckless disarmament and misguided pre-Korean War Republic of Korea Army development. All represented lack of military professionalism, the expected outcome of civilian military incompetence.

Senselessly, the US advisory Korean Military Assistance Group (KMAG) reported not to the Defense Department, but the State Department, whose civilians assessed and decided on adequacy of South Korean military preparation. Incompetence bred incompetence.

Of course, civilian interference in military affairs did not cease with Korean War armistice but grew ever stronger. Today it compromises US military effectiveness throughout the world.

CUTTING LEADERSHIP LEGS FROM COMBAT EXCELLENCE

As expected and desired by tradition-haters, American military leadership underwent a retrograde movement in professionalism. Tight politicizing civilian control brought sycophants to top echelons of military command. Budding military leaders quickly perceived the "political leadership" model as the ladder to success. Unfortunate features of this system are rampant dishonesty, micro-management, general contempt for people, and strict top-down control of decisions. These are also prime characteristics of Soviet-style management.

Since organizational leadership standards are set from the top, aggressive career-minded officers could not fail to note the Joint Chiefs' "Five Silent Men" example. Self-serving commanders placed personal careers ahead of loyalty to nation, mission accomplishment, and protection of their troopers. Non-political true warriors usually failed to rise above the rank of colonel. Often frank, honest, and abrasive in personal style, unwilling to sacrifice revered standards of professionalism, including ethical and moral principles, such real fighters represent a threat to political agendas and cannot be tolerated.[33] For too many presidents and top advisors, ability to fight and win wars is secondary to propagation of political power.

One true American warrior, then-Marine Brig. Gen. "Chesty" Puller, who broke through the colonel ceiling, joined another, Army Col. Glover S. Johns, in attempting to force truth on the American people:

> "The Army took a hell of a beating in Korea, and the greatest part was *after* the heavy fighting was over. First there was the 'no-win war' spirit. Then the political limitations imposed on us during peace negotiations. The Army meekly submitted, raising higher and ever higher the point of responsibility for the smallest action. As regimental commander I couldn't even send out one patrol without Army Corps approval of the plan, submitted 48 hours in advance. It made company and battalion commanders messenger boys. You had no authority."[34]

A JCS member might utter similar words of exasperation about the same mindless, obsessive, top-down control.

CHINESE-STYLE POLITICS

Betrayal of field commanders by politicians was not solely an American phenomenon. Marshal Peng, who served Chairman Mao so loyally in Korea for War's entirety, ran afoul of the Great Leader in 1959 and lost his PRC Defense Minister position. Peng made the mistake of criticizing

Mao's "Great Leap Forward" economic development plan. John Toland reported that 10 years later Peng was "tortured to death during the Cultural Revolution."[35] Chang and Halliday related his "decency and decorum," and shyness at "fighting for power for himself." Peng couldn't "match Mao in mud-slinging and political smearing."[36]

According to *New York Times* China correspondent Fox Butterfield, Mao's great 1960s Cultural Revolution social upheaval claimed 400,000 lives and spared no segment of society. Persecution included hundreds of thousands of teachers, scientists, and health professionals.[37] We again note Communist proclivity for liquidating whole classes of people. Chang and Halliday accused Mao of responsibility for "over 70 million deaths in peacetime, more than any other 20th-century leader."[38]

In similar deadly vein, Butterfield reported executions of "three million former landlords, Kuomintang officials, and army and police officers" during the Chinese land-reform campaign of 1949-51.[39] The massacre occurred during CCF Korean War fighting, a throwback to Soviet Russia's 1937-39 Great Purge that crushed a million lives and a host of Red Army officers, shortly to be missed as world war began. Slaughtering of army officers may have compromised CCF leadership and contributed to the Spring 1951 rout. Revolutionary purification seemed to take precedence over practical needs and underscored superiority of ideology over humanity in the Communist system, and chilling obsession with class conflict.

MILITARY EDUCATION IGNORES KOREAN LESSONS

The Korean War proved the inability of air power to shut off, or markedly restrict, enemy supply. Nor could air bombing destroy heavily entrenched enemy front line units, isolate the battlefield through denial of logistical flow and reinforcements, or penetrate deep underground infantry and artillery emplacements. Sparse allocation of America's best jet fighters, inadequate maintenance resources, and lack of jet-capable airfields added to Korean woes. These facts became especially apparent in the War's latter two years.

Ground war had its own problems, among them minimal US infantry strength, Red artillery ascendance, Chinese territorial sanctuary, the troop rotation policy, and attritional fighting favoring Communists.

Instead of raising soldierly standards to meet Red threat, the post-Korean War era saw watering down of Army training to minimize civilian complaints of unnecessary brutality. Realistic combat scenarios were too risky – some recruits had died in training, likely from drill instructor incompetence. Surprisingly, the regression took place in the presidency of Dwight Eisenhower. The Marine Corps resisted the trend toward recruit leniency.

It wasn't just press and politicians who papered over significance of Korean War outcomes. Senior Army generals felt embarrassed by July - August and November - December 1950 combat debacles, and two years of fruitless static war that deeply chaffed their sense of professionalism and traditional focus on victory. War's end then brought self-imposed military cover-up, truth too discomforting to acknowledge.[40]

Tragically, the practical consequence was that military services in the Eisenhower (1953-61), Kennedy (1961-63), and Johnson (1963-69) administrations "learned nothing from the Korean experience, only to carry the same non-lessons into the next war [Vietnam] to blow it all over again."[40]

D. Clayton James and Anne Wells noted pre-Second World War failure of American officers to learn and appreciate important distinctions in military and national strategies. Success in war meant sensitive attention to host-country political and economic matters. International policies of *all* nations, including those related to war, always reflect internal politics. Unfortunately, American military education appeared to under-emphasize or ignore such factors.

George Kennan mentioned absence of formal American politico-economic war standards as hampering State Department efforts to develop a comprehensive post-World War II war doctrine. State Policy Planning Staff resorted to literature of Clausewitz and other century-old (or more) classic strategists for needed advice. The deficiency "contributed to the *muddled strategy* in Korea" (italics added).

James and Wells strongly indicted military education for ignoring Korea in the 11 years leading up to Vietnam, revealing, "The senior military colleges offered virtually nothing about the lessons of the Korean War and the confusion of military and national strategic objectives to prepare the upcoming senior leaders of America's forces in the Vietnam War." It boiled down to "failure of the curriculum and teaching of the top service schools."[41]

Secretary of Defense McNamara, who like Acheson took pride in running roughshod over military or civilian opponents, brushed off the Korean War as representing only US "unpreparedness, and rashness by MacArthur."[42] In McNamara's mindset, educators offered nothing of substance to the Vietnam situation: "Those that can, do – those that can't, teach."

FANCY-FOOL LEADERS: IGNORANCE AND DISRESPECT OF ENEMY

The time's fawning praise heaped on "brilliant" McNamara, and his stature as heavyweight champion of defense, readily melded with the view of North Vietnamese incapability of resisting American machinations and waging effective war. Northern leaders would never be so foolish as to take on the great American military. "They wouldn't stand a chance," even though Hanoi inflicted a sound beating on the French, who fielded a half-million men in Indo-China and lost 48,000 dead and 132,000 wounded, figures scarily close to American Vietnam casualties. As Dwight Eisenhower later observed, more French officers were killed in Vietnam in one year than graduated from France's national military academy, Saint Cyr.[43] Unbridled McNamara hubris and a hefty dose of racial chauvinism made a dangerous brew.

McNamara had bullied his way through corporations and Government, achieving great success by American standards. But author David Halberstam correctly pegged the vaunted Defense Secretary: "Intelligent, forceful, everything but wise."[44] Identical qualities applied to Secretary Acheson. *For the third time in 23 years*, racial chauvinism provoked "underestimation of Asian fighting capabilities."[45] Physically-small, primitive, black-pajama-clad yellow Asians could never compete with white greatness. Halberstam blamed an American leadership sense of superiority as preventing true North Vietnamese assessment – the "enemy did not register in terms they could visualize and understand."[46] Hence McNamara could ignore a December 1961 report on Vietnam by respected Army Gen. Maxwell Taylor and political operative Walt Rostow, that described North Vietnamese as "arrogant and contemptuous toward their foe, with a distinguished record against a previous Western challenger."[47]

Before France's humiliating 1954 final defeat at Dien Bien Phu, Gen. Marcel LeCarpentier explained that "Vietnamese would not understand sophisticated war, it would be easy to fool them."[48] A French officer colleague joined in denigrating Ho Chi Minh's Communist army: "They have no artillery, and even if they did, they do not know how to use it."[49] One can envision culturally-superior Carthaginians voicing similar ill-advised, dangerous sentiments about primitive Romans before start of the First Punic War (264 BC).

Underestimating an enemy is a most costly war mistake. American and French social sophistication proved incapable of overcoming a relatively primitive but fierce and unyielding enemy, willing to spend endless lives to achieve victory.

US Army Gen. Norman Schwarzkopf's military autobiography dealing with the first Iraqi war (1991), and Robert McNamara's Vietnam-era statements, allow appreciation of the misperceived association in part of US military culture between tallness, imposing physical appearance, and combat prowess. Effective war fighters are supposed to resemble John Wayne characters. This of course reflects parochialism and deep ethnocentrism.

Unfortunately for haughty Secretary McNamara, and tragically for the American people, North Vietnamese revolutionaries were not impressed by American standards. Ho Chi Minh had successfully dealt with Western arrogance before in forcing France from Indo-China. North Vietnamese *will* was not amenable to breaking like those who might challenge and lose to McNamara in Washington. And so McNamara utterly failed to impose *his* will on North

Vietnam. Brilliance of Washington figures didn't matter to Hanoi leaders. Their system and combat strong points lay outside the realm of American leader influence and understanding.

A final irony in the form of deadly reality awaited great McNamara. After committing a half-million American troops to Vietnam, and gaining a fully established war quagmire with 200-plus American killed-in-action each week, the Secretary lamented, "If only we had known more about the enemy, more about its society, if we had more information ...."[50] Halberstam hammered the hypocritical blood-stained big-shot: "Of course one reason there was so little knowledge about the enemy was that no one was as forceful as he in blocking its entrance into the debates."[50]

Meanwhile, lies came in abundance from Vietnamese battlefields, American colonels and generals wanting to look good to their big bosses. Loyalty was to career, not Constitution, truth, morality, or subordinate officers and men with lives at risk. South Vietnamese were said to be growing in military strength, able to fight off the North without American combat presence. "Body counts" held sway among field leadership. North Vietnamese Communists were quite adept at sacrificing bodies, but not nearly as many as Washington reported. Worshipping at the political altar, US civilian and military war leadership bent objective truth in the quest to create favorable, and false, war reality.[36] This worked in the Soviet system, but not for US war-fighting.

As David Hackworth knew, the only hope for America in Vietnam was to out-guerrilla the guerrillas. It happened sometimes, but not frequently enough to achieve military victory.

Recently, Edward Marolda summarized American leadership failure in the Vietnam War. Our nation's "best" civilian and military brains, and their presidents and cabinet secretaries, ignored vital lessons from Korea and conducted another tragic Asian war under the flawed premise "that North Vietnam had neither the will nor the capacity to make war against the United States."[51] As in Korea, American military operations then suffered under the mistaken policy of

> "graduated escalation. Fearful of Chinese or Soviet intervention, President Johnson and Secretary McNamara undercut their own chosen path by limiting the application of

force, imposing tight restrictions on operations, and micromanaging the campaign from afar. US military leaders must share the blame for endorsing and even championing this strategic approach … and operations that were clearly failing to deliver intended objectives."[51]

Marolda described inability of "US civilian and military leaders to reassess the wisdom of their overall strategic assumptions" as a great war tragedy.[51] Identical words apply to the Korean War.

Chapter 41: Bitter Korean Fruit

"Along the weary battle line, green and hot with the midsummer of 1953, UN troops licked their wounds and wondered if they dared hope. A hundred times in two years the peace rumors had waxed strong; a hundred times they had been cruelly dashed. And while they wondered, the big guns continued to flame."[1]

- T.R. Fehrenbach, This Kind of War.

On July 27, 1953, six months after Eisenhower assumed office, the Korean War ended. Gen. Clark reported sadness at being the first American commander to sign an armistice agreement that did not represent military victory and would require unceasing vigilance to preserve.[2] No South Korean signed the document.

Clark's prophecy stood the test of time. North Korean hostility remained a permanent fact. Keeping his promise to President Rhee, at War's end Eisenhower stationed two reinforced American Army divisions in South Korea, originally numbering 62,000 troops, gradually reduced to some 30,000 today.[3] The PRC continues to serve as the North's chief, and mighty, supporter.

For 63 post-War years, duty along the Korean Demilitarized Zone (DMZ) has been quite dangerous. On a number of occasions, North Koreans physically attacked and sometimes killed US and ROK soldiers. In fact, from the July 27, 1953 armistice signing until only 1976, 49 Americans, 1,000 South Koreans, and some 600 North Koreans died in border clashes.[4]

The August 1976 beating and hacking to death of US Army Major Arthur Bonifas and Lt. Mark Barrett brought to President Gerald Ford "the greatest threat of all-out war from the 1953 armistice to the nuclear crisis of the 1990s."[5] In 1967, during Lyndon Johnson's presidency, North Korean boats attacked and captured the US Navy spy-ship *Pueblo* in the Sea of Japan, imprisoning and brutalizing 90 officers and crew for one year, one of whom died. The ship is still in northern hands, used as a propaganda display.

A special risk for the past 10 years is North Korean nuclear attack on American and South

Korean troops and cities. Ominously, the Korean War precipitated "huge expansion of US and Soviet nuclear arsenals," which facilitated the horrible national strategies of "Mutual Assured Destruction," or the apt acronym, "MAD."[6] The standoff lasted until the 1990-91 dissolution of the Soviet Union. The War also served to galvanize Chinese desire to develop a potent nuclear arsenal. Until the 1960 Moscow-Beijing falling out, the USSR helped in this effort, along with Manhattan Project spies Joan Chase Hinton and Klaus Fuchs.

Beyond question, PRC agents have continually plundered America's nuclear weapon laboratories and programs. Since nuclear age advent, atomic secrecy has been "mission impossible" for the United States. As mentioned, in the 1990s, China stole critical US secrets about the miniaturized thermonuclear (H-bomb) warhead known as "M-88." Today's PRC strategic missile arsenal includes the latest in Multiple, Independently-targeted Re-entry Vehicles (MIRVs), each capable of holding a miniaturized five-megaton, region-busting warhead. Land-based, mobile Chinese intercontinental ballistic missiles armed with MIRVs are an especially deadly combination and nearly impossible to destroy before use.

Should Islamic or other terrorists manage to obtain one or more of these compact society-killing warheads for use against America, millions of civilian casualties and regional devastation and contamination would signify "game over" for the constitutional government and society founded by Washington, Jefferson, Franklin, and Madison. Despite use of deceptive labels, dictatorial government and decades-long police-state rule would rapidly follow, placing American living standards and world influence in steep nosedive.

TARGET: US SUPERCARRIERS

Currently, China's economic muscle fuels a potent military production and purchase program aimed at neutralizing American Far Eastern naval power. Much money and effort have poured into offensive battle systems designed to destroy US Navy aircraft carrier battle groups, showcases of American military might, Beijing-perceived as the major impediment to PRC projection of regional and world power. Just one instance of Chinese gain is restriction of US carrier battle groups from the Formosan Straits because of adjacent and very strong mainland Chinese missile forces dedicated to their destruction.

China's anti-US-carrier battle plan calls for saturation attacks by thousands of conventional high-explosive ballistic and cruise missiles. Sea-skimming "Sunburn" missiles are a dangerous and near-indefensible part of the PRC anti-carrier arsenal.[7] Another devoted carrier killer is the newly-deployed WU-14 "anti-ship ballistic missile, designed to evade the Aegis sea-based missile defense system guarding our ... carrier battle groups."[8] A third element is the land-based, mobile ballistic missile DF-21D, a system designed and deployed "to target and track aircraft carrier battle groups with the help of satellites, unmanned aerial vehicles [drones], and over-the-horizon radar."[8] After launch, the DF-21D travels into space and blazes toward its ship target at almost 8,000 miles per hour.

Even if US ship defenses, including Aegis-class guided missile cruisers, shoot down 90% of the barrage, enough would get through to disable or sink supercarriers and support ships. Continual war-gaming of the scenario produces the same result: US Navy crews face reality of multiple destructive hits on their battle-group vessels. Human loss could easily reach 5,000 to 10,000 sailors and Marines *per group.* China would then be unstoppable and unopposed in the Pacific.

Despite attending political spin from Washington, such US defeat would represent first-rank military, national, and international disaster, ending the "Age of the Supercarrier," along with America's over-used and misplaced "superpower" descriptor. Despite reflexive political cover-up, the defeat would formally acknowledge shift in the Pacific and global power balance in China's favor and its de facto standing as "world's most powerful nation." In only a few years, all Pacific nations, islands, and bases, including Hawaii, would recognize PRC dominance, America's West Coast serving as the new, de facto national defense line. The 50th state would be a Communist Chinese protectorate.

GLOBAL STRATEGIC NUCLEAR THREAT

Almost 15 years ago, Institute for Defense and Disarmament Studies analyst Frank W. Moore predicted China would deploy 576 submarine-based nuclear warheads, with the "minimal number likely to be on station and capable of striking the United States [of] 192 – enough to saturate the "light" Alaska/California-based US missile defense system.[9,10]

Surely, America could develop counter-measures against the host of Chinese naval and strategic missile attack vehicles. The real question is whether American leaders have the *will* to protect their people, and take on and defeat Reds in major war. The author finds an economically and militarily weaker America, its leadership consumed with achievement of "social justice," beset with multi-trillion-dollar debt to China, as unfit in character and courage to confront and defeat a dedicated, strongly-armed, technologically-superior Chinese host. The US could not achieve this in Korean War, despite infinitely greater strategic advantage, and will surely fail a far more difficult 21st-century challenge.

Leftist power is fully comfortable with this outcome. Domestic rulers, including President Obama, perversely view world-humbled America as more "just" than before. Legions of politically-influential radical leftists would be thrilled at the prospect. Political correctness will tacitly acknowledge Chinese military supremacy and need for US avoidance of the fearsome foe, while impressing on the American people the farce of Sino-American "equality" and maintenance of American "superpower" status in the Pacific and world. Labels are such handy and effective weapons with which to beat people!

Akin to 5th-century AD Roman trembling at sight of Gothic hordes, Washington will simply make the necessary concessions and carry on the campaign of lies. As long as people don't think about the outcome and continue to indulge in moronic bread and circuses, they won't know any better. Why face unpleasant truth when numbing artificial reality is always at hand?

POWERHOUSE ON THE MARCH

A recent expression of Red Chinese military muscle is the East China Sea – Yellow Sea "Zone of Influence" proclaimed November 2013, prohibiting foreign aerial over-flight without prior

Beijing permission. Also disputing possession of islands held by Japan, The Philippines, and Vietnam, and proclaiming maritime spheres of dominance in East and South China seas, the PRC sends daily runs of warships and aircraft to intimidate claimed territories and countries. Russia's example of Crimean invasion, prelude to Ukrainian re-incorporation into a reformed Moscow-led Eurasian empire, encourages similar Chinese power grab. The Republic of China on Formosa is another potential low-risk target. Obviously, China seeks to *project* military power deep into the Pacific. For America the humble, the balance of Pacific and world power flows East.

Journalist David Ignatius reported on the February 2014 Stockholm China Forum annual meeting, co-sponsored by the PRC's Shanghai Institutes for International Studies and a private US fund. A Chinese military official spoke of "the inevitability of rising PRC power in the Pacific. In 10 years, we will be much stronger."[11] Beijing's expanding military strength scares adjacent nations, prompting that same official to remark, "You think we are a bully. We think we are a victim."

Both sides agreed on the reality of a central point – "tensions in the Pacific are rising, and China and neighbors cannot seem to find a way out." Forum delegates openly discussed "the danger of war in the Pacific."

A week before Stockholm, US Navy Capt. James Fanell told a San Diego meeting about Chinese "training for a 'short, sharp war' to assert primacy over islands claimed by Japan … and China …. I do not know how Chinese intentions could be more transparent." Capt. Fanell described Beijing's mantra of "protection of maritime rights" as "Chinese euphemism for coerced seizure of coastal rights of China's neighbors."[12]

As Ignatius related, the Shanghai meeting "dispelled … the hope that China will continue deferring to a powerful US. Instead, we're clearly heading for a period of greater Chinese assertiveness, especially in maritime issues." America has a treaty obligation to "defend Japanese administrative control in the disputed Senkaku Islands" and "has plans to defeat any

Chinese 'short, sharp war' there." In the broader South China Sea, Beijing's goals revolve around the so-called "Nine-Dash Line," an ill-defined assertion of "maritime claims almost to the coasts of Vietnam, Malaysia, and Philippines," not recognized at present by the US.[11]

Ignatius characterized the common Chinese international meeting pitch of "win-win cooperation" as "soothing … elevator music" meant to portray a "spirit of compromise." Unfortunately, no signs of compromise are yet evident in Far East Pacific maritime disputes.[11]

MACARTHUR THE REALIST

As his military career ended, Douglas MacArthur spoke the visionary words, "In war, there is no substitute for victory." He predicted "100 years of difficulty for America" in Asia. We are 60 years in, with no positive end in sight. Despite regular predictions of economic collapse, North Korea is not going away and continues development of nuclear and missile forces. Soon its nuclear-armed (let us hope *not* with hydrogen bombs) intercontinental ballistic missiles will be able to strike most American cities.

For its part, China is close to achieving global economic primacy and rapid translation into military superiority. Deployment of nuclear-powered ballistic missile submarines off US East and West coasts will soon be a reality, each holding dozens of multiple hydrogen-bomb warhead-tipped rockets. Warning of attack on American cities and bases will be reduced to minutes. At that point the United States, in a strategic sense, will be neutralized as a nuclear power.

Close alliance with Japan helps America equalize the Far Eastern balance of power as China continues to project military force into the Pacific. No stranger to sacrifice, China will pay any price to preserve its security and achieve dominance. US naval defeat would of necessity push Tokyo into the Red sphere.

Chapter 42: Korean War Outcomes –   Very Good, Very Bad

North Korean leader Kim Jong Un "boasts of his ability to

'burn Manhattan down to ashes.'"[1]

- The Economist, May 28, 2016.

Koreans proved tough, resolute people, enduring years of death and material devastation, yet rising from ashes to build lasting nations. The North acted the role of continually-belligerent police state, the South's despotic government yielding to market-driven expansion and social vibrancy.

Saving South Korea from Red control is the Korean War's greatest success. As retired Gen. James Van Fleet observed, "Millions live in freedom because of what we did." America deserves principal thanks for this reality, President Truman the lion's share of credit.

Communism failed to capture South Korea, permitting its development as a capitalist power. In South Korea, paternalistic US influence helped create a "stable local political class," which encouraged a highly successful free-market economy.

In contra-distinction, Peter Wright observed success of North Korea's Bolshevik model in creating stable if reprehensible political leadership, while utterly failing in the economic realm. The People's Republic of China is a prominent exception to typical Communist economic disaster.

Tens of millions of South Koreans survived primitive physical conditions in the 1950s and 60s to enjoy a much-improved standard of living. Within 40 years post-War, the South's per capita income rose from $100 per year to $10,000, its economy the world's 11th largest. South Korea's capital, Seoul, holds some 10 million people, Pusan close to three million, Taegu and Inchon over one million. Robust automobile, ship, and electronic consumer goods manufacture help provide a strong economic base.

Unfortunately, the fore-mentioned North Korea – South Korea Demilitarized Zone, or DMZ, is referred to as "The most dangerous and heavily fortified border in the world."[2] The dictatorial Democratic People's Republic is the reason why. Except for its showcase capital, Pyongyang, northern living conditions are far behind the South. Like the former Soviet Union, strengthening of military forces has always been preferred to humanitarian development.

Authors Robert Scalapino and Chong Sik Lee describe North Korea as "perhaps the most highly militarized society in the world today."[3] Perennial stories of hunger prompt Western food shipments, which may be diverted to military personnel. The same is true regarding provision of heating oil.

One thriving enterprise is Northern hostility, unabated over 63 postwar years. Heavy concentrations of NKPA artillery target Seoul, said able to destroy the city. The North's nuclear bomb arsenal is now 10 years old, estimated to contain 20 atomic bombs; "every six weeks or so it adds another."[4] Five test explosions have been conducted, backed by intercontinental ballistic missiles (ICBMs) fired over Japanese airspace. Even worse, Pyongyang now flirts with thermonuclear, hydrogen bomb development. Threats of ballistic missile atomic attack are not limited to South Korean and American bases and Japanese cities, but now include Washington and New York.

On the bright side, the Korean War served as an important element in Japan's economic resurgence. America is again credited with encouragement of stable political leadership and healthy free market economy. Extensive military-related repair services, together with scores of thousands of American servicemen and essential ports and airbases, boosted industry and employment, pushing Japanese manufacturing to its feet from World War II devastation. European countries also enjoyed a time of economic boom from Korean military build-up.

For Taiwan, the Republic of China island holding the Nationalist Government remnant, the Korean War spared Red Chinese invasion and take-over, for which planning and preparation were underway. Small Formosan Straits islands Quemoy and Matsu knew Red artillery barrages and threats in the mid-1950s, but Mao did not press for elimination of Nationalists from Formosa. Nonetheless, Sino-American tensions rose toward prospects for another war.

At the time, a reporter asked President Eisenhower, at a White House press conference, if the US would use nuclear weapons against China. The answer was an unreserved "yes, for purely military targets."[5] It seemed the President wanted to convey a message of resolve to Beijing. Crisis abated. Today, America walks a fine line as a major Taiwan arms supplier, while trying to avoid great offense to the People's Republic of China.

In similar vein, Eisenhower sent a clear message to Moscow:

> "It seemed clear that only by the interposition of our nuclear weapons could we promptly stop a major Communist aggression …. My intention was firm: to launch the Strategic Air Command immediately upon trustworthy evidence of a general attack against the West."[6]

Unfortunately, war in Korea encouraged rapid growth of US and Soviet nuclear arsenals. Mutual distrust dominated relations, including the Sino-American situation. Cold War reached a fearsome level, from which it would not subside until the late 1960s and 70s.

Fortunately, hatred between Beijing and Washington did not blind either side to necessity of establishing reliable communications. President Nixon's historic 1972 overture to Mao Zedong, skillfully managed by Henry Kissinger and Zhou En-lai and key to the US "triangulation" policy with Beijing and Moscow, signaled permanent thaw in hostility and quick establishment of diplomatic relations, hopefully based on mutual respect.

DOMINO THEORY TAKES HOLD IN WASHINGTON

War in Korea forced America into a phase of military strengthening. Not for entirety of Cold War would US military force sink to the 1945-1950 level. Ominously for America and the world, North Korean attack on the South also immediately resulted in increased US military assistance to Indo-China (Vietnam, Laos, and Cambodia) and The Philippines. America became more active in helping French troops resist, unsuccessfully, Ho Chi Minh's Viet Minh forces. "Stopping the advance of Communism" in Southeast Asia became a rallying cry, even after 1954 French surrender at Dien Bien Phu.

The Far East Asian theme of north-south division featuring intense ideological opposition brought two Vietnamese nations, with Communist control centered in the North at Hanoi and Saigon-based "democratic" government in the South. The Korean mess was set up all over again, official US consciousness fixed on the "domino theory:" if South Vietnam toppled to Communism, all Southeast Asia would follow.

Interestingly, Dwight Eisenhower observed that end of Korean War stopped a major drain on People's Republic of China military and economic resources, allowing important increase in support for Ho's Viet Minh.[7]

Secretary Acheson cited telling words of State colleague John Ohly, who many years before the Vietnam War warned that America was "moving into a position in Indo-China (South Vietnam) in which our responsibilities tend to supplant rather than complement those of the French" and South Vietnamese. The US "could be sucked into direct intervention. These situations have a way of snowballing."[8] In 10 years Ohly's prophecy came to horrible fruition. Over 58,000 Americans gave lives in Vietnam fighting.

FALLING OUT BETWEEN RED GIANTS

The Korean War set Communist China and North Korea in stone. But Moscow insistence on being paid for weapons and supplies necessary to Chinese war effort created hard feelings in Beijing. While Mao may have thought endless Soviet shipments of guns, planes, and supplies represented brother-to-brother kindness, Moscow thought otherwise. Without Soviet help, the People's Army could never have fought the US Army to a draw. Thus began the process of schism between Red giants. Mao learned at his first Moscow meeting with Stalin (December 1949) the mandate of "only one international high-priest of world Communism, and that would be Stalin."[9]

In 1960 the rift deepened. Soviet Party Chairman Khruschev removed the host of technical advisors from China, while border clashes took place between Russian and Chinese troops. The PRC became a prime target for Soviet espionage, second only to the United States, a KGB division devoted to the task. Moscow even considered pre-emptive nuclear attack on Chinese bases and cities, feeling out Washington on the matter. The PRC did not yet have a credible nuclear deterrent. Eisenhower and Kennedy strongly objected to the drastic step. America preserved the opportunity of Chinese Communist independence from Moscow, rightly seeing great self-advantage in split between titanic Red regimes.

REVOLUTIONARIES ADAPT TO NEW ENVIRONMENT

Killing and wounding of American boys in the first shooting war between World War II allies caused domestic Communism to suffer loss of favor. Soviet Chairman Khruschev landed another blow in a secret 1956 speech to Party leaders criticizing Stalin's murderous methods, acknowledging the bloody crimes committed. Once word leaked out, any façade of righteousness and respectability vanished from American Communism. CPUSA membership plummeted. But in its 1930s – 40s heydays, serious damage had been visited on American institutions, along with planting of numerous radical leftist budding revolutionaries in political, governmental, educational, legal, and communication landscapes. These did *not* decline in numbers and influence. Their progeny includes at least 40 current US Democratic and "Independent" (read "Socialist") senators, 100 Democratic congressmen, and one sitting president, all advancing the Red ball at every opportunity.

After the costly War, China, recipient of US and Soviet nuclear threats, decided it must develop atomic weapons, setting out on a determined scientific and intelligence effort. American nuclear traitor Joan Chase Hinton and British counterpart Klaus Fuchs helped make Communist China a nuclear power in 1964, then thermonuclear-capable just three years later. Today the PRC wields the world's third largest nuclear arsenal, after the US and USSR-successor Russian

Federation, and possibly the most advanced of all. PRC nuclear forces become more sophisticated and deadly with each passing year. The recent and excellent Stillman and Reed book provides ample details.

NECESSARY POLITICAL DECEPTION

The Korean War also served as impetus for fancy leftist political footwork. The American ruling class decided to erect a wall between serious Roosevelt and Truman Far East Asian mistakes and public knowledge thereof. Politically-harmful truth must be kept from the people. A script was created, a story line that brooked no editing. Simplistically couched in terms of good versus bad, the line ignored the key issue: Roosevelt's creation of two Koreas through insistence on massive Soviet Far East invasion.

Immediate post-World War II Red occupation of vast Asian territories must be banished from popular understanding, along with the disastrous effect of concurrent US military disarmament. Americans learned that "bad North Koreans" caused the Korean War, then "good Americans" came to rescue South Korea. Truman enjoyed hero status in stepping up to the challenge.

New political labels had to be created and publicized to fool the public. Since Korean War blood had stained credibility of domestic Communism, the descriptor grew out of favor. "Communism" could not be commonly associated with liberalism, nor with Internationalism. Then the word "Red," widely used as a Communist synonym, might remind people of Russia and Moscow, now undesirable associations to many Americans, so it too became *verboten*.

Despite its powerful influence on American Government decisions and the people's lives, the term "Internationalism" never gained public traction – it might provoke needless thinking, and accurate reflection on non-American, or anti-American, emphasis. Accuracy and truth tend to impede political power. But "Progressive" had a certain comfort, safeness, simplicity. "Progress" was good. Most people liked and believed in progress. Likewise, "Liberal" connoted "giving" and concern about people, especially when linked to popular savior Franklin Roosevelt.

While leftist political parties, such as the pink American Liberal Party and Red-as-a-beet American Labor Party, could turn out deciding votes in northern industrial state presidential and congressional elections, and keep Roosevelt and Truman in the White House, the movement did not catch fire with the public. So professional anti-Americans had to find shelter under the Democrat Party umbrella. Everyone knew Democrats stood for the common people, the "little man." Hatred for traditional America could then be somewhat shielded from view, deception maintained.

Socialist success *always* depends on deceit. That deceit now gained a Party haven. Class envy could be used as a brutal club, injustices exposed as proof of capitalism's wickedness, permanent underclass dependence sustained as a vital political base. All would be well, revolution could proceed, holy *Manifesto* script still the master plan. People could be kept in the dark where they belong. As long as they voted left, let them spill worthless blood on distant battlefields and violent streets. After all, prophet Lenin preached revolutionary flexibility as wise strategy. President Lyndon Johnson's 'Great Society' sounded so encouraging, but left tens of millions in dire straits.

To Reds and friends, America is a tough case, entrenched in antiquated beliefs and obsession with freedom. But little by little, revolution makes its way. One by one, foundational institutions such as law and religion, and "absurd socio-economic-based" moralities such as traditional marriage and families, are battered until they fall. Harsh, life-expendable Lenin and Stalin tactics lived on. The new tool of television promised unlimited mind bending and dumbing down. Give them bread and circuses, make them happy sacrificial lambs.

NUCLEAR-ARMED NORTH KOREA

The North received valuable help from Pakistan in developing atomic weapons. As reported in the August 25, 2005 *New York Times*, Pakistani President Pervez Musharraf related the role of nuclear scientist A.Q. Khan in providing Pyongyang key information on separation of bomb-grade uranium (U-235) from U-238, the common uranium isotope.[10] Natural deposits of U-238 contain only about 1% of fission-sustaining U-235. The technology for separating bomb-grade uranium and plutonium (a byproduct of nuclear power reactors) from spent nuclear reactor rods, ostensibly used to generate electricity and for other "peaceful" purposes, is one assured path to atomic bomb development.

In 2004, three years after America's 9/11 nightmare, 110 nuclear reactors around the world still used highly enriched uranium. Besides North Korea, Khan also shared bomb manufacturing processes with Libya, Iraq, and Iran. PRC help in making Pakistan a "Muslim Bomb" nuclear power reflected desire to counter perceived-competitor India's nuclear weapon program.

North Korean Communist Party chief Kim Jong Un, grandson of Korean War-era dictator Kim Il Sung, announced in April 2016 a 'successful' hydrogen bomb test explosion. Some Western nuclear scientists dispute the boast, believing the device a souped-up fission bomb. Yet, the reality is that every nuclear power has sooner rather than later become a thermonuclear power.

One vital nuclear issue bears repeating. For world safety, especially that of Korea, America, Japan, and China, may North Korea's nuclear bombs be restricted to fission types. Japan proved that nations can survive limited nuclear attacks. A single Nagasaki-strength, 20-kiloton atomic bomb, exploded in Seoul, is estimated to kill or wound 420,000 residents.[11] But should the North master, or purchase, and use fusion-based thermonuclear or hydrogen explosives, no nation could survive the incredible destructiveness and severe shock. Present civilizations will cease to exist, with widespread incineration and radiation sickness killing and maiming hundreds of millions.

Obviously, the depressing fact is that America and the West are proved helpless in deterring Northern nuclear bomb and missile warhead programs, and their H-bomb progeny. American, Asian, and European feet will be planted in Hell with Pyongyang hydrogen bombs.

There is no other conclusion: North Korean and PRC permanence and today's nuclear-

thermonuclear threat flow directly from Korean War outcome. Leadership of revered Franklin Roosevelt and Harry Truman decisively brought the current North Korean and Chinese Communist nightmare. Wimpish Korean War conduct of Truman and Secretary Acheson left Communist malignancy intact. Now it has metastasized to frightening proportions. We live with an apparently unsolvable, multiple-holocaust dilemma. Only unusually-competent American and Western leadership may save our hides.

TODAY'S US – SOUTH KOREAN – NORTH KOREAN STANDOFF

An important and largely secret assumption underlies deterrence to North Korean use of nuclear and hydrogen weapons against South Korea, Japan, and the US. The author believes such use *must* bring undoubted, rapid, and overwhelming US nuclear counterstrike against the North. Any deviation from this standard represents a large step toward American and Far Eastern suicide.

The lesson is clear: not a hint of presidential hesitation to utterly destroy North Korea may be perceived by Pyongyang. Northern leader Kim Jong Un may be tempted to launch nuclear first strike should he expect post-attack White House stand-down.

Since presidential approval is necessary for effective nuclear counterstrike, and given President Obama's world bent, there is doubt the US would promptly, or ever, retaliate to destroy North Korea. Influential leftists consumed with social justice would do their best to prohibit American reprisal. Non-response would be seen as proper anti-American action. Doubt, fear, specter of world war, environmental contamination, and ideological sympathy with oppressed masses may inhibit presidential counterstrike. Presidential and military leader *politics* defying common sense, logic, and national best interests is on-going national-international reality.

LATE SCOOP ON KOREAN MILITARY SITUATION

The Washington-based Center for Strategic and International Studies held a January 21, 2014 conference on the current Korean peninsula military confrontation. Panelists included three former US commanders-in-chief of the "Combined Forces Command" of UN, ROK, and US troops based in South Korea: retired generals James Thurman, Walter Sharp, and John Tilelli.

Commanders agreed on the significant threat posed by North Korean long-range artillery aimed at the South, some 8,400 pieces strong. The ROK capital Seoul and its millions of residents are highly vulnerable to northern cannon striking. Likewise, given the North's 2,400 multiple rocket launchers, broad-scale missile defense is an important feature of the allied military system.[12]

Generals proclaimed the US "nuclear umbrella" protecting both South Korea and Japan as "strong." The shield is comprised of multiple-warhead, nuclear ballistic missile submarines, land-based ICBMs, and B-2 bombers. Unsaid by commanders is the umbrella's complete dependence on presidential will. As stated, any president may choose to fold the umbrella, to delay or refuse response to Northern atomic or conventional strike. Nothing short of military revolution could change this fact. The commander-in-chief rules the military roost. Fates of 300 million Asians and tens of millions of Americans lie in his, or her, hands.

Chinese defeat of US carrier battle groups, and subsequent Chinese and North Korean nuclear threat to America, Japan, and South Korea, would encourage presidential folding in Korea and Japan, freeing the field for Sino-North Korean regional aggression. Shorn of US nuclear umbrella, Japan must either risk war with, or capitulate to, China and North Korea. If the former, Tokyo is likely to promptly develop its own nuclear/thermonuclear striking forces.

The conference reported no US nuclear weapons stored on South Korean soil, a remarkable change from the 1950s, 60s, and 70s. As author Gary Oberdorfer related,

> "Throughout the four decades since the armistice of 1953, the US military considered renewal of war in Korea to be one of its most dangerous potential challenges. Since the Vietnam War's 1975 end, American military planners had consistently identified Korea as the most likely spot for Asian hostilities involving the United States. Starting December 1957, President Eisenhower ordered Korean deployment of nuclear warheads on Honest John missiles and 280-millimeter long-range artillery."[13]

According to nuclear authority William Arkin, by 1972 the US had amassed a peak Korean arsenal of 763 atomic warheads.[14]

On another level, General Thurman reported risk of accidental atomic explosion at North Korean bomb development sites as "severely threatening" to the PRC, Japan, and entire Korean peninsula. All participants emphasized Japan's key role in joint preparations to meet any North Korean military threat. The North's long-range ballistic missiles are routinely "tested" over Japanese soil.

Most Americans assume their civilian and military leaders want to do what is best for nation and people. "We the People" are advised that assumption is the lowest form of knowledge. As proven by Korean War decision-making, satisfaction of political interests always comes first, national and popular interests last. Power is the magic elixir. We stand in great peril before matters of war and peace.

Part VIII:

Plain and Undeniable:

Red Control in Government,

Labor, and Academia,

1945 – 2016

Chapter 43: Emerging Truth of Dual Power, Two Governments –

Part 1

"Anyone who has studied totalitarian espionage recognizes that its chief function is in being a weapon for the formulation of policy."[1]

- Isaac Don Levine, Plain Talk.

MEET PATRIOT JOHN H. AMEN – WHO?

We now bust down any remaining wall separating leftist revolutionary power in America and associated Soviet espionage, from prominent Korean War leadership influence. Put in Biblical terms, the issue is not a speck in America's eye, but a plank. May readers carefully weigh the following facts.

Sworn US Senate committee testimony given in "Executive Session" is protected from public scrutiny for at least 50 years. Of course most or all political blowback from very belated negative information would then hardly be noticed. Also, Congressional transcript records are often thousand-page monsters chocked full of small-font paragraphs and dazing insignificant detail, a dish fit only for the hearty and strong-eyed. Online viewing does not eliminate pain.

Information revealed below was generated by the 83rd Congress in 1953, but not released until January 2003 by the 107th Congress.[2] Politics rules all.

One of the key State Department cogs driving the Red Government machine was John Carter Vincent, born in China and serving there from April 1924 to February 1936, and again from March 1941 to August 1943. Such long tenure in one location is a diplomatic rarity.[3]

Biographer Robert Beisner told of Dean "Acheson's appointment of old China hand Vincent to head the Office of Far Eastern Affairs," which "prompted wholesale resignations" within the division.[4] These actions took place after Acheson assumed the post of Secretary of State in

1948. Vincent and Acheson were ideological twin brothers, a reality not subject to refute, even by leftists.

In 1953, former CPUSA member and *Daily Worker* editor Louis Budenz, who later worked closely with the FBI, testified under oath in Executive Session before the Senate Permanent Subcommittee on Investigations. Budenz swore to John Carter Vincent's Communist Party membership, and Vincent's mission to achieve maximum Government penetration. Budenz testified, "Communists were eager to have Vincent obtain a key position in the State Department where he could influence policy."[5]

Following Budenz, State Department personnel specialist John H. Amen gave additional revealing testimony about Vincent before the same Senate Subcommittee. Amen brought credibility to the witness stand. A former US Army colonel, he served as trial counsel and American chief of investigation at the 1946 Nuremberg war crimes trials. He also performed investigative work in New York City for Governor, later Senator, Herbert Lehman.

Held under rules of Executive Session, Amen's testimony verbally detailed and synthesized a host of facts about Vincent's disloyalty to the United States. He also submitted a concise written report containing ordered statements about Vincent's wrongdoing. Unfortunately, Amen's full-page, hard-hitting statement was published in tiny font in the official 2002 US Government Printing Office transcript.[6] Relegating Amen's exceptional synopsis to "the small print" seemed to message unimportance to readers, and discouragement of attention to unpleasant facts. In reality the statement plainly and undeniably laid out the steps involved, and one man's vital complicity in, successful Red capture of one section of American Government.

George Kennan, unequaled in describing the brutal Soviet character and system, knew the overarching Red aim of placing agents in positions where they could actually set US national policy. Amen described such achievement in Vincent's holding of "an exceptionally high position in the Department of State having to do with the formulation of US Chinese policies." Amen cited direct sworn Congressional testimony from a number of credible witnesses, among them former Ambassador to China Gen. Patrick Hurley, China military advisor Gen. Albert Wedemeyer, Navy Adm. Miller, and State's Far East section chief Mr. Duman, to prove "Vincent's opposition to the declared China policy of the US Government."

Amen refreshed the memory of Ambassador Hurley's 1945 resignation and public statement condemning pro-Communist interference within the State Department in implementing US China policy. Hurley's charges triggered pro-Red press elements to strident defense of "highly-loyal and patriotic" China hands. Defenders included *Time* magazine China correspondent Theodore H. White, CBS News foreign correspondent and future prominent television personality Eric Severeid, and Annalee Jacoby.

The record included a second investigation of Vincent carried out by the Senate Committee on the Judiciary. After lengthy hearings, this Committee "… unanimously concluded that John Carter Vincent for many years had been the principal fulcrum of Institute of Pacific Relations (IPR) pressures and influences in the State Department." One of hundreds of US Communist front groups, in fact holding a "remarkable number of Communists and pro-Communists," the CPUSA described the IPR as "the Little Red Schoolhouse for teaching certain people in Washington *how to think* about Chinese and Far Eastern matters" (italics added).[7] It was headquartered at 125 East 52nd Street, New York City.

Amen disclosed Red use of the IPR "to promote the interests of the Soviet Union in the United States, the vehicle used by Communists to orient American Far Eastern policy toward Communist objectives." He testified to "Vincent's influence in bringing about a change in US policy favorable to the Chinese Communists" that evidenced "uniform and strict adherence to the Communist line of ideology." Vincent's achievement represented a textbook Soviet foreign operation, straight from teachings of Marx and Bolshevik organizational principles of Lenin and Trotsky.

FOLLOW THE LEADER: NEW US GAME-PLAN FOR CHINA

Moscow created the new Far Eastern line. All Party elements, including the spy apparatus, must 100% support the line. Starting in 1944, vital shift in US policy entailed withdrawal of support for the Nationalist Chinese government while embracing Mao's Communist movement. Now, the labels "corrupt" and "feudal" were glued to Chiang's leadership, with Mao's cohorts blessed as "pure" and "democratic." An obliging press and pro-Red writers Theodore White, Edgar Snow, Agnes Smedley, and Owen Lattimore pitched glowing accounts of Mao's humanitarianism. The Comrade Chairman quickly appreciated the valuable help "Western journalists could be to his cause."[8] The American ship of state steered in hard-left rudder mode.

A 400-page propaganda book on new China might contain a half-page of tempered Red criticism, the rest unfettered Communist praise. Then crooked authors and reviewers could claim fair coverage of both sides of pertinent issues. The word came forth: Old China was finished, doomed to defeat in civil war, the New heralded as people's saviors, destined to rule. Theodore White later enjoyed popular acclaim writing quadrennial books on "The Making of the President," starting with the tight 1960 Kennedy-Nixon race.

On the state of Chinese military affairs, "Vincent's reports to the State Department on the relative strength and activity of the Chinese Communists and of the army of Chiang Kai-shek differed substantially from official US Army intelligence information." The new line falsely emphasized great Red Chinese fighting against the Japanese, while Mao himself admitted allotting only 10% of Communist energies toward that end ("expansion" commanded 70% and fighting Chiang 20% of Red resources.)[9] Famed author Ernest Hemingway observed the same, stating, "The role of the Nationalists in combat against Japan has been 100 times that of the Communists."[10] Pro-Communist White House aide and Soviet agent Lauchlin Currie successfully implored Hemingway not to publicize the distasteful fact. Truth may never be allowed to block progress.

REDS ENGULF FAR EAST ASIA MAINLAND

Chinese Communists reaped a bonanza from August 1945 Soviet occupation of North China and Manchuria. Revolutionary opportunity of a lifetime presented – heavens now rained gold. Following in Russian footsteps, Mao's forces took surrender of defeated Japanese and inherited their armories, plus at least 240,000 Chinese Kwantung soldiers who now swelled Red People's Army ranks. Red Chinese forces in Manchuria quadrupled in a matter of months, along with subjected territories and peoples.[11] As predicted by former Roosevelt Undersecretary of State Sumner Welles, Nationalist China was doomed.

Despite the stacked deck, in early 1946 Nationalists had Communists on the run, taking control of the key Manchurian city of Harbin. Reflecting the unpleasant military situation, Mao then proclaimed a switch from conventional to guerrilla operations. The US came to Red rescue as Truman sent esteemed Gen. George Marshall to China to insist on a cease-fire, reluctantly agreed to by Chiang Kai-shek. But cease-fire proved a sham. To force coalition government with Communists and peace between warring parties, a seven-month US arms embargo on Nationalists followed. Soviets never stopped arming Chinese Communists. *America did what was best for Red Chinese and Soviet interests, not those of America and the free world.* Dual Power worked wonders for Reds throughout the world.

The next sworn Congressional witness, Mr. Duman, chaired the important Far Eastern Subcommittee of State, War (Department), and Navy (Department), succeeded in that position September 1, 1945 by John Carter Vincent. Duman testified before the Senate Permanent Subcommittee on Investigations about changes made after his resignation in various State Department documents dealing with terms of Japanese surrender. Document changes reflected "a complete shift of emphasis to the Communist line from the documents originally drafted by Duman and approved by State Department officials."

The new policy called for immediate removal of all US troops from China. This of course hurt Chiang's Nationalists and smoothed the Red path. Comrade Vincent assured nothing should impede Red revolutionary success.

CARVING OUT TRUTH 70 YEARS LATER

Amen concluded that with Vincent, *"There emerges ... a general pattern of Communist activities and sympathies entirely at variance with the declared and established policy of the Government of the United States. The pattern is clear and unequivocal* (italics added)."[12] No other witness countered the truth and accuracy of Amen's testimony. *Democrat* Senator Styles Bridges publicly and accurately stated that Vincent "approved the Communist program in China, opposed support of the Nationalist Government and furthered extension of the influence of Russia in China."[13]

The cup of political incorrectness now overflowed. The name of John H. Amen joined the host of truth speakers condemned to everlasting, or at least 50-year, obscurity. When you can't beat them, bury them.

As it turned out, American Communist foreign service professional Vincent headed the State Department's Far East working division, not a figurehead politician. Responsible for developing the nuts and bolts of official policy, he was positioned to inflict severe damage on American Far East interests. Vincent did just that. He also greatly assisted, with fellow State Department traitors Service, Davies, Rosinger, and others, in facilitating the Korean War.

News stories attending 2003 revelation of long-secret Senate testimony naturally emphasized Sen. McCarthy's abuses as the only valid object of attention. McCarthyism is always ready to be dusted off and brought front and center, an icon of political correctness. John Carter Vincent's high State Department treason received not a mention. The American people are completely unaware of the conspirator's harmful behaviors on behalf of Communism that encouraged lop-sided shift in the Far East Asian power balance, Korean War, millions of dead Koreans, and 54,262 dead Americans.

The message is clear: keep the people from thinking about truth.

In December 1952, a three-to-two decision of the Truman-created Loyalty Review Board found Vincent disloyal. Two prior Board reviews gave him a clean bill. Just prior to Eisenhower's inauguration, "Acheson took the question to Truman, and got permission to appoint a new so-called board chaired by esteemed Judge [Learned] Hand. There was no precedent for any such proceeding, but it was just done."[14]

With changing of the presidential guard, new Secretary of State John Foster Dulles dissolved Hand's board, issuing a summary statement relieving Vincent of State Department employment and merely accusing him of *poor judgment* in job performance. Vincent kept his Government pension, always a leftist-press favored son until his 1972 death. Unsurprising given Vincent's history, Robert Beisner related his preference for the Socialist Party in US national elections.[14]

Political houses must be very fragile, if a documented, outright Soviet Russian agent cannot be truthfully described in public. The identical descriptive limitation exists today, although the left commonly refers to tradition-minded Americans as "right-wing extremists and nut-jobs." It is most incorrect to label Pelosi, Reid, Leahy, and Durbin as "socialists" or Reds. Of interest, J. Edgar Hoover and Eisenhower Attorney General Herbert Brownell used the same language, "poor judgment," in describing Truman's mishandling of Red federal employees.

UNMASKING A TRAITOR

As the Carl (Aldo) Marzani case demonstrated, firing a disloyal federal employee, even with overwhelming evidence, proved exceedingly difficult.[15] Reds played the American judicial system like a beloved musical instrument.

Dean Acheson related President Truman's August 31, 1945, Office of War Information closure and "transfer of its functions to State and to Inter-American Affairs."[16] Hundreds of former OWI workers, a strong dose of hammer and sickle blood, infused State. New invaders included slick editor Marzani, whose New York publishing house long accepted Moscow Center support money. In total, State absorbed some 25,000 employees from World War II-related federal agencies, a great bureaucratic metastasis.[17]

Immediately after World War II, Deputy Assistant Secretary of State J. Anthony Panuch assumed responsibility for processing the numerous host into State slots. Marzani's records showed prior OWI charges of disloyalty and attempted firing, but under oath he made fools of incompetent examiners in evading heavy Red connections. The newly created State Department "Security Office" did not work with the FBI and "... excluded from its membership State's outstanding expert on Communist doctrine and subversive techniques of infiltration."[18]

Within New York City Police Department Anti-Subversion Squad files, Panuch found a highly credible eyewitness account of Marzani's Red dealings, secured fresh witness testimony, and brought charges of lying under oath. The Red domestic legal apparatus then swung into high gear for valuable asset Marzani, such Government interference intolerable. As revealed by close surveillance, Marzani kept in constant touch with top Reds throughout America, with the Party's New York brain trust responsible for his defense strategy.

Trial defense came straight from the Party line, emphasizing "witch-hunting" by FBI Director Hoover and Congressional committees, equating "a firm foreign policy as anti-Soviet," blaming "liberals as the real subversives."[19]

Deputy Assistant Secretary Panuch proved "Marzani lied under oath about his Communist affiliations to the FBI in 1942, the Civil Service Commission in 1943, and the Department of State in 1946."[20] The dogged official surmounted numerous frustrations in finally securing a jury trial verdict of guilty and Marzani's dismissal from State. One less Communist walked the halls, but it took determined legal effort. Would the average American "realize the tremendous amount of planning, professional skill, and sheer tenacity on the part of all concerned which had been required to convict Marzani the hard way – in open court and before a jury ...?"[21]

RED CONTROL IN VOICE OF AMERICA RADIO

The Senate Subcommittee on Investigations shortly heard testimony of Voice of America (VOA) employee Larry Bruzzese. In theory, VOA beamed radio programming to promote America throughout Europe, South and Central America, and other regions. In practice, much air time went to putting America down. Reds infested management of a number of VOA foreign language operations, always sensitive to the importance of steering mass communications.[22]

Mr. Bruzzese worked in Italian language broadcasting. He told the Subcommittee on Investigations, "I consistently heard sneering and derogatory broadcasts and comments about America. An entirely anti-American attitude existed with four or five employees in the Italian section."[23] He then mentioned a surprising comment heard at the station: "In news coverage of General Eisenhower's nomination for president July 12, 1952, a VOA editor said, 'I think we better mention Nixon's name (the vice-presidential candidate) because Eisenhower will die, we hope, pretty soon.'"

Another politically-inspired experience caught Bruzzese's attention. "One day in August 1951, the lead story to the Italian audience related to the Korean War. UN negotiation chief Adm. Joy had complained to the Communist delegation at Kaesong about armed Red soldiers [patrolling the site], a violation of the truce conference agreement. The pro-Red VOA editor crossed out these scripted words and told me, 'The US should get back to the 38th Parallel and give back to the Communists the territory that belongs to them.'"[23] The comment mirrored official Moscow policy, as related by Dean Acheson.[24] America could be bad-mouthed at will, audiences shielded from anti-Communist news and views.

The VOA French section proved equally hostile to America, also run by Reds and pro-Reds. Anti-American attitude bothered one employee, Nancy Lenkeith, who told the Senate Subcommittee words of a sympathetic supervisor: "Your experience here with un-Americanism is only beginning."[25] Lenkeith was fired after broadcasting a complementary story about Whittaker Chambers' book *Witness* that contained anti-Communist commentary. Four VOA officials joined the meeting that resulted in her sacking. Lenkeith testified to six traitors running the French section: "Messers Auberjonois, Ogle, Troup Mathews, acting chief of section; and Marcelle Henry, Rene Erville, and Raymond Haugher."[25]

Lenkeith told the Subcommittee, "Vigorously anti-Communist material was strictly prohibited" from broadcast. For American media and academia, this point of view remains unchanged 70 years later; anti-Communism is still readily equated with "Fascism." Lenkeith accused the VOA as

> "bent on substantiating Communist myths about the US and France.[25] Red script portrayed Americans as incapable of serious thought. They are children who struck oil and are happy, but light-headed, cheerful, and only like light entertainment. Americans are incapable of serious intellectual or cultural effort, and have no imagination."

Station managers instructed Lenkeith to keep broadcasts "with as little substance as possible." Founders and continuers of American television broadcasting must have attended the same school of ideology. Truth is a harsh, intolerable light.

A Subcommittee senator commented, "The material being beamed out as the Voice of America sounded more like the Voice of Moscow."[25]

VOA "bad guys" were usually naturalized American citizens. Most were atheists, the "official" Internationalist faith, with very few Christian or Jewish practitioners. Given Red bent, and widespread Catholicism at the time in France, stand-alone, religious-themed Christmas programs were forbidden. All faiths and sects had to be represented on air "to be fair and Constitutional." This of course rings a contemporary bell. Management told employees, "VOA listeners hate any kind of religion." Lenkeith reported "the Catholic population in France as the nation's most active anti-Communist group."[25] There was the rub. "The lie, the lie, everywhere the lie …."

Today we see adoption of the line's anti-religious component as powerful and correct domestic political doctrine, culturally immune from charges of discrimination. Vicious insults to Christianity and Judaism are not considered discriminatory statements. Reds simply can't tolerate competing influence.

An important arm of US Government world communication, the Voice of America, had been taken over by America's Red arch-enemies. Boldly and confidently, Moscow minions filled the air with anti-Americanism. Uncovering the travesty reflexively equaled Fascist oppression.

We currently call such fine people "progressives." They run our cultural, legal, political, academic, and media agendas.

PULLING A 'FAST' ONE

In 1942-43, prominent American Communist author Howard Fast worked at the Office of War Information overseas radio division, recruited by fellow Communist Jerome Weidman. Fast's works were favorites of OWI libraries around the world. He earned almost $10,000 for his year at OWI, a sum close to $120,000 today. Before the Senate Subcommittee on Investigations in 1953, he repeatedly invoked the Fifth Amendment when asked about Communist Party membership and Red support for his publications.[26] Fast later confessed to Party membership during the 1940s.

Eastern Europe received its share of Red-tinged broadcasts. Jan Ciechanowski's book, *Defeat in Victory*, told, "Of all the US Government agencies, the Office of War Information under director Elmer Davis, had very definitely adopted a line of unqualified praise of Soviet Russia."[27] Author Anthony Kubek mentioned repeated protests by Ciechanowski about "pro-Soviet propaganda broadcasts to occupied Poland." Apparently, OWI "received directives straight from the White House" for such programming.[28]

STANDING AGAINST THE 'MAIN ENEMY' – ALAN CRANSTON AND FRIENDS

Herbert Romerstein and Stanislav Levchenko revealed fascinating information about OWI leadership during World War II, illustrating classic Bolshevik clandestine control in United States Government, and related evolution of "legitimate" leftist political power.

Starting in 1940, 26-year-old Alan Cranston of California served as OWI Foreign Language Division chief, a post held until 1944, during the Italian, French, and Polish Red radio bonanza. Cranston admitted to hiring pro-Communist writer David Karr, a life-long friend. Karr regularly published articles in the *Daily Worker*.[29]

There is evidence of pro-Moscow actions in Cranston's Foreign Language Division role. He publicly denied any Communist link in the murder of activist Carlo Tresca, who opposed Red membership in the domestic Italian-American Victory Council supported by OWI. Soviet intelligence had ordered hundreds of Italian-speaking agents into the US to maximize Red influence in Italian affairs and counter Tresca's efforts. Control of Italy seemed torn between Moscow and Washington. Many believed Reds killed Tresca, including his family.[30] We question whether a US Government official should defend Communist actions, or lack thereof, in America. Was there something to hide?

Cranston then squelched Polish-language American radio broadcasts implicating Soviets in the Katyn Forest Massacre of 11,000 Polish Army officers. As Joseph Lang, manager of New York radio station WHOM, testified before Congress, "Cranston felt the Polish news commentators had taken a rather antagonistic attitude toward Russia in this matter – Cranston wanted the situation 'straightened out.'" Romerstein and Levchenko noted that "Cranston served the Soviet purpose in covering up a Soviet atrocity."[31]

Stanford graduate Cranston, born into a wealthy northern California land investment and home-building family, went on to a remarkable political career, the only candidate to win four consecutive terms as California US Senator (1969-1992). Prior political experience included the 1949-52 presidency of the United World Federalists, a one-world-government agency, and a successful campaign for California State Legislature endorsement of US Congressional amendment to the Constitution permitting "federal world government."[32] Internationalists strongly push the 'One-World' agenda.

In 1983, Cranston threw his hat in the ring for the Democratic presidential nomination. Future leftist Washington State US Senator Maria Cantwell moved to California to run his caucus effort. Poor primary showings caused abandonment of presidential aspirations.[33] Cranston defeated prostate cancer and died at age 86 on New Year's Eve, 2000.

Extensive national and regional press coverage of Cranston's four-decade political career never touched his pro-Red background, or One-World-government passion. Californians and all Americans should have known these proclivities, valid subjects of voter consideration.

Should the mainstream press practice political neutrality, stories featuring Internationalist backgrounds would appear for the current Red crop of US senators, representatives, president, and aspirants. But journalistic eyes look elsewhere for news. Censorship is guaranteed for favored elites as Moscow's baton passes on. Labels change, but the deception-destruction game plan continues in high gear.

Obviously, communication control is the heart of leftist power. Communication control makes possible the grand public deception upon which Communism, Internationalism, and Socialism flourish. It assures unimportance of truth in the political arena.

THE CASE OF NATHANIEL WEYL – RED LABOR AND ACADEMIC MUSCLE

Educated at Columbia University and the London School of Economics, Nathaniel Weyl held a number of economist-related federal positions, starting with Franklin Roosevelt's Agricultural Adjustment Administration (1933-35). He then served on the Federal Research Board (1940-41), the Board of Economic Warfare (1941-43), and in the Department of Commerce (1945-47).[34]

On February 23, 1953, in Executive Session before the Senate Subcommittee on Investigations, Weyl testified to 1930s Communist Party membership, and activity during that time in a Washington-based Soviet spy cell, one of at least two rings busy plundering the Capitol.

As former Red spy Whittaker Chambers revealed to Assistant Secretary of State Adolph Berle in September 1939, Weyl belonged to the Harold Ware Group, along with cell members Lee Pressman, attorney John Abt, and Nathan Witt. Abt served as chief counsel to the Civil Liberties Subcommittee of the US Senate Education and Labor Committee, chaired by Wisconsin progressive Robert La Follette.[35,36] Haynes, Klehr, and Firsov asserted that by Second World War's end, "CIO [Congress of Industrial Organizations] unions with Communist-aligned leaders represented 1.37 million members, one-fourth of CIO total membership."[37]

Weyl's revelations were old and incorrect news. On August 12, 1938, the US House Un-American Affairs Committee, chaired by Texas congressman Martin Dies, established the mature and extensive state of Communist labor movement penetration in America. Testimony by union leader John Frey

> "named 238 full-time Communist *organizers* in the CIO (italics added). Frey exposed 200 front organizations. Backed up by Party membership books, police records, and informants high in the Party, Frey's testimony was unimpeachable."[38]

The Dies Committee had the audacity to publish a list of Red subversives.[38] For the first time, the American people learned, albeit briefly, of extremely damaging key spy Nathan Gregory Silvermaster. Communist Party member Silvermaster gave up open activity for more important spy work. A US Civil Service Commission report noted

> "considerable testimony indicating that in 1920 Silvermaster served as an underground agent for the CPUSA. He was known and listed in the files of Seattle and San Francisco police departments, the Thirteenth (West Coast) Naval District, FBI, Naval Intelligence, and military intelligence as a Communist Party member and leader. The overwhelming amount of testimony indicates beyond reasonable doubt that Nathan Gregory Silvermaster is a Communist Party leader and very probably a secret agent of the OGPU [the main branch of Soviet intelligence]."[39]

On July 16, 1942, the Civil Service Commission recommended the traitor be barred from government employment "for the duration of the national emergency."[39] But numerous friends allowed Reds to routinely bypass incriminating government reports. Given White House connections, including powerful Roosevelt aide Lauchlin Currie (1939-45), mere Civil Service advice did not impede espionage ring chief Silvermaster's plundering one bit, nor his ability to secure Government employment anywhere he wished, or more accurately, as Moscow wished.

Traitor Silvermaster served the Farm Security Administration from 1935-38, the Maritime Labor Board from 1938-40, four subsequent years in the Department of Agriculture, and wound up with a 1944-46 stint as Treasury Department economist. He also represented the US in important post-World War II international financial support meetings.

Unsurprisingly, Chairman Dies and his Committee came under massive leftist press bombardment, smeared with every possible degrading name. Author Ted Morgan called the "systematic vilification ... a backhanded homage to its exposure of Party activities."[40] It is *never* permissible to expose true liberal-leftist destruction.

Along with many others, Weyl broke with Communism in 1939 after the Hitler-Stalin pact. By the early 1950s, acting with cultural incorrectness, he had written two books highly critical of Marxism and Soviet Russia. One, entitled *Treason*, tellingly described typical American and Canadian Soviet agents as "highly intelligent, of superior education and seemingly unimpeachable moral character. For the intellectual with a conscience, it was easy to become a 'trusted soldier of the revolution,' and live in the elevated world of a quasi-religious brotherhood."[41] Former spy Hede Massing wrote of the identical phenomenon. Naturally, Weyl's name is unknown to the American people.

The Subcommittee, chaired by Sen. Joseph McCarthy, heard Weyl's sworn statements about extensive Communist penetration at Columbia in 1932-33 that included the National Student League and Columbia Social Problems Club, both under Party control.[42] Another Columbia Communist front, the International Labor Defense, contained student and faculty members and served as the "legal defense arm of the Communist Party USA."[43] This group had been founded in America in 1925!

SPECIAL TARGET: ACADEMIA

Weyl emphasized the broad scope of such organizations. They were not limited to Columbia University, but represented a *national* student movement within the context of Moscow's Communist International or "Comintern" bureau. A hundred or more prominent American academic institutions served as recruiting agencies for the "top fraction," described by Weyl as the Communist movement's key Party members who "guide or direct the policies of whole organizations" of front groups.

An important detail overlooked by most historians, Weyl testified about personal 1930s spy cell work with notorious Alger Hiss. Harvard-educated lawyer Hiss rose to an important State Department post, Director of Special Political Affairs. He served as Roosevelt's personal Yalta Conference advisor, and chaired formational meetings of the United Nations. Hiss also served prison time for a perjury conviction related to false sworn Congressional testimony about ties to confessed Washington spy cell colleague Whittaker Chambers, and spent a lifetime denying obvious Communist affiliation.[44] Venona findings sealed Hiss's guilt.

Religious background did not preclude radical leftist bent. The pulpit held its share of fellow travelers. Harry Freeman Ward, Professor of Christian Ethics at Union Theological Seminary, publicly viewed Communism as an "extension of democracy, democracy advancing to a higher field."[41] Early-1930s forced collectivization of Ukrainian peasant farmers (kulaks) resulting in mass starvation, along with Stalin's murderous 1937-39 Great Terror, could easily be ignored by devoted Marxist ideologue Ward. So the outrageous irony of a seminary professor advocating for a governmental system whose DNA mandated crushing of religious practice. Correct credentials allowed Ward to assume the American Civil Liberties Union chairmanship in 1940.

CPUSA JUST A POLITICAL PARTY? NO!

Testimony such as Weyl's proved American Communism, even at the student level, anything but a casual endeavor, but instead a meticulously planned, heavily-invested, metastatic-like generational mission meant to take control of US Government and people. As seen from the above, serious planting began during Calvin Coolidge and Herbert Hoover Republican presidencies. Advent of Roosevelt administrations brought blooming flowers and ripening fruits. Fields of toil remained intact under Truman. Moscow left not a single stone unturned.

One large Red operation, the American League for Peace and Democracy, was described as "the mother of all front groups."[45] Its ranks included 563 federal employees, among them Assistant Secretary of the Interior Oscar Chapman, and National Labor Relations Board members Edwin Smith and Nathan Witt, part of the Communist cell that ran the Board. Numerous Reds and pro-Reds worked in federal agencies and on Congressional committee staffs.

After leaving office, President Eisenhower wrote that by 1953-54, "8,008 suspected subversives had been identified by properly appointed boards." Of these, 5,000 resigned from Government or related private employment before their cases were heard, the remainder dismissed as security risks after official hearings.[46] Assuredly, these still mostly represented the above-ground element. Red roots were too widespread and deeply embedded politically, legally, and academically to eradicate.

Venona decryptions, drawn from a sample of less than 3% of World War II Soviet-US spy cable traffic, identified 350 Soviet agents working in America, many known only by code name. Based on the 10% rule, this easily translates into 3,500 Reds infesting Government, industry, and mass communication, and is in harmony with subversive numbers reported by Eisenhower. A good-sized Red regiment had infiltrated Executive, Congressional, and Judicial branches, plus business, unions, education, media, and politics.

RUSE – EMPHASIS ON MCCARTHYISM, NOT DEADLY TREASON

Radical leftists could not have thrown a more effective cover over their mischief than McCarthyism. Republican Sen. McCarthy of Wisconsin chaired the Subcommittee on Investigations for four years. He discourteously treated many committee witnesses, many of them hostile to begin with. McCarthy's tenure on the American stage is popularly characterized as a political travesty that "ruined careers and blacklisted innocent people from employment." Eisenhower despised him and believed his approach counter-productive to promoting national security. The Senate ultimately voted to censure him, and alcohol helped kill the two-term senator at age 48.

McCarthy favored the tactic of alleging large numbers of Communists in various federal agencies. Press coverage gave much publicity and ridicule to his speeches. Estimates of Red presence in Government were painted as gross exaggerations, manifestations of misplaced "hysteria" gripping the nation. President Truman endorsed the deceptive view with his 1948 "red herring" campaign charge. Instead of righteously treating the issue as a vital national security matter, Truman's politicizing confused American understanding of massive Soviet treason for almost 40 years.

For example, the public knows nothing about Communist Party member Lawrence K. Rosinger, who served as State Department China policy advisor to Secretary Acheson in 1949. Brought before McCarthy's Senate Internal Security Subcommittee, Rosinger took the Fifth Amendment, "refusing to answer testimony of three previous witnesses that he was a Party member."[47] Communists did not sit in official government capacities as bystanders – they felt passionate obligation to constantly advance Soviet Russian interests at any price to America.

Reading transcripts of the Senator's Subcommittee meetings reveals a heavy hand to people innocent under the law but likely participants in treason or disloyalty. Many day-long Committee sessions were mired in unimportant, needlessly repetitive, even boring subjects.

While McCarthyism generated headlines, *the charge shifted attention from the reality of widespread treason and foreign control of Government to "abuses" of legislative oversight.*

In the main, McCarthy was right about the massive extent of Soviet influence in all departments of Federal Government, including the White House. Unfortunately, "McCarthyism" became of far greater national significance than the basis of the Senator's crusade: rampant Red treason.

Carpet-bomb press treatment assured that McCarthyism saved traitorous hides from public scrutiny for decades to come, if not permanently. We are not supposed to think about atomic bomb-related Red treason facilitating Korean War and a great many American dead, or about Washington's decided tilt toward Communist ascendance in China under Roosevelt and Truman. How many did McCarthy kill, how many nations did he subject to totalitarian rule?

On March 21, 1954, Internationalist standard-bearer David Lilienthal pitched the politically-accepted line relegating reality of treasonous control to "hysteria" and "violent, nasty vilification: There is so little evidence of a real communist threat in the United States that the point [of McCarthyism] simply disappears. The extent of that threat, among so prosperous and patriotic a people as the Americans, is almost invisible."[48] No doubt Kremlin leaders took comfort in Comrade Lilienthal's defense.

TREASON'S PROOF IN OUTCOMES

Tragedy attending the shower of attention generated by McCarthy's actions holds to this day. Communists, Socialists, and Internationalists *did* invade all parts of Federal Government, including every Executive Branch department, the armed services, plus Congress and the Judiciary (the US Supreme Court in particular). Many traitors reached high office and helped direct US policy on a number of vital levels. Roosevelt set the pattern maintained by Truman of routinely favoring Soviet interests over American. Stalin indeed had his hand on the American tiller.

Soviet-favored policies shut down the postwar US nuclear program, gave all nuclear secrets to Moscow, sapped conventional military strength, placed a chokehold on professional military leadership, and favored China's fall to Communism. Such policies created an internationally-level media playing field which ignored Soviet mass murder and permitted Reds to compete for world hegemony with true democracies.

Red hand in Washington brought world political disaster to the efforts of World War II, with half the globe under Communism, followed by a 45-year Cold War and "the greatest military confrontation in history" along Europe's Iron Curtain. From the groundwork rose hot wars in Korea and Vietnam.

In the case of Korean War, Internationalism put brakes on American victory. Ideologically-driven, high-placed American Red agents, icons of Government respectability, took the Dual Power baton, rushing toward desired Moscow policy objectives. Then the US did what Soviets and compatriots wanted. From presidents Roosevelt and Truman on down, America proved easy pickings. Moscow set the direction, the over-arching aim. Its minions held the keys to turning America's ship of state. Foreign rule, in reality Bolshevik rule, joined that of American: the concept plain and simple, the results devastating.

Chapter 44: Emerging Truth of Dual Power, Two Governments –

Part 2

"And there shall be a bridle in the jaws of the people."[1]

-    Isaiah, Chapter 30, Verse 28.

Revelation of two earth-shaking spy operations confirms potent Red-handed Washington power. Both center on White House and Executive Branch leadership action supporting vital Communist interests while ignoring bloody consequences to America. The first guaranteed US entry into World War II, the second, war in Korea.

MOSCOW'S 'OPERATION SNOW' – KEEPING JAPAN OFF RUSSIA'S BACK

Given massive Nazi invasion launched June 21, 1941, national survival became Moscow's most important policy goal. Japan represented a dangerous threat to Russia's Far East flank. With hands full fighting Germans, a second front against Japan must be avoided at all costs. East Asian Red troops had been mobilized for action against Nazi armies and could not be spared to fight Japan. But great Lenin's words solved the dilemma: "Contradictions between the imperialist powers should always be ruthlessly exploited in the interests of Communism."[2]

Memoirs of high-ranking KGB agents, plus opened Soviet intelligence archives, provide strong evidence of the slick Red operation to discourage Japan from attacking the USSR at its most vulnerable moment. American-based legal and illegal agents joined US Government traitors to get the Soviet Union off the two-front hook.

NKVD (KGB predecessor) "Operation Snow," set in motion by Stalin's chief of secret police Lavrenti Beria, promoted maximum hostility between Japan and America. The plan aimed to "divert Japanese aggression away from Siberia by aggravating the strained relations between the US and Japan."[3] Top Treasury official Harry Dexter White, prolific Washington spy Nathan Gregory Silvermaster, and Roosevelt White House aide Lauchlin Currie served as key American assets assuring operational success.

Japan invaded China in 1932, conquering huge northern and coastal regions. Although Chiang Kai-shek's Nationalist Government suffered grievous troop losses, it stayed in the fight 13 years. Many Japanese troops were tied up in China's vast reaches. *More Chinese resistance meant less Japanese ability to threaten Far Eastern Soviet Russia.* Should China fold, Moscow faced the specter of massive Japanese attack and dreaded second war front. At that time, the Kremlin considered Chiang's Guomindang leadership politically correct, and soon became China's largest arms supplier.

Interestingly, in 1995 retired NKVD intelligence official Lt. Gen. Vitali Pavlov "published the first [public] revelation of Operation Snow in the Russian monthly newspaper *News of Intelligence and Counterintelligence,* followed the next year by a book on the same subject."[4] More Russian scholarship on Operation Snow surfaced January 21, 2000, in the Moscow publication *Independent Military Review*. Respected author and highly-decorated retired GRU (military intelligence) Col. Vladimir Karpov boldly stated that "War in the Pacific could have been avoided. Stalin managed to prevent an attack against the USSR from a second front in the Far East …. *Stalin was the real initiator of the [US] ultimatum to Japan,*" subsequent attack on Pearl Harbor, and Pacific War between Japan and America (italics added).[5]

Above sources document Pavlov's Moscow meeting with Harry Dexter White's Red superior, chief KGB illegal officer in America Iskhak Akhmerov, to "thoroughly analyze … the progress of the operation …. We could be sure that [White] accepted our piece of advice and by all means would use it."[6] White fully appreciated Operation Snow as "framed to lead America into war with Japan." Charged by Treasury Secretary Henry Morgenthau, Jr. with responsibility for all international financial matters, White wrote many provisions of America's harsh Japanese trade embargo.

Before Pearl Harbor attack, New York-based Soviet intelligence officer Pastelniak, code-named "Luka," cabled Moscow about White's faithful discharge of Soviet instructions. As revealed in

Project Venona, Pastelniak's "agents Robert [Silvermaster] and Richard [White] were actively participating" in recommendations to Roosevelt "to prevent and impede Japan from acting against the Soviet Union." Venona also revealed Lauchlin Currie's key role in the Silvermaster apparatus. Cutting off oil shipments represented a major blow to a nation lacking this important resource.

Roosevelt sought to goad Tokyo into attacking the US Pacific Fleet as a *causus belli* to overcome strong domestic isolationist sentiment and pave America's entrance into world war. A week before Pearl Harbor, he admitted the provocation to Secretary of War Henry Stimson. By mid-summer 1941, American diplomats demanded Japanese evacuation of dominated Asian territories and announced the oil shipment embargo, made in full knowledge Tokyo acceptance would be impossible. The punishing stance brought direct attack on the US Pearl Harbor fleet and death to thousands of Army, Navy and Marine personnel. Japan must now concern itself primarily with America. The US rescued Russia in a big way.

After Hitler's surprise June 21, 1941 attack on Russia along an unprecedented 1,500-mile front, no time could be wasted securing Red Far Eastern flank safety. US embargo on Japan began July 26, 1941. Tokyo responded as expected. Stalin's intelligence army and its US Government agents rapidly confronted the dire threat. The United States obligingly played the role of lightning rod for the Kremlin, making an offer Tokyo had to refuse, a perfect coincidence to Roosevelt's plan for US entry into World War II.

Jerrold and Leona Schecter personally asked retired Gen. Pavlov about Moscow's reaction at the time to Japan's Pearl Harbor attack. Pavlov admitted, "We sighed a deep sigh of relief."[7]

The Schecters neatly summed up Harry White's mission philosophy, shared by all US Government Reds: "His agenda was to keep in mind Soviet interests and inject them into American policy, making it appear that peace was his only objective."[6]

Recently, a few authors noted an emerging "new clarity ... showing the effect of Soviet espionage on American foreign policy."[8] Clear vision by a small number, yes; widespread understanding and cultural acceptance, not even close. Knowledge of Operation Snow, and the vital traitorous role played by important US Government leaders, is of course highly politically incorrect. The radical left finds such truth, *any* truth, unacceptable. Unreality is the preferred political domain. So the Red mission and its huge consequences are unknown to Americans.

ANOTHER LESSON IN AMERICAN RED POWER

A striking, unappreciated example from the Pacific theater illustrates the intimate relation of World War II and war in Korea. Linkage includes well-established functioning of Communist influence within Washington decision-making.

America entered the fourth year of Pacific War facing an important question: How strong was Japan's armed force? The answer would determine intensity of war fighting, extent of US killed and wounded, and War's duration.

At great cost in blood, the US had thrown Japan from a series of Central and South Pacific islands, and sunk almost all its aircraft carriers and heavy warships in a string of naval and amphibious victories. Air bombing of Japan's home islands grew in frequency and intensity. One massive April 1945 incendiary air attack by American B-29 bombers destroyed 11 square miles of Tokyo. The shrinking Imperial Navy testified to enemy inability to produce major combat vessels or aircraft at anywhere near the rate needed to counter American destruction. Winston Churchill concluded that "… by the end of July the Japanese Navy had virtually ceased to exist."[9] A shade descended over the Empire of the Rising Sun.

Japan kept armies in vast conquered areas of North and coastal China, and Manchuria. A number of Western and Asian intelligence sources spied on these forces in hopes of learning their strength. Besides US military intelligence using aerial and ground reconnaissance, and separate Office of Strategic Services operations, agents from Nationalist China, Communist regions of China, Russia, Great Britain, and Australia worked to assess Japan's military situation.

INTELLIGENCE FAILURE, IGNORING ACCURATE INTELLIGENCE, OR POLITICS ABOVE ALL

Given ample sources, it appeared abundant "raw" information flowed to Allies about Japanese armed force. Then came the issue of analysis. Aside from the Soviets, intelligence masters who devoted huge resources to such matters, and Chinese directly facing the Japanese, it is unknown if other nations properly analyzed the gatherings. And for America at least, in the end political factors would trump any intelligence, no matter its accuracy. This simply meant that regardless of America's best interests, great white father Roosevelt would do whatever he wanted in the Far East.

Political reality's immediate consequence was the ruling out of any unilateral American peace agreement with Japan. Blind to human cost, Pacific War must last until the Soviet Union could jump in with both feet. According to Roosevelt's mantra, Soviets were "equal partners" with America, despite their very late entry into Pacific action. After all, they had "borne the lion's share" in defeating Nazi Germany and deserved to reap Far Eastern rewards.

The fact that Soviets supported Hitler's war effort for almost two years must be overlooked. The same mental gymnastics must be performed on the 1939 Hitler-Stalin Pact kicking off World War II, and the April 1941 peace treaty between Japan and Soviet Russia freeing large Japanese military forces to make war on America.

Always sticking to his Russian policy of "concession without reciprocation," Roosevelt appeared to give no thought to the East Asia balance of power and regional and world effect attending Soviet control of vast reaches of China, Manchuria, and Korea. As astute observers David Dallin, James Forrestal, and Sumner Welles knew, Communist domination of China must follow.[10] Despite American military victory over Japan, from 1945 on, the Far East would be closer to war than peace. A preparatory campaign of words must soften the blow.

Starting November 1944, endless domestic propaganda pounded home Soviet reasonableness and desire to work with the US and Britain in founding the United Nations. All would be well in the world of Internationalism. As Roosevelt said, "Make the Russians satisfied and they will work with us to build a world of peace and democracy." Charming yet inexcusable innocence, or unflattering stupidity, attended such wishful thinking, as if one meal could satisfy ravenous Communist world revolutionary appetite. How easy to envision solutions to vexing problems when polar-opposite complicating details are factored out.

Superb historian Barbara Tuchman joined colleagues William Manchester, D. Clayton James, Richard Dunlop, John Toland, and OSS chief William "Wild Bill" Donovan in decrying politically-encouraged American military intelligence mistakes about Japanese capability in the last year of war.[11,12,13] Presidential political power ruled the day. The issue serves as a perfect example of mass disinformation meant to steer American war policy toward Soviet interests.

ABOVE ALL, LOYALTY TO MOSCOW

The upper-echelon Washington line, shared with the public through ample and expected press attention, portrayed Japan as still possessing potent military force. Her Kwantung armies in mainland China, Manchuria, and Korea supposedly held 700,000 to a million troops, the majority Chinese conscripted in over 13 years of Sino-Japanese fighting. The preferred story posed the Kwantung as crack combat outfits, well-armed and supplied, ready to pound American infantry should the two collide. "Hundreds of thousands" of American boys would perish.[14]

Likewise, American Reds and pro-Reds pitched Japan's home islands as loaded with fanatical warriors ready to die for imperial honor. Supermen lay in wait to push hated Americans from Japanese beaches. In the face of "prolonged resistance," US assault on Japanese heartland would surely result in "millions" of American casualties, so the story told.

What, or who, could prevent such bloodbath? The atomic bomb would not be tested for another 10 months, and the story line told that US strategic bombing of Japan had not yet inflicted damage sufficient to deflate the "fanatical martial powerhouse."

According to Washington, retained Japanese military power could easily assure continuation of

Pacific War another 18 months after Germany's defeat. What could a president and top civilian and military leadership do to "save American lives" and yet deal effectively with the dire threat?

At least one US agency avoided the proffered bait. John Toland is among a handful of authors relating a contrary opinion on the matter of Kwantung Army strength. Investigation by Capt. Ellis Zacharias and cohorts at US Naval Intelligence revealed Japan's mainland Army to be a largely spent force, its "cream of troops" skimmed off in transfer to Leyte in The Philippines and other Pacific sites of Japanese need. Artillery and armor had likewise been shipped elsewhere. Capt. Zacharias believed the continental force to "exist primarily on paper."[15] Roosevelt, then Truman, and top brass, ignored advice of Naval Intelligence, an incorrect truth.

OPENING EASTERN GATES TO COMMUNISM

Alas, brave, "peace-loving and democratic-principled" peoples of Soviet Russia held keys to salvation. Showing unmatched mettle in driving back barbaric German Nazism, "Christian gentleman" Stalin could perhaps be persuaded to come to America's aid (Roosevelt used the perverse words, "There is something of the Christian gentleman in Stalin, perhaps from his experience in the seminary," at a post-Yalta cabinet meeting. No wonder he forbade taking of minutes at any meeting he attended). What other solution existed? No other ally had ground resources to match and overwhelm the *powerful, elite* Kwantung of vicious Japanese Fascists.

To preserve the all-important element of surprise and deny Tokyo warlords time to prepare adequate defense, request to Comrade Stalin for Soviet invasion forces must be made in utmost secrecy. It would be natural to balance the transaction with reasonable in-kind rewards for Red sacrifice. Stalin had his own people to please, they would perhaps expect a bit of territory and other gifts in return for blood.

With Moscow always attuned to necessity of intelligence excellence, it was fitting that America's official World War II spy agency, the Office of Strategic Services (OSS), held the highest percentage of Soviet spies of any US department. According to authors Christopher Andrew and Oleg Gordievsky, the latter a retired KGB agent, Truman's post-war closure of OSS temporarily deprived at least 20 Red agents of employment. US spy chief Donovan, who out of desperation hired many Communists for OSS work, believed Roosevelt erred in blindly trusting the Soviets. *After* the war, Donovan described America's perception of great Japanese military strength as a costly mistake, attributed to misreading of intelligence.[16] He would never publicly accuse Roosevelt of intentionally favoring Red Russia.

In a great historical irony detailed by prize-winning author Simon Montefiore, even Stalin believed Japan defeated by July 1945. He privately criticized US atomic bombing of Hiroshima and Nagasaki as unnecessary.

As mentioned earlier, from the mid- to late-1930s, it became in Soviet interest to arouse anti-Japanese sentiment in America and Western Europe, and stimulate Nationalist China's will to resist Japan. Hitler posed a disturbing European threat, while Japan could make war on Russia from the Far East. Soviet leadership never placed much value on diplomatic agreements – despite the April 1941 Soviet-Japanese peace treaty, Moscow worried mightily about risk of two-front war. The Communist Party USA (CPUSA) and world Communism quickly toed the line. So did the Roosevelt Administration in ever more harsh embargoes of oil and raw materials against Japan, and freezing of financial assets.

November 1944 saw marked change in Soviet Far Eastern attitudes. Two-front war had receded as supreme threat. With Germany on the ropes, Reds no longer feared Japanese opening of an Asian front. With Japan itself reeling from relentless American attack (this could not be publicly voiced), Moscow no longer needed the Nationalist China counterweight.

So a new story emanated from the Kremlin, a series of deprecating comments about recent ally Nationalist China, and glowing words for "valiant Chinese Communists" under Comrade Mao. Foreign Minister Molotov told US China specialist Donald Nelson that Moscow and Chungking, seat of Nationalist government, had parted ways. Moscow's many friends rallied to the new cause. The fresh line gained great traction in the American press and Executive agencies.

Of course, intelligence reports didn't matter – Soviet interests demanded participation in the Pacific War and share in spoils. Allied effort was a joint effort, one for all, all for one. The Russian people had made huge sacrifices, far greater than Americans or British. According to correct politics, whatever gains gallant Reds accrued from Far East Asia would be most deserved. Whatever losses accrued to America and the West in Communist domination of China, Manchuria, and northern Korea, would be publically ignored. Red interests always came before those of America and its people.

No higher good, no good at all, would attend mention of war risk in Korea, a most-incorrect fact.

MOSCOW INVENTS AND SPREADS 'TRUTH'

New Truth always originated in, and emanated from, the Kremlin. "Truth" went out to foreign Communist parties and agents not as advice or suggestion, but fact to be perfectly followed. Actual happenings were bent, pounded, twisted, turned upside down, seasoned with pots of accessory lies. All was considered normal, acceptable behavior. No moral constraints prevented crushing of truth and spreading of gargantuan lies.

According to Churchill, "Russians had no understanding of the words 'honesty,' 'honor,' 'trust,' and 'truth,' regarding them as negative virtues." This was the Red way, enshrined in Marx's *Manifesto,* Lenin's embellishments, and Stalin's practical applications. Communist foundational writings are brutally frank on necessary revolutionary actions, such as "despotic inroads" on traditional society and sanctity-of-life's zero consequence. With encouragement from home, agents within and without distant governments spread the word. Pro-Red press continually shielded audiences from monstrous truth. Foreign government endorsement of Moscow's line provided the greatest testament to revolutionary success.

Red-Internationalist crews at State and Treasury departments and White House parroted the end of 'evil Chinese Nationalist feudalism' and ascendance of 'enlightened, democratic Chinese Communism.' Associated public relations barrage included a host of previously mentioned Moscow-directed, pro-Mao-and-company books and articles. Gate-keeper editors at many American publishing houses, along with book reviewers, relished the opportunity of promoting these 'authoritative, fact-filled' tomes. It was one big, happy family.

As the February 1945 Yalta Conference approached, Moscow word percolated through Washington. American leaders by the boatload heartily concurred in the misperception of vast continental Japanese military strength. Such key support played so well into the desired pitch: only large-scale Soviet military presence in north China, Manchuria, and Korea could prevent wholesale American slaughter. The Red Army would "pin down Japanese armies on the mainland." American generals George Marshall and Douglas MacArthur were said to favor such assistance. As John Toland related, on January 23, 1945, "the Joint Chiefs of Staff formally advised Roosevelt that Russia's entry into the war against Japan was vital to US interest."[17] Justification had come full-circle. Moscow stood ready to sweep the board clean of World War II spoils. Communism would explode on the world scene.

Prospect of assault on Japan's home islands provided nightmare enough, "a fight to the last man." So went the story. Only two weeks remained until Roosevelt would personally, and secretly, present the invitation to Stalin at Yalta. Churchill did not receive an invitation to this "Big Two" meeting.

NO TO JAPANESE PEACE PROPOSAL

Also starting November 1944, Japan made peace feelers to the US through Sweden. South Pacific Commander Gen. MacArthur received a prospective peace agreement early 1945, passed to Roosevelt through White House Chief of Staff Admiral Leahy. Fortunately for posterity, Leahy copied the proposal before sending it to the Commander in Chief, figuring Roosevelt would deep-six the document. Political correctness mandated no peace allowed until the Soviet Union had a chance to enter the war and benefit from that entry. Premature end of fighting, though it might save a host of American lives, could not be accepted. Securing Soviet interests trumped prospective American dead.

Adm. Leahy gave the peace proposal copy to *Chicago Tribune* reporter Walter Trohan with the proviso it not be made public until Japan surrendered. The Japanese offer was nearly identical to that formally signed on the battleship *Missouri* September 2, 1945, its Chicago publication mostly ignored. Nothing could disturb the national party. Roosevelt, of course, never disclosed the peace feeler. Since Soviet interests *always* came before American, 12,520 US Marines and soldiers killed and 36,631 wounded in the battle for Okinawa could be ignored as a necessary price for "future world peace."[12]

SOVIET RUSSIA'S SIX – DAY WAR

A 1.6-million-strong, three-pronged Soviet Army invasion, launched August 9, 1945, overwhelmed all Japanese resistance. *Five* days later, "fearsome" Japanese forces surrendered. Pacific War fighting had ended. The vaunted, mainland Asian-based Japanese Kwantung Army capitulated directly to Soviet and Chinese Red forces. Soviets turned over captured armories and troops to Chinese Communists, quadrupling People's Army manpower within a few months. China, Manchuria, half of Korea, and 650 million people would know Red control, and that was that. For years, Russian press accounts gave the USSR full credit for defeating Japan, albeit in only six days; "the atom bomb played no role."

Former US Ambassador to Soviet Russia William Bullitt documented dutiful CPUSA adherence to Moscow's line through its New York-based official newspaper, the *Daily Worker*. Articles appearing in July and early August 1945 emphasized unspent, fearful Japanese military might so requiring Soviet help to overcome. After the Red Army walked through the decrepit Kwantung, *Daily Worker* articles and editorials encouraged US forces *to leave China forthwith*, lest they impede creation of "people's democracies."

Perversely, Moscow now stood as an authority on democratic government. US Reds also pressed for immediate demobilization of powerful American armed forces. Truman willingly obliged on both counts. Roaring Socialist Sidney Hillman had put him in power! Truth meant nothing. As shown time and again by Bullitt, should Soviet leadership order a diametrically new course, *Daily Worker* editorialists would perform somersaults in endorsement.[18]

American military leaders did not factor atomic weapons into the "retained Japanese might" equation. To naturally conservative American Joint Chiefs and the Combined Chiefs of British and American services, nuclear bombs represented "untried weapons." With pats on the back from Roosevelt, they felt it necessary to bring Russians into the Pacific War as soon as possible.[17] That the atomic bomb made Red Pacific War contribution unnecessary could not be allowed to interfere with the grand plan. Backward military thinking and political kow-towing, combined with Red power within US and British governments, assured continued favoring of Soviet interests.

Americans, soon to pay heavily for pro-Communist policies, so easily ignored Roosevelt-guaranteed reality of "complicated postwar settlement in Asia." Instead, grand World War II military victory must be celebrated, political defeat ignored.

A key fact is that in Franklin Roosevelt, Reds had the greatest friend imaginable. James and Wells put it mildly, in typically subdued historical style: "The Anglo-American alliance of World War II attained total victory but *dubious postwar political gains* (italics added)."[19] How casually is world disaster treated! With Roosevelt at the helm, no other outcome was possible.

Chapter 45: Internationalist – Communist Solidarity

"The Left proposed to tackle ... problems ... with one prescription – the centralization of power of all kinds in Washington. Those who advocated centralization believed they were infallible. They liked power, and they lacked faith in people. History taught that such a course could lead only to ruin – we would in the process also lose our freedoms."[1]

- Dwight D. Eisenhower, Mandate for Change.

The Venona Project conducted by the National Security Agency (NSA) managed to decrypt all or part of 2,900 secret messages exchanged by American-based Soviet espionage leaders and Moscow intelligence headquarters.[2] We know these represented less than 3% of total World War II cable traffic between the two.

As expected, Russians were tipped off about Venona findings in 1947-48 by agents within the NSA, including supervisor William Weisband and British spy Kim Philby. Weisband spent a year in jail rather than reveal Soviet contacts, never criminally tried for his body-blow treason. Long after the fact, master decrypter Meredith Gardner recalled pipe-smoking arch-spy Philby looking over his shoulder as he worked unraveling codes. Washington did not publicly acknowledge Venona until 1995.

As disclosed in a deciphered May 16, 1944 New York-to-Moscow cable, upper-level KGB agent Vladimir Sergeevich Pravdin met with American Internationalist co-founder and prominent American journalist Walter Lippman. The KGB assigned Lippman the code-name "Imperialist."

The message to Moscow spy headquarters noted,

> "Imperialist continues to consider the question of participation of the USSR in the war against Japan a stumbling block in Soviet-American relations. Imperialist does not conceal that *our future interests in this matter are considered in responsible circles in the United States to be a deciding factor in the policy of the United States*" (italics added).

The statement proves the reality of Two Governments/Dual Power in Washington. Soviet interests, not American, were decisive in highest US policy regarding Red Pacific War participation. America did what was best for Soviet Russia in the matter, regardless of hurt inflicted on its own, Chinese, and world interests. Communists had achieved their hard-won goal, ability to set policy within US Government. Reds ran key parts of American Government. *Anti-Americanism ruled America.* Treason became official policy.

Lippman also shared with Pravdin secret US plans for invading and occupying key Pacific islands in the quest to defeat Japan. As a respected member of the press, Lippman learned these from direct talks with top admirals and generals in Washington. Ideological brother Moscow so wished to be informed about such matters.

Historian Ted Morgan told of Lippman's Communist-affiliated Washington secretary, Mary Price, a highly-productive Red agent. Price joined the CPUSA while living in North Carolina. Confessed spy Elizabeth Bentley told of receiving secret Government files from Price and delivering them to cell supervisors for shipment to Moscow. Price mentioned to Bentley a highly-placed Red source in the CIA fore-runner Office of Strategic Services, one Duncan Chapin Lee.[3]

Reared in China by US missionary parents, Lee came to America at age 12. In typical Soviet agent pattern, he graduated valedictorian from the University of Virginia Class of 1935. While a Rhodes scholar at Oxford, he "married and honeymooned in Moscow."[3] (Four 'Red Flags' have popped up). Yale Law School then beckoned, followed by employment at the New York law firm headed by William J. Donovan. As World War II dawned and Roosevelt called on Donovan to head US intelligence efforts, Lee became his chief OSS assistant. Shortly after, Lee joined the important Jakob Golos New York-based spy apparatus, for which Elizabeth Bentley worked.

According to Venona discovery, Golos messaged Moscow on Lee's unique intelligence status: "All the OSS agent information from Europe and the rest of the world comes through his hands. He joined the Party at Yale [Law School] in 1939; his wife joined the Party at the same time …. He will make notes and pass them to Mary Price."[3] So Lee joined the infective Red host, whose esprit de corps reflected "confidence of their superiority over all others."[4]

Lee's background mirrored common espionage agent themes: graduation from schools producing America's ruling class; spouses and family as Communist Party (CP) members; early ideological commitment; personal connection to Russia; loyalty to Stalin, not Roosevelt or Truman; duty to promote Red revolution, whatever the risks; and display of chutzpah-like indignation if ever questioned about Red actions.

Agents were a cut above regular CP members. Through indoctrination to Bolshevik operating principles, they had been transformed into disciplined, ruthless soldiers in a true revolutionary cadre, "combat party."[5] Affinity for communication-related work and espionage produced a strong host at the Fort Monmouth, NJ US Army Signal Corps. Roosevelt's obliging executive order mandating placement of Communist radio operators on US Navy warships furthered the quest. As mentioned, Reds ran much of the World War II Office of War Information and Voice of America radio operations.

The Soviet spy network in America reached incredible heights of organization, penetration, and strength. Following Lenin and Trotsky tenets, Reds controlled whole sections of Federal Government, especially within State and Treasury departments. Reality of this accomplishment is recognized by words of only a handful of historians – "Spies hired each other, promoted each other, and wrote admiring reports about each other."[4]

Confessed spy Whittaker Chambers was one of many who left the Communist movement upon news of 1939 Soviet-Nazi partnership. His book *Witness* described

> "an entirely new type of Communist …[,] a small intellectual army [who] would help to shape the country's domestic and foreign policies …. They would, at last, in a situation unparalleled in history, enable the Soviet Union to use the American State and Treasury departments as a terrible engine of its revolutionary purposes, by the calculated destruction of powers vital to American survival (like China)."[6]

The Washington situation under presidents Franklin Roosevelt and Harry Truman is easy to summarize. We borrow the fitting exclamation of Julius Rosenberg brother-in-law, spy cell member, and convicted atomic traitor David Greenglass: "All power to the Soviet Union!" (Greenglass died in 2014 at age 92). Internationalists and companions knew only loyalty to Moscow. The Soviet Union represented "a heaven … brought to earth in Russia."[7] The US, its people and institutions, simply didn't count.[8]

Chapter 46: Stronger Than Ever

"In the final analysis, the issue now joined in Korea is whether Communism or individual freedom shall prevail; whether the flight of fear-driven people we have witnessed shall be checked, or shall at some future time, however distant, engulf our own loved ones in all its misery and despair."[1]

- Gen. Matthew B. Ridgway, The Korean War.

"... take pains to read history – it is only from the past that one can judge the future ...."[2]

- Winston S. Churchill, Triumph and Tragedy.

The March 12, 1945 *Daily Worker*, official American Communist Party organ, carried Chairman Earl Browder's comments on the important Communist effort in the 1944 presidential election:

> "Our own policies and work contributed essentially to the victory of November 7, and therefore directly to the consummation at Yalta .... Our political influence within the labor and progressive organizations and communities has grown far wider and deeper than it ever was before. We are gradually breaking down and dissolving the barriers built up against us over a generation by the dominant forces in American society ...."[3]

If Browder lived to the year 2016, he could with prideful accuracy state, *"We* are now the dominant force in American society!"

George Kennan knew that "Success of a local Communist party, any advance of Communist power anywhere, had to be regarded as an extension of the Kremlin. Precisely because Stalin maintained so jealous, so humiliating a control over foreign Communists, all the latter had to be regarded as vehicles of his will ..., as instruments of Soviet power."[4]

In the six years following World War II, the FBI developed a clear view of extensive Soviet penetration of US Government and damage done to American interests, including "subversion of our politics and culture."[5] Among former American Soviet agents cooperating with the FBI were Elizabeth Bentley, Thomas Black, Whittaker Chambers, Max Elitcher, Harry Gold, David and Ruth Greenglass, Hede Massing, Robert Miller, Jacob Morros, Jack and Myra Soble, and Nathaniel Weyl. They risked lives and often had a hard sell convincing American authorities, press, and historians of the truth.

On the plane of daily action, presence of Two Governments simply reflected the reality of many disloyal Americans occupying key Federal Government posts. The FBI identified 206 domestic agents actively involved in Soviet espionage. These are only *discovered* enemies – a great many more eluded identification.[6]

On a broader plane, widespread treason represented strong American leftist-socialist power, "a great political force bent on our destruction."[7] Starting in heady 1915 Washington Internationalist days, pressure for socialist control and hostility to America never ceased. A poking, prodding, viciously-worded campaign targeted institutions and people and succeeded. The century-old theme is clear and straight from the Red playbook: "*Such evil as exists in the world has its seat in the United States, which doesn't want to understand*" (emphasis in original).[8]

Internationalist thesis held sway with Supreme Court justices Holmes, Brandeis, Frankfurter, Benjamin Cardozo, and William O. Douglas; protégés Dean Acheson, David Lilienthal, J. Robert Oppenheimer, and Harry Hopkins; important press figures Joseph Harsch, Walter Lippman, and James Reston; and presidents Franklin Roosevelt and Harry Truman. Great wealth of Ford, Carnegie, and Rockefeller foundations pushed the One-World agenda.

The Truman Administration had to conduct war in Korea within powerful leftist constraints. Rulers ordained America would not and could not win the War. Far more important issues presented: success of the United Nations and the collective security policy; preservation of Communist China; and global Red power sufficient to prevent American world hegemony.

Since "All Kremlin leaders endorsed policies decidedly hostile to the United States," shadow government had no choice but to aggressively back these policies.[9] As Arthur Schlesinger, Jr. correctly diagnosed, "Despite illusions to the contrary, the CPUSA was firmly in the grip of the Kremlin."[10]

Isaac Don Levine added core leftist common-ground:

> "It is impossible to understand the mentality and policy of progressives unless one takes into account the fact that the Communist Manifesto is their manual and holy writ, the only reliable source of information about mankind's future as well as the ultimate code of political conduct. *Any antagonism between Communism, Socialism, and New Dealers is about the means to be resorted to for attainment of all-round central planning and the entire elimination of the market economy* (italics added).

> From the Manifesto they learned that the coming of Socialism is inevitable and will transform earth into the Garden of Eden. They call themselves progressives and opponents 'reactionaries' precisely because, fighting for the bliss that is bound to come, they are borne by the 'wave of the future' while their adversaries are committed to the hopeless attempt to stop the wheel of Fate and History. What comfort to know that one's own cause is destined to conquer.

> Then the progressive professors, writers, politicians, and civil servants discover in the Manifesto a passage which especially flatters their vanity. They belong to that 'small section of the ruling class,' to that 'portion of the bourgeois ideologists' who have gone over to the proletariat, 'the class that holds the future in their hands.' Thus they are members of the elite."[11]

Reactionaries such as Republican presidential candidates Sen. John McCain (2008) and Gov. Mitt Romney (2012) tried with futility to explain "progressive policies as economically insufficient and untenable," believing points of righteousness could be made with the American people. Levine reminded, "How wrong they are! In the eyes of progressives the excellence of these policies consists in the very fact that they *are* 'economically insufficient and untenable,' and will act to achieve the desired destruction of capitalist society."[11]

Current Republican presidential candidate Donald Trump appears to be grounded in reality in seeing leftist political power bent on destroying free enterprise and personal freedom. Wired in Red ideology, what else could leftist revolution stand for?

During Truman's presidency, this ideology meant putting brakes on US nuclear weapons, rapid military demobilization, shutting the door on Nationalist China while embracing Communist China, continuing Soviet espionage, and destroying the American family along with the evil of organized religion – the Communist agenda for visiting total catastrophe on America as prelude to raising the Red banner.

Distinguished, realistic diplomat and adroit communicator Kennan envisioned behind-the-scenes control in American governmental functioning. He described a "Long shadow cast by the towers of the Kremlin," within which "forces beyond our vision guided our footsteps and shaped our relations with Russia.[8] The more I see of this international society the more I am convinced that it is in the shadows rather than the substance of things that move the hearts, and sway the deeds, of statesmen."[12]

Unfortunately, Kennan's espousal of truth never gained traction. It ran completely opposite to the politically-correct version. Guiding hand works best in darkness. Awful political truth of World War II could never be revealed. Kennan realized America

> "won a war in Europe – on the battlefield. It cost us far more than we realized – it cost the stability of our international environment. Worst of all, it was not a complete victory. The Anglo-American world was not strong enough to put down all the forces that threatened our existence. We were forced to ally ourselves with a part of them [Soviet Russia] in order to defeat the other part [Nazi Germany, Italy, and Japan]. We deceived ourselves and our people as to the nature of that alliance."[13]

Grand deceivers ran what they wanted in US Government, creating and sustaining warped historical-political views of World War II and aftermath. Distorted popular understanding enabled global competition between Soviet Communism and Western democracy. If truth be known, there could be no contest. Who wished generalized murder and repression? Stalin's advice assured an easy fix: "We alone determine what is true, and what is not true." Befitting proper loyalty, a sympathetic American press fell in line.

DIFFERENT STRIPES, SAME TIGER

We are five generations deep in Internationalism's unrelenting attack on America. Today's front features the prominence of Pelosi, Reid, Schumer, Durbin, Feinstein, Boxer, Sanders, consecrated Obama, the Clintons, and hundreds of prominent national politicians, all fonts of utmost respectability, reasonableness, even patriotism. Flags cover their backs. Old distasteful labels are gone, replaced by continual "good people" portrayals, in the fight for economic and political justice, equality, and better life for all.

Yet, all the while, today's Red revolutionists relentlessly push classic "Despotic inroads on the old social order." Grand Ruse masters, they preach "sound and desirable principles, followed by words of restriction and procedural limitation that nullify the principles."

Night yields to day, the campaign of destruction slickly waged. Evils of individualism, personal freedom, rights of property, an antiquated Bill of Rights, and religious practice must be wiped out. Innate personal dignity means nothing. People mean nothing. Elite orders and instructions will be obeyed. Rulers must be secure, their power unchallengeable.

In ending his fine 1946 book, *The Great Globe Itself,* Ambassador William Bullitt, Franklin Roosevelt neighbor and contemporary, quoted words from ancient Greek dramatist Euripides (484 – 406 BC):

> There be many shapes of mystery;
>
> And many things God makes to be,
>
> Past hope or fear.
>
> And the end men looked for cometh not,
>
> And a path is there where no man thought,
>
> So hath it fallen here.[14]

Ambassador Bullitt cast mystery aside in ending his book with excerpts from great Stalin's 1939 work, *Problems of Leninism*. Stalin sandwiched personal wisdom and zeal around prophetic Lenin mandates, the war-cadre's marching orders:

"... revolution victorious in one country must not consider itself a self-contained entity, but a support, a means of speeding the victory of the proletariat in other countries.[15,16]

"... dictatorship of the proletariat is the most unconditional and most merciless war of the new class against its more powerful enemy, the bourgeoisie, whose resistance is increased ten-fold when overthrown ...[;] proletarian dictatorship is a stubborn fight – bloody and bloodless, violent and peaceful, military and economic, educational and administrative – against the forces and traditions of an old society."[17,18]

"... there is not the least possibility of realizing all these tasks in a short period of time, of accomplishing this in a few years. Dictatorship of the proletariat, the transition from capitalism to communism, must therefore not be regarded as a brief moment of 'super-revolutionary' deeds and decrees, but as an entire historical period, with civil wars and foreign conflicts, of constant organizational work and economic reconstruction, of attacks and retreats, of victories and defeats."[18]

"... dictatorship of the proletariat is the domination of the proletariat over the bourgeoisie, unobstructed by law and based on violence, enjoying the sympathy and support of the working and exploited masses. [It] must be a state that is democratic in a new way, for the proletariat and the poor at large, and dictatorial in a new way, for the bourgeoisie ...."[19,20]

Solutions to America's ills are only found in truth. Deceit means morass, not foundation. As authors Klehr, Haynes, and Firsov warned, "Whatever prevents us from accepting the past will also prevent us from making reasoned decisions in the future."[21] Two-thousand seven-hundred years before, the prophet Isaiah urged the people to, "Open the gates, that the righteous nation which keeps the truth may enter in."[22]

Author Emily Hahn lived many years in China and in plain English emphasized the intentionally-distorted American view of pending Communist struggle for ascendance and Nationalist inhumanity. Her conclusion applies to the entire 101-year (1915-2016) leftist revolutionary movement in America: "The public has been fooled. It frightens me. Is it too late to start telling the truth?"[23]

Let those cherishing freedom rebel against slavery, no matter the price.

- end -

✝

Appendix: Proofs of Dual-Power/Two Governments, and Major American Players

1. Washington encouragement of US-Japan hostility to prevent Japanese attack on Far Eastern Soviet Russia, facilitating American entry into World War II: Harry Dexter White, Lauchlin Currie, FDR, Henry Morgenthau, Jr., Nathan Gregory Silvermaster.

2. US refusal to accept late-1944 Japanese peace offer that would save almost 13,000 American lives in Okinawa fighting: FDR.

3. Post-World War II Soviet political bonanza and US political disaster – Communism replaces Nazism and Fascism as world threat: FDR, HD White, Currie, Alger Hiss, Silvermaster.

4. Pro-Communist US China policy 1944-50, including propaganda campaign 1944-46: FDR, Truman, Acheson, John Paton Davies, John Carter Vincent, John Stuart Service, Currie, Michael Greenberg, Solomon Adler, V. Frank Coe.

5. Pro-Communist results at Yalta and Potsdam conferences: FDR, Truman, Harry Hopkins, Hiss, Currie, Earl Browder.

6. Truman appointments of known Communists Harry Dexter White and V. Frank Coe to important International Monetary Fund positions: Truman, Acheson.

7. Venona decryptions proving massive Red infiltration of US Government: FDR, Hopkins, Silvermaster, Duncan Lee, White, Currie, Hiss, Maurice Halperin (OSS).

8. Venona message about paramount Soviet interests in Roosevelt decision to ask massive Red Army invasion of Far East Asia, assuring Communist ascendance in China: FDR, Truman, Walter Lippman, White, Currie.

9. Released sworn testimony of State Department personnel administrator John H. Amen about details of John Carter Vincent's treason – Bolshevik Dual Power in action: Acheson, JC Vincent, Lawrence Rosinger (State Department).

10. Soviet co-ownership of "super-secret" Manhattan Project, including Super-Lend-Lease provision to Moscow of uranium and a dozen other nuclear bomb components: FDR, Hopkins, J Robert Oppenheimer, Truman, Acheson, David Lilienthal, Steve Nelson, Joseph Woodrow Weinberg, Martin David Kamen, David Hawkins, Theodore Hall.

11. Shut-down of US nuclear weapons program after World War II to allow Russian catch-up: Truman, Acheson, Lilienthal, Oppenheimer.

References

Dean Acheson. Present at the Creation. New York: W.W. Norton and Company, 1969.

Joseph Albright, Marcia Kunstel. Bombshell – The Secret Story of America's Unknown Atomic Spy Conspiracy. New York: Times Books, 1997.

Christopher Andrew, Oleg Gordievsky. KGB – The Inside Story. New York: Harper Collins Publishers, 1990.

Christopher Andrew, V. Mitrokhin. The Sword and the Shield. New York: Basic Books, 1999.

Roy E. Appleman. Escaping the Trap: The US Army X Corps in Northeast Korea, 1950. College Station, TX: Texas A & M Press, 1990.

Roy E. Appleman. South to the Naktong, North to the Yalu: United States Army in the Korean War. Washington: Office of the Chief of Military History, Department of the Army, 1961.

Rick Atkinson. The Long Gray Line. Boston: Houghton Mifflin Company, 1989.

Lee Ballenger. The Outpost War – US Marines in Korea. Vol. 1: 1952. Washington: Brassey's Inc, 2001.

Robert L. Beisner. Dean Acheson – A Life in the Cold War. New York: Oxford University Press, 2006.

Robert L. Benson. The Venona Story. Center for Cryptologic History, National Security Agency; 9800 Savage Road, Suite 6886, Fort George G. Meade, MD 20755-6886.

Elizabeth Bentley. Out of Bondage. New York: The Devin-Adair Company, 1951.

bioguide.congress.gov./scripts/biodisplay.pl?index=C000877. [Alan Cranston].

Stanley F. Bolin, John S. Cowings, Kim Nam Che. Twelve Hungnam Refugees. Seoul: Headquarters, Eighth United States Army, 1975.

Robert H. Bork. Slouching Towards Gomorrah – Modern Liberalism and American Decline. New York: HarperCollins Publishers, Inc., 1996.

Catherine Drinker Bowen. Yankee from Olympus. Boston: Little, Brown and Company, 1944.

Oman N. Bradley, Clay Blair. A General's Life. New York: Simon and Schuster, 1983.

501, **REFERENCES**

Bernard Brodie. War and Politics. New York: The Macmillan Company, 1973.

William F. Buckley. Odyssey of a Friend. New York: G.P. Putnam's Sons, 1969.

William C. Bullitt. The Great Globe Itself. New York: Charles Scribner's Sons, 1946.

William C. Bullitt. How We Won the War and Lost the Peace. Life Magazine: Sept. 6, 1948. pp. 86-103.

James Burnham. The Web of Subversion. New York: John Day, 1954.

Fox Butterfield. China – Alive in the Bitter Sea. New York: Times Books, 1982.

Brian Catchpole. The Korean War 1950-53. New York: Carroll and Graf Publishers, 2001.

Whittaker Chambers. Witness. New York: Random House, Inc., 1952.

Winston S. Churchill. A Roving Commission – My Early Life. New York: Charles Scribner's Sons, 1930.

Winston S. Churchill. The Second World War. Vol. VI: Triumph and Tragedy. Boston: Houghton Mifflin Company, 1953, 1985.

Jan Ciechanowski. Defeat in Victory. New York: Doubleday and Company, 1947.

Clark Clifford, Richard Holbrooke. Counsel to the President. New York: Random House, 1991.

J. Lawton Collins. War in Peacetime – The History and Lessons of Korea. Boston: Houghton Mifflin Company, 1969.

Blanche Wiesen Cook. Eleanor Roosevelt. Vol. 2: 1933-1938. New York: Penguin Books, 1999.

John Costello. Mask of Treachery. New York: William Morrow and Company, 1988.

John Costello, Oleg Tsarev. Deadly Illusions. New York: Crown Publishers, 1993.

Alan Cranston biography. bioguide.congress.gov/scripts/biodisplay.pl?index=C000877.

Alan Cranston biography. en.wikipedia.org/wiki/Alan_Cranston.

David J. Dallin. Soviet Espionage. New Haven, CT: Yale University Press, 1955.

David J. Dallin. Soviet Russia and the Far East. New Haven, CT: Yale University Press, 1948.

502, **REFERENCES**

Robert Dallek. Franklin Roosevelt and American Foreign Policy, 1932-1945. New York: Oxford University Press, 1979.

Robertson Davies. For Your Eye Alone. New York: Penguin Books, 2002.

Burke Davis. Marine! The Life of Chesty Puller. New York: Bantam Books, 1964.

Raymond De Jaegher, Irene C. Kuhn. The Enemy Within. Garden City, NY: Doubleday & Company, 1952.

Ralph de Toledano. J Edgar Hoover – The Man in His Time. New Rochelle, NY: Arlington House, 1973.

Ralph de Toledano. The Greatest Plot in History. 2nd Edition. New Rochelle, NY: Arlington House Publishers, 1977.

Ralph de Toledano, Victor Lasky. Seeds of Treason: The Strange Case of Alger Hiss. London: Secker and Warburg, 1950.

Discoverthenetworks.com – a guide to the political left.

Dennis J. Dunn. Caught Between Roosevelt and Stalin: America's Ambassadors to Moscow. Lexington, KY: The University Press of Kentucky, 1998.

The Economist, London: May 28, 2016.

Dwight D. Eisenhower. Crusade in Europe. Garden City, NY: Doubleday & Company, 1948.

Dwight D. Eisenhower. The White House Years – Mandate for Change 1953-1956. Garden City, NY: Doubleday and Company, 1963.

en.wikipedia.org/wiki/Alan_Cranston.

Federal Bureau of Investigation. Elizabeth Bentley Investigation. http://vault.fbi.gov/Rosenberg-case/elizabeth-bentley/Elizabeth-t-bentley-part11-of.

Federal Bureau of Investigation. Underground Soviet Espionage Organization (NKVD) in Agencies of the United States Government. Oct. 21, 1946. Washington, DC. http://vault.fbi.gov/william-remington/william-remington-part-16-of.

Federal Bureau of Investigation. Klaus Fuchs Investigation. http://vault.fbi.gov/rosenberg-case/klaus-fuchs/klaus-fuchs-part-69-of/at_download/file.

503, **REFERENCES**

Federal Bureau of Investigation. Sen. Joseph McCarthy.
http://vault.fbi.gov/Sen%20Joseph%20(joe)%20McCarthy/Sen.%20Joseph%20(Joe)20McCarthy%20part%2038%ofo/o2056at_download/file.

Federal Bureau of Investigation. Sen. Joseph McCarthy. https://vault.fbi.gov/Sen. Joseph (Joe) McCarthy/Sen. Joseph (Joe) McCarthy part 46. p.34/100.

Federal Bureau of Investigation. J. Robert Oppenheimer Interview.
http://vault.fbi.gov/rosenberg-case/klaus/klaus-fuchs-part-110-of/at_download/file.

Federal Bureau of Investigation. Summary Memorandum to Director Hoover on Soviet Espionage. Oct. 26, 1950. Washington, DC.

T.R. Fehrenbach. This Kind of War – A Study in Unpreparedness. New York: The Macmillan Company, 1963.

R.H. Ferrell, editor. The Eisenhower Diaries. New York: W.W. Norton and Company, 1981.

John T. Flynn. The Roosevelt Myth. 50th Anniversary Ed. San Francisco: Fox & Wilkes, 1998.

Robert F. Futrell. The United States Air Force in Korea 1950 – 1953. Washington, DC: Revised Edition, Office of Air Force History, United States Air Force, 1983.

Edward Gibbon. The Decline and Fall of the Roman Empire. Vol. 1. Everyman's Library, Alfred A. Knopf, Inc, 1993.

Bill Gilbert. Ship of Miracles – 14,000 Lives and One Miraculous Voyage. Chicago: Triumph Books, 2000.

O. Gilbert. Marine Corps Tank Battles in Korea. Havertown, PA: Casemate, 2003.

Mikal Gilmore. Bob Dylan – The Rolling Stone Interview. *Rolling Stone:* Sept. 27, 2012; issue 1166, p. 48.

John Grigg. 1943, the Victory that Never Was. New York: Hill & Wang, 1980.

Russell A. Gugeler. Combat Actions in Korea. Washington, D.C.: Office of the Chief of Military History, United States Army, 1970.

Mireille Hadas-Lebel. Flavius Josephus – Eyewitness to Rome's First-Century Conquest of Judea. Translated by Richard Miller. New York: Macmillan Publishing Company, 1993.

Emily Hahn. China to Me. Boston: Beacon Press, 1988.

504, **REFERENCES**

Kim Hakjoon. Russian Foreign Ministry Documents on the Origins of the Korean War. Paper presented at a conference conducted by the Korean Society, Korea-American Society, and Georgetown University. Washington, DC, July 24 – 25, 1995.

David Halberstam. The Best and the Brightest. New York: Random House, 1972.

J.A. Hammerton, ed. Outline of Great Books. New York: Wise & Company, 1936.

Robert T. Handy. Patrick J. Hurley and China, 1944-1945.
pdxscholar.library.pdx.edu/open_access_etds/1462/

Max Hastings. The Korean War. New York: Simon and Schuster, 1987.

Alden Hatch. General Ike – A Biography of Dwight D. Eisenhower. Chicago: Consolidated Book Publishers, 1944.

David A. Hatch, Robert Louis Benson. The Korean War: the SIGINT Background. Washington: The Center for Cryptologic History, National Security Agency, 2000.

John Earl Haynes, Harvey Klehr. In Denial: Historians, Communism, and Espionage. San Francisco: Encounter Books, 2003.

John Earl Haynes, Harvey Klehr. Venona: Decoding Soviet Espionage in America. New Haven, CT: Yale University Press, 1999.

John Earl Haynes, Harvey Klehr, Alexander Vassiliev. Spies: The Rise and Fall of the KGB in America. New Haven, CT: Yale University Press, 2009.

Francis H. Heller, ed. Korean War: A 25-Year Perspective. Lawrence, KS: The Regents Press of Kansas, 1977.

Richard Hirsch. The Soviet Spies: The Story of Russian Espionage in North America. 1947.

Edwin P. Hoyt. The Bloody Road to Panmunjom. New York: Stain and Day Publishers, 1985.

Bong Hak Hyun, Marian Hyun. Christmas Cargo: A Civilian Account of the Hungnam Evacuation. Norfolk, VA: The General Douglas MacArthur Foundation, 1997.

David Ignatius. Beijing Creating Rising Tensions in South Pacific. Investor's Business Daily: Feb. 27, 2014, p. A13.

Harold L. Ickes. The Secret Diary of Harold L. Ickes. Vol. III, The Lowering Clouds, 1939 – 1941.

505, **REFERENCES**

Fred Charles Iklé. Annihilation from Within – The Ultimate Threat to Nations. New York: Columbia University Press, 2006.

Robert Jackson. Air War in Korea 1950-1953. Osceola, WI: Motorbooks International, 1998.

D.Clayton James. The Years of MacArthur. Vol. III. Boston: Houghton Mifflin Company, 1985.

D. Clayton James, Anne Wells. Refighting the Last War – Command and Crisis in Korea 1950-1953. New York: The Free Press, 1993.

C. Turner Joy. How Communists Negotiate. New York: Macmillan, 1955.

E. J. Kahn, Jr. The China Hands. New York: Viking Press, 1975.

Oleg Kalugin. The First Directorate. New York: St. Martin's Press, 1994.

George F. Kennan. Memoirs 1925-1950. Boston: Little, Brown and Company, 1967.

George F. Kennan. Sources of Soviet Conduct. Foreign Affairs. July, 1947.

Melanie Kirkpatrick. Inside North Korea's Gulag. Wall Street Journal. June 16, 2009. p. A13.

Henry Kissinger. Diplomacy. New York: Simon & Schuster, 1994.

Harvey Klehr, John E. Haynes, F.I. Firsov. The Secret World of American Communism. New Haven, CT: Yale University Press, 1995.

Korean War Project.

Anthony N. Kubek. How the Far East Was Lost, 1941-49. Chicago: Henry Regnery, 1963.

Robert Lamphere, Tom Shachtman. The FBI-KGB War – A Special Agent's Story. New York: Random House, 1986.

Isaac Don Levine. Plain Talk. New Rochelle, NY: Arlington House Publishers, 1976.

David E. Lilienthal. The Journals of David E. Lilienthal. Vol. III. New York: Harper & Row Publishers, 1966.

Jiawei Lou. US Nuclear Threats During the Korean War. Journal of Jixi University 9 (3): 105, 2009.

Douglas MacArthur. Reminiscences. Annapolis, MD: Naval Institute Press, 1964.

506, **REFERENCES**

MacArthur Story: No Substitute for Victory – Lessons of the Korean War. US News and World Report. April 20, 1964: Vol. 56, No. 16. pp. 38-41.

William Manchester. American Caesar. Boston: Little, Brown and Company, 1978.

William Manchester. Goodbye Darkness: a Memoir of the Pacific War. Boston: Little, Brown, and Company, 1980.

Edward J. Marolda. Grand Delusion: US Strategy and the Tonkin Gulf Incident. Naval History. Vol. 28, No. 4, August 2014. pp. 24-31.

S.L.A. Marshall. Pork Chop Hill. New York: William Morrow edition 1956, Berkley Books, 2000.

S.L.A. Marshall. The River and the Gauntlet. New York: Time Reading Program, 1953, 1962.

S.L.A. Marshall. A New Strategy for Korea? The Reporter, March 3, 1953. pp. 17-21.

S.L.A. Marshall. Our Mistakes in Korea. The Atlantic Monthly. Sept. 1953. pp. 46-49.

Hede Massing. This Deception. New York: Duell, Sloan and Pearce, 1951.

David McCullough. Truman. New York: Simon & Schuster, 1992.

Alice V. McGillivray, Richard M. Scammon. America at the Polls 1920 – 1956 – Harding to Eisenhower.

H.R. McMaster. Dereliction of Duty. Lyndon Johnson, Robert McNamara, the Joint Chiefs of Staff, and the Lies that Led to Vietnam. New York: HarperCollins Publishers, Inc., 1997.

Robert S. McNamara. In Retrospect: the Tragedy and Lessons of Vietnam. New York: Vintage Books, 1996.

Francis Trevelyan Miller. War in Korea and the Complete History of World War II. Made in the United States of America, 1953.

Walter Millis, ed. The Forrestal Diaries. New York: The Viking Press, 1951.

Yuri Modin. My Five Cambridge Friends. New York: Farrar, Straus, and Giroux, 1994.

Simon S. Montefiore. Stalin – The Court of the Red Tsar. New York: Vintage Books, 2003.

Ted Morgan. Reds: McCarthyism in 20th Century America. New York: Random House Trade Paperbacks, 2003.

507, **REFERENCES**

J.R. Moskin. Mr. Truman's War. New York: Random House, 1996.

Daniel Patrick Moynihan. Secrecy: The American Experience. New Haven, CT: Yale University Press, 1998.

William L. Neumann. After Victory: Churchill, Roosevelt, Stalin, and the Making of the Peace. New York: Harper and Row, 1967.

Verne W. Newton. The Cambridge Spies: the Untold Story of Maclean, Philby, and Burgess in America. Lanhan, MD: Madison Books, 1991.

Don Oberdorfer. The Two Koreas – A Contemporary History. Reading, MA: Addison-Wesley, 1997.

Matthew Pennington. North Korea Resumes Testing of Missiles. Associated Press: The Palm Beach Post, May 10, 2015. p. A3.

Barrie Penrose, Simon Freeman. Conspiracy of Silence: the Secret Life of Anthony Blunt. New York: Farrar Straus Giroux, 1987.

Joseph E. Persico. Roosevelt's Secret War – FDR and World War II Espionage. New York: Random House, 2001.

John M. Pratt. Revitalizing a Nation. Chicago: The Heritage Foundation, Inc, 1952.

Thomas C. Reed, Danny B. Stillman. The Nuclear Express – A Political History of the Bomb and its Proliferation. Minneapolis: Zenith Press, 2009.

David Rees. Harry Dexter White – A Study in Paradox. New York: Coward, McCann & Geoghegan, 1973.

Matthew B. Ridgway. The Korean War. New York: Da Capo Press, 1967.

Herbert Romerstein, Stanislav Levchenko. The KGB Against the "Main Enemy" – How the Soviet Intelligence Service Operates against the United States. Lexington, MA: Lexington Books, 1989.

Martin Russ. Breakout – the Chosin Reservoir Campaign, Korea 1950. New York: Penguin Books, 1999.

St. Paul's Abbey. newtonosb.org/mid=history.

Roger Sandilands. The Life and Political Economy of Lauchlin Currie: New Dealer, Presidential Advisor, and Development Economist. Durham, NC: Duke University Press, 1990.

508, **REFERENCES**

Jerrold Schecter, Leona Schecter. Sacred Secrets: How Soviet Intelligence Operations Changed American History. Washington: Brassey's, Inc., 2002.

Arthur M. Schlesinger, Jr. The Age of Roosevelt – the Politics of Upheaval. Boston: Houghton Mifflin Company, 1968.

Philip Selznick. The Organizational Weapon: A Study of Bolshevik Strategy and Tactics. Glencoe, IL: The Free Press of Glencoe, 1960.

Charles Shallcross. Modernizing China's Military. Oakland, CA: University of California Press, 2004.

Neil Sheehan. A Bright Shining Lie – John Paul Vann in Vietnam. Amazon.com, 1988.

William Shirer. The Rise and Fall of the Third Reich. New York: Simon and Schuster Touchstone Book, 1981.

Katherine A.S. Sibley. Red Spies in America. Lawrence, KS: University Press of Kansas, 2004.

Henry DeWolf Smyth. Atomic Energy for Military Purposes: The Official Report on the Development of the Atomic Bomb Under the Auspices of the United States Government, 1940-1945, with a New Foreword by Philip Morrison and an Essay by Henry DeWolf Smyth. Stanford, CA: Stanford University Press, 1987.

Henry D. Sokolski. Best of Intentions – America's Campaign Against Strategic Weapons Proliferation. Westport, CT: Praeger, 2001.

Spirit Filled Life Bible. New King James Version. Nashville, TN: Thomas Nelson Publishers, 1991.

Josef Stalin. Problems of Leninism (Voprosy Leninizma). Moscow: OGIZ, 1939.

Pavel Sudoplatov. Special Tasks: Memoirs of an Unwanted Witness – a Soviet Spymaster.

Addison Terry. The Battle for Pusan – A Korean War Memoir. Novato, CA: Presideo Press, 2000.

Christopher Thorne. Allied of a Kind. New York: Oxford University Press, 1978.

John Toland. The Rising Sun – The Decline and Fall of the Japanese Empire 1936-1945. Vol. 2. New York: Random House, 1970.

John Toland. In Mortal Combat – Korea, 1950-1953. New York: Quill William Morrow, 1991.

Leon Trotsky. The Defense of Terrorism. London: George Allen & Unwin, 1935.

509, **REFERENCES**

Harry S. Truman. Memoirs, Vol. 1. Year of Decision. Garden City, NY: Doubleday and Company, 1955.

Harry S. Truman. Memoirs. Vol. 2: Years of Trial and Hope. Garden City, NY: Doubleday and Company, 1956.

Harry S. Truman Library. Oral Interview with Philleo Nash. Conducted by Jerry N. Hess. Washington, DC, 1969. pp. 771-777.

Barbara W. Tuchman. Stilwell and the American Experience in China 1911 – 1945. New York: Grove Press, 1971.

United States Congress. Sen. Joseph McCarthy. Congressional Record: Aug. 9, 1951, Vol. 97, Number 146, p. 9918.

United States House of Representatives, Select Committee to Investigate the Federal Communications Commission, *Study and Investigation of the Federal Communications Commission*, Vol. 1, p. 388.

United States House of Representatives, Select Committee on the Katyn Forest Massacre. Final Report, p. 5.

United States House of Representatives, Select Committee on the Katyn Forest Massacre. Transcript, Part 7, pp. 2174-2195; 2272-2293.

Edward Van Der Rhoer. The Shadow Network. New York: Charles Scribner's Sons, 1983.

James Van Fleet. Life Magazine. May 11, 1953; May 18, 1953. pp. 127-142, 156-172.

Venona Project. http://vault.fbi.gov/Venona.

www.businessinsider.com/chinese-us-military-comparison-2016-8/#chinas-navy-7. Aug. 5,

2016. How World's Largest Military Stacks Up to US Armed Forces.

www.nsa.gov/about/_files/cryptologic_heritage/publications/coldwar/venona_story.pdf.

www.nsa.gov/public_info/declass/venona/may_1944.shml.

www.nsa.gov/public_info/declass/venona/dec_1944.shtml.

Allen Weinstein, A. Vassiliev. The Haunted Wood: Soviet Espionage in America. New York: The Modern Library, 2000.

Richard Whelan. Drawing the Line – The Korean War, 1950-1953. Boston: Little, Brown and Company, 1990.

510, **REFERENCES**

Theodore H. White, Annalee Jacoby. Thunder Out of China. New York: William Sloane Associates, 1946.

Robert Whymant. Stalin's Spy: Richard Sorge and the Tokyo Espionage Ring. New York: St. Martin's Press, 1996.

Peter Wright. Spy Catcher – the Candid Autobiography of a Senior Intelligence Officer. New York: Viking Penguin Inc., 1987. www.bardcollege.edu.

www.posse.gatech.edu/sites/posse.gatech.edu/files/Nuclear.

Tong Zhao. Signaling at China's Perception About Nuclear Threat: How China Handled Nuclear Threats in the Cold War. Sam Nunn School of International Affairs, Georgia Institute of Technology, 2009.

Zhou Ziyang. Prisoner of the State: The Secret Journal of Premier Zhou Ziyang. Translated and edited by Bao Pu, Renee Chiang, Adi Ignatius. New York: Simon & Schuster, 2009.

Notes and Comments

Chapter 1: Politically – Dominated War Leadership

1. George Kennan, Memoirs 1925-1950. Boston: Little, Brown and Company, 1967. p. 526.

2. Ibid, p. 521.

3. Ibid, p. 528.

4. Ibid, p. 529.

5. Omar Bradley, Clay Blair. A General's Life. New York: Simon and Schuster, 1983. pp. 557, 582.

6. William Manchester. American Caesar. Boston: Little Brown, and Company, 1978. pp. 628, 630.

7. The International Student Bible for Catholics. Nashville: Thomas Nelson Publishers, 1999. Book of Proverbs, Chapter 9, Verse 6.

8. Ibid, Letter of St. Paul to the Ephesians, Chapter 5, Verse 11.

9. Ibid, Verses 8, 9.

Chapter 2: Two Governments – Dual Power

1. Mikal Gilmore. Bob Dylan, the *Rolling Stone* Interview. Issue 1166, Sept. 27, 2012. P. 48.

2. http://vault.fbi.gov/rosenberg-case/klaus-fuchs-klaus-fuchs-part-110-of/at_download/file.

3. Kennan, Memoirs, p. 71.

4. Ibid, p. 339.

5. Ibid, p. 55.

6. Daniel Patrick Moynihan, Secrecy, pp. 49, 152.

7. Simon Montefiore, Stalin, pp. 302, 335.

8. William Bullitt, The Great Globe Itself, p. 107.

9. Kennan, Memoirs, pp. 69, 70.

10. Katherine A.S. Sibley. Red Spies in America. p.243.

11. Ibid, p. 179.

12. Christopher Andrew, Oleg Gordievsky. KGB – The Inside Story. New York: Harper Collins Publishers, 1990. p. 367.

13. Ralph de Toledano. J. Edgar Hoover – The Man in His Time. New Rochelle, NY: Arlington House, 1973. p. 247.

14. http://vault.fbi.gov/Venona. The Red Menace. p. 7. Memo Mr. Ladd to Hoover, Feb. 28, 1950.

15. Kennan, Memoirs, p. 517.

16. Ibid, 546.

17. Ibid, p. 548.

18. Ibid, p. 7.

19. George Schuyler, in Isaac Don Levine, Plain Talk. p. 397.

20. Walter Millis, Forrestal Diaries, pp. 14, 54.

21. Millis, pp. 47, 53.

22. Kennan, p. 521.

23. Ibid, p. 226.

24. Ibid, pp, 250, 546.

25. de Toledano, J. Edgar Hoover, p. 247.

26. Ted Morgan, Reds, p. 249.

27. Harry S. Truman Library. Oral History Interview with Philleo Nash (Special Assistant to President for Minority Problems). By Jerry N. Hess, Washington, DC, 1969. pp. 771 – 777.

28. http://vault.fbi.gov/Sen.%20Joseph%20(joe)%20McCarthy/Sen.%20Joseph%20(Joe) 20 McCarthy%20part%2038%ofo/o2056at__download/file. p. 32/61.

29. Ralph de Toledano, Victor Lasky. Seeds of Treason – the Strange Case of Alger Hiss. p. 153.

30. Dennis J Dunn, Caught Between Roosevelt and Stalin, p. 128

31. Kennan, Memoirs, p. 292.

32. Andrew, Gordievsky, p. 281.

33. http://vault.fbi.gov/Venona, message number 1822.

34. Morgan, p. 254.

35. de Toledano, Hoover, pp. 243, 245-247, 253.

36. Ibid,, p. 241.

37. David J. Dallin, Soviet Espionage, p. 441.

38. http://vault.fbi.gov/Sen%20Joseph%20(joe)%20McCarthy/Sen.%20Joseph%20(Joe)2
0McCarthy%20part%2038%ofo/o2056at_download/file. p. 27/61.

39. John Earl Haynes, Harvey Klehr, Alexander Vassiliev. Spies – the Rise and Fall of the KGB in America. New Haven, CT: Yale University Press, 2009. p. 258.

40. Memorandum to Director Hoover 10-26-50, FBI, on Browder's help with espionage, p. 74.

41. FBI report, "Underground Soviet Espionage Organization …", p. 55/150. This comprehensive document is largely based on Elizabeth Bentley's detailed and extensive comments. Finally released under the Freedom of Information Act, it is heavily redacted.

42. Ibid, on Halperin's delivery secret messages, pp. 26, 86, 106, 107/150.

43. David Dallin, Soviet Espionage, on Duncan Chapin Lee and wife, p. 474. Also see FBI "Underground Soviet Espionage Organization …" for personal details on Lee.

44. de Toledano, J Edgar Hoover, p. 223.

45. Ibid, p. 247, Brownell statement, "Records available to me fail to show anything done to impede Red operations …."

46. Robert T. Handy. Patrick J. Hurley and China, 1944-1945. pdxscholar.library.pdx.edu/open_access_etds/1462/.

47. Millis, The Forrestal Diaries, pp. 98, 99.

48. Kennan, Memoirs, p. 238.

49. EJ Kahn Jr. The China Hands, p. 192. *Democrat* Sen. Styles Bridges noted Vincent's "approval of the Communist program in China, opposition to Nationalist Government, and furthering extension of Russian influence in China."

50. Isaac Don Levine, Plain Talk, on Alfred Kohlberg allegation of Roosevelt-Truman insistence on coalition government ("United Front") in China, p. 142.

51. Barbara Tuchman, Stilwell and the American Experience ..., "Far East beyond reach ...," pp. 530, 531.

52. Levine, p. 148.

53. Ibid, p. 149.

54. Kahn, p. 141. US military advisor to Republic of China, Lt. Gen. Albert Wedemeyer, noted State Department "sympathy for Chinese Communists is obvious from their reports and ... recommendations that we back the Communists instead of the Nationalist Government."

55. Millis, Forrestal Diaries, p. 112. Forrestal cabled Gen. Wedemeyer November 1945, "The State Department does not wish to support Chinese Nationalist Government against the Communists" (p.109, Millis).

56. FBI, Elizabeth Bentley file, traitor Ted Hall statement, "I did the right thing ....", p. 86.

57. Joseph E. Persico, Roosevelt's Secret War, p. 438. Stalin's personal library contained thousands of pages of nuclear-related documents, most stolen from America.

58. Montefiore, p. 497. Stalin's Manhatten Project spies, including Klaus Fuchs, promptly reported to intelligence boss Lavrenti Beria America's first-ever successful atomic bomb test, July 1945. Stalin knew about A-Bomb three years before Truman.

59. de Toledano. The Greatest Plot in History, p. 151.

60. Sibley, p. 141.

61. de Toledano, The Greatest Plot in History, p. 62

62. Ibid, pp. 40, 147, 155.

63. Sibley, p. 155.

64. Persico, p. 408.

65. Sibley, p. 134.

66. Ibid, p. 134.

67. Ibid, p. 147.

68. Ibid, p. 163.

69. Harry S. Truman. Memoirs, Vol. 2: Years of Trial and Hope. p. 299.

70. Ibid, p. 301. Oppenheimer's statement strongly favoring Soviet sharing of nuclear secrets reflected official US Government policy, stated in the seminal 1946 Acheson-Lilienthal atomic policy paper.

71. Kennan, Memoirs, pp. 296, 297. Kennan could not accept outright nuclear sharing with Moscow, appreciating the grave dangers.

72. Ibid, p. 300.

73. https://vault.fbi.gov/Sen. Joseph (Joe) McCarthy/Sen. Joseph (Joe) McCarthy part 46. p.34/100. *New York Times* article of Feb. 16, 1946 shown; FBI file reveals Jessup membership and leadership roles in numerous Communist front organizations, among them the Institute of Pacific Relations Research Advisory Council, IRP Board of Trustees, and the publication *Far Eastern Survey*.

74. Montefiore, p. 502.

75. de Toledano, The Greatest Plot in History, pp. 285, 286. Most literature incorrectly gives David Lilienthal credit for 1946 discovery of nuclear impotence at Los Alamos. Dr. Bacher later told Congress that no US uranium inventory took place until July 1950. Lilienthal told Congress the Atomic Energy Commission didn't buy uranium because it would drive up the world price. In sum, Moscow must be given the chance to atomically catch up.

76. Omar N. Bradley, Clay Blair. A General's Life. p. 474.

Chapter 3: Tragic World War II Leadership Begets Korean War

1. Matthew B. Ridgway. The Korean War. New York: Da Capo Press, 1967. p. 250.

2. Francis Trevelyan Miller. War in Korea and the Complete History of World War II. Made in the United States of America, 1953. P. K-3.

3. Fox Butterfield. China – Alive in the Bitter Sea. New York: Times Books, 1982. p. 454.

4. Ibid, p. 455.

5. Barbara Tuchman. Stilwell and the American Experience in China 1911-1945. p. 132.

6. Butterfield, p. 353.

7. J.A. Hammerton, ed. Outline of Great Books. Political Testament. New York: Wise & Company, 1936. p. 1186.

8. Simon S. Montefiore. Stalin. p. 623.

9. Miller, p. K-2.

10. Gene C. Fant Jr. The Liberal Arts – A Student's Guide. p. 62.

11. D. Clayton James and Anne Wells. Refighting the Last War – Command and Crisis in Korea 1950 – 1953. The Free Press, 1993. p. 9.

12. Ibid, p. 6.

13. Harry S. Truman. Memoirs. Vol. 2, Years of Trial and Hope. p. 329.

14. Peter Wright. Spycatcher. p. 45.

15. Montefiore, p. 139.

16. David J. Dallin. Soviet Russia and the Far East. New Haven, CT: Yale University Press, 1948. P. 384.

17. Book of Proverbs, Chapter 9, verse 6.

18. Letter of St. Paul to the Ephesians, Chapter 5, verses 15-16.

Chapter 4: North Korean Surprise Attack

1. David E. Lilienthal. Journals of David E. Lilienthal. p. 71.

2. Omar N. Bradley, Clay Blair. A General's Life. p. 530.

3. Isaac Don Levine. Plain Talk. p. 156.

4. David A. Hatch, Robert Louis Benson. The Korean War: the SIGINT Background. Center for Cryptologic History, National Security Agency, 2000.

5. Ibid, p. 22. British counter-intelligence officer Peter Wright stated that 'Weisband gave away the greatest intelligence secret in the Western world.'

6. Simon S. Montefiore. Stalin: the Court of the Red Tsar. p. 609. "Stalin was pulling the strings in Korea."

7. Jung Chang and Jon Halliday. Mao, the Unknown Story. p. 359. "January 30, 1950, Stalin wired a message to Kim Jong II, 'prepared to help him on this.' This is the first documented evidence of Stalin's agreeing to start war in Korea."

8. Bradley and Blair, p. 476.

9. William Manchester. American Caesar. p. 169.

10. Bradley and Blair, p. 528.

11. Manchester, p. 539.

12. Bradley and Blair, pp. 535, 557. "Korea had been written off. Our greatest concern militarily was the possible loss of Europe."

13. D. Clayton James and Anne Sharp Wells. Refighting the Last War – Command and Crisis in Korea 1950-1953. p. xii.

Chapter 5: Twin Albatrosses – United Nations "Legitimacy" and Revised Chain of Command

1. George Kennan. Memoirs 1925-1950. p. 490.

2. Bradley and Blair, p. 582. Bradley's statements reflect deep, even excessive consideration for Great Britain's views, perhaps a reflection of the General's World War II experiences.

3. James and Wells, p. 150. Authors refer to "UN façade," and "allied influence with Washington far exceeding battlefield contributions."

4. D. Clayton James. The Years of MacArthur. Vol. III. p. 525. "State Department canvass of UN members involved in Korea revealed overwhelmingly negative sentiment regarding

air force pursuit of the enemy across the Manchurian border."

5. James and Wells, p. 212.

Chapter 6: Military Reality – Outgunned, Outnumbered, Undertrained

1. RH Ferrell, ed. The Eisenhower Diaries. New York: W.W. Norton and Co., 1981. p. 139.

2. Bradley and Blair, p. 474.

3. Ibid, p. 475.

4. Walter Millis. The Forrestal Diaries. New York: The Viking Press, 1951. p. 81.

5. Ibid, p. 129. "Truman should level with the American people."

6. Bradley and Blair, p. 473.

7. Harry S. Truman. Memoirs. Vol. 2: Years of Trial and Hope. Garden City, NY: Doubleday and Company, 1956. p. 345. The "cover one's behind at all costs in truth" nature of political memoirs is illustrated.

8. James and Wells, p. 135.

9. David McCullough, 785.

10. Tim Sullivan. Now You See It. National Geographic, vol. 224, no. 4, October 2013. p. 115.

11. Addison Terry. The Battle for Pusan – A Korean War Memoir. Novato, CA: Presidio Press Inc., 2000. p. 111.

12. Ibid, p. 75.

13. Russell A. Gugeler. Combat Actions in Korea. Washington: Office of the Chief of Military History, United States Army. US Government Printing Office, Second Edition, 1970. p. 3.

14. David Hackworth and Julie Sherman. About Face – the Odyssey of an American Warrior. New York: Simon & Schuster, 1989. p. 91.

15. Rich Atkinson. The Long Gray Line. p. 205.

16. Gugeler, p. 4.

17. Ibid, p. 3.

Chapter 7: American Combat Begins

1. Bradley and Blair, p. 539. The US made the identical huge mistake in Vietnam.

2. Ibid, p. 582. Sheer stupidity, leftist political pressure, or both, can only account for Truman's failure to order heavy military mobilization, as recommended in NSC-68.

3. Gugeler, p. 6.

4. Ibid, p. 3. Pentagon and press reports falsely claimed US troops were fighting with great bravery and effectiveness.

5. Ibid, p. 8.

6. Ibid, p. 9.

7. Ibid, p. 11.

8. Ibid, p. 12.

9. Hackworth and Sherman, p. 226.

10. Ibid, p. 137.

11. Ibid, p. 37.

12. Ibid, p. 816.

13. Burke Davis. Marine! The Life of Chesty Puller. New York: Bantam Books, 1964. p. 165.

14. Gugeler, p. 18.

15. Hackworth and Sherman, p. 816.

16. Ibid, p. 160. Platoon leaders in all American 20th- and 21st-century wars had fragile life expectancies.

17. Gugeler, p. 27.

18. Matthew B. Ridgway. The Korean War. New York: Da Capo Press, 1967. p. 85.

19. Ibid, p. 87.

20. Ibid, p. 88.

21. Ibid, p. 101.

22. Ibid, p. 102.

23. Gugeler, p. 13.

24. Hackworth and Sherman, p. 776.

25. Ibid, p. 140.

26. Terry, p. 42. Brig. Gen. SLA Marshall's Korean War book, *Pork Chop Hill,* notes the US Army's battle record of "almost invariable collapse of communications" (p. 6).

27. Ibid, p. 28.

28. Ibid, p. 43.

29. Gugeler, p. 13.

30. Terry, p. 195. The 24th Regiment (25th Division) was a mostly black unit. The author agrees with Hackworth on responsibility of regimental leadership for its poor combat performance.

31. Ibid, p. 14.

32. Ibid, p. 30.

33. Ibid, p. 69.

34. Ibid, p. 200.

35. Ibid, pp. 112, 113.

36. Gugeler, p. 10.

37. Gugeler, p. 13.

38. Hackworth, p. 816.

Chapter 8: Combat Second Phase – Naktong Perimeter

1. Terry, p. 231.

2. Ibid, p. 37.

3. Ibid, p. 119.

4. Brian Catchpole. The Korean War. New York: Carroll and Graf Publishers, 2001. p. 107.

5. Gugeler, p. 17.

6. Ibid, p. 31.

7. Terry, p. 73.

8. Ibid, p. ix.

9. Ibid, p. 153.

10. Ibid, p. 233.

11. Ibid, p. 172.

12. Gugeler, p. 31. NK close to total victory.

13. Terry, p. 13.

14. Ibid, pp. 40, 41.

Chapter 9: Phase 3 – MacArthur and Inchon

1. Hammerton, p. 1192.

2. Manchester, p. 575. MacArthur had a flair for dramatic statements. His former staff officer Dwight Eisenhower once said, "I studied drama under MacArthur for four years." MacArthur returned the favor in stating, "Eisenhower was the best clerk I ever had."

3. Toland, In Mortal Combat, pp. 187-88. Toland does not address American and British Red spying as responsible for Mao's knowledge of Inchon invasion. He gives Mao undeserved credit for the discovery and its passage to Kim Il Sung.

4. Oleg Kalugin. The First Directorate. New York: St. Martin's Press, 1994. p. 133.

5. John Costello. Mask of Treachery. New York: William Morrow and Company, 1988. pp. 501, 544.

6. Christopher Andrew, Oleg Gordievsky. KGB: The Inside Story. New York: Harper Collins Publishers, 1990. p. 392.

7. Joseph E. Persico. Roosevelt's Secret War – FDR and World War II Espionage. New York: Random House, 2001. pp. 19, 21, 23.

8. Toland, In Mortal Combat, p. 188.

9. Davis, p. 235.

10. Ibid, p. 239.

11. Ibid, p. 247.

12. Ibid, p. 260.

13. Clifton La Bree. The Gentle Warrior – Oliver Prince Smith, USMC. Kent, OH: Kent State University Press, 2001. pp. 1, 134. Smith's words are a kind way of blaming MacArthur for not insisting on better plans for sealing egress of the NKPA from South Korea.

14. Hearing Before The Subcommittee on Korean War Atrocities of the Permanent Subcommittee on Investigation of the Committee on Government Operations, United States Senate. 83rd Congress, First Session. Pursuant to Senate Resolution 40. Part 3, December 4, 1953. United States Government Printing Office, Washington: 1954.

Chapter 10: Genius Run Amok: Push to the Yalu

1. Bradley and Blair, p. 568.

2. John Toland, In Mortal Combat. p. 251.

3. James and Wells, p. 183.

4. Bradley and Blair, p. 560.

5. Ibid, p. 565.

6. Manchester, American Caesar, pp. 546, 547.

7. Gugeler, p. 1. To Truman, war with Russia represented American disaster. Without conventional military strength, the US must resort to widespread nuclear attack, or face rapid Red conquest of Western Europe.

8. Bradley and Blair, p. 467. More than one historian noted "the NSC wanted to abandon all US bases west of Hawaii."

9. Manchester, p. 584.

10. Bradley and Blair, p. 586.

11. Ibid, p. 592.

12. Ibid, p. 594.

13. La Bree, p. 141. Wisdom of Smith's simple observation was continually proven in Korean battle.

14. SLA Marshall. From River to Gauntlet. New York: Time Reading Program Special Edition, 1962. pp. 276 – 322.

15. Bradley and Blair, p. 578.

Chapter 11: Traditional Mistreatment of the Chinese People

1. Barbara W. Tuchman. Stilwell and the American Experience in China, 1911-1945. p. 147.

2. John M. Pratt, ed. Revitalizing a Nation – A Statement of Beliefs, Opinions and Policies Embodied in the Public Pronouncements of General of the Army Douglas MacArthur. p. 32.

3. Ibid, p. 33.

4. Tuchman, p. 58.

5. Fox Butterfield. China – Alive in the Bitter Sea. p. 459.

6. Tuchman, p. 105.

7. Ibid, p. 86.

8. John Toland. The Rising Sun – The Decline and Fall of the Japanese Empire 1936-1945. p. 515.

9. Chang and Halliday, p. 291.

10. Tuchman, pp. 58, 105.

Chapter 12: Colossal Presidential Fraud – Red Russia Takes Far East, Central and East Europe

1. Hammonton, p. 1166.

2. William L. Neumann. After Victory: Churchill, Roosevelt, and Stalin and the Making of the Peace. p. 93.

3. Ibid, p. 65. Publicly unknown, Peter Wright revealed Churchill's huge and unwise courtesy to Stalin in ordering all British anti-Soviet intelligence work to cease during World War II partnership (starting June 1941). Wright, Spy Catcher, p. 182.

4. Ibid, p. 43.

5. Ibid, p. 50.

6. Ibid, p. 117.

7. Ibid, p. 118.

8. Ibid, p. 123.

9. Ibid, p. 124.

10. Ibid, p. 125.

11. John Toland. The Rising Sun – the Rise and Fall of the Japanese Empire 1936 – 1945. Vol. 2. p. 580.

12. Neumann, p. 68.

13. Ibid, p. 101.

14. James and Wells, pp. 154, 155.

15. Neumann, p. 52.

16. Ibid, p. 53.

17. Simon S. Montefiore. Stalin: the Court of the Red Tsar. p. 302.

18. Neumann, p. 100.

19. Ibid, p. 89.

20. Ibid, p. 87.

21. Ibid, p. 137.

22. Ibid, p. 54.

23. Ibid, p. 181.

24. Henry Kissinger. Diplomacy. pp. 55, 75.

25. Neumann, p. 95.

26. Ibid, pp. 95, 96.

27. Ibid, p. 97.

28. Ibid, p. 103.

29. Ibid, p. 55.

30. Joseph E. Persico. Roosevelt's Secret War – FDR and World War II Espionage. pp. 404, 405.

31. David J. Dallin. Soviet Russia and the Far East. p. 228.

Chapter 13: Communist Friends in American News Media

1. John Earl Haynes, Harvey Klehr, Alexander Vassiliev. Spies – The Rise and Fall of the KGB in America. p. XXX.

2. Neumann, p. 90.

3. Ibid, p. 91.

4. Ibid, p. 92.

5. Dallin, Soviet Russia and the Far East. p. 229.

6. Owen Lattimore. Solution in Asia. pp. 108, 109, 139.

7. Dallin, Soviet Russia and the Far East. pp. 229, 230.

8. Ibid, p. 230.

9. Harvey Klehr, John E Haynes, and Fl Firsov. The Secret World of American Communism. p. 60.

10. Robert Whymant. Stalin's Spy: Richard Sorge and the Tokyo Espionage Ring. p. 320.

11. Klehr, Haynes, and Firsov, p. 232.

12. Ibid, p. 196.

13. Ibid, p. 299.

14. Ibid, p. 324.

Chapter 14: Russian Zenith, American Nadir

1. Hammerton, p. 1192.

2. William C. Bullitt. How We Won the War and Lost the Peace. pp. 86-103.

3. Henry Kissinger. Diplomacy. p. 416.

4. Dallin, Soviet Russia and the Far East. p. 232.

5. Toland, The Rising Sun. p. 583.

6. Philip Selznick. The Organizational Weapon: A Study of Bolshevik Strategy and Tactics. p. 237.

7. Leon Trotsky. The Defense of Terrorism. p. 55.

8. Tuchman, p. 132.

9. Toland, The Rising Sun. p. 792.

10. Millis, The Forrestal Diaries. p. 112.

11. Manchester, American Caesar. pp. 534-37.

12. Chang and Halliday, p. 231.

13. Toland, The Rising Sun. p. 793.

14. Chang and Halliday, p. 278.

15. Neumann, p. 159.

16. Kennan. p. 259.

17. Ibid, p. 261.

18. Dallin, Soviet Russia and the Far East. p. 214.

19. Ibid, p. 212.

20. Chang and Halliday, p. 283.

21. Dallin, Soviet Russia and the Far East. p. 213.

22. Ibid, p. 233.

23. Ibid, p. 282.

24. Kennan, Memoirs, p. 390.

25. Ibid, p. 395.

26. Dallin, Soviet Russia and the Far East. p. 219.

27. Dwight D. Eisenhower. Mandate for Change – 1953-1956. p. 446.

28. Dallin, Soviet Russia and the Far East. p. 236.

Chapter 15: Ill Wind – Communist Triumph in China

1. Toland, The Rising Sun. p. 793.

2. Dallin, Soviet Russia and the Far East. p. 263.

3. Jonathan Spence. Mao Zedong. New York: Penguin Group, 1999. p. 91.

4. Chang and Halliday, p. 233.

5. Tuchman, p. 86.

6. Chang and Halliday, p. 295.

7. Spence, p. 102.

8. Chang and Halliday, p. 283.

9. Ibid, p. 290.

10. Spence, p. 81.

11. Ibid, p. 98.

12. Ibid, p. 107.

13. Chang and Halliday, p. 5.

14. Kennan, Memoirs, pp. 373 - 375. Kennan's belief of Japan as far more significant than China in economic development potential, and therefore more worthy of US concern than China, appeared to reflect the feelings of many US Government leaders.

15. Millis, Forrestal Diaries, p. 112.

16. Harry S. Truman. Memoirs. Vol. 2. Years of Trial and Hope. p. 77.

17. Burke Davis. Marine! The Life of Chesty Puller. p. 242.

18. Dean Acheson. Present at the Creation. p. 735.

19. David J. Dallin. Soviet Russia and the Far East. p. 206.

20. Ibid, p. 208.

21. Churchill, Triumph and Tragedy, p. 480.

22. Acheson, p. 744.

23. Ibid, p. 745.

24. Chang and Halliday, p. 291.

25. Ibid, p. 295.

26. Tuchman, p. 531.

Chapter 16: Politics Rules – Truth of Global Threat Kept from People

1. Manchester, American Caesar, p. 631.

2. Tuchman, p. 94.

3. Ibid, p. 105.

4. John Toland. In Mortal Combat – Korea, 1950-1953. p. 305.

5. Tuchman, p. 144.

6. Dallin, Soviet Russia and the Far East, p. 300.

7. Ibid, p. 285.

8. Millis, Forrestal Diaries, p. 140.

9. George Kennan. Memoir. p. 500.

10. Douglas MacArthur. Reminiscences. pp. 320, 385.

Chapter 17: Stalin's Englishmen – Gentlemen Traitors Beyond Suspicion

1. Barrie Penrose, Simon Freeman. Conspiracy of Silence: the Secret Life of Anthony Blunt. p. 333.

2. Ibid, p. 359.

3. John Costello. Mask of Treachery. p. 544.

4. Peter Wright. Spycatcher – The Candid Autobiography of a Senior Intelligence Officer. p. 238. Regarding Philby's spying as 'the greatest treachery of the 20th century,' Wright told that his 'deception had been a second skin for 30 years' (p. 194).

5. Penrose and Freeman, p. 329.

6. Ibid, p. 322.

530, **NOTES AND COMMENTS**

7. Ibid, p. 339.

8. Costello, p. 501.

9. Oleg Kalugin. The First Directorate. p. 133.

10. Christopher Andrew, Oleg Gordievsky. KGB – The Inside Story. p. 394.

11. Manchester, American Caesar, p. 596.

12. David Dallin. Soviet Espionage. p. 441.

13. Costello, p. 474.

14. Ibid, p. 475.

15. Wright, p. 182. Venona discovered less than 3% of US – Moscow World War II Soviet cable traffic.

16. Ibid, p. 187.

17. Ibid, p. 237.

18. Ibid, p. 288.

19. Ibid, p. 289.

20. Ibid, p. 194.

21. Ibid, p. 121. Many agents remained loyal to Stalin after World War II.

22. Ibid, p. 122.

23. Ibid, p. 166.

24. Ibid, p. 235.

Chapter 18: Communist China Enters the War

1. Raymond De Jaegher, Irene Kuhn. The Enemy Within. As Father De Jaegher mentioned, "The Communist army was never called the 'Communist Army,' always the 'People's Army.' It grew larger, bolder, more skillful, and tougher all the time." This was obviously the prime objective of Mao Zedong and Chinese Communism.

2. Bernard Brodie. War and Politics. p. 73.

3. Isaac Don Levine. Plain Talk. p. 154.

4. James and Wells, p. 185.

5. Toland, In Mortal Combat, p. 236.

6. Brodie, p. 73.

7. Toland, In Mortal Combat, p. 235.

8. E. J. Kahn. The China Hands. p. 226.

9. James and Wells, p. 16.

10. Toland, In Mortal Combat, p. 249.

11. James and Wells, p. 44.

12. Ibid, pp. 184, 185.

13. Toland, In Mortal Combat, pp. 252, 253.

14. Bill Gilbert. Ship of Miracles – 14,000 Lives and One Miraculous Voyage. p. 41.

15. Robert Frank Futrell. The United States Air Force in Korea 1950 - 1953. Revised ed. pp. 228, 229.

16. Toland, In Mortal Combat, p. 271.

17. William Manchester. American Caesar. p. 602.

Chapter 19: CCF Potent Foe – Old Defeats New

1. Manchester, American Caesar, p. 607.

2. Tuchman, p. 422.

3. Jonathan Spence. Mao Zedong. p. 116.

4. David J. Dallin. Soviet Russia and the Far East. p. 120.

5. Ibid, p. 124.

6. De Jaegher, Kuhn. p. 212.

7. Toland, In Mortal Combat, p. 279.

8. La Bree, p. 142. Wind chill factors easily reached 40-50 degrees below zero.

9. Hackworth and Sherman, p. 102.

10. Davis, p. 267.

11. Manchester, American Caesar, p. 601.

12. Edwin P. Hoyt. The Bloody Road to Panmunjom. p. 27.

13. Toland, In Mortal Combat, p. 351.

Chapter 20: The Night the Chinese Came

1. Eisenhower, Mandate for Change, p. 483.

2. Hackworth and Sherman, p. 146.

3. Winston Churchill. A Roving Commission. p. 186.

4. Ibid, p. 187.

5. Ibid, p. 193.

6. Davis, p. 309. Puller would not allow accompanying press to photograph the battle debacle.

7. Hackworth and Sherman, p. 48. Given paucity of use in Korean War literature, the accurate description is too embarrassing and politically incorrect to publicly emphasize.

8. Futrell. p. 261.

9. SLA Marshall. From River to Gauntlet. pp. 272-275.

10. Ibid, p. 178.

11. Neil Sheehan. A Bright Shining Lie – John Paul Vann and America in Vietnam. p. 466.

12. Davis, p. 281.

13. LaBree, p. 172.

14. Hoyt. pp. 100, 101. In the author's words, "The men of Company F, 7th Marine Regiment, had spent the day at the top of Toktong Pass preparing for an enemy night attack. They collected weapons and ammunition from dead Marines and dead Chinese, including, from the latter, Thompson submachine guns and Springfield 1903 rifles – bits of the Beijing government's inheritance from US aid to Chiang Kai-shek."

15. LaBree, p. 168.

16. Hoyt, p. 144. "Marines and a handful of Army men of the 7th Division had made the trek from Hagaru to Hamhung, … carrying packs, parkas, sleeping bags, and their weapons across frozen roads and hillsides, pelted by snow and icy winds. They had mauled half a dozen Chinese Ninth Army Group divisions to the point of exhaustion."

17. Davis, p. 290.

18. Gilbert, p. 178.

19. La Bree, pp. 164-165.

20. Hoyt, p. 120.

21. La Bree, p. 160.

22. Davis, pp. 290, 296.

23. Hoyt, p. 138. As described by the author, "One US Marine division, reinforced by remnants of the Army's 7th Division, against 10 enemy divisions – those were the odds."

24. Futrell, p. 276.

25. Davis, p. 287.

26. Ibid, p. 289.

27. LaBree, p. 185.

Chapter 21: Comparing US Army and Marine War Performance November – December 1950

1. Lee Ballenger. The Outpost War – U.S. Marines in Korea. Vol. 1: 1952. p. 137.

2. Hackworth and Sherman, p. 94.

3. Edward Gibbon. The Decline and Fall of the Roman Empire. Vol. 1. p. 15.

4. Ibid, p. 14.

5. Hackworth and Sherman, p. 140.

6. Davis, p. 242.

7. Hackworth and Sherman, p. 360.

8. T.R. Fehrenbach. This Kind of War. p. 188.

9. Ibid, p. 189.

10. Ibid, p. 192.

11. Ibid, p. 519.

12. Ballenger, p. 28.

Chapter 22: "Greatest Sea Rescue in History of Mankind"

1. Gilbert. Ship of Miracles. p. 85.

2. Ibid, p. 106.

3. Ibid, p. 121.

4. Bok Hak Hyun, Marian Hyun. Christmas Cargo: A Civilian Account of the Hungnam Evacuation.

5. Gilbert, p. 94.

6. Ibid, p. 113.

7. Ibid, p. 105.

8. Ibid, p. 115.

9. Ibid, p. 122.

10. Ibid, p. 131.

11. Ibid, p. 139.

12. Ibid, p. 140.

13. Ibid, p. 142.

14. Ibid, p. 143.

15. Stanley F. Bolin, John S. Cowings, Kim Nam Che. Twelve Hungnam Refugees.

16. St. Paul's Abbey. newtonosb.org/mid=history.

17. Gilbert, p. 178.

Chapter 23: Shell-Shocked Washington Weighs Surrender

1. Hammerton, p. 241.

2. William Manchester, American Caesar, p. 611. Manchester cited the British as "wanting to quit … to protect commercial interests in China," and on page 620 reported, "The Chiefs never say in so many words that they are prepared to leave the Chicoms in possession of the field …." Acheson mentioned "The hysteria about evacuation …."

3. Bernard Brodie. War and Politics. p. 80.

4. Ibid, p. 79.

5. H. R. McMaster. Dereliction of Duty. Lyndon Johnson, Robert McNamara, the Joint Chiefs of Staff, and the Lies that Led to Vietnam. p. 108.

6. Ibid, p. 416.

7. J. Lawton Collins. War in Peacetime – the History and Lessons of Korea. p. 229.

8. Ibid, p. 241.

9. Bradley and Blair, p. 558.

10. Ibid, p. 582.

11. Truman, Memoirs Vol. 2, p. 408.

12. Collins, p. 266.

13. Ibid, p. 263.

14. Ibid, p. 331.

Chapter 24: Field Command Hand of Fate – Ridgway the Savior

1. Matthew B. Ridgway, p. 101.

2. Acheson. Present at the Creation. p. 512.

3. La Bree, p. 192.

4. James and Wells, p. 3.

5. Ballenger, p. 206. During the last few days of October 1952, "Some 34,000 rounds of CCF artillery were used to soften the [Outpost Hook] position before seizure, and when the enemy assault came, there were few Marines left able to resist."

6. Ibid, p. 225.

7. Hackworth and Sherman, p. 240.

8. Brian Catchpole. The Korean War 1950-53. p. 153. After each day's march in hostile territory, Romans built a ditch- and stockade-surrounded camp, allowing 90 feet of open ground within walls. Soldiers could enjoy relatively peaceful rest and relaxation. Pack animals carried loads of wooden stakes from one camp to the next.

9. Ibid, p. 107.

10. Ibid, p. 106.

11. Ibid, p. 109.

12. Ibid, p. 111.

13. Ridgway, pp. 106, 107.

14. Catchpole, p. 112.

15. Brodie, p. 80.

16. Ridgway, p. 112.

17. La Bree, p. 203.

18. Ibid, pp. 191, 192.

Chapter 25: Truman Sacks MacArthur, Chinese Do-Or-Die

1. Davis, pp. 320, 321.

2. Pratt, p. 41.

3. Hackworth and Sherman, p. 88.

4. Brodie, p. 91.

5. Hackworth and Sherman, p. 113.

6. Ibid, p. 100.

7. Ibid, p. 112.

8. James and Wells, p. 218.

9. Hackworth and Sherman, p. 135.

10. Acheson, pp. 517-18.

11. Philip Selznick. The Organizational Weapon: A Study of Bolshevik Strategy and Tactics. pp. 212, 213.

12. Ibid, p. 217

13. Ibid, p. 257, 258, 273.

14. Brodie, p. 94.

15. Toland, In Mortal Combat, p. 465.

16. Ibid, pp. 465-466.

17. Brodie, p. 95.

18. Pratt, p. 54.

19. Harry S. Truman. Memoirs. Vol. 2, Years of Trial and Hope. pp. 378, 391, 416. In great dereliction of presidential responsibility as Commander in Chief, Truman stated (p. 345), "In 1945-46 the American people had chosen to scuttle their military strength. I was against hasty and excessive demobilization at the time. The press and Congress drowned us out."

20. Kissinger, Diplomacy. p. 487.

21. James and Wells, p. 23.

22. Manchester, American Caesar, p. 542.

23. Ibid, pp. 535, 542.

24. James and Wells, p. 221.

25. Ibid, p. 225.

26. Collins, p. 304.

27. Ibid, p. 305.

28. James and Wells, p. 223.

29. Ibid, p. 225.

Chapter 26: Acheson's Explanation for Going on the Defensive

1. Acheson, p. 652.

2. Robert Beisner. Dean Acheson – A Life in the Cold War. p. 24.

3. Acheson, p. 517.

4. Ibid, p. 529.

5. Beisner, p. 2.

6. James and Wells, p. xi.

7. Ibid, p. 15.

8. Ibid, p. 230.

9. Ibid, p. 242.

10. Acheson, p. 514.

11. Pratt, p. 55.

12. Acheson, p. 515.

13. Ibid, p. 516.

14. Ibid, p. 517.

15. Pratt, p. 49.

16. Ibid, p. 57.

17. Ibid, p. 58.

18. Ibid, p. 19.

19. Ibid, p. 17.

20. Ibid, p. 59.

21. Beisner, p. 13.

22. Ibid, p. 14.

23. Pratt, p. 80.

24. Ibid, p. 60.

25. Ibid, p. 92.

26. Ibid, p. 61.

27. Ibid, p. 84.

28. Ibid, p. 79.

29. Bradley and Blair, p. 560.

30. Acheson, p. 518.

31. James and Wells, p. 218.

32. Hackworth and Sherman, p. 270.

33. James and Wells, p. 227.

34. Catchpole, p. 216.

35. James and Wells, p. 228.

36. Ibid, p. 229.

37. Catchpole, p. 320.

38. Acheson, p. 519.

39. Collins, p. 299.

40. Ibid, p. 301.

41. Acheson, p. 520.

42. Ibid, p. 527.

43. Ibid, p. 529.

44. Brodie, p. 93.

45. Ibid, p. 94.

46. Ibid, p. 95.

47. Saul Alinsky. Rules for Radicals, p. 128.

48. Acheson, p. 529.

49. Ibid, p. 532.

50. Ibid, p. 533.

51. Montefiore, p. 636.

52. Acheson, p. 534.

53. Ibid, p. 535.

54. Beisner, p. 14.

55. Ibid, p. 18.

56. James and Wells, p. 21.

57. Acheson, p. 538.

58. Ibid, p. 696.

59. Ibid, p. 536.

60. Ibid, p. 537.

61. Ibid, p. 538.

62. Ibid, p. 697.

Chapter 27: America's Masters – The Internationalists

1. Eisenhower, Mandate for Change, p. 128.

2. Manchester, American Caesar, p. 535.

3. Eisenhower, Mandate for Change, p. 453.

4. John T. Flynn. The Roosevelt Myth. 50th Anniversary Edition. p. 345.

5. Manchester, American Caesar, p. 492.

6. Catherine Drinker Bowen. Yankee from Olympus. p. 385.

7. Ibid, p. 413.

8. Blanche Wiesen Cook. Eleanor Roosevelt. Vol. 2, p.177.

9. Bowen, p. 393.

10. Robertson Davies. For Your Eye Alone. The Spengler-Toynbee 'dying-West' clarion well-fit champions of proletarian revolution. The movement had a firm and prestigious academic base.

11. John Earl Haynes, Harvey Klehr, F.I. Firsov. In Denial: The Secret World of American Communism. p. 210.

12. www.bardcollege.edu.

13. Discoverthenetworks.org. – a guide to the political left. Corliss Lamont.

14. Joshua Muravchik. American Enterprise Institute. www.weeklystandard.com/content/public/article/000/000/013/783zfoqh.asp.

15. Universityofwashington.edu. Harry Bridges Center.

16. Haynes and Klehr, p. 231.

17. Hede Massing. This Deception. p. 313.

Chapter 28: Dual Power - A Great Nation's Undoing

1. Fred Ikle, p. 70.

2. Ibid, p. 71.

3. Wright. Spycatcher. p. 158.

4. Andrew, Gordievsky. KGB - The Inside Story, p. 249.

5. Wright, p. 207.

6. Ibid, p. 172.

7. Ibid, p. 185.

8. Ibid, p. 187.

9. Selznick, p. XII.

10. Ibid, p. 19.

11. Ibid, p. XIV.

12. Blanche Wiesen Cook. Eleanor Roosevelt. Vol. 2: 1933-1938. pp. 7, 562, 644.

13. William Bullitt. The Great Globe Itself, pp. 278, 279.

14. Ibid, p. 279.

15. Kennan, p. 526.

16. Ibid, pp. 556, 557.

17. Gilbert, p. 57.

18. Robert Dallek. Franklin D. Roosevelt and American Foreign Policy 1932-1945. p. 501.

19. David J. Dallin. Soviet Russia and the Far East, p. 221.

20. Ikle, p. 75.

21. Ibid, p. 77.

22. Montefiore, pp. XIX, 33.

Chapter 29: Korean Battle-Fix, Part II

1. S.L.A. Marshall. Our Mistakes in Korea. pp. 46-49.

2. John Toland. In Mortal Combat, p. 466.

3. Montefiore, p. 636.

4. Francis T. Miller, pp. K3 – K6.

5. Collins, p. 303.

6. Hackworth and Sherman, p. 270.

7. James and Wells, p. 218.

8. Ibid, p. 7.

9. Fehrenbach. This Kind of War, pp. 603, 604.

10. Hackworth and Sherman, p. 236.

11. Lee Ballenger. The Outpost War – US Marines in Korea, Vol. 1: 1952. p. 47.

12. Toland, In Mortal Combat, p. 484.

13. James and Wells, p. 7.

14. Harry S. Truman. Memoirs, Vol. II: Years of Trial and Hope. p. 391.

15. David McCullough. Truman, p. 919.

16. Toland, In Mortal Combat, p. 556.

17. Fehrenbach, p. 504.

18. Hackworth and Sherman, p. 243.

19. Fehrenbach, p. 514.

20. Ridgway, p. 221.

21. Ibid, p. 526.

22. Fehrenbach, p. 521.

23. Ibid, p. 529.

24. Ibid, p. 505.

25. James and Wells, pp. 124, 125.

26. Toland, In Mortal Combat, p. 487.

27. Brodie, p. 97.

28. Ridgway, p. 238.

29. Ibid, p. 200.

30. Toland, In Mortal Combat, p. 486.

31. Hackworth and Sherman, p. 239.

32. James and Wells, p. 126.

33. Ibid, p. 75.

34. Fehrenbach, p. 508.

35. James and Wells, p. 8.

Chapter 30: Horse Power Stops Atomic Power

1. Collins, pp. 296, 307.

2. Hoyt. The Bloody Road to Panmunjom, p. 105

3. Collins, pp. 298, 299.

4. Ibid, p. 301.

5. Ibid, p. 303.

6. Ibid, p. 307.

7. Ibid, p. 289.

8. Ibid, p. 331.

9. Ibid, p. 371.

10. Winston Churchill. Triumph and Tragedy, p. 483.

Chapter 31: Air Power's Failure

1. Davis, pp. 318, 319.

2. William L. Shirer. The Rise and Fall of the Third Reich, pp. 282, 946-954, 1009.

3. Futrell. The United States Air Force in Korea 1950-1953. Revised Edition, p. 175.

4. Ibid, p. 146.

5. Ibid, p. 136.

6. Hackworth and Sherman, p. 240.

7. Ibid, p. 277.

8. Futrell, pp. 241-242.

9. Ibid, p. 404.

10. Ibid, p. 402.

11. Ibid, p. 412.

12. Ibid, p. 419.

13. Ibid, p. 411.

14. Ibid, p. 69.

15. Ibid, p. 229.

16. Ibid, p. 692

17. Ibid, pp. 285, 402.

18. Ibid, pp. 576, 577.

19. Ibid, p. 578.

20. Ibid, p. 581.

21. Ibid, p. 583.

22. Ibid, p. 588.

23. Ibid, p. 589.

24. Ibid, p. 592.

25. Ibid, p. 593.

26. McCullough, Truman, p. 764.

27. Clark Clifford, Richard Holbrooke. Counsel to the President, p. 177.

28. Katherine A.S. Sibley. Red Spies in America, p. 195.

29. Futrell, p. 493.

30. James and Wells, p. 134.

31. Gugeler, p. 3.

32. Ballenger, p. 34.

Chapter 32: Evaluating Washington War Leadership

1. Fehrenbach, p. 527.

2. Brodie, p. 452.

3. Kennan, p. 525.

4. James and Wells, p. 5.

5. Ibid, p. 22.

6. Tuchman, p. 132.

7. Gannon, p. 57.

8. Tuchman, p. 58.

9. Bullitt. The Great Globe Itself, p. 193.

10. Millis. The Forrestal Diaries, pp. 14, 54.

11. Brodie, p. 299.

12. Ibid, p. 445.

13. Ibid, p. 433.

14. R.H. Ferrell, ed. The Eisenhower Diaries, p. 195.

15. Winston S. Churchill. Memoirs of the Second World War. Vol. VI: Triumph and Tragedy. Abridgement of The Second World War, p. 988. Regarding deep Soviet incursion into Europe, Churchill stated, "The real time to deal with these issues was when the fronts of the mighty Allied armies faced each other in the field, and before the Americans, and ... British made their vast retirement on 400-mile front to a depth ... of 120 miles, giving the heart ... of Germany over to the Russians. It was impossible to gather American support for this ...."

16. Kennan, pp. 214, 215.

17. Tuchman, p. 515.

18. Brodie, p. 438.

19. Ibid, p. 446.

20. Sheehan, A Bright Shining Lie, p. 637.

21. Churchill, Triumph and Tragedy, pp. 399, 400. The Prime Minister wrote of Allied military victory, "This climax of apparently measureless success was to me a most

unhappy time. I moved amid cheering crowds … with an aching heart and a mind oppressed by forebodings." Regarding the Roosevelt-Truman transition, Churchill related (p. 418), "It seemed to me extraordinary, especially during the last few months, that Roosevelt had not made his deputy and potential successor thoroughly acquainted with the whole story and brought him into the decisions which were being taken. This proved of grave disadvantage to our affairs."

22. James and Wells, p. 22.

23. Brodie, p. 447.

24. Ibid, p. 458, p. 91.

25. McMaster. Dereliction of Duty, pp. 305, 330, 331. "Joint Chiefs had become technicians whose principal responsibility was to carry out decisions already made rather than fully participating in the planning and advisory process." McMaster noted that by July 1965, "The administration's lies to the American public had grown in magnitude as the American military effort in Vietnam escalated. The president's plan of deception depended on tacit approval or silence from the JCS. [JCS Chairman Gen.] Wheeler lent his support to the president's deception of Congress. The 'five silent men' on the Joint Chiefs made possible the way the United States went to war in Vietnam. Wheeler in particular allowed his duty to the president to overwhelm his [sworn] obligations under the Constitution."

26. Brodie, p. 93.

27. Ibid, p. 94.

28. Ibid, p. 96.

29. Fehrenbach, p. 33.

Chapter 33: Politics, Military Failure, and Treason

1. Ridgway, p. 22.

2. de Toledano. The Greatest Plot in History, p. 252.

3. Ibid, pp. 266, 285, 287.

4. Dallek, p. 471.

5. de Toledano, The Greatest Plot in History, p. 289.

6. James and Wells, p. 139.

7. Ibid, p. 230.

8. Venona, general picture:
    www.nsa.gov/about/_files/cryptologic_heritage/publications/coldwar/venona_story
    .pd f. Peter Wright called Venona "by far the most reliable intelligence on massive
    Soviet penetration of Western security" (Wright, p. 238).

9. Venona, file decryption specifics:
    www.nsa.gov/public_info/declass/venona/may_1944.shml.

10. Center for Cryptologic History, National Security Agency, Fort George G. Meade, MD.

11. Philip Selznick. The Organizational Weapon: A Study of Bolshevik Strategy and Tactics,
    pp. XIV, 19, 21, 28, 46.

12. Herbert Romerstein, Stanislav Levchenko. The KGB Against the "Main Enemy" – How
    the Soviet Intelligence Service Operates Against the United States, pp. 3, 5, 24, 103,
    106, 107.

13. Edward Van Der Rhoer. The Shadow Network, pp. 2, 6, 13, 152, 227, 228.

14. Flynn. The Roosevelt Myth, p. 231.

15. Alice V. McGillivray, Richard M. Scammon. America at the Polls 1920-1956 – Harding
    to Eisenhower. New York Election Notes, p. 545.

16. Romerstein and Levchenko, pp. 79, 81.

17. Jerrold Schecter, Leona Schecter. Sacred Secrets: How Soviet Intelligence Operations
    Changed American History, pp. 191, 193.

18. Romerstein and Levchenko, p. 3.

Chapter 34: American Largess to Chinese Communism

1. Hoyt. The Bloody Road to Panmunjom, p. 230.

2. Brodie, p. 94.

3. Ibid, p. 96.

4. Bradley and Blair, p. 582.

5. Ibid, p. 95.

6. Ibid, p. 69.

7. Selznick, p. 46.

8. Brodie, p. 85.

9. Ibid, p. 86.

10. Toland, In Mortal Combat, p. 493.

11. Ibid, p. 494.

12. de Toledano, J. Edgar Hoover, pp. 223, 241, 243, 244, 247.

13. Ibid, p. 272.

14. Toland, In Mortal Combat, p. 486.

15. Brodie, p. 97.

Chapter 35: Truth Versus Deception

1. Montefiore, pp. 230, 231; 139, 623.

2. Brodie, p. 94.

3. Robert H. Bork. Slouching Towards Gomorrah – Modern Liberalism and American Decline, p. XIII.

4. Ibid, p. 330.

Chapter 36: National Leadership Theme: Inconsistency

1. Hoyt, p. 283.

2. Ibid, p. 285.

3. Acheson, p. 706.

4. Sibley, p. 176.

5. Acheson, p. 726.

6. Ridgway, p. 238.

7. Futrell, p. 402

8. Truman. Memoirs, Vol. I, p. X.

9. Churchill. A Roving Commission, p. 47.

10. Ibid, p. 58. Ironically, Churchill ordered all British anti-Soviet intelligence work to cease during the World War II alliance, a boon to deep Moscow infestation of London agencies (Wright, p. 182).

Chapter 37: POW Problem

1. Catchpole. The Korean War 1950 – 1953, p. 207.

2. Appleman, South to the Naktong, North to the Yalu, p. 76.

3. Richard Whelan. The Korean War, 1950 – 1953 – Drawing the Line, pp. 330, 331.

4. James and Wells, p. 5.

5. Catchpole, p. 88.

6. Toland, In Mortal Combat, p. 499.

7. Ibid, p. 535.

8. United States Senate. Hearing Before the Subcommittee on Korean War Atrocities of the Permanent Subcommittee on Investigations of the Committee on Government Operations. 83rd Congress, First Session. Part 3 – December 4, 1953. pp. 150-159.

9. Ibid, p. 150.

10. Ibid, p. 152.

11. Toland, In Mortal Combat, pp. 255, 256.

12. Ibid, p. 257.

13. Ibid, p. 258.

14. Ibid, p. 259.

15. Ibid, p. 262.

552, **NOTES AND COMMENTS**

16. http://www.army.mil/medalofhonor/kapuan.

17. http://www.frkapuan.org/about.html.

18. Catchpole, p. 213.

19. Ibid, p. 214.

20. Ibid, p. 216.

21. Korean War Project, p. 196.

22. Senate Subcommittee on Korean War Atrocities, pp. 188-190.

Chapter 38: Ike's War

1. Dwight D. Eisenhower. Crusade in Europe, pp. 468, 470.

2. Alden Hatch. General Ike – A Biography of Dwight D. Eisenhower, p. 83.

3. Eisenhower, Mandate for Change, p. 95.

4. Ibid, p. 180.

5. Fred Charles Ikle. Annihilation from Within, p. 121.

6. Truman, Memoirs. Vol. 2, p. 391.

7. Iklé, p. 44.

8. Futrell, pp. 401, 402.

9. Eisenhower, Mandate for Change, p. 181.

10. Montefiore, p. 609.

11. Hackworth and Sherman, p. 243.

12. Ballenger, pp. 217, 251.

13. S.L.A. Marshall. A New Strategy for Korea?, pp. 17-21.

14. S.L.A. Marshall. Our Mistakes in Korea, pp. 46-49.

15. Ballenger, pp. 202-206.

16. Ibid, pp. 212, 213.

17. Toland, In Mortal Combat, p. 568.

18. Eisenhower, Mandate for Change (p. 96), "There was general agreement with my conclusion that we could not tolerate the indefinite continuance of the Korean conflict; the United States would have to prepare to break the stalemate."

19. Ibid, p. 181. "Lack of progress in the long-stalemated talks ... and the nearly stalemated war both demanded, in my opinion, definite measures on our part to put an end to these intolerable conditions."

20. Ibid, p. 123. "... it put the Chinese Communists on notice that the days of stalemate were numbered; that the Korean War would either end or extend beyond Korea. It thus helped, I am convinced, to bring that war to a finish."

21. Ibid, p. 479. "Zhou En-lai estimated that in a war with the United States, Red China might lose 100 million people and still have 450 million left – apparently believing that this would constitute victory for his side."

Chapter 39: Nuclear Explosives and the Korean War

1. Ridgway, p. 236.

2. Eisenhower, Mandate for Change, pp. 180, 181.

3. George Will, *The Palm Beach Post,* July 28, 2007.

4. Mark Clark. From the Danube to the Yalu, P. 267.

5. Brodie, p. 104.

6. Tong Zhao. Nuclear Signaling of China's Perception About Nuclear Threat: How China Handled Nuclear Threats in the Cold War, p. 3.

7. Jiawei Lou. US Nuclear Threats During the Korean War. Journal of Jixi University 9 (3), p. 105.

8. Brodie, p. 64.

9.   Iklè, p. 52.

10. Ibid, p. 53.

11. Reed and Stillman, pp. 195, 206.

12. Iklè, p. 55.

13. Ibid, p. 54.

14. Ibid, p. 63.

15. Matthew Pennington, Associated Press. North Korea Resumes Testing of Missiles, p. A3.

16. Iklè, p. 122.

17. Ibid, p. vii.

18. de Toledano, The Greatest Plot in History, p. 286.

19. Brodie, p. 64.

20. Truman, Memoirs, Vol. II, p. 299.

21. Ibid, p. 301.

22. Henry DeWolf Smyth. Atomic Energy for Military Purposes: The Official Report on the Development of the Atomic Bomb Under the Auspices of the United States Government, 1940-1945, with a New Forward by Philip Morrison and an Essay by Henry DeWolf Smyth.

23. Iklè, p. 79.

24. Morgan, p. 229.

25. J.E. Haynes, H. Klehr, A. Vassiliev. Spies, p. 58.

26. Jerrold Schecter, Leona Schecter. Sacred Secrets: How Soviet Intelligence Operations Changed American History, p. 199.

27. Ibid, p. 205.

28. Ibid, p. 206.

29. Ibid, p. 300.

30. Iklé, p. 79.

31. Jerrold Schecter, Leona Schecter, p. XIX.

32. Reed, Stillman, p. 31.

33. Max Hastings. The Korean War, p. 337.

Chapter 40: War's End

1. Ballenger, p. 250.

2. James and Wells, XII.

3. Ibid, p. 14.

4. Ibid, p. 17.

5. Ibid, p. 25.

6. Ballenger, p. 251.

7. Ibid, p. 153.

8. Ibid, p. 247.

9. Ibid, p. 249.

10. Ibid, p. 197.

11. Ibid, p. 152.

12. Ibid, p. 134.

13. Ibid, p. 83.

14. Ibid, p. 36.

15. Toland, In Mortal Combat, p. 588.

16. Hastings, p. 329.

17. Ibid, p. 328.

556, **NOTES AND COMMENTS**

18. James and Wells, p. 22.

19. Manchester, American Caesar, pp. 533 – 537.

20. Truman, Memoirs Vol. 2, p. 378.

21. Ibid, p. 383.

22. Ibid, p. 395.

23. Manchester, American Caesar, pp. 535, 542.

24. Hackworth and Sherman, p. 135.

25. Brodie, p. 112.

26. Ibid, p. 104.

27. Toland, In Mortal Combat, p. 486.

28. Ibid, p. 530.

29. Ibid, p. 494.

30. James and Wells, p. 127.

31. Hackworth and Sherman, p. 289.

32. Brodie, p. 106.

33. Hackworth and Sherman, p. 615.

34. Ibid, p. 357.

35. Toland, In Mortal Combat, p. 593.

36. Chang and Halliday, p. 151.

37. Butterfield, p. 394.

38. Chang and Halliday, p. 5.

39. Butterfield, p. 394.

40. Hackworth and Sherman, p. 816.

42. Sheehan, p. 554.

43. Eisenhower, Mandate for Change, p. 167.

44. David Halberstam, The Best and the Brightest p. 213.

45. James and Wells, p. 153.

46. Halberstam, p. 183.

47. Ibid, p. 170.

48. Ibid, p. 135.

49. Ibid, p.136.

50. Ibid, p. 137.

51. Ibid, pp. 258, 259.

52. Ibid, p. 280.

53. Hackworth and Sherman, p. 832.

54. Edward J. Marolda. Grand Delusion: US Strategy and the Tonkin Gulf Incident, p. 31.

Chapter 41: Bitter Korean Fruit

1. Fehrenbach, pp. 647, 648.

2. Ibid, pp. 649, 650.

3. Don Oberdorfer. The Two Koreas – A Contemporary History, pp. 74, 83, 95.

4. Rick Atkinson. The Long Gray Line, p. 420.

5. Oberdorfer, p. 75.

6. Iklé, p. 43.

7. Charles Shallcross. Modernizing China's Military, pp. 98-125.

558

8. Investor's Business Daily, March 12, 2014, p. A12.

9. www.businessinsider.com/chinese-us-military-comparison-2016-8/#chinas-navy-7. Aug. 5, 2016. How World's Largest Military Stacks Up to US Armed Force. "China on course to deploy greater quantities of missiles with greater range than those systems employed by US Navy against them. China on track to have quantitative parity or better in surface-to-air missiles and anti-ship cruise missiles." For Chinese combat philosophy, "preemptive first strike is preferable, sets stage for remainder of conflict and puts aggressor in distinct position of advantage."

10. www.comw.org/cmp/fulltext/iddschina.html.

11. David Ignatius. Beijing Creating Rising Tensions in South Pacific. Investor's Business Daily, Feb. 27, 2014, p. A13.

Chapter 42: Korean War Outcomes - Very Good, Very Bad

1. The Economist, London: By the Rockets' Red Glare. Vol. 419, No. 8991; May 28, 2016, p. 19.

2. Oberdorfer, p. 2.

3. Ibid, p. 59.

4. The Economist, May 28, 2016, p. 11.

5. Eisenhower, Mandate for Change, p. 477.

6. Ibid, p. 453.

7. Ibid, p. 168.

8. Acheson, p. 674.

9. Montefiore, p. 607.

10. Iklè, p. 124.

11. The Economist, May 28, 2016, p. 22. Even if US-supplied Patriot and THAAD (Terminal High-Altitude Area Defense) anti-ballistic missiles destroy 90% of North Korean missile barrage, Seoul and other population centers will be largely destroyed by the untouched 10%. Northern smuggling of compact nuclear-thermonuclear bombs into South Korean cities and military bases is another worry.

559

12. Oberdorfer, p. 313.

13. Ibid, p. 311.

Chapter 43: Dual-Power – Two Governments in Action, Part 1

1. Levine, p. 43.

2. Executive Sessions of the Senate Permanent Subcommittee on Investigation of the Committee on Government Operations. Vol 1. Eighty-Third Congress, First Session, 1953. Made public January 2003, (107th Congress, Second Session). www.gpo.gov/fdsys/pkg/CPRT-107SPRT83869.pdf.

3. Ibid, pdf file p. 945/950; Senate Vol. 1, p. 908.

4. Beisner, p. 25.

5. Senate Permanent Subcommittee on Investigation, Executive Sessions, 1953. Vol. 1. pdf file p. 946/950; Senate Vol. 1, p. 907.

6. Ibid, pdf pages 942-950, Senate, pp. 903-911.

7. Costello. Mask of Treachery, p. 476.

8. Chang and Halliday, p. 234.

9. Dallin, Soviet Russia and the Far East, p. 221.

10. Chiang and Halliday, p. 233.

11. Ibid, pp. 283, 284.

12. Senate Executive Sessions, Vol. 1. Pdf pp. 946-7; Senate, pp. 907-8.

13. Kahn, p. 192.

14. Biesner, p. 303.

15. Levine, pp. 170-183.

16. Acheson, p. 127.

17. Levine, p. 171.

18. Ibid, p. 177.

19. Ibid, p. 181.

20. Ibid, pp. 178, 180.

21. Ibid, p. 183.

22. Senate Executive Sessions, Vol. 1, p. 562. www.gpo.gov/fdsys/pkg/CPRT-107SPRT83869/pdf/CPRT-107SPRT83869.pdf.

23. Ibid, pp. 562-563; pp. 601-602/950, pdf.

24. Acheson, p. 536.

25. Senate Executive Sessions, Vol. 1. pp. 606-7/950 pdf; Senate, pp. 567-8.

26. Senate Executive Sessions, Vol. 1, p. 610/950 pdf; Senate, p. 571.

27. Jan Ciechanowski. Defeat in Victory, pp. 115, 116.

28. Anthony Kubek. How the Far East was Lost, 1941 – 1949, p. 53.

29. Romerstein and Levchenko, p. 122.

30. Ibid, p. 141.

31. Ibid, p. 228.

32. bioguide.congress.gov./scripts/biodisplay.pl?index=C000877.

33. en.wikipedia.org/wiki/Alan_Cranston.

34. Senate Executive Sessions, Vol. 1, p. 573.

35. Ibid, p. 613/950 pdf; Senate, p. 574.

36. Ibid, p. 526/950 pdf; Senate, p. 486-7.

37. John Earl Haynes, Harvey Klehr, F.I. Firsov. In Denial ..., p. 96.

38. Morgan, p. 189.

39. de Toledano, Victor Lasky, Seeds of Treason, pp. 143, 144.

40. Morgan, p. 209.

41. Ibid, p. 206.

42. Senate Executive Sessions, Vol. 1. P. 654/950 pdf; Senate, p. 615.

43. Senate Executive Sessions, Vol. 1. P. 658/950 pdf; Senate, p. 619.

44. de Toledano and Lasky, pp. 278, 279.

45. Ibid, p. 128.

46. Eisenhower. Mandate for Change, p. 315. Red spy infestation proved a continually-pressing tide – in *1963,* Peter Wright trumpeted 'large scale and high-level Soviet penetration in Britain and the US since World War II ', including 'continuous penetration of Western signals intelligence organizations since the great war' (Wright, pp. 206, 207). NSA spies Martin and Mitchell defected to the Soviet Union in 1960.

47. Senate Executive Sessions, Vol. 1, pp. 616, 618.

48. David E. Lilienthal. The Journals of David E. Lilienthal. Vol. III, p. 492.

Chapter 44: Dual Power, Two Governments in Action, Part 2

1. Spirit Filled Life Bible. New King James Version. Isaiah, Chapter 30, v. 28, p. 1001.

2. Kennan, Memoirs, p. 518.

3. Jerrold Schechter, Leona Schechter, p. 21.

4. Ibid, p. 44.

5. Ibid, p. 43.

6. Ibid, p. 24. Key Roosevelt insider Harold Ickes wrote in his diary, 'Dean Acheson brought in a statement of exactly the policy I had been struggling for … with respect to shipments of oil to foreign ports from the US. Of course oil and gasoline should not be shipped to Japan' (Ickes, p. 547). Soon after, Ickes revealed, 'Acheson telephoned me in great triumph. The President just signed orders greatly restricting the flow of oil and gasoline between the US and Japan' (Ickes, p. 591). Harry White had a loyal colleague in Acheson.

7. Ibid, p. 45.

8. Ibid, p. XXV.

9. Churchill. The Second World War – Triumph and Tragedy, p. 641.

10. Millis, ed. The Forrestal Diaries, pp. 112, 145, 175.

11. Tuchman, pp. 515, 518.

12. Manchester, American Caesar, p. 431.

13. Toland, The Rising Sun, pp. 792, 793.

14. Manchester, American Caesar, pp. 436, 437.

15. Toland, The Rising Sun, pp. 787, 788.

16. Neumann. After Victory: Churchill, Roosevelt, Stalin, p. 154.

17. Toland, The Rising Sun, p. 787.

18. Bullitt. The Great Globe Itself. Appendix II, pp. 233-292.

19. James and Wells, p. 22.

Chapter 45: Communist-Internationalist Solidarity

1. Eisenhower. Mandate for Change, p. 51.

2. Morgan. Reds: McCarthyism in 20th-Century America, p. 224.

3. Ibid, p. 243.

4. Ibid, p. 246.

5. Selznick. The Organizational Weapon, pp. 254, 257-263.

6. E.J. Kahn. The China Hands, p. 197.

7. Harvey Klehr, John E. Haynes, F.I. Firsov. The Secret World of American Communism, p. 324.

8. www.nsa.gov/public_info/files/venona/1944/16may_sergej.pdf.

Chapter 46: Stronger Than Ever

1. Ridgway, p. 265.

563, **NOTES AND COMMENTS**

2. Churchill. Triumph and Tragedy, p. 769.

3. William Bullitt. The Globe Itself, p. 278.

4. Kennan, Memoirs, p. 366. The distinguished diplomat defined "Soviet power" as "the system of power organized, dominated, and inspired by Joseph Stalin. [It was] a monolithic power structure, reaching through the network of highly disciplined Communist parties .... Stalin was the only center of authority in the Communist world."

5. John F. Fox, Jr. The Red Menace. FBI: Venona, Highlights of history/article/Venona.

6. FBI Summary Memorandum 10-26-50 to J. Edgar Hoover, p. 74.

7. Kennan. Memoirs, p. 351.

8. Ibid, pp. 249, 261, 300.

9. Bullitt, The Globe Itself, p. 99.

10. Arthur Schlesinger Jr. The Age of Roosevelt – the Politics of Upheaval, p. 189.

11. Levine. Plain Talk, p. 378.

12. Kennan, Memoirs, p. 230.

13. Ibid, p. 518.

14. Bullitt, The Globe Itself, p. 217.

15. Ibid, p. 293.

16. Stalin. Problems of Leninism (Voprosy Leninizma), p. 385.

17. Bullitt, The Globe Itself, pp. 293, 294.

18. Stalin, pp. 173, 190.

19. Bullitt, The Globe Itself, p. 294.

20. Ibid, p. 295.

21. Klehr, Haynes, Firsov, p. 326.

22. Spirit Filled Life Bible. Isaiah, Chapter 26, v. 2, p. 993.

23. Emily Hahn. China to Me, p. 199.

Index

A

566

G

H

623

635

L

651

    donates $1 million to fund endowed chair in his name at Columbia, 287

Lamphere, Robert, FBI agent documenting US shipments of secret nuclear hardware to Soviet Union, 362

Lane, Arthur B., US Ambassador to Communist Poland, 54

Lang, Joseph, New York radio station manager, testifes before Congress about Red control, 466

Laos, nuclear reactor recipient, 409, 366

LaRue, Master Leonard, captain cargo ship SS *Meredith Victory*, saved 14,000 North Korean civilians, 216-220

    becomes Benedictine monk Brother Marinus, receives highest decoration from Merchant Marine for exceptional civilian rescue, 220

      lived at St. Paul's Abbey, Newton, New Jersey, 220

    told Pusan could not accept any more refugees, to proceed to island Koje Do, 218

      refugee mass transferred to LSTs to make landfall, 219

        'God's own hand at helm of my ship,' 220

Lash, Joseph, American Communist, great friend of Eleanor Roosevelt, 293

Laski, Harold, head British Labour Party, early Internationalist in America, 283

Latvia, 145

Lattimore, Owen, pro-Red author, academician, politician, 150, 170, 458,

    praises Red Chinese election system, 150

    'Soviet Union stands for democracy!', 150

leadership, 8, 9, 23-25, 57, 58, 63, 64, 68, 116-118, 155, 169, 170, 174, 188-190, 201, 204, 205, 208-216, 219-222, 228, 271, 272, 276-279, 282, 292, 293, 301, 330, 331, 351, 353, 354, 356, 361, 425, 426, 433, 436,
    American flop in Korea, 190

    Americans overvalue national leadership, 353

    Churchill and Dallin bemoan poor World War II-era American presidential leadership, 118 presidential

      war decisions may have very long-lasting effects, 279, 331

        Eisenhower's Atoms for Peace program becomes 'Atomic Weapons for War,' 330, 331

          today's PRC – North Korea dilemma, 279

653

654

675

692

694

Q

702

712

713

744

W

✝

Made in United States
Orlando, FL
29 October 2024

53239586R00417